CRITICAL INSIGHTS

Isabel Allende

CRITICAL INSIGHTS

Isabel Allende

Editor
John Rodden

Salem Press
Pasadena, California   Hackensack, New Jersey

Cover photo: AP/Wide World Photos

Published by Salem Press

© 2011 by EBSCO Publishing
Editor's text © 2011 by John Rodden
"The *Paris Review* Perspective" © 2011 by Michael Wood for *The Paris Review*

∞ The paper used in these volumes conforms to the American National Standard for Permanence of Paper for Printed Library Materials, Z39.48-1992 (R1997).

Library of Congress Cataloging-in-Publication Data
Isabel Allende / editor, John Rodden.
    p. cm. — (Critical insights)
Includes bibliographical references and index.
ISBN 978-1-58765-699-6 (vol. 1 : alk. paper)
1. Allende, Isabel—Criticism and interpretation. I. Rodden, John.
PQ8098.1.L54Z696 2011
863'.64—dc22
                                                                2010030137

PRINTED IN CANADA

Contents_____

Career, Life, and Influence_____

Critical Contexts_____

Critical Readings_____

Resources

About This Volume_____

John Rodden

This collection presents a wide and rich selection of criticism about an internationally recognized woman of letters and the best-selling female writer in the world. Given Allende's prolific achievement as a novelist, a short-story writer, a young adult book writer, and an essayist and memoirist, the essays in this volume necessarily cover only a representative sample of her vast and ever-expanding body of work.

After a general section that paints Allende's history and impact in broad strokes ("Career, Life, and Influence"), the collection is divided into two parts. Addressing the diverse milieus ("Critical Contexts") and interpretations ("Critical Readings") of her work, each part presents critical essays about Allende, several of which have been specially commissioned for this collection. The volume opens with my editor's introduction, which furnishes a historical and conceptual overview of Allende's achievement, thereby providing a thematic focus for the critical essays that discuss the specific contexts and texts of Allende's corpus. Following a biographical sketch of Isabel Allende by Amanda Hopkinson, which relates Allende's colorful life to her oeuvre, this first section closes with Michael Wood's *Paris Review* essay addressed to Allende's literary achievement and stature.

The "Critical Contexts" section consists of essays devoted to Allende's major works, to their historical and political contexts, and to her critical and popular reception both in the English-speaking world and in Latin America. Beth E. Jörgensen's valuable critical overview of Allende's reception and impact takes the story of her growing reputation up to 2002, thus covering her first two decades as a published writer. Jörgensen offers a review and reassessment of both Allende's fiction and nonfiction, testifying to the broad variety and high caliber of criticism written about Isabel Allende. In an original essay for this volume, Charles Rossman contributes a close reading of Allende's first novel, *The House of the Spirits*, providing a compelling analysis of its narrative, characters, settings, and historical-political context (e.g., the coup led by Augusto Pinochet that deposed Salvador Allende on September 11, 1973, and led to his death). Rossman also discusses the novel's relationship to Gabriel García Márquez's *One Hundred Years of Solitude*, the writing style known as magical realism, and the so-called Boom in Latin American literature and its major writers (García Márquez, Carlos Fuentes, Julio Cortázar, and Mario Vargas Llosa). Giving particular attention throughout to Allende's especially sensitive treatment of her female characters, Rossman situates Allende's evolving canon within the larger context of the Boom and beyond, also discussing briefly her fiction after *The House of the Spirits* as well as her memoirs.

This part of the volume concludes with two important reprinted essays. In an unusual and stimulating study in comparative criticism, María Roof discusses Allende in relation to the Caribbean novelist Maryse Condé, whose best-selling two-volume family saga *Ségon* (1984-85) possesses interesting similarities with Allende's trilogy. Carrie Sheffield then takes up questions similar to those raised by Rossman, but from a different angle, specifically locating her discussion of historical memory in the political context of Chile in the 1970s and later.

The "Critical Readings" section chiefly features reprinted essays that demonstrate the scope both of Allende's oeuvre and of the critical approaches taken toward it. It unfolds chronologically, beginning with Allende's fiction of the 1980s. The section opens with an article about *The House of the Spirits*, Allende's first and most famous novel, by distinguished Allende scholar Sara E. Cooper. Cooper takes a psychological approach to the novel, explaining how the theory of "family systems" illuminates its main themes and furnishes insight into Allende's treatment of the history and politics of Chile. Next is an essay on Allende's best-known and most-beloved heroine, Eva Luna. Barbara Foley Buedel considers how both the novel *Eva Luna* and Allende's short-story collection *Cuentos de Eva Luna* exemplify magical realism, focusing on fateful moments and circumstances in the narratives when the transformative or transcendent enters.

The next essays in this section include critical studies that focus on Allende's nonfiction masterpiece *Paula* rather than on her fiction. Linda S. Maier underscores the significance of emotion in *Paula*, explaining how the act of writing *Paula* functioned as a cathartic experience of therapeutic healing for Allende. Cherie Meacham also highlights the mother-daughter connection in *Paula*, placing Isabel and Paula's relationship in the context of important themes and motifs in *The House of the Spirits*.

The immediately following essays address the other two novels in Allende's great trilogy, both of them composed in the wake of her maternal loss and the challenge of literary renewal after Paula's death. I explore how Allende's *Daughter of Fortune* casts not only its heroine but also Isabel Allende herself as a star-crossed child of fate and circumstance. Nadia Avendaño concentrates on Allende's subversions of conventions of gender in the same novel, explaining how her heroine traverses both geographical and gender boundaries (via practices such as cross-dressing). My subsequent discussion of the autobiographical dimension of *Portrait in Sepia* broadens beyond its reflections on the novel to pursue larger questions about the relationship between biography and fiction in Allende's oeuvre.

The "Critical Readings" section closes with a group of essays possessing a rich, dual focus that alternately examine important yet lesser-known individual works and take a broad view of Allende's work. Two essays commissioned for this volume lead off, both of them raising significant issues about Allende's entire career. Linda Gould Levine explores a central theme in Allende's writings: the erasure of boundaries and the creation of fictional terrains marked by the traversal of lines that have traditionally separated human beings. Through an examination of selected passages from Allende's memoirs and from *The House of the Spirits*, *The Infinite Plan*, *Daughter of Fortune*, *Inés of My Soul*, and *La isla bajo el mar*, this essay highlights how Allende's characters defy social conventions and traverse neighborhoods, countries, and continents in search of a space of belonging. Levine shows how Allende's characters overcome barriers of gender, class, ethnicity, race, religious beliefs, and ingrained views of nationalism and how Allende's tightly knit literary universe exhibits narrative scenarios that dramatize how violence and oppression are redeemed by acts of love and solidarity. Drawing upon Allende's biography and her own traversals (or transgressions) of boundaries, Levine also illuminates how a hybrid sensibility and ethos form part of Allende's utopian agenda for social change. This agenda rests on her conviction that human destiny is not fixed or determined by absolute categories, but is rather pregnant with unexpected, manifold possibilities.

Vincent Kling advances an innovative, provocative reading of Allende's sensibility for paradox and for a complex "balance of opposites." Kling argues that her fiction traffics in oppositions, dichotomies, and seeming contradictions that both enable her work to transcend ideology and reconcile themselves at the level of myth and archetype. Often patronized and dismissed as merely a writer of literary soap operas, Allende is a victim of her own popularity, Kling maintains, which induces critics to make shallow snap judgments based on false categories. They mislabel her as an ideologue, by turns a Marxist and a feminist feebly aping the magical realism of other authors. Applying more appropriate categories that capture the full range of Allende's art, Kling concludes that Allende is a sophisticated literary artist who resolves paradox by holding the contradictory terms in harmonious, creative tension and taking seeming contradictions intact into a yet more encompassing reality. Thus her art shows that paradox cannot dwell with monolithic ideology but rather comes into its full meaning as a vehicle for archetypal experience. *The House of the Spirits*, for instance, enacts the alchemical process of purification and renewed life, and Kling's "alchemical reading" discloses dimensions of her art not evident if an interpretation stops short at Marxist or feminist elements (which are indeed present, but as parts of a deeper, wider whole).

The trio of reprinted essays that follow represent the variegated criticism on Allende's somewhat neglected later works. Philip Swanson offers a nuanced essay that discusses Allende's *Zorro*, a spirited sequel to the original novel about the famed "masked man." Luz María Umpierre considers questions of immigration and social justice as she offers an in-depth analysis of Allende's short story "Dos palabras" ("Two Words"). Don Latham discusses Allende's three young adult novels and how they exemplify magical realism. The section concludes with my own broad overview of Allende's self-presentation (and self-advertisement) in the numerous interviews that she has granted since the 1980s.

CAREER, LIFE, AND INFLUENCE

On Isabel Allende_____

John Rodden

Isabel Allende's literary career was launched thirty years ago in the 1980s with *The House of the Spirits* (*La casa de los espíritus*, 1982) and continues to flourish into the second decade of the twenty-first century, a span of time during which she has written seventeen books, including not only award-winning novels but also highly acclaimed memoirs and even books for young adults. Indeed, more than fifteen million copies of her books have been published in twenty-seven languages, making her the best-selling woman writer in the world today.

Equally astounding, this extraordinary literary career began quite unexpectedly, even adventitiously, given that her first novel, *The House of the Spirits*, was not planned as a work of publishable fiction at all, but rather emerged from a series of letters Allende wrote to her dying grandfather, Agustín Llona. "People die only when they are forgotten," her beloved grandfather had once told her. In exile from Chile, after having flown from her native Santiago following the coup and death of her second cousin (and godfather) Salvador Allende in September 1973, Isabel was writing missives back home trying to tell her grandfather in Santiago what life was like in faraway Venezuela.

Isabel Allende's leftist political stance was born in the throes of a crisis occasioned by the assassination and her subsequent flight into exile. Before 1973, Allende had been a prominent television host and journalist in Santiago; she had been known as an interviewer rather than as a political or literary figure. Since the publication of *The House of the Spirits*, she has become an internationally recognized champion of feminism and socialism, and commentators have given substantial critical attention both to the radical themes interwoven within her fiction and to her impact on the larger culture, both as a Latina feminist and as a leftist.

Allende's imaginative career is animated by a passion for social justice. In *The House of the Spirits*, she told the multigenerational story of the Trueba family, a saga worthy of Balzac or Galsworthy that indicted the patriarchal and reactionary establishment of Chile in the nineteenth and early twentieth centuries. In *Of Love and Shadows* (*De amor y de sombra,* 1984), Allende elaborated on her critique of reactionary political regimes with an attack on counterrevolutionary politics. As she shows in both novels, the enemies of justice are often the law, the military, and the police as they are embodied in corrupt institutions.

Allende moved in a different direction to more overtly feminist themes in her next two works, *Eva Luna* (1987) and *The Stories of Eva Luna* (*Cuentos de Eva Luna*, 1990). In these works, she created a feminist heroine who is essentially a projection of Allende's own ego ideal, a Latina Scheherazade who served both as a model and as an inspiration to millions of young women readers who came to identify with her in the early 1990s. Allende followed up these works with *The Infinite Plan* (*El plan infinito*, 1991), a heavily autobiographical novel based on the life story of her new husband (California attorney William Gordon) and his itinerant, Bible Belt preacher-father, from whose breast-beating religious tract of the 1930s Allende takes her title. This was also the first Allende work whose setting was in the United States, chiefly in San Francisco and Berkeley, California.

Publication of *The Infinite Plan* in Europe in December 1991 coincided with the shocking collapse of Allende's daughter, Paula Frías, and her descent into a permanent coma in a Madrid hospital, the result of a rare enzyme deficiency known as porphyria. Paula never awoke from her coma. The tragic loss of her twenty-eight-year-old daughter on December 6, 1992 (a year to the very day after she fell ill), plunged Allende into a deep depression, and the trauma not only threatened to end her literary career but also blighted her new marriage and family.

With tenacity and perseverance, Allende worked her way through this protracted crisis and eventually published an amusing work of nonfiction in the form of a cookbook-cum-sex manual, *Aphrodite: A Memoir of the Senses* (*Afrodita*, 1997). Its emphasis on physical appetite and erotic pleasure—the sensuality of food, the excitement of sexual passion—awakened her own senses and eventually triggered an imaginative spark, thereby reviving the emotional state crucial for her mode of impassioned fiction. But first she would pen a memoir to her beloved daughter, a book that arose in circumstances similar to those of *The House of the Spirits*. Published in 1994, it is titled simply *Paula*, and it mushroomed from a series of letters that Allende began writing to Paula just days after the coma began, when Allende still had the highest hopes that her daughter would fully recover. Unlike the case with her grandfather, however, this correspondence was aimed at saving Paula, not mourning her. Isabel's idea at this time was to furnish a very personal epistolary record that Paula could read later to find out everything she had missed during her coma.

It is indeed all that and much more: *Paula* is a gripping, searingly personal account of Allende's tumultuous past life and her daughter's losing fight with death. The memoir also introduces the reader to the dramatic events and larger-than-life family members who have formed the basis of Allende's rich tapestry of fiction and shows that Isabel Allende has led a life as adventurous and dramatic as any of her heroines or heroes. Or as one British reviewer observed, "It gives magical realism a human face."

With her fictional powers restored, Allende now shifted her attention to complete a projected trilogy of novels devoted to the themes originally advanced in *The House of the Spirits*. As it turned out, *The House of the Spirits* would ultimately form the third and final work of the trilogy, so that Allende's two new novels represented essentially the prequels to her first great book. In *Daughter of Fortune* (*Hija de la fortuna*, 1999), Allende highlights her heroine's struggles during and after the 1849 California gold rush and against the backdrop of immigration from Chile to the United States. Combining a storytelling sensibility blessed both with swashbuckling gusto and with Dickensian theatricality, Allende constructs the narrative of Eliza Sommers as an alternative myth in which what comes to matter is not one's pedigree but one's innate qualities of goodness and nobility. In *Portrait in Sepia* (*Retrato en sepia*, 2000), whose narrative history ranges from 1862 to 1910, Allende portrays the colorful del Valle family and showcases the gender, sexual, ethnic, and cultural challenges confronting an immigrant heroine in the United States.

Allende branched out in numerous new directions during the last decade. Among her feats has been to write two new volumes of memoirs, *My Invented Country* (*Mi país inventado,* 2003) and *The Sum of Our Days* (*La suma de los días*, 2007), the novel *Zorro* (2005), three young adult books, and another major new novel, *Island Beneath the Sea* (*La isla bajo el mar*, 2009). Yet because Allende has so often been cast in the role of a popular novelist and a writer of realistic fiction, scant attention has been devoted to her thematic and conceptual innovations. Allende is no formal experimentalist; she is committed to powerful storytelling and to writing readable, plot-driven prose that is always accessible to a wide audience. Nonetheless, if we examine the arc of her career during the past three decades, the degree of innovation in her work is striking.

In the mid-1980s, during the first phase of her career—after the publication of *The House of the Spirits*, *Of Love and Shadows*, and *Eva Luna*—Allende was heralded as inaugurating the Latin American post-Boom and as an exponent of magical realism. She was judged as heavily indebted to Gabriel García Márquez, especially to his path-breaking novel *One Hundred Years of Solitude,* which is often regarded as the defining work of the Boom and indeed the greatest Latin American novel of the twentieth century, an achievement on a par with Joyce's *Ulysses* and Proust's *À la recherche du temps perdu*. Even though Allende eschewed extensive formal experimentation in the mid-1980s, she showed a flair for innovation in her willingness to shift from a family saga to a political thriller to a romance featuring an intrepid (and autobiographical) heroine. Thereafter, Allende became even more daring, moving from genre to genre in search of the best way to communicate her art. After writing these three successful novels, she turned to short stories and proved that she was a masterful storyteller in *The Stories of Eva Luna*.

Then, as the 1990s opened, rather than repeat herself, Allende took a major risk. Drawing on her old skills as an interviewer and journalist, she set her next novel, *The Infinite Plan*, in the United States and portrayed the American West of her new husband's family heritage. After the tragedy that befell Paula, Isabel once again embraced a new form and experimented with nonfiction in *Paula* (and subsequently in *Aphrodite* and in her two memoirs). Each of these works exhibits a bold readiness to break with past work and enter unfamiliar territory, often both in subject matter and literary form. Allende is willing to write in genres and modes that she has never tried before, though she usually prefers the straightforward and carefully plotted realism characteristic of nineteenth-century fiction. (Allende has always said, ever since her days as a television personality in Santiago, that her dream was to become a scriptwriter for a Latin American soap opera, a *telenovela*.)

Whereas Allende's writings of the 1980s—all of them works of realistic fiction—showed her developing her literary sensibility in tandem with her radical politics and feminist vision, Allende coped with tremendous upheaval throughout the 1990s as she searched for suitable forms and themes in which to discover herself as a writer and as a woman. The decade might be divided into "pre-Paula" (1990-1994) and "post-Paula" (1994-1999). As I have suggested, during the first half of the decade, Allende continued her pattern from the 1980s yet developed her art in new directions, especially as she integrated her experience of marriage and stepmotherhood into *The Infinite Plan*. Paula's death marked a terrible divide in the middle of the decade, during which time Allende's fictional voice fell silent. Between 1993 and 1999, she wrote no fiction at all. But she did manage to write two books of nonfiction that reawakened her dormant literary powers and recalibrated her voice in a new register, from which she would write major new novels during the next decade. Beginning in 1999-2000, Allende recovered her voice and vision, which eventually resulted in her completing two more great novels as part of her trilogy. With renewed ambition, she also went on to experiment in innovative ways in her young adult books and in her novels *Zorro* and *Inés of My Soul* (*Inés del alma mía*, 2006).

As Latin American literature has evolved further and further away from the Boom period of the 1960s and 1970s, and even beyond the post-Boom of the 1980s and 1990s, Allende herself has also ranged more freely, sometimes playfully subverting the recognized conventions of realist fiction and so-called magical realism. In her twenty-first-century fiction, even when she has stayed within the limits of the tradition of the realistic novel, Allende has pushed these limits with a sense of audacity, resourcefulness, and pragmatism.

In the final analysis, Isabel Allende has grown enormously during the last three decades, both as a woman of letters in general and as a novelist in particular, refining her art as she ventures new innovations in genre and form—and all the while promoting a radical politics and a feminist vision as foundations for social awareness and collective responsibility. If she had only written *The House of the Spirits*, she would be justly regarded as an important writer in contemporary Latin American literature. But that masterpiece was only the first landmark in what has turned out to be a surprising, eventful career worthy of a real-life Eva Luna. Indeed, Allende's biography, featuring a remarkable history of adventures (and misadventures), attests that life *is* sometimes stranger than fiction. Without question, Isabel Allende's Technicolored life is no portrait in sepia. She can justly be called "the Chilean Scheherazade."

Biography of Isabel Allende_____

Amanda Hopkinson

Like a great many authors, Isabel Allende uses her life in her fiction. However, the games she plays in so doing, and those she plays with her interviewers, have caused critics to assume that she is fictionalizing her life experiences. In fact, Allende remains consistently clear about the difference—if not the separation—between reality and fiction, while insisting on her right to write subjectively of either. It is no coincidence that she describes *Paula*, the story of her daughter's tragic death, as "journalism." (The first magazine Allende worked on was also called *Paula*.) Nor that her Chilean memoirs, recalled in her California home, are called *My Invented Country.* This essay focuses on Allende as the author of both her life and her books—seventeen of them, along with hundreds of articles and stories.

In Spanish, both history and story are referred to by the same word: *historia*. In oral cultures, the hi/stories alter not only with the teller but also with the telling: it would be boring, and may prove impossible, to relate the same tale exactly the same way twice. In the course of my first interview with Allende, in 1992, I asked how she came to meet her present husband, Willie Gordon. She told me, first, that they had been introduced by a mutual friend; then that their eyes had met across a crowded restaurant; finally that she had jumped off the Golden Gate Bridge to rescue a man from drowning. (She had previously told me that she did not know how to swim.) Amused, I asked whether such tales were intended for mere amusement: "You could just say that I enjoy telling lies, although never about anything important," she responded (Interview). The notion that fiction can be mendacious, while real life demands the truth, was instantly upended as Allende acknowledged that she is an unreliable narrator of both fiction and her life.

Isabel Allende Llona was born in Lima, Peru, on August 2, 1942, to a family whose origins are rooted in Castile, Portugal, and the Basque country. Though a Chilean citizen, she was born in Peru because her father (Tomás Allende) was the Chilean ambassador to Peru at the time. Allende's mother (Francisca "Panchita" Llona Barros) came from an aristocratic background with a strongly matriarchal tradition, and her parents vigorously disapproved of her choice of spouse. Allende's family life afforded material for her first best seller, *The House of the Spirits*, which is based largely on her grandmother's stories.

When Allende was only three years old, her father "vanished," an event that Allende has recounted in several imaginative variations, which she later explained as an outgrowth of her need to "therapise" herself through her writing, perhaps to exorcise the ghosts of her past, even to attempt to fill "the great lacuna in my life" left by her father's departure (Cox 2). In time, Allende learned that her father had acquired expensive (if largely concealed) tastes and was living well beyond even an ambassador's means in Lima. Vanishing was apparently a way for him to avoid the inevitable scandal and humiliation.

Panchita Allende, her one daughter, and two sons were assisted by another Chilean diplomat, Ramón Huidobro, in their return to Santiago, Chile, where they took up residence with Isabel's maternal grandparents. Huidobro—although already married and with four children of his own—allegedly pledged himself to look after the beautiful Panchita "forever." In the short term, however, the high-bourgeois Panchita found herself obliged to live as a single parent and take a day job as a bank clerk, then spend her nights sharing her bedroom with her three children. It was no doubt the example of this exceptional resourcefulness that stood Isabel in good stead when her own turn came to be the mainstay in the support of her own children. At the same time, since a secular divorce was unavailable to her, Panchita went through the long and laborious process of getting her first marriage annulled by the Church (in the 1940s such matters were dealt with not, as now, by the local bishop, but by the Pope himself).

In 1948, Panchita joined Ramón Huidobro in a clandestine reunion, soon after which he left his post as attaché to the Chilean embassy in Bolivia and returned to Santiago. There he made a home for his adoptive family while waiting for the furor fomented by the older generations on both sides to die down. Nearly eight years passed before the two legally married. As an adult, Isabel was to recognize that she had as many difficulties as most children in adapting to a new stepfather and that she deeply resented sharing her mother with him. However, she gradually learned not only to call him "Tío [Uncle] Ramón" but also to respect his qualities as well as his authority and even to love him dearly. She would even dedicate some of her later books to him, calling him "father," for it was he who fulfilled the paternal role throughout her formative years.

Like her mother before her, Panchita had, apparently, started recounting tales to her Isabel while she was still in the womb. For her children, curious about the old-fashioned nature of their first home in Santiago—and aware from an early age that their grandfather, whom Isabel came to adore, had been raised without electricity or running water—Panchita composed a patchwork family tree, using her active imagination to color in the branches of which she had little or uncertain knowledge. In a period before television, when even radio programs were for adults, storytelling was not merely a domestic but still a normal, even national, pastime. Yet Panchita brought a particular seriousness to the medium, and early on young Isabel determined to adapt and adopt her mother's skills. As she later recalled of a preschool birthday party, though her family had hired entertainers, all of the children were drawn to Isabel as she told them story after story.

Once married, the couple and the three children moved, first to Bolivia, where Ramón had been reassigned, then on to Beirut. During this five-year period, Allende's education was largely in English: in Bolivia she attended a U.S. school and in Beirut, an English one. Here, she discovered for herself the joys of reading Shakespeare and Scheherazade's *One Thousand and One Arabian Nights*, which Tío Ramón kept out of the children's reach in a cupboard, though Isabel secretly removed it. Although it did not contain anywhere near the number of lewd passages she had hoped for, she discovered sensuality in the feel of the book's beautiful binding and liberation in its fantastic stories.

In 1958, two years into the Suez Canal crisis, the whole family returned to Chile for a visit. When they returned to the Middle East, Isabel undertook a spell of home education with her respected—and adored—grandfather and then completed high school. She later claimed that she had had no thoughts of continuing on to university: it was not what her patriarchal grandfather expected of a young woman and not what Allende demanded of herself. Nor was it the role model provided by her own mother.

As the only daughter in the family, Isabel was always immensely close to her mother, with whom she shared bedtime stories that, even though they may have passed through printed editions, were best related rather than read aloud. Then, while the rest of her family was abroad, the custom of a daily exchange of letters with her mother began, one that has persisted to this day. It has stood her in immensely good stead ever since, not only as a source of advice, solidarity, and inspiration but also as an archive of past events and thoughts, as at the end of each year Isabel now collects back her own letters and binds them together with her mother's replies. No doubt, both sides of this near-unique correspondence will one day become many fascinating volumes describing a writer's-eye view of life in its most frightening, confusing, joyous, and intimate moments—and without recourse to the devices of narrative fiction, unreliable or otherwise.

Each one of Allende's novels has an epistolary element—from her first, *The House of the Spirits*, which began as a letter to her beloved grandfather during her political exile in Caracas, to the tales of Eva Luna, to the missives she read aloud to her comatose daughter, Paula, during Paula's last illness. Even the largely autobiographical *The Sum of Our Days*, which takes up where *Paula* left off, is prefaced by a letter that begins "Dear Booksellers." Between its polite opening thanks and its tempting closing promise ("I have to tell the whole story"), Allende includes the admission: "I am a born liar, so fiction is my territory: I create the story and I shape the destinies of my characters. . . . My only problem with fiction is to make it believable. A memoir, however, is an attempt to tell the truth, and truth usually is less believable than fiction."

In 1959, at the age of just seventeen, Allende accepted a secretarial post with the United Nations Food and Agricultural Organization (FAO), where she continued working until 1965. By this time she had been married three years, to Miguel—whom she called "Michael" out of respect for their shared Anglophilia—Frías, whom she had met when he was an engineering student in Santiago. They traveled in Europe together, visiting England before both winning fellowships to study in Brussels, where Isabel continued working for FAO. Their daughter, Paula, was born in 1963 and their son, Nicolás, on their return to Santiago in 1966. Isabel gave up working at FAO in 1965 and began translating highly sentimental "pink romances" from English into Spanish. Where she found Barbara Cartland's prose repetitious and her heroines tame, Isabel could not resist improving on the original, introducing not only feisty passages of verbal dexterity but also imposing endings in which the heroines become independent rather than wed. Before long, these rewrites were noted, and Allende's career as a literary translator was over.

Allende realized her personal interests and literary style were better suited to the feminist than the romantically feminine. She joined the women's paper *Paula* as a columnist and editor; contributed to children's magazines (most notably *Mampato*, where she rose to become editor); and began making television documentaries, including a series for the "humour channel." At the recommendation of the great Chilean poet Pablo Neruda, whom she met in 1972, she edited her satirical columns into her first book. Her name was becoming known throughout the media, even while she still considered herself primarily a mother, wife, and caregiver. She remained largely a conformist product of her background, however eccentric; she understood herself to be a woman of her class and of her time. Her personality was questing rather than rebellious; her interests cultural rather than political.

Nonetheless, in the polarized Latin America of the 1960s and 1970s there was to be no such thing as apolitical. A period of increasingly repressive regimes, many initiated by military putsches, left little political space for a "middle way," or for publicly stated libertarian attitudes. And traditional culture was also being buffeted by the winds of change: feminism was a force to be reckoned with, one that would (however many years later) impact domestic laws, for Chile was the last Latin American country to finally legislate to allow divorce and abortion.

Conversely, the 1960s saw the rapid growth of the movement known as the Latin American Boom, with authors such as Gabriel García Márquez (Colombia), Mario Vargas Llosa (Peru), Carlos Fuentes and Octavio Paz (Mexico), and Jorge Luis Borges and Julio Cortázar (Argentina) achieving sudden and substantial international reputations with a type of writing commonly called magical realism. While its name was first applied by Alejo Carpentier to the particularly baroque style of his native Cuba, and exemplified by the modernist/populist character of the Guatemalan Miguel Ángel Asturias's *Men of Maize* in the 1950s, the term originated with Christopher Columbus to describe the hyperreal beauty of the Caribbean isle he named Hispaniola but which he believed to be at least a whole new continent, at best "the shores of paradise." Allende, as wholly European in her family background as almost all her fellow Latin American writers, still shared some of that wonder at both the luxuriant nature and the strangely grafted cultures of her native region. She was different, however, in being a woman, and although women writers were also making their names, none received anything like the accolades the male writers of the Boom received.

In 1970 Salvador Allende, leader of the Socialist Party, was elected president of Chile. It was his third bid for power, and he was a man already advanced in years. To Isabel, this rare senior male relative from her father's side of the family was "Uncle" Salvador. Strictly speaking, he was her father's cousin, making him her cousin once removed, but in extended families—and especially where members are clearly of different generations—a term such as "uncle" can swiftly substitute for a much more cumbersome name. In any case, the Spanish for "first cousin once removed" back-translates as *uncle to the second degree*."

On September 11, 1973, General Augusto Pinochet deposed "uncle" President Salvador Allende, in a bloody CIA-backed coup in which Allende was shot dead in the presidential palace, La Moneda. Pinochet was to remain in power for seventeen years, until voted out on a referendum he then sought to repudiate. Throughout that period, organized workers and liberal intellectuals found themselves among the tens of thousands of Chileans targeted for "disappearances." These disappearances, meticulously executed by the three armed forces, generally involved the abduction and torture of their targets in clandestine detention centers before their summary executions—which were frequently carried out through such extrajudicial methods as being thrown out of helicopters or abandoned at sea.

Isabel and Miguel became drawn into a network that helped those most at risk evade the death squads, the country, or both. Panchita and Ramón, as diplomats who had served under Salvador Allende, only narrowly avoided assassination, and soon Isabel herself began to receive death threats. Her critical play, *El embajador*, performed in 1973, attracted unwanted political attention. The magazine *Paula*, on whose editorial board Allende now sat, was first heavily censored, then summarily shut down. Feminism was now deemed tantamount to the Communism of which Salvador Allende stood accused. When, in 1974, a family friend and the former commander-in-chief of the armed forces was assassinated in Argentina—where he had fled, but where the military were increasingly collaborating with the Chilean armed forces—Isabel's parents sought asylum in Venezuela. Isabel, Michael, and the children, by now also the victims of death threats, followed them to Caracas.

Isabel always said that she thought this was a temporary move. In any event, she remained in Venezuela for thirteen years and was never to resume living in Chile. Her career as a freelance columnist was launched in exile, and she entered the mainstream as a reporter for the prestigious daily *El Nacional*. Pablo Neruda had told her she had too much imagination to be a proper fact-finding journalist. Thus it was under the duress of exile that, on January 8, 1981, she learned her beloved 99-year-old grandfather was dying in Santiago and began writing a letter to him.

Five hundred pages later, almost all written at night, this "letter" became the typescript of *The House of the Spirits* (1982), Isabel's first novel, born of the fantastical stories that together constituted a fabulous version of her family history. Yet she claimed the ghosts she was exorcising were those the Pinochet regime was responsible for "disappearing." The book also referred to the real murdered heroes of the Chilean Left (the singer Victor Jara, the poet Miguel Enríquez), described the horrors of illegal detention and torture, and quoted Salvador Allende's farewell broadcast to his people from the besieged La Moneda palace. Because of its imaginative weaving of Allende's homeland's contemporary history with the direct experiences of its author and of those she knew, the book has been accused of imitating the already immensely successful version of Latin American culture propounded by García Márquez's first best seller, *One Hundred Years of Solitude*. But in making the ever-resourceful Clara, whose notebooks record and connect a dynasty of powerful and sensual women, the main narrator, Allende not only effects the more radical shift from fantasy to reality but also relates the narrative through a series of women's voices.

While thus engaging with her own recent past and her country's immediate present by night, Allende held down a job as the financial administrator and admissions registrar of the Marrocco School, where she worked double shifts from 1979 to 1983 to make ends meet. Her marriage was, however, coming under increasing stress. Leaving home and living abroad, even in a country that shared some of the constraints of church and family of her homeland, Allende was encountering a period of sexual liberation. In 1978 she had followed a lover to Spain, a move that was short-lived, but indicative of a permanent change in her personal relationships. Although she returned to live with Michael, and they were to remain lasting friends, she was increasingly leading her life as an individual rather than as a wife.

Her own account of this period says much of the impact of these political, personal, and cultural changes on her career, without her ever having consciously chosen it.

> On 8th January 1981 . . . I received a phone call that my beloved grandfather was dying. I began a letter to him that later became my first novel. . . . It was such a lucky book from the very beginning, that I kept that date to start [every other book I have written]. ("Questions and Answers" para. 88)

It was a work that harnessed all her established patterns of writing: like an investigative journalist, Isabel kept files on all her characters, and the important events of their times; and, as always, she consulted her mother at every stage, and took Panchita's advice about ordering and expanding her material. From then on, Panchita was to be her first reader and most trusted critic and editor. Panchita also proved crucial in finding an agent for the work at a time when Allende was receiving only rejections. Carmen Balcells, the pioneering Spanish founder and director of her eponymous agency, read *The House of the Spirits* in one sitting and took it—and Isabel Allende—on board immediately.

The book at once became a global best seller. In Chile, where it was banned, it was secretly circulated in photocopied form, a technique commonly known as *samizdat* during the days of the Soviet Union. Exactly two years later, Isabel commenced *Of Love and Shadows* (1984), a very different work. While *The House of the Spirits* crossed conventional boundaries between high and low art (or, in a Latin American context, between the intellectual and the popular) and was retailed through both university bookshops and supermarket stores such as Woolworth's, her second book was more recognizable as a midlist novel. Allende herself described it as "a police story that could have been written by a journalist." It was also to be the work that prompted her second husband, Willie Gordon, to request an introduction.

In 1987, Isabel and Michael definitively separated and divorced amicably. In August of that year, a fellow exiled author, Celia Correas Zapata, then living in California, managed at last to bring Allende to the United States to give a lecture to her university class and to give an interview for the biography she was planning to write. Celia also gave Gordon, a friend and a San Francisco attorney, a copy of the book. He wrote back to her that "the author understands love in the same way as I," and, when Allende arrived in the States, they met together in a restaurant. In characteristic style, Allende describes how "Willie appeared in front of me that very day, and from then on we never separated. I left everything behind me in Venezuela, to stay with this *gringo* with Irish looks, who spoke Spanish like a Mexican film bandit, and at the end of six months I convinced him, not without difficulty, I admit, to marry me" (Correas Zapata 14).

Allende drew up not a proposal but a contract, which she faxed to him on her return to Caracas. After all, what better to send a lawyer than a contract? Yet the numerous clauses she included were less concerned with what has since become the substance of prenuptial agreements than with the essence of what would be their future life together. She expected a marriage, she explained, to include mutual respect and shared amusement and to be based on common assumptions about love. Once he had signed, Allende packed up and relocated to California, where they married on July 17, 1988. Interestingly, Allende would later describe the book that had brought them together as born of "years of anger at dictatorship, not just in Chile, but across the whole of Latin America."

That each of Allende's books explores a new genre, even a new ethos, is less a matter of literary devices and the desire to experiment than an outcome of the fact that Allende relates each one to a different period in her own autobiography. Following *Of Love and Shadows* were two companion volumes, *Eva Luna* (1987) and *The Stories of Eva Luna* (1990), whose unlikely heroine—poor, ill educated, rough around the edges—is a feminist protagonist. How far Isabel identified with a personage in many superficial senses her own opposite is suggested by the fact that Eva, too, gives birth to another volume of tales of her own.

The next book was again the fruit of an enforced life change, her daughter Paula's fatal illness. In 1991, one year into her marriage to a young Spaniard named Ernesto, Paula, who was then twenty-seven, fell into a porphyria-induced coma. Allende recounts that the book named for her daughter (1994) was "written during the interminable hours spent in the corridors of a Madrid hospital and in the hotel room where I lived for several months, as well as beside her bed in our home in California during the summer and fall of 1992" (*Paula* 1). Isabel believed, against medical opinion, that her comatose daughter might hear, even if she could not respond. So while she nursed Paula, she related the tales belonging to the world of her own childhood, right up until Paula's death on December 6, 1992.

Typically, each of the stories of *Paula* begins with: "Listen, Paula. I am going to tell you a story, so that when you wake up you will not feel so lost" (3). Yet there is always a level beyond the simply personal: Allende invokes an ancient Greek myth, that of the goddess Demeter, who is compelled to pursue her daughter, Persephone, through the halls of Hades (in Allende's case, the pursuit is through the corridors of the hospital and hotel). Compelled to bear her daughter's affliction as her own—for Paula's doctors insisted that Paula was insentient in her unconsciousness—Allende found even the all-consuming *porphyria*, which means the funereal color of purple, redolent of her own mourning.

Allende treats Paula's death as a tragedy of classical dimensions, even one of religious symbolism, whose central relationship is that of the agnostic mother seeking to recover and retain her Christian daughter. (Paula's last words, just before slipping into the coma, were "I go looking everywhere for God, but He slips away from me, Mama," followed by, "I love you, too, Mama" [*Paula* 19, 20].) Isabel would come to regard this episode as having as great an impact on her life as Pinochet's coup: both appeared to arrive like thunderbolts, and she had no choice or control in either case beyond what she herself could create out of the experience. To date, the intensely moving account that is *Paula* has sold more than any other of Isabel's books. In 1995, the British Broadcasting Corporation produced the film *Listen, Paula*, which closely tracks the life stories of the two Allendes, mother and daughter, through the pages of the book.

The launch party for *The Infinite Plan* (a title that says much about Allende's own philosophy) in Madrid on December 8, 1991, had coincided with the news of Paula's admission to hospital. It was Allende's first book to engage with her move to California and the many contradictions it generated. This reconstruction of her experiences in a literary form epitomized what Allende calls her "therapeutic writing"—and a means of differentiating the Chilean from the Argentinean tradition of taking all of one's experiences to a psychoanalyst for dissection. Paradoxically, it was only when Willie and Isabel hit repeated crises in their own relationship (which is arguably inevitable in a stepfamily in which both daughters have died—Willie's daughter, Jennifer, through a heroin addiction), and their sons were also having difficulty, that they plunged into joint therapy at a point where otherwise they would surely have separated.

While Allende was suffering from depression and writer's block, films of both *The House of the Spirits* (starring Jeremy Irons and Meryl Streep, 1993) and *Of Love and Shadows* (starring Antonio Banderas, 1994) appeared. Isabel's own move, however, was not from one medium to another but, in the first instance, geographical. She took a long boat trip up the Amazon River, which she wrote about in an essay, just to get herself writing again. No sooner had she accomplished this than she returned to base, creating a highly original "recipe book" she called *Aphrodite: A Memoir of the Senses* (1997). The flyleaf notes, "I dedicate these erotic meanderings to playful lovers and, why not? also to frightened men and melancholy women." Part celebration, not only of the senses of taste and touch but also of eroticism and advancing maturity (Isabel calls "the fiftieth year of our life, like the last hour of dusk" [7]), this book is also her first collaboration. In it, the almost edible illustrations are supplied by Robert Shekter and the recipes by her mother, who is credited as Panchita Llona. It contains also a long dedication to Carmen Balcells, not only for her encouragement and efficacy as an agent but also for her Catalan soups, her spicy blood sausage, and her ever-welcoming and groaning spread table. The whole functions as much as a celebration of Allende's extended family, embracing friends and colleagues, as of food and sex.

The ludic aspect lay as much in its reception as in its production. Allende confesses having to laugh at the seriousness with which she was cross-examined by the media on the supposed aphrodisiac properties of her dishes, which she only later revealed were largely made up on the spot. Nonetheless, the rediscovery of laughter, after nearly three years in mourning for Paula, helped precipitate her return to writing novels.

This time, *Daughter of Fortune* (1999) followed its author in relocating to California. Like its sequel, *Portrait in Sepia* (2000), it pursues three generations of the same family, beginning at the time of the 1862 gold rush and continuing up until 1910. The story does not properly stop here, however, since the main protagonists are in fact grandparents to those in *The House of the Spirits.* Living in a state such as California, with its long tradition of Chicanos and Latinos, its immigrants and now its wealthy Latin residents, it was near-inevitable that in making a break with grief and the past Allende would move on to a different kind of an epic, one involving immigration north and south of the Rio Grande. Enormous quantities of research were called for, particularly in the Bay Area libraries and bookshops, and the historical novel came of age in Allende's bibliography.

Another kind of transformation took place with her next book, *City of the Beasts* (2002), for which the Amazonian journey also served. Again the start of a trilogy, it was pitched at a new teenage audience at just the point in time when Allende's own grandchildren (through her son, Nicolás, now on his second marriage) were growing into adolescence. Following it were *Kingdom of the Golden Dragon* (2003) and *Forest of the Pygmies* (2004), all of them major successes targeted in the youth market.

At the same time, Allende was experimenting again. The result, *My Invented Country* (2003), contains an epigram from the poet who so inadvertently, in criticizing her journalism, started her on her fantastical journeys. In 1972, the year they met, Pablo Neruda wrote, "For some reason or other, I am a sad exile. In some way or other, our land travels with me and with me too, though far far away, live the longitudinal essences of my country" (qtd. in *My Invented Country* epigraph).

What seems to have precipitated this book is Allende's final acceptance of the opposite: while writing might be nostalgia (or "a constant exercise in longing" [*My Invented Country* xi]) for her, she is ultimately no longer just Chilean, or even Latin American, but simply American. Many Latin Americans have long and deeply resented the United States' appropriation of the term *America*, which is derived from the name of the early cartographer Amerigo Vespucci, who charted all the Americas. To Allende the symbiosis came of age with the destruction of the Twin Towers of the World Trade Center on the same date, and at almost the same hour, as the destruction of Salvador Allende's democratically elected civilian government, twenty-eight years earlier. Like her compatriot author and fellow U.S. resident Ariel Dorfman, Allende sees the coincidence as ineluctably linking her fate with that of her adopted country, now her home. This long last look back at Chile, then, is in part a moving (if intermittently invented) reminiscence, in part a song of praise to the place and people of her land of origin.

In search of new heroes and heroines, Allende went on to excavate the life story of *Zorro* (2005), the masked swashbuckler of eighteenth-century epic history and son of a Southern Californian Shoshone mother and a Spanish aristocrat. Here, for the first time, Allende deliberately crosses the adolescent/adult divide, something underlined by the book's subsequent adaptation as a stage musical "for all the family." A year later there followed *Inés of my Soul* (2006), the tale of a Spanish *conquistadora* in the unlikely setting of sixteenth-century Chile and Peru. Again, much rigorous research into the better-known lives of the conquistadors Pedro de Valdivia (who becomes Inés's lover) and Francisco Pizarro is matched by the dazzling extravagance of an extraordinary, somewhat wild, and highly courageous woman.

In 2007, Allende brought her readers up to date with *The Sum of Our Days*. She uses her multi-American family (minus one of Willie's sons, who requested that his part be removed), and their neighbors and friends as her cast of characters. The book opens with the exuberantly titled chapter "The Capricious Muse of Dawn" and with the phrase, "There is no lack of drama in my life, I have more than enough three-ring-circus material for writing" (1). In three hundred pages, it tells the story of how an extended dysfunctional family can begin to be welded into one "small tribe," despite two deaths, numerous births, and a running subtext of drugs and divorce, separations and exiles. It triumphs, finally, in a slow exploration of the delights and comforts of older age and, if not utter harmony, at least mutual acceptance. Even the journey through Indian mysticism resonates in the concluding sentence: "The sum of our days, our shared pains and joy, was now our destiny" (297).

Allende's mining of her own life and family history has brought her public rewards, awards, and accolades. Indeed, it could almost be said that Allende has been as much written about as writing, yet she has never been truly a writer's writer. Her severest critics have probably been from within Latin America and include her fellow Chilean the late Roberto Bolaño (whose enormous success has mainly come posthumously) and Gabriel García Márquez himself. Yet she has been honored in the United States with the Dorothy and Lillian Gish Prize; in

France with the Grand Prix d'Evasion and with being named a Chevalier des Arts et Lettres; in Italy with the Bancarella Prize; and, finally, in Latin America with the Gabriela Mistral Prize.

Bibliography

Allende, Isabel. *Aphrodite: A Memoir of the Senses*. New York: HarperPerennial, 1998.

_____. *Conversations with Isabel Allende*. 1999. Ed. John Rodden. Austin: U of Texas P, 2004.

_____. Interview with Amanda Hopkinson. April 2008.

_____. *My Invented Country: A Memoir*. New York: HarperCollins, 2003.

_____. *Paula*. New York: HarperCollins, 1995.

_____. "Questions and Answers." Isabel Allende Web site. 1 Apr. 2010. http://www.isabelAllende.com/curious_frame.htm.

_____. *The Sum of Our Days*. Hammersmith, England: Fourth Estate, 2008.

Correas Zapata, Celia. *Isabel Allende: Life and Spirits*. Trans. Margaret Sayers Peden. Houston, TX: Arte Público Press, 2002.

Cox, Karen Castellucci. *Isabel Allende: A Critical Companion*. Westport, CT: Greenwood Press, 2003.

McNeese, Tim. *Isabel Allende*. New York: Chelsea House, 2006.

PARIS
REVIEW

The *Paris Review* Perspective_____

Michael Wood for *The Paris Review*

The style of Gabriel García Márquez constitutes a whole narrative school, and its star pupil is Isabel Allende. When she leaves school, as pupils must, she remains a fluent and inventive storyteller but becomes, paradoxically, a little less herself. She moves from the magical, mythological history that marks so marvelously *The House of the Spirits* (1982), *Of Love and Shadows* (1984), and *Eva Luna* (1987) to the more straightforward romantic history of *Daughter of Fortune* (1999), *Portrait in Sepia* (2000) and *Inés of My Soul* (2006). The shift, compelling and necessary, no doubt, for the writer, leaves the reader admiring but mildly nostalgic for the old intricacies.

Even as a pupil, however, Allende made clear her differences from the master Márquez. If his writing rests, as he has suggested, on the memory of his grandmother's storytelling, her writing demonstrates that we all have storytelling grandmothers—and that we live among their stories. The question is simply whether we listen to them and whether their mythologies allow the writers among us to do things that old-fashioned realism manifestly does not. (The question is as important for Toni Morrison and Salman Rushdie as it is for Allende, and of course García Márquez himself attended the great school of supposedly unreliable ancestral narrative, that of William Faulkner.)

These mythologies work best in fiction when they are in open dialogue with official or rational history or any kind of history that has no time for grandmothers' tales. In this kind of fiction, fables and myths subvert the notional truths of that history and offer truths of their own amid the hyperactive claims made by fantastical tales. The tales are real without being literal, although their narrators often pretend that the extravagant doings they recount are literally true. The pretense and the extravagance are both important, and their combination produces something quite different from either realism or fantasy. This result has a name—magical realism—that has become virtually meaningless through sheer wear and tear. But, as Allende reminds us, we should hang on to the concept of reality haunted by magic, magic that is wrestling constantly with obdurate realities.

The House of the Spirits begins with this passage:

> Barrabás arrived in the family by sea, little Clara noted in her careful handwriting. Even then she had the habit of writing down important things, and later, when she became dumb, she wrote down insignificant things too, without suspecting that fifty years later her notebooks would help me to rescue the memory of the past and to survive my own terror.

This opening, at the beginning of her very first book, already bears Allende's signature—in its emphasis on writing, the textual trace that leads the present back to the past. There is a neat instance in the recent novel *Inés of My Soul*, where the narrator not only insists on the fact of her writing but also tells us when the ink and the writing hand change: "I get tired now after a few lines and prefer to dictate to you; my handwriting looks like a tangle of flies but yours, Isabel, is subtle and elegant. You like the rust-colored ink recently brought from Spain."

Allende's stories declare their own provenance, the direct relation from person to person that brings the past to us, even if most—and in some cases all—of the protagonists of the story are dead. The very obliquities of narrative method Allende has so brilliantly learned from García Márquez—in the passage from *The House of the Spirits* we cannot yet know who Barrabás is, why Clara becomes dumb, who is narrating, or what her terror was—lead to a territory that is very much her own: a place that is often named only indirectly but is unmistakably Chile, with a history that belongs far more fully to its characters than any history in García Márquez does and an open reflection on destinies and events that boldly breaks all rules of narrative discretion. "Now I doubt my hatred," the narrator of *The House of the Spirits* writes, after a detailed account of the terror promised in the first lines of the book, speaking for Allende as much as for herself. A little later she explains herself more fully: "I look for my hatred and can't find it. . . . It will be difficult for me to avenge all those who need to be avenged because my vengeance would only be another part of the same inexorable ritual. I want to believe that my task is life."

Like Julio Cortázar, García Márquez combined literary disenchantment with radical activism: there is nothing in their fictional work to contradict the most depressing prognostications for Latin America. On the contrary: the despair in the work demands some sort of action in the world. Allende's stance is quite different and altogether more positive on the page. It is not that she does not have her forms of irony—when she writes, at the start of *Inés,* of avoiding "panic among my possible readers," there is plenty of wit and self-awareness in the words "panic" and "possible." But when she writes, in the same note, that "any resemblance" between the contents of her novel and the "facts and persons of the conquest of Chile is not accidental," she is acknowledging the stern reality of recent experience and consciously rejecting any revisionist program, whether built on despair or the preaching of progress.

In Allende, history is what it is. The Spanish murderers of indigenous populations, she proposes, were noble figures, some of them, and not all people who live in criminal times are criminals. None of them are saints, either, though some of them are survivors, and certain forms of human decency survive with them, especially forms that allow us to transcend hatred. It is the voice of those survivors that we constantly hear in her fiction, those who have endured through a form of historical magic. If Allende has left magical realism behind, it is no doubt because that magic itself no longer needs separate advertisement. We cannot think of history without it.

CRITICAL CONTEXTS

"Un puñado de críticos":
Navigating the Critical Readings
of Isabel Allende's Work_____

Beth E. Jörgensen

This project of the *Latin American Literary Review Press* pays a significant scholarly tribute to the literary phenomenon known as Isabel Allende. The unexpected success of her first novel in 1982, her astonishing rise to popularity among readers in Latin America, Europe, and the United States, the widespread translations of her books, and her steady production of fiction and memoir over the past twenty years place her at the center of Latin American literature. Both the writer as a public figure and her work have been met by a varied and polemical critical response that involves journalists and scholars from many countries and the author herself. Three manifestations of literary study engage in an ongoing dialogue: interviews with Allende, book reviews, and research articles and books. In this essay I address the primary trends in the English and Spanish-language criticism and analysis of Allende's writings from *La casa de los espíritus* (1982) to *Retrato en sepia* (2001). Limited references to selected interviews and book reviews will provide a point of departure for a more in-depth examination of scholarly books and articles that have made a significant contribution to our understanding of Allende's texts and the contexts of their production and reception. From the outset it should be acknowledged that the vast majority of the criticism is highly favorable, with few dissenting voices. Allende's novels are widely praised for a variety of qualities, including most notably their feminist perspective, their strong female protagonists, and a generous capacity for good, "old-fashioned" storytelling. My objective is to explore the points of convergence and conflict in the criticism and, in concluding, to signal aspects of Allende's work, including some problematical qualities, that have not received due attention. I start by accounting for the large body of criticism on *La casa de los espíritus*, *De amor y de sombra*, and *Eva Luna*, and the well-known debate over *Casa*, and then I focus on the relatively few articles that treat her books published from 1991 to 2001. In this way I hope to provide a critical context within which to read and appreciate the new essays brought together in this volume.[1]

It is impossible to undertake a broad review and analysis of this kind without considering the author's own famously negative opinion of critics and criticism. Even a cursory look at a selection of the published interviews with Isabel Allende finds numerous examples of her dissatisfaction with critics, which occasionally borders on contempt. I borrowed a phrase from a recent interview to use in my title: "No creo que un puñado de críticos tenga más autoridad moral o literaria que los lectores. ¿Quiénes son? Gente que no sabe escribir. Escritores frustrados que les gusta lo hermético. Si una cosa se populariza, ya le tienen desconfianza. Les da rabia que yo venda porque ellos no venden" (Rosendo González 68). On other occasions she has poked fun at the whole project of literary study, for example by expressing sympathy for students who must spend their time "looking for symbols and metaphors in a book of mine where there were no symbols and metaphors intended" (Carrión interview, in Rodden 310). To be sure, her novels have been the object of controversy and debate, and at the time of each book's publication a mix of reviews has appeared in the press that includes highly favorable ones and others that are more skeptical.[2] Nevertheless, overall Allende has been well served by critics, scholars, and their students, who, as we will see, have given her writing careful, perceptive readings and have helped argue the case for her prominent stature among contemporary writers.

Research articles on Isabel Allende's first three novels started appearing by the mid 1980s, and they comprise at least eighty percent of the criticism to date. Of these, the analyses of *La casa de los espíritus* vastly outnumber all the rest combined, although *De amor y de sombra* (1984) and *Eva Luna* (1987) have each received considerable scrutiny from a variety of critical perspectives. It hardly needs mentioning that the single most commonly—and hotly—debated question for about a decade was the relationship of *Casa* to Gabriel García Márquez's *Cien años de soledad*. Is *La casa de los espíritus* "parody or piracy," a case of legitimate intertextuality or just "imitation García Márquez," literary innovation or literary debtor? Virtually every article on the novel addresses this question at least in passing, and many interviewers have asked Allende to comment on the influence of García Márquez's magical realist masterpiece on her own first novel. It is the hot button issue that has most persistently energized and polarized her readers. Setting aside book reviews, some of which dismissed *Casa* because of its strong initial resemblance to *Cien años*, the critical studies that treat the matter with care generally provide a balanced accounting of both the textual correspondences and the divergences between them. The process of examining this question has revealed important aspects of Allende's writing style and thematic concerns, and it has also given us new ways to read García Márquez. If it is tempting sometimes to view the controversy as the proverbial six-hundred-pound gorilla that we all just wish would go away, the truth is that those who have confronted it directly have contributed to our understanding and evaluation of *La casa de los espíritus* and to the larger debate over the meaning of originality and tradition in literature.

Early articles by Marcelo Coddou, Juan Manuel Marcos, and Mario Rojas (all 1985) refer to the obvious similarities between the two novels and they acknowledge, in Rojas's phrase, that "el 'espíritu' de *Cien años de soledad* flota constantemente en *La casa de los espíritus*" (917). Marcos's position that *Casa* represents an original and captivating treatment of the Latin American family saga and magical realism is frequently cited in later studies. However, a detailed analysis of the numerous "afinidades y corespondencias" must wait until Robert Antoni's excellent 1988 article, "Parody or Piracy: The Relationship of *The House of the Spirits* to *One Hundred Years of Solitude*." In addition to Antoni, I will look at four other key essays that contribute to the debate. "Parody or Piracy" parts from the hypothesis that Isabel Allende either consciously or unconsciously began writing her novel squarely within the García Márquez tradition of magical realism. The first chapter of *Casa*, in particular, is paradigmatic of literary reworking in the form of parody. Antoni creates an impressively complete list of the similarities between the two books that the earlier articles alluded to and that later critics will reiterate: the striking resemblance between the opening lines; the similar use of the literary devices of hyperbole, oxymoron, personification, flashback and prolepsis (all typical of magical realism); the family saga; and parallel characters, to name some of the most important ones. However, Antoni's point is not to make the case for parody. On the contrary, his thesis is that Allende begins in parody, but gradually substitutes her own language and her own vision for that of García Márquez. Allende's significant innovations include the counterpoint of masculine and feminine voices through the inclusion of Esteban Trueba's narrating I; the predominance of female characters and a feminine tradition of writing (what is often referred to as the feminocentric quality of the novel); and the way in which *Casa* changes from a magical-realist story into an ever more realistic retelling of "the tragic political history of Chile" (21). Ultimately, tragedy replaces comedy and history replaces magic as *La casa de los espíritus*, "which began as an attempt to rewrite *One Hundred Years of Solitude* . . . discovers itself as a unique statement" (25).

Robert Antoni's defense of the originality of Allende's first novel is taken up by the other critics who pursue elements of his argument from different perspectives. Lyana María Amaya R. and Aura María Fernández R. use the principles of deconstruction in a study of the characters of the two novels. By comparing Úrsula and Clara, José Arcadio Buendía and Esteban Trueba, and the pairs José Arcadio/Aureliano and Jaime/Nicolás they demonstrate how the matrilineal family structure of *Casa* subverts García Márquez's patriarchal text and leads to an ending that projects into the future, as opposed to the "vía de extinción" portrayed in *Cien años de soledad* (195).

Nicasio Urbina's 1990 article carries out a fairly complete comparative analysis of the two novels along the lines of Antoni's work, in order to show that both share "un modelo retórico común" in their representations of a common Latin American reality. Without in any way effacing the influence of *Cien años de soledad* and Macondo in *La casa de los espíritus*, he refers to Harold Bloom's "anxiety of influence" as a reminder that the notion of literary originality is a cultural construct and that absolute originality does not exist. *Cien años de soledad* employs already existing literary codes, and Allende then reworks them in her own effective manner. Without finally including Allende in his list of "auténticos revolucionarios en su arte," a list comprised of García Márquez, Cervantes, Homer, Shakespeare, and Darío, Urbina does characterize Isabel Allende as an accomplished creative artist who "logra excelentes resultados en una senda abierta por un precursor" (228).

Laurie Clancy, in turn, pushes Antoni's argument a little further in her 1995 analysis. She agrees with him that Allende is conscious of initially writing a "parasitic" text, or a deliberate recovering of the earlier novel's terrain. Clancy's thesis is that Allende challenges García Márquez's "fatalistic submission" to Latin American history and replaces his circular, pessimistic view with an image of meaningfulness, change, and transformation informed by her feminism and her Marxism (42-43). Finally, Ray Keck looks beyond the *Casa-Cien años* pairing to address both novel's relationship to *Don Quijote* through the parallel figures of Cide Hamete, Melquíades, and Alba Trueba. Keck concludes that the device of the literary frame is most successfully employed by Allende in her creation of Alba as narrator, editor, chronicler, and participant in the family and the national saga.

All of the articles discussed ultimately defend the value and the originality of *La casa de los espíritus*. Facile dismissals and accusations of imitation play no role in these scholars' interpretations of the novel, in spite of the easily identified similarities between the two works. If I have one fault to find, it is that in an effort to draw a clear line between the two texts, the critics tend to downplay or even ignore the historical and political dimensions of *Cien años de soledad*. That is, almost all of the articles point out the strongly referential, realistic character of the second half of *Casa* as a major difference from *Cien años*. In doing so, they seem to have forgotten the many and important ways in which García Márquez represents and critiques specific, identifiable episodes in Colombian history in his depiction of political violence (the decades-long clash between liberals and conservatives); economic imperialism (the banana companies); and the repression of workers (the massacre of the strikers). These are powerful components of the story of Macondo, and it is wrong to omit them in an effort to enhance the reading of Allende's novel. I would also suggest that a conscientious, open-minded reader may still react negatively to the many similarities that these critics point out, in spite of their conclusions. Perhaps one person's creative intertextuality is another reader's imitation, and perhaps the difference depends on each one's formation as a reader, attachment to cultural ideals of originality, capacity for recall, and preference for new versus familiar reading experiences.

The second controversial issue surrounding *La casa de los espíritus*, also extending to *De amor y de sombra* and to a lesser degree *Eva Luna*, concerns the ideological value of the texts. No one disputes Allende's abilities as a storyteller, no one denies her creation of feminocentric fictional world, and no one argues with her success in adapting popular literary genres to new uses, but opinion is deeply divided on the relative liberalism or conservatism of her novels' politics. Again, most studies praise Allende's writing by emphasizing its forward-looking optimism and its feminist critique of patriarchal social structures and cultural codes. These cannot be said to be conservative values. Nevertheless, a skeptical voice was raised early on by Gabriela Mora in her 1985 article on *La casa de los espíritus* and *De amor y de sombra*. Her rebuke of Allende's "confused" and "suspiciously bourgeois" ideology (Shaw 71) quickly became a catalyst for equally fervent defenses of the novels on ideological grounds.

Mora puts together the remarkable success of *La casa de los espíritus* and the grave historical moment in which it was written, and Allende's feminist credentials to create a basis from which to justify asking some hard questions about the novel's political content. Mora demands that we judge with particular care the ideological value of a popular literary work that portrays a time of social crisis. Her premise is that from a feminist point of view, literature, because it has some power to "propulsar y fijar ideologías" (53), has a responsibility to contribute to social progress. And as a reader in search of socially aware and committed texts, Mora identifies a series of problematical aspects in *Casa*, and even more in *De amor y de sombra*. First she acknowledges a number of positive political dimensions: support for the Unidad Popular government, criticism of Pinochet, the representation of social class and gender divisions, and feminine solidarity. Under "objectionable" elements Mora mentions the feminine affinity for magic and nature, the passivity of subaltern characters, and the ending of the novel, which grants Esteban Trueba a peaceful death and leaves Alba waiting at home for better times to arrive. Perhaps the most serious ideological lapse that Mora identifies is the way in which the novel's conclusion privileges acts of individual forgiveness and solitary recuperation over a continuing struggle for justice.[3]

Other tendencies that Mora identifies as essentially conservative elements in *Casa* and *De amor y de sombra* include the creation of characters built upon essentialized and stereotypical qualities, the emphasis on predestined events, the recurrence to love as a motive for social action, and the overblown egotism of the characters toward whom the reader is made to feel sympathetic. No other critic has taken such a strong position against Allende's first two novels, but among the many admiring voices, a few other objections have been raised. Patricia Hart finds *De amor y de sombra* to be a far weaker work than *Casa* owing to the failure to create suspense, the recycling of material from the first novel, the hackneyed love scenes, and the unsuccessful attempt to combine love story and political drama (137-140). In his chapter on Isabel Allende as a novelist of the post-Boom, Donald Shaw takes a different approach that nonetheless adds fuel to Mora's fire. Without assuming an overt political stance from which to judge Allende's texts, and without judging certain aspects as good or bad, he invites readers to draw their own conclusions about such issues as the role of determinism, the melodramatic polarization of good and evil and its strong emotionalism, the idealization of the oppressed classes, and the privileging of love over activism and individual initiative over collective action (55-62). Among the post-Boom writers that Shaw studies (Puig, Valenzuela, Skármeta, Giardinelli and others), he calls Allende the most "reconciled to the system" (66), which may help to account for her popular appeal, but does not enhance her credentials as a feminist and a social progressive.

The two debates that I have reviewed lurk under the surface of most Isabel Allende criticism and analysis, and the other important trends in the studies of Allende's first three works have already been seen in the playing out of these controversies: Allende's creation of female protagonists and feminocentric fictional worlds; the relationship of myth and history; the hallmarks of attractive storytelling and readerly accessibility; the presence of the popular genres of melodrama, romance, and journalism; magical realism; the testimonial value of some of her writing; and the autobiographical nature of much of her novelistic material are recurring objects of study. Without providing an example of each of these trends, I will highlight a few outstanding and influential analyses. One prominent tendency in Allende criticism is toward thematic, content-driven readings, but I will continue to focus on books and articles that pursue a well thought-out theoretical angle.

Lloyd Davies's monograph on *La casa de los espíritus* is the single most extensive treatment of the novel. In the introduction, Davies clearly states his aim to "reinforce the perception of her as a serious feminist writer" (17). The strengths of his book are the substantive chapters on the historical context and the literary background for reading *Casa*, and the analysis in chapter four of magical realism, myth, and carnival. These three terms are both celebrated and opposed throughout the novel, and Davies concludes that Allende acknowledges their conservative potential while using her female characters to oppose them and to vindicate their liberating power.

Patricia Hart's book on "magical feminism" in *La casa de los espíritus*, *De amor y de sombra*, and *Eva Luna* is notable for the in-depth consideration of the author's unique contribution to the tradition of magical realism. Hart defines magical feminism as Allende's blending of magic and the tall tale with realism and history in feminocentric texts. She calls her hybrid a new category, not to be conflated with García Márquez's brand of magical realism. One of Hart's principal insights is that in Allende's narratives the real consistently undermines the magical and proves to be the more powerful force. Her final chapter overturns the conventional notion of literary influence by reminding us that once *Casa* was published, it began to influence the way we read *Cien años*. Hart further claims that *El amor en los tiempos de cólera* can be seen as magical feminism influenced by Isabel Allende.

Among the articles on *De amor y de sombra*, Monique J. Lemaitre employs a well-defined theory of her key terms, "deseo, incesto y represión." She uses Gilles Deleuze and Felix Guattari's *Anti-Oedipus* to examine the complex interplay of desire and/of repression, and desire and/of incest, and to elucidate ways in which Allende self-censures her portrayal of the characters Gustavo Morante and Professor Leal. Lemaitre, like Shaw, concludes that in spite of a thematics of political denunciation, *De amor y de sombra* supports solutions that remain within the boundaries of the status quo.

In her book published in 2000, Leasa Y. Lutes carries out a comparative study of *Eva Luna* and novels by Fanny Buitrago and Alessandra Luiselli as feminine manifestations of the *Bildungsroman*. Lutes characterizes *Eva Luna* as the most optimistic of the three novels, with the protagonist who undergoes the most complete and successful process of evolution toward feminine autonomy and agency. Her conclusions are well in line with other assessments of the novel that see it as Allende's most celebratory and upbeat book, reflecting perhaps the cultural milieu of its Venezuelan setting and the author's oft-stated affection for and identification with the novel's protagonist.[4]

Isabel Allende published five books from 1991 to 2000: the novels *El plan infinito* (1991), *Hija de la fortuna* (1999), and *Retrato en sepia* (2000); the memoir *Paula* (1994); and *Afrodita: Cuentos, recetas y otros afrodisíacos* (1997), a mixed media memoir/treatise on culinary and sexual pleasures. Given the lengthy and slow publishing pipeline in the humanities, it is not surprising that relatively few articles on these newer works have appeared to date in journals and edited collections of essays. Nevertheless, some criticism is available, and Allende has answered numerous questions about her recent work in interviews. The existing articles explore very different aspects of each text, avoiding the inevitable overlap of the criticism on *Casa*. It has not yet been possible for readers to enter into a dialogue with other critical work, with the result that each essay stands alone and stakes out its own territory.

El plan infinito, Allende's first novel to feature a male protagonist and a contemporary California setting, is compared with Leslie Marmon Silko's *Ceremony* (1977) in Daniel P. Hunt's 1993 article "Women Writing Men." Hunt studies both novels as challenges to the traditional *Bildungsroman*, and he discovers a common element in the portrayal of a male protagonist who makes real progress in his life only when he rejects individualism and cosmopolitanism in favor of communal values. It is interesting to see a comparative study of Allende and a non-Latin writer, but I would question his ascribing a position of marginality *vis-à-vis* mainstream U.S. society to the popular Chilean author. At the very least it should be acknowledged that Allende lives and writes from a highly privileged "marginality" in which all doors are open to her.

Ignacio López-Calvo convincingly shows the presence of Octavio Paz's concept of Mexican identity and the theories of liberation of Gustavo Gutiérrez and Paulo Freire in Allende's novel. This is a new aspect of intertextuality for Allende's writing, because it consists of discerning a philosophical subtext rather than a reworking of characters, story, and style from prior texts. A third essay, Catherine Perricone's "*El plan infinito*: Isabel Allende's New World," starts by highlighting the intimate connection between life and art, i.e., Allende's new life in California and her new novel. Perricone's primary focus, however, is on narrative technique in the novel, and she shows that *El plan infinito* offers "an extraordinarily complete and life-like image of modern life" through its successful counterbalancing of third and first-person narrators, the economical use of dialogue, manipulation of temporal perspectives, and a limited use of magical realism (55). All three articles praise the novel for its thematic innovation, continuing the line of positive evaluations of Allende's work.

Isabel Allende began writing the notes and letters that would become the memoir *Paula* during the year that her daughter was in a coma, first in a hospital in Madrid and later in Allende's California home, where Paula Frías died in December 1992. The book combines family history, a portrait of her daughter and, most of all, Isabel Allende's autobiography. María de la Cinta Ramblado Minero opens her analysis of maternity in four novels by Allende by observing that when she started to read *Paula* she had "la sensación de que ya lo había leído," and that this book could be seen as "una selección de los mejores momentos de la ficción de Allende" (53). This allusion to the repetitive nature of Allende's writing serves as a point of departure for identifying the similar concept of maternity found in *La casa de los espíritus*, *Eva Luna*, and *Paula*. The article concludes that Isabel Allende's feminism is fundamentally essentialist, and yet it resists a perpetuation of the status quo by constituting "una forma de rebelión camuflada" (96). In focusing on essentialism, Ramblado Minero takes a somewhat different approach to the widely treated topic of the author's feminism, although she arrives at the same positive conclusion as many other readers.

Two other articles address the truth value of *Paula* as a work of nonfiction. Verónica Cortínez confronts the impression that the memoir is actually largely about Isabel Allende and not her daughter. She contends that, content aside, in this text Allende takes on her daughter's voice and sacrifices her own in homage to Paula's life and spirit. Cortínez perceives this act of literary ventriloquism in the nonfiction quality and the relatively "simple," "unadorned" writing style of the book that are said to be true to Paula's personality. This somewhat convoluted interpretation (Isabel's life told in Paula's voice as a tribute to Paula) depends on an underdeveloped concept of the distinction between fiction and nonfiction, and an unquestioning acceptance of the author's statements that in this book she is attempting to be honest and true to reality. Catherine Perricone strikes a similar note by identifying a combination of nonfiction genres in the book (memoir, biography, autobiography, confession, testimony), and by claiming, without any apparent irony intended, that Allende brings to the book "her own unique objectivity, deriving from her many years as a journalist" (44).

Cortínez and Perricone do not engage the rich body of theory on memoir and autobiography that would complicate their claims for confessional sincerity and autobiographical transparency. Their articles also show a common trait in Allende criticism that I will discuss again later in this essay: the tendency to read the life-art, autobiography-fiction relationship in virtually unmediated terms, and also to take Allende's interviews as authoritative sources of insight into her life and her writing.

To conclude the overview of essays published on this decade's work, Joy Logan has written an analysis of *Afrodita: Cuentos, recetas y otros afrodisíacos* called "Aphrodite in an Apron." She characterizes *Afrodita* as a "travelogue of carnal delights" and places it within the tradition of the encyclopedia, a compendium of human knowledge that strives for an image of completeness. Logan's thesis is that Allende is concerned less with defining the objects of her writing (sex and food), and more with "the evocation of the creative act and the autoerotics of representing the self" (687). Logan's treatment of self-representation effectively employs the vocabulary of travel, space, and mapping, and that of food and feasting to trace Allende's "textual and culinary voyage" through the realms of pleasure toward (an always delayed) satiety. Allende's self-inscription "as the goddess of love and storytelling" takes the narrative spotlight in a gesture that can be found in much of her prior work.

The many published interviews with Isabel Allende since the mid 1980s constitute an additional evolving commentary on the writer's work and on her life. Inés Dölz-Blackburn and Violeta Sulsona's 1992 article "Isabel Allende a través de sus entrevistas" and John Rodden's introduction to his edited collection of thirty-four interviews conducted from 1984 to 1995, provide excellent overviews of the copious interview material. I will not repeat here their identification of common themes and anecdotes and their variations. Nonetheless, a consideration of the interviews does point us toward the tendency mentioned above to use the writer's own statements as authoritative guides to the proper interpretation of her books. Frequently quoted and rarely contested, Allende's interview responses are most often shown to correlate directly with the work under study. As a consequence, Allende criticism has a strong biographical orientation, with her interviews signaling the correspondences to be drawn between life and text, and between author and character or narrator in an abundant reiteration of identity markers.

John Rodden pays tribute to Allende's "fundamental openness and straightforwardness" as a celebrity interviewee (2), but he quickly reminds us—and documents—that she freely admits to inventing and reinventing herself by changing her stories over time and making things up (3-4). For example of the twenty or perhaps even fifty versions of how she met her second husband, one rather prosaically claims that she encountered him in a restaurant, while in another she saves him from drowning in the San Francisco Bay (Rodden 4). Rodden therefore cautions against taking the interviews at face value, seeing in them a literary process of self-transformation and performance in their own right, as well as an act of remembering. This observation can be applied to the interviews with any writer, or to any other means by which a writer comments on his or her own work, but in the case of Allende the reminder may be especially apropos.

I have kept for last a seminal book on Allende's writing, because it stands alone among the rest of the criticism in scope and completeness. Linda Gould Levine's book *Isabel Allende*, published in the Twayne World Authors Series in 2002, makes a singular contribution to the scholarship by providing a comprehensive, up-to-date study of all of the writer's fiction and her memoir *Paula*. Levine leaves the nonfiction *Afrodita* out of her study, but she carries out a systematic analysis of the rest of her titles, devoting a chapter to each one. The introductory chapter "Weaving Life into Fiction" (republished in this special issue) suggests the overarching concept of Levine's reading of Allende: that autobiographical and historical referents are the "primary" (not to say "raw") materials of her narrative art in a particularly pronounced fashion. This is not a new approach to take. In fact, it seems almost inevitable given Allende's love of telling stories about herself, but Levine explores the connection between autobiography and fiction with great care and insight. She also discusses aspects of Allende's narrative style such as the reworking of popular genres into "serious literature," and she provides extensive information on the sources researched by Allende while writing *De amor y de sombra*, *El plan infinito*, and *Hija de la fortuna*.

Levine's analysis takes into account the existing criticism and she consistently defends the artistic and ideological value of Allende's writing against any negative or skeptical view. The overwhelmingly positive tone of the study matches the message that Allende is to be admired for writing optimistic, socially committed stories that affirm, time and again, the power of love, human goodness, individual transformation, and a feminist agenda of gender equality. Offering as well an annotated bibliography and a previously unpublished interview that she conducted with Allende in August 2000, Levine's book is the single most complete guide to understanding this author and her place in contemporary Western literature.

The critical work realized in the past fifteen years reflects the extraordinary enthusiasm and the sheer enjoyment created in many readers by Isabel Allende's fiction. The two principal controversies surrounding *La casa de los espíritus* and, to a lesser extent, *De amor y de sombra*, seem to have lost their momentum with time and with the publication of eight more books. Scholarly analysis has yielded largely favorable interpretations of her artistry and her ideology, as I indicated at the beginning of this article. In light of her popular success, some critics have felt a need to make the case for regarding Allende as a serious literary author, as well as a talented storyteller. Linda Gould Levine, in covering all of the fiction up to 2001, mounts the strongest defense of Allende's contribution to literature and even to humanity. In my own reading and teaching of Allende's writing and its criticism, I have observed certain aspects that I believe merit further study and debate. Several of the articles that I have cited already allude to the elements of her style and her thought that I would like to raise in concluding this review, but with the exception of Gabriela Mora, they have not engaged them in a sustained way.

Judgments about style are perhaps the most personal and idiosyncratic ones that a reader can make. There is no successful theory of literary aesthetics by which to measure "good" or "bad" writing. It's not enough to say "you know it when you see it," although any individual usually does know what suits his or her own private taste. Allende is generally praised for being a masterful storyteller, one who captivates both academic and "common" readers. Occasionally someone will mention an overdependence on clichés and stereotypes, "florid" language (especially in the love scenes), and highly contrived plots, without these perceived weaknesses making any real difference in the critical reception. My own reading preferences and habits rebel against an aspect that a few readers see as a virtue, and most simply seem to ignore: the extraordinary amount of repetition from one book to the next.

At the level of plot, characterization, and theme, the similarities cannot be denied, and the use of language often verges on the formulaic. By the second or third book, stylistic tics such as her use of prolepsis, hyperbole, rambling sentences and paragraphs, repetition of images, and restatement of important points already clearly expressed, threaten to reach the level of self-parody. As a consequence, for this reader the potential for pleasure is limited to the real but easy pleasure of the familiar, and has not to date provided the more challenging reward of an encounter with the new and the unexpected.[5]

In terms of ideas and content, Allende is almost universally recognized as a feminist, socially conscious, and progressive writer for obvious and well-documented reasons. There are, however, elements of her fiction that warrant a harder look. Gabriela Mora identified one key issue in *La casa de los espíritus* that those who reject her conclusions fail, in my mind, to address adequately: the question of justice. What happens to justice in a novelistic universe in which love (heterosexual or maternal love), hope, and individual powers of forgiveness are the privileged solutions to institutionalized violence and oppression? In rejecting revenge, it is true that one kind of cycle of violence may be interrupted. Nonetheless, a solution that only denounces revenge without attending to the demands of justice is not only shortsighted, but it also comes uncomfortably close to the self-serving rhetoric reconciliation espoused by the very kind of regime against which a writer like Allende so rightly protests.

From a feminist perspective, a third and final problematical element that is little examined is the recurrence to stereotypes, especially in depicting lower-class characters. To mention just one example that is particularly egregious for feminism, consider the representations of subaltern women in their role as caregivers to wealthy children. The maternal politics of paid domestics and their "unconditional" love for their charges is a complex issue that requires a more serious and nuanced treatment than Allende has achieved thus far. The good-humored reproduction of worn-out stereotypes of wise, all-comforting Indian nanas (*Casa*) and black women with ample bosoms (*Plan*) who save high-strung white children from their loneliness and their fears can no longer be read as great storytelling. The real stories to be told are somber and sober, and they may pose a genuine challenge to the status quo, literary or otherwise.

To return to the beginning of this paper, a careful look at the scholarship reveals a respect, admiration, and enjoyment of Allende's writing that is virtually unprecedented with regard to any other Latin American woman writer. Contrary to Allende's scolding of envious critics and killjoy scholars, it is difficult to identify very many contemporary writers who can match her critical and popular reception worldwide. In reviewing a substantial portion of the English and Spanish-language criticism on Isabel Allende, including many items that I was unable to mention in this article, my own reading and appreciation of her texts have been enhanced and challenged by the thoughtful readings undertaken by others. The new essays published here promise to continue the critical dialogue and controversy in original and productive ways.

From *Latin American Literary Review* 30, no. 60 (2002): 128-146. Copyright © 2002 by the Latin American Literary Review Press. Reprinted with permission of the Latin American Literary Review Press.

Notes

1. Two articles appearing in 1996 purport to address the existing academic criticism on Isabel Allende. Susan Frenk proposes to look at the critical reception of Allende's work in terms of two key terms: femininity and motherhood. Her article does not primarily evaluate the criticism, however. Instead it offers its own analysis of those two terms as themes in Allende's writing. L. Teresa Valdivieso discovers the "continuidad poética" of Allende's writing through a review of criticism, which she defines as our "ejercicio del entusiasmo levantado por una obra" (305). She groups existing articles into three categories: those that compare *Cien años de soledad* and *La casa de los espíritus*; feminist analyses; and studies focusing on the referential function and the historical dimension of Allende's narratives.

2. A careful analysis of book reviews published around the world is outside of the scope of this essay, but my own impression of the mix of positive and negative opin-

ions is confirmed by the references to reviews of Allende's early works in Patricia Hart's well-known book on "narrative magic" (33-36).

3. Philip Swanson offers the most direct counterargument to Gabriela Mora's "drubbing of Isabel Allende" in his article "Tyrants and Trash." I don't find his reading of class struggle in the novel to be as convincing as Mora's critique of the perpetuation of bourgeois norms.

4. *Los cuentos de Eva Luna*, a collection of twenty-three stories published in 1989, has not received a great deal of critical attention to date. Of the handful of studies available, the most useful are the corresponding chapter in Linda Gould Levine's book, *Isabel Allende*, and Patricia Hart's 1993 essay that follows the pattern of her earlier study on magic feminism in Allende's work.

5. The Argentinian writer Ana María Shua identifies the Allende "recipe" in a short column published alongside an interview with Allende in the May 17, 2001 issue of the periodical *3 Puntos*. Without at all denying her popular appeal and her storytelling talent, Shua also calls attention to the repetitive quality of her texts.

Works Cited

Amaya R., Lyana María and Aura María Fernández R. "La deconstrucción y la crítica feminista. Lecturas posibles de *Cien años de soledad* y *La casa de los espíritus*." *Nuevo Texto Crítico* 2.4 (1989): 189-95.

Antoni, Robert. "Parody or Piracy: The Relationship of *The House of the Spirits* to *One Hundred Years of Solitude*." *Latin American Literary Review* 16.31 (1988): 16-28.

Clancy, Laurie. "Isabel Allende's Dialogue with García Márquez: A Study in Literary Debt." *Antípodas: Journal of Hispanic and Galician Studies* 6-7 (1994-95): 29-43.

Coddou, Marcelo. "*La casa de los espíritus*: De la historia a la Historia." *Texto Crítico* 11.33 (1985):165-72.

Cortínez, Verónica. "*Paula*: Memorias en silencio." *Antípodas: Journal of Hispanic and Galician Studies* 6-7 (1994-1995): 63-75.

Davies, Lloyd. *Isabel Allende: La casa de los espíritus*. London: Grant and Cutler, 2000.

Dölz-Blackburn, Inés and Violeta Sulsona. "Isabel Allende a través de sus entrevistas." *Revista Interamericana de Bibliografía/Inter-American Review of Bibliography* 42.3 (1992): 421-30.

Frenk, Susan. "The Wandering Text: Situating the Narratives of Isabel Allende." *Latin American Women's Writing*. Ed. Anny Brooksbank Jones and Catherine Davies. Oxford: Clarendon P, 1996. 66-84.

Hart, Patricia. "Magic Feminism in Isabel Allende's *The Stories of Eva Luna*." *Multicultural Literatures Through Feminist/Poststructuralist Lenses*. Ed. Barbara Frey Waxman. Knoxville: University of Tennessee Press, 1993. 103-36.

_____. *Narrative Magic in the Fiction of Isabel Allende*. London and Toronto: Associated University Presses, 1989.

Hunt, Daniel P. "Women Writing Men: Leslie Marmon Silko's *Ceremony* and Isabel Allende's *El plan infinito*." *Selecta* 14 (1992): 16-19.

Keck, Ray M. "Cide Hamete, Melquíades, Alba Trueba: Marco narrativo y tema en Cervantes, García Márquez y Allende." *Crítica Hispánica* 18.2 (1996): 313-23.

Lemaitre, Monique J. "Deseo, incesto y represión en *De amor y de sombra* de Isabel Allende." *Letras Femeninas* 18.1-2 (1992): 31-37.

Levine, Linda Gould. *Isabel Allende*. New York: Twayne Publishers, 2002.

Logan, Joy. "Aphrodite in an Apron or the Erotics of Recipes and Self-Representation in Isabel Allende's *Afrodita*." *Romance Languages Annual* 10 (1999): 685-89.

López-Calvo, Ignacio. "Las premisas ideológicas de *El plan infinito* de Isabel Allende: El pensamiento de la liberación y el de Octavio Paz." *Narrativa hispanoamericana contemporánea: Entre la vanguardia y el post-boom.* Ed. Ana María Hernández de López. Madrid: Pliegos, 1996. 293-303.

Lutes, Leasa Y. *Allende, Buitrago, Luiselli: Aproximaciones teóricas al concepto del 'Bildungsroman' femenino.* New York: Peter Lang, 2000.

Marcos, Juan Manuel. "Isabel Allende: *La casa de los espíritus*." *Revista Iberoamericana* 51.130-131 (1985): 401-6.

Mora, Gabriela. "Las novelas de Isabel Allende y el papel de la mujer como ciudadana." *Ideologies and Literature* 1.3 (Fall 1985): 53-61.

Perricone, Catherine R. "*El plan infinito*: Isabel Allende's New World." *SECOLAS Annals* 25 (March 1994): 55-61.

_____. "Genre and Metarealism in Allende's *Paula*." *Hispania* 81.1 (March 1998): 42-49.

Ramblado Minero, María de la Cinta. "La madre de todas las historias: Representación de la maternidad en la obra de Isabel Allende." *Reflexiones: Ensayos sobre escritoras hispanoamericanas contemporáneas.* Vol. 1. Ed. Priscilla Gac-Artigas. New Jersey: Ediciones Nuevo Espacio, 2002. 53-71.

Rodden, John, editor. *Conversations with Isabel Allende.* Austin: University of Texas Press, 1999.

Rojas, Mario A. "*La casa de los espíritus* de Isabel Allende: un caleidoscopio de espejos desordenados." *Revista Iberoamericana* 51.132-133 (1985) 917-25.

Rosendo González, Pablo. "Isabel Allende: secretos de mujer." *3 Puntos* 4.203 (May 17, 2001): 61-70.

Shaw, Donald L. *The Post-Boom in Spanish-American Fiction.* Albany: SUNY P, 1998.

Swanson, Philip. "Tyrants and Trash: Sex, Class and Culture in *La casa de los espíritus*." *Bulletin of Hispanic Studies* 71.2 (1992): 217-37.

Urbina, Nicasio. "*La casa de los espíritus* de Isabel Allende y *Cien años de soledad* de Gabriel García Márquez: Un modelo retórico común." *Escritura* 15.29 (1990): 215-28.

Valdivieso, L. Teresa. "Palabras sobre 'la palabra' de Isabel Allende." *Narrativa hispanoamericana contemporánea: entre la vanguardia y el post-boom.* Ed. Ana María Hernández de López. Madrid: Pliegos, 305-12.

The House of the Spirits:
A Twentieth-Century Family Chronicle_____

Charles Rossman

Isabel Allende has described the genesis of her first novel: "On January 8, 1981, I was living in Venezuela and I received a phone call that my beloved grandfather was dying. I began a letter for him that later became . . . *The House of the Spirits*" ("Questions and Answers"). Allende's letter-cum-novel was published in Barcelona just a year and a half later and quickly became a literary sensation in the Spanish-speaking world. German, French, and Italian editions appeared in 1984, and an English translation followed in 1985. All four were best sellers and Isabel Allende suddenly found herself, in her early forties, the most famous female Latin American writer of the late twentieth century. To grasp the import of her sudden fame and her novel's astonishing popularity requires some historical background.

The "Boom" and Beyond

During 1962 and 1963, twenty years before the publication of *The House of the Spirits,* four Latin American male writers published a novel each.[1] So began a period of exceptional fertility and commercial success in the Latin American novel. That period reached its peak in 1967 with the publication of García Márquez's *One Hundred Years of Solitude,* a hugely admired and influential work that paved García Márquez's way to the Nobel Prize.[2]

This "Boom" in Latin American fiction, as the movement soon became known, brought unprecedented international publicity to its major writers. Before the Boom, Latin American literature had remained, from the perspective of North American and European readers and critics, largely a regional matter. Suddenly, new books by García Márquez and Vargas Llosa were reviewed in the *New York Times* or the *Times* of London or *Le Monde*. Fiction by the Boom writers was quickly translated and heavily promoted by North American and European publishers, and the writers themselves won international prizes and were offered visiting professorships at distinguished universities. It was an exhilarating time, a marvelous flowering of genuine literary genius. But the Boom remained almost exclusively a male affair; tellingly, all five of the most frequently cited Boom writers are men.[3]

Isabel Allende published *The House of the Spirits* fifteen years after the major impact of the Boom, whose writers cleared a path for her in at least three specific ways. First, the Boom writers provoked unprecedented international curiosity about Latin American literature and its authors. Second, they created a huge market for Latin American fiction. And, finally, the very success of Allende's male predecessors drew attention to an increasingly obvious literary absence, the voice of a Latin American *female* novelist.

The fiction of the Boom, albeit undeniably engrossing, is unequivocally male centered. It is typically narrated from a male perspective and predominantly concerned with the fulfillment or frustration of the loves, goals, and struggles of male protagonists. Notable examples are Cortázar's postadolescent victims of angst in Paris and Buenos Aires in *Rayuela*; Vargas Llosa's adolescent cadets in *The Time of the Hero*; Fuentes's massively egocentric and corrupt business tycoon and womanizer, Artemio, in *The Death of Artemio Cruz*; and García Márquez's dazzling array of Buendía men, distributed over several generations in *One Hundred Years of Solitude.* In this fictive context of unrelenting *machismo* and the mainly subordinate women who enable their men's follies, Isabel Allende's *The House of the Spirits* offered readers the rare novelistic experience of four generations of self-actualizing *women*—Nívea, Clara, Blanca, and, finally, Alba, who at the book's end is about to give birth to a child that she presumes will be a daughter. Allende herself has described the essential qualities of her protagonists: "All the women in my book are feminists in their fashion; that is, they ask to be free and complete human beings, to be able to fulfill themselves, not to be dependent on men" (Rodden 41).

Despite the widespread celebrity of *The House of the Spirits,* the many similarities and parallels between Allende's novel and *One Hundred Years of Solitude* troubled some critics. For instance, Gene Bell-Villada commented that "in prose and format [Allende's novel] was mostly imitation García Márquez" (23). In Allende's defense, other critics rightly pointed out that, because it is mostly narrated from the perspective of strong, triumphant women, and stresses the misogynistic and brutally tyrannical nature of Esteban Trueba, the book's male protagonist, *The House of the Spirits* can be interpreted as a counter-narrative to *One Hundred Years of Solitude.* Properly understood, these critics argue, Allende's novel is a *critique*, not an imitation, of García Márquez's work. Indeed, the feminist perspective adds a crucial *corrective* to the ideologically reductive representations of dominant men and subordinate women that characterize most Boom fiction, not just García Márquez's.

Two other charges unsympathetic critics brought against Allende were that she derived the narrative device of the "family chronicle" from *One Hundred Years of Solitude,* as well as the technique now known as magical realism. But, in fact, both criticisms ignore literary history. Well before García Márquez appeared on the scene, the so-called family chronicle—a depiction of two or more generations that explores both the characters' interpersonal conflicts and their complex interaction with historical events—was a common novelistic means for simultaneously dramatizing the evolution of characters and of their culture. Similarly, magical realism—which is basically the interweaving of realism, or verisimilitude, with fantasy, and treating both the empirically "real" and the fantastical as equally valid objective experiences—had a long history in both theory and practice before García Márquez made the technique a familiar aspect of Boom fiction.[4]

In any case, the mid-1980s dispute over Allende's indebtedness to García Márquez has been rendered moot by her long and distinguished writing career. The novice whose first novel drew heavily from her influential predecessor has manifestly established her own confident and compelling voice.

What follows is an analytical close reading of *The House of the Spirits,* which may ultimately prove to be Allende's most influential and enduring work of fiction. We begin with some basic facts about the novel's setting, characterization, and point of view, before turning to more comprehensive matters of plot, structure, and meaning.

Setting

The House of the Spirits is set in an unnamed country that is nonetheless readily identifiable as Allende's homeland, Chile. By not naming the country, Allende achieves a valuable simultaneity of references. On one hand, the novel is a *generalized* national history of deadly political crises provoked by totalitarian rule, which reflects the actual history of several Latin American countries in the twentieth century. On the other hand, *The House of the Spirits* invites readers to interpret its dramatized political struggles as an allegory of Chile's election of Salvador Allende as president, in 1970, and his overthrow during a coup led by General Augusto Pinochet in 1973.

The novel's events unfold in three specific locations. The chief site is the country's unnamed capital city, where the central characters have their principal residence, and where a violent, right-wing coup d'état and the subsequent torture of dissenters take place. A second major site is Tres Marías, Esteban Trueba's hacienda in a valley to the south, an overnight train trip away from the city. A third but only fleetingly important locale is the remote mining district in the northern desert, where Trueba nearly strikes it rich in the book's opening chapter. Each of these settings is characterized by its unique populations and activities. The mines are a dirty, minimally civilized place where men seek to realize their materialistic dreams through long hours of hard physical work. The hacienda Tres Marías is populated by humble, uneducated peasants at the service of a rich landowner—

Esteban Trueba—who is at once their master and their *patrón*, a pattern intrinsic to the historical arrangement in Latin America of landowners and serf-like peasants. Only the capital city has the diversity of social classes, the mass education, the institutions, the wealth, and the leisure time that bespeak an evolved, more or less "modern," civilization.

Main Characters

The House of the Spirits traces over a span of approximately seventy years the overlapping lives of four upper-class women and, to a lesser extent, their husbands and lovers. The first of the women is Nívea del Valle, wife of Severo del Valle and bearer of fifteen children, of whom eleven are alive as the novel opens, just after the turn of the twentieth century. Nívea sets the stage for the unconventional and self-determining Trueba women who follow her. She is anticlerical, bored by talk of heaven and hell, a supporter of her husband's political aspirations, and an impassioned proponent of women's suffrage. She is clearly the antithesis of the conventional wife who, confined to the domestic role of mother, derives her status from her husband's achievements and social position. The second generation of women includes Nívea's daughters: the green-haired beauty, Rosa, who is eighteen years old and betrothed to Esteban Trueba as the story opens but who dies before marrying him; and "Clara the clairvoyant," who is eight years younger than Rosa and marries Trueba some nine years after Rosa's death. Clara—the main female character for the first third of the novel—possesses unique mental powers, such as psychokinesis, mind reading, and the ability to foresee the future. Clara is also the writer of elaborately detailed diaries that her granddaughter, Alba, and husband draw on as narrators of *The House of the Spirits*. Notably, Clara marries Trueba without love and without conceding to the male authority implied by the traditional notion of marriage. Although Clara and Esteban share intense sexual intimacy, she is otherwise distant from him throughout most of their married life. The third generation of women is represented by Clara's only daughter, Blanca, who does not share the social and political will that propelled both her grandmother and mother. Rather, Blanca expands the family's concept of womanhood in a new way—she is more earthy, sensual, and passionately sexual. In defiance of her patriarchal father, Blanca finds deeply personal fulfillment outside of traditional marriage and conventional social roles in a lifelong love affair with Pedro Tercero, her childhood playmate from Tres Marías.

The last of the Trueba women is Blanca's only daughter, Alba, who also takes a lover outside of marriage. Alba is the first woman in her family to experience an extended formal education, including ten years in a "British school for young ladies" where "she learned to eat boiled vegetables and burnt rice . . . sing hymns . . . read the Bible, play tennis, and use a typewriter" (Allende 255). Alba hates the British school, but thrives at the university, where she comes alive intellectually by studying philosophy and music, and where she falls in love with Miguel, a law student and revolutionary who is ardently committed to social justice. Like her great-grandmother Nívea and her grandmother Clara, Alba devotes herself to the enhancement of women's rights and to seeking a more just social and political order. Like her mother, Alba fulfills her sexual desires without regard to religion or cultural mores. As the Trueba women set aside the traditional roles imposed by their patriarchal culture, the significance of patrilineal lines inevitably fades. For years, Alba doesn't know that Pedro Tercero is her father, and at book's end it does not matter that she cannot determine if the father of the child she carries is her lover, Miguel, or one of the rapists who tortures her in prison. For Alba, the sperm donor is incidental—the child is *her* event, the principle of continuity is her womb.

Allende explains in an interview her own understanding of the three Trueba women, and how their names suggest their natures:

The fact that all the names in *The House of the Spirits* mean the same thing—Clara, Blanca, Alba—is like saying that Clara is the great spiritual mother of us all. She is not concerned with braiding the hair of her daughters or whether they are going to get married or not. On the other hand, Blanca is the great earthly mother, she fulfills all the household tasks. Alba is the great intellectual mother. (Rodden 133-34)

Here Allende consciously "mythologizes" her female characters, speaking of them in archetypal terms that link them with powerful images of women from ancient mythologies. In claiming that the names of the women all "mean the same thing," Allende emphasizes the overtones of whiteness (Nívea means "snow," Blanca means "white"), clarity (Clara), or luminosity (Alba means "dawn") that, taken together, radiate an aura of freshness, of feminist renewal. Allende further comments, "I wanted to symbolize a state of purity, not the purity that means virginity, normally assigned to women, but the purity of facing the world with new eyes, free from contamination, open and tolerant" (Rodden 79). These are women imbued with an intrinsic, explicitly female agency that is apart from and counterbalances the authority of men.

A fifth woman of major importance in the novel, even though she appears in only four brief scenes, is Tránsito Soto. As her name implies, Tránsito successfully navigates the half century of social, political, and economic upheavals that Trueba himself barely survives. She is a remarkably strong-willed prostitute and astute businesswoman, whom Trueba visits in times of need—for sex, for emotional comfort when he feels unbearable loneliness, and, finally, after she has become rich and influential, for help in saving Alba's life and preserving something of Trueba's own well-being. In the end, Tránsito's power raises her to a status equal to Trueba's.

Esteban Trueba, who is prominent throughout the novel as the *macho* patriarchal figure, is the major male character. At the outset, he is twenty-five; he dies at the age of ninety. Trueba often throws uncontrollable fits of rage, expounds bigoted and self-serving political and economic opinions, rabidly smashes things, injures people, and rapes at will (exercising his *droit de seigneur*) the young women in the countryside surrounding Tres Marías. For much of the novel, and in many ways, Trueba is simply a monster who elicits hatred even from his family. Yet, in the end, he saves Blanca and her lover, Pedro Tercero, from the brutal agents of the right-wing coup, and he uses his waning political power to help them flee the country. To save Alba from the same dark forces as the crisis worsens, he seeks Tránsito Santo, confesses his powerlessness, and humbly but urgently asks for her help. The nature and depth of Trueba's sudden humility at the end of the book poses a major crux for the reader.

Point of View

Two unique and sustained narrative strands weave through *The House of the Spirits,* each told by a different voice from a distinct perspective. The initial and predominant voice of the novel poses one of the earliest interpretive puzzles that a reader encounters. In the opening paragraph, this voice appears to be a first-person, dramatized narrator, like the one Esteban Trueba will later become. The first speaker remarks that "I" used Clara's "notebooks" to "reclaim the past and overcome terrors of my own" (Allende 1). But readers do not encounter this narrative "I" again for more than sixty pages and, until the epilogue, self-referential words like "I" and "me" recur only about ten times altogether during this narrative strand—nearly always to comment on the narrator's sources in Clara's manuscripts. It is only in the epilogue that Alba suddenly identifies herself as the first-person narrator and informs the reader that all the events of her narrative strand have been filtered through her mind.

The second narrative strand is the voice of Esteban Trueba, who uses the first-person "I" to tell his story. It begins when he is about twenty-five years old and working in the northern gold mines, hoping to get rich enough to become worthy of marrying Rosa del Valle.

Trueba narrates eleven brief sections of the novel, for a total of only forty-seven pages, mostly to justify himself, to assert his will and opinions, and to vent his rage. He is an "unreliable" narrator in the ironic sense that his effort to elicit the sympathy of the reader more often evokes the reader's negative judgment. Trueba is "unreliable" also in that when his memory fails him he must rely on Clara's notebooks. Moreover, he does not even begin to write his *apologia* until twenty years after Clara's death, when his memory is surely fading. Trueba's voice offers a bold counterpoint to the second (female) narrative perspective. Yet, at the age of ninety, he remains less interested in "truth" or self-awareness than in easing his conscience. The reader inevitably has to make an independent judgment of whether to accept Trueba's self-assessment at face value.

The reader faces the same problem with Alba's narrative. Up until the epilogue, the rarity of first-person self-references in Alba's narration invites the reader to regard her narrative as a traditional, omniscient, third-person narration. When she finally reveals herself, it takes some critical effort—some willed suspension of disbelief—to accept her authority as first-person narrator, even though she acknowledges that she had relied on Clara's notebooks and letters and consulted with her coauthor, Trueba. Allende herself seems aware of the problem of Alba's reliability as a narrator. Allende comments, in an interview: "Initially, the whole book was written in the third person. I told the book." Allende notes that she revised the book to enhance Alba's authority:

> So how can Alba, who is writing the book, know all these things? It was too easy and artificial that she should know them. So at the end of the novel, Alba says: "I have written this book based on the diaries of my grandmother." (Rodden 134)

Media guru Marshall McLuhan famously claimed, "Art is anything you can get away with." Many readers might well ask if Allende "gets away with" blending the ostensible third-person omniscient narrator with Alba's claim in the epilogue of being, all along, the first-person narrator.

Plot and Structure

As previously mentioned, the plot of *The House of the Spirits* is based on a staple convention of nineteenth-century realism, the family chronicle. To this simple structure, Allende adds flourishes of magical realism (such as Clara's ability to predict earthquakes or to move salt shakers and dishes by mental power), occasional bits of near-farce (such as the escapades of Uncle Marcos and the brief history of Clara's dog, Barrabás), and an especially complex interweaving of the family's fate with the coeval political tragedy of their country.

The story begins on a Holy Thursday, just after the turn of the twentieth century. Severo and Nívea del Valle attend the noon mass. Counting the eleven children, the del Valle family takes a full row of benches near the front of the church. Father Restrepo rants against a catalog of modern sins—such as legalizing "bastards and civil marriage" and "putting women on an equal footing with men"—all of which, he claims, undermine "the family, the fatherland, private property, and the Church" in defiance of "the law of God" (Allende 5). Severo del Valle is an atheist, but he harbors political ambitions and therefore attends mass just to be seen. Nívea has her own notion of God and distrusts the teachings of the Church but supports Severo's political ambitions as a means of securing women's suffrage. Severo's plans advance when he is invited to be the Liberal Party candidate in the approaching congressional elections, a party allegiance that goes against the conservative political traditions of his social class. One day, his political supporters send a gift of a roast pig to the del Valle home, and a bottle of brandy arrives concurrently. Three days later, Clara has a premonition of a death in the family, a death that will be a "mistake." That night Clara's older, incredibly beautiful sister, Rosa, develops a chill and takes to her bed in great discomfort. To help Rosa sleep, a servant opens the bottle of brandy, mixes some with lemonade, and gives it to Rosa. The next day, a servant discovers Rosa lying dead upon her bed. Dr. Cuevas and his assistant perform a grisly autopsy on a counter in the del Valle's kitchen. The doctor determines that Rosa was killed by the brandy, which had been poisoned, apparently by a political opponent of Severo's, with the intention of killing the candidate. Severo immediately renounces his candidacy, resigns from the Liberal Party, and vows to forgo all future public deeds and political activity—thus demonstrating that political terrorism can be quite effective.

Clara, who cannot sleep during the night of her sister's autopsy, leaves her bedroom seeking company. Seeing a light in the kitchen, Clara climbs on a wooden box in the courtyard to peek through the kitchen window as the autopsy is being performed. Mesmerized, she watches the outlandish behavior of the doctor's young assistant, who kisses Rosa "on the lips, the neck, the breasts, and between the legs" (35). Clara is traumatized by what she has witnessed, both the cutting into the corpse of her sister and the necrophilia of the medical assistant. She remains frozen in place until dawn, after which "silence filled her utterly," and she does not utter a word for the following nine years (35).

The death of Rosa is more than a family tragedy. It resonates throughout the novel in various ways. Political assassinations were unknown in the country before Rosa's death, and the botched attempt on Severo del Valle's life foreshadows the unbridled violence of the reign of terror that will overtake the country in the novel's final chapters. Similarly, the mutilation of Rosa's corpse prefigures several instances of violations of the female body. Some, although grisly and grotesque, the women consent to, such as the abortion performed by Jaime Trueba on his brother's lover, or the cesarean deliveries of Clara's children. But many other acts against women are simply brutal impositions of male power, such as the rapes of peasant women in Tres Marías and the rape and mutilation of Alba Trueba while Colonel Esteban García holds her captive late in the novel.

At the time of Rosa's death, Esteban Trueba has just finished his second year as a gold prospector in the north. He goes to the capital to attend Rosa's funeral and, rather than return to the mines, decides to go south to his hacienda, Tres Marías, the last remnant of the family fortune that his drunken father had squandered. When he arrives at Tres Marías, he finds the abandoned main house in tatters. The tenant peasants have remained on the property, however, and Trueba selects from among them a vigorous and responsible young man, Pedro Segundo García, as his foreman and begins the long task of reversing the hacienda's decline. After nine years of intense effort, Tres Marías becomes the most prosperous and respected hacienda in the region.

Despite the peasants' tireless efforts, Trueba barely acknowledges their humanity. He regards them at best as children, at worst as "a bunch of donkeys" (56). He therefore sees no reason to accord them basic civil rights, pay them reasonable wages, grant them a humane workload, let them organize unions, or even allow them to vote in governmental elections. Trueba scoffs at the notion of women's rights in general, but with special scorn regarding the rights of peasant women. He brands all such ideas as "degenerate" or "communism." In effect, he regards the peasants as quasi property: men he exploits and women he rapes at will and often impregnates. When a woman shows up at his door claiming that he is the father of her child, he gives her a few banknotes and threatens to drive her off with a whip if she bothers him again. A male relative who intervenes on behalf of such a woman might end up with a bullet in his head. As a result of Esteban's frequent and inexplicable fits of anger and his harsh, autocratic treatment, the peasants—including the foreman, Pedro Segundo García—all bristle with resentment and hatred of him.

One particular event in Esteban Trueba's early days at Tres Marías especially contributes to the downfall of the Trueba family. Trueba rapes Pancha García, the fifteen-year-old sister of his foreman, and takes her away as his servant and concubine. When Pancha becomes pregnant, Trueba casts her out, thus sowing in the Garcías the vindictive rage that endures for generations. It is Esteban García, Pancha's grandson, who becomes Trueba's nemesis and eventually extracts retribution by incarcerating, raping, and disfiguring Trueba's granddaughter, Alba.

When Clara decides to speak again after nine years of silence, it is to utter another premonition—that she will soon marry Rosa's fiancé, Esteban Trueba. As Clara predicts, Trueba returns to the city from Tres Marías to propose to her, and they soon become engaged. During their year of engagement, Clara prepares for the wedding as Trueba builds for her the mansion in the city that will become known as "the big house on the corner." During this interlude, Trueba's sister, Férula, a spinster who has devoted her life to caring for him and their mother, befriends Clara. Trueba and Clara marry and spend their honeymoon in Italy. The newlyweds were not in love when they married, but Trueba becomes enthralled by Clara within their second day on the boat; when they return after three months, Clara is pregnant. Férula cares for Clara tenderly, bathing her, rubbing her with cologne, and powdering her. When Trueba goes away to Tres Marías on business, Clara and Férula establish an exclusively female daily routine centered on Clara. Trueba's absence means little to Clara, who is detached from mundane concerns and lives in her ethereal world of spirits. But Férula, who is starved for human warmth, feels an increasing attachment to Clara and abhors the thought of Trueba returning to shatter the harmony between her and her sister-in-law. Férula even confesses to a priest that she has become obsessed with Clara, a passion that causes her to feel shame, and suggests to the priest that she may harbor repressed lesbian desires. But soon Trueba returns from Tres Marías; their daughter, Blanca, is born; and Clara (who knows nothing of Férula's sexual angst) and Trueba rekindle their impassioned, distinctly heterosexual lovemaking. Férula's plight is overshadowed by the whirl of events.

Trueba had wanted a son to bear his name, but, through her clairvoyance, Clara foresees both the baby's gender and her predetermined name. Blanca will be the third generation of women with luminous names, and she will inherit their intuitive sense of justice, their intelligence, and their passionate sensuality. She is still a child, perhaps three years old, when the whole family goes for the first time to spend a summer in Tres Marías. They arrive to find all the tenants awaiting them in the courtyard, as if to welcome royalty. Among the welcomers is Pedro Tercero García, the foreman's son, who is about the same age as Blanca. Delighted at the sight of a new playmate, Blanca immediately pulls off her fancy clothes and runs out to play with Pedro Tercero; their bonding is instantaneous. The children exchange kisses, share their food, and finally fall asleep under the dining room table, with the boy on his back and Blanca's head "on the round belly of her new friend" (90). Some two decades later, Blanca will be found in the same position, equally naked and passionately in love with Pedro Tercero— who will pay a terrible price for loving Blanca across racial and class lines and for the couple's Rousseau-like belief that natural instincts take priority over the corrupting effects of civilization.

During that first summer in Tres Marías, Clara intuits the peasants' resentment toward her husband and begins to make inferences about his past and his true character. She becomes aware of the misery of the women and children in the hacienda and devotes herself to improving their lot—she treats their mange and lice, teaches them to read and to sing, and urges the women to resist the men's violent and tyrannical behavior. Clara does remember, however, how her own mother's efforts to help the poorest women and children in the city, many years before, had prompted Clara as a child to write "with formidable intuition that charity had no effect on such monumental injustice" (71). She feels the same hopeless ineffectuality again in Tres Marías when the women nudge each other and smile slyly, humoring Clara but realizing that their husbands would beat them if they implemented Clara's ideas. Soon after, her own husband flies into a rage and threatens that if Clara persists in following her mother's feminist footsteps, he "would pull her pants down and give her a good spanking" (92). It is their first serious quarrel. Later in the summer, Clara becomes pregnant again and foresees that she will have twin boys, neither of whom will be named Esteban, again thwarting Trueba's wish to name a son after himself. Furious at her, Trueba goes to a brothel, where he finds Tránsito Soto, a prostitute he had visited years before. Tránsito echoes Clara's sentiments by decrying bullying men and timid women. She declares that although women "need a man to feel secure . . . they don't realize that the one thing they should be afraid of is men" (100). Tránsito, clearly prosperous now, offers to repay Trueba the fifty pesos he lent her years before. But Trueba refuses to take the money, preferring that she continue to be in his debt—a debt that he will call in at the end of the book, when he is powerless to rescue Alba from her torturer and needs Tránsito's help.

Over many subsequent summers, the Truebas return to Tres Marías, where the affection between Blanca and Pedro Tercero evolves from childish pleasures through their emerging adolescent sexuality until, by the age of fifteen, they become lovers. Clara senses their physical intimacy but finds nothing in it to fault, and several years pass with the young couple taking pleasure in their sexuality. During this calm interlude, Pedro Tercero develops skills as a songwriter and minstrel while becoming increasingly aware of the social inequality and injustice bred by the country's racism and rigorous class structure. The stability is shattered when the area suffers a severe earthquake and tsunami (as Chile did in 1939) that causes major damage to the hacienda. Pedro Tercero is reluctant to help rebuild Tres Marías, declaring that the peasants were breaking their backs to restore Trueba's wealth while they themselves would continue to live in squalor. Trueba himself is incapable of working, owing to injuries suffered during the earthquake. His complaints and outrage provoke Clara's contempt, especially in contrast to Pedro Segundo's serenity amid the damage and chaos. Soon after that, Trueba banishes Pedro Tercero from the property because of his communist ideas, promising to "blow his brains out" if he ever returns (146). When Clara intercedes, Trueba, in a fit of rage, strikes her with his cane, knocking a soup bowl out of her hands. In response,

Clara puts a lock on her bedroom door, which might have immediately precipitated further violence but for two subsequent events.

First, the return of Clara's twin boys, Jaime and Nicolás, who have completed twelve years of the local British School, slows the family's momentum toward disaster. The young men have come home to Tres Marías to bide their time before choosing professions. Another event that momentarily quells Trueba's rage is the arrival of a French visitor, Count Jean de Satigny, who ingratiates himself by asking for Blanca's hand in marriage. But Blanca, now twenty-four years old and deeply in love with Pedro Tercero, loathes both her father and the improbable Count and refuses to have anything to do with either. Piqued, Satigny spies on Blanca and uncovers the love affair between her and Pedro Tercero, which he promptly reports to Trueba. Totally out of control, Trueba beats Blanca brutally, threatens to castrate Pedro Tercero, and, in his fury, strikes Clara viciously, knocking out several of her teeth. Feeling that her marriage has been irretrievably shattered, Clara leaves Tres Marías with Blanca to return to her house in the city, where she takes off her wedding ring, abandons her married name, and vows never to speak to her husband again.

Left alone in Tres Marías, Trueba blames Pedro Tercero for the family's dissolution and, eager for revenge, offers a reward for information about his hiding place. Pancha García's grandson, Esteban García, now only ten years old, steps forward with the information. Trueba finds him, a scuffle follows, and Pedro Tercero barely escapes as Trueba swings an axe, cutting off three of the young man's fingers. When Esteban García asks for his reward, an enraged Trueba reneges on the agreement with the words "There's no reward for traitors!" (176). Eventually, Trueba will pay dearly for cheating the ten-year-old; more than a decade later, Colonel Esteban García gets his revenge by arresting, jailing, and savagely torturing Alba.

Back in the capital city, Blanca confesses that she is pregnant, and Trueba rushes home from Tres Marías to engineer a coerced marriage between Blanca and Satigny. Blanca resists, but gives in out of fear of her father and because she believes Trueba's claim that he has killed Pedro Tercero. A stickler for the traditions and appearances that Blanca despises, Trueba arranges a formal wedding in the cathedral, with the blessing of the bishop and a traditional wedding dress that cleverly disguises Blanca's pregnancy. After the ceremony, Trueba presents Satigny with a check to fund the newlyweds in a comfortable life and whisks them off to the north. As the couple leaves, Clara reveals to Blanca that Pedro Tercero is alive. With that news, Blanca dries her tears and regains a glimmer of hope that all is not lost. Later, to Blanca's relief, her new husband confesses that he has no interest in marital sex. When she also learns that Satigny is involved in elaborate sexual variations and entanglements, she senses danger and hastily leaves Satigny to return home. She reaches the capital two days later, barely before the delivery of her baby, Alba.

Unlike her grandmother and her mother, Blanca does not openly engage in the struggle between social classes or the crucial fight for equal rights for women. Rather, her unique contributions to the evolution of the Trueba women are essential matters of *being*—that is, her spontaneous and guiltless joy in sensuality and her indifference to such cultural and religious mandates as paternal rights and institutionalized marriage. Blanca does not seek her freedom, she lives it. As Allende herself puts it in an interview, Blanca is a "less flamboyant" character than Nívea or Clara, but, unlike them, she "has the experience of a great love" through which she "escapes a humdrum life" (Rodden 43).

What Is Over When the Book Is Over? Alba, the "Terror," and a New "Dawn"

Alba embodies the fourth generation in the Trueba's matrilineal line. Her mother and grandmother display an almost metalinguistic awareness of her birth as a *textual* event. Blanca wants to name the child "Clara," a proposal that Clara herself rejects because it would create "confusion in her notebooks that bore witness to life." Clara and

Blanca find the word "Alba" in a thesaurus and regard the name as "the last in a chain of luminous words" (Allende 223). It is as though the two women, as they search for a name that implies a "dawn," are simultaneously characters in the novel and authors of it.

And indeed, there are auspicious signs in Alba's early life to suggest that she is destined to be an illuminating force in the history of the Trueba family. She is born feet first, a sign of good luck; she has a tiny star-shaped birthmark, a sign of happiness; her time and place of birth mesh propitiously for her astrological chart. Moreover, Alba's mere presence brings a sparkle to her grandfather's eye, and Trueba seems altogether transformed into a kinder, gentler man. He lavishes Alba with presents and frets over her if she cries. She is homeschooled by adoring relatives and enlightened visitors. Alba's childhood is charmed like that of a princess in a fairy tale.

But there is something merely *willed* about the family's celebration of Alba as harbinger of a new dawn for the Truebas: not enough darkness has preceded Alba's birth to give meaning to the light. Accordingly, the novel's last chapters overturn the early optimism by charting Alba's passage through a "dark night of the soul" (or perhaps more aptly, "a dark night of the *body*") before she can emerge as a "light" dispelling the horrible darkness that befalls both the Trueba family and their country.

An early sign of the darkness looming in Alba's future occurs when she is six years old and Esteban García knocks at the door of the Big House in the city, seeking money from Trueba, who is by then a senator. As García waits for Trueba in the library, Alba enters the room. García instinctually hates her as the embodiment of the wealth and status he can never attain. Boldly, he approaches the child, fondles her legs and neck, feels her braid touch his wrist, and fantasizes about strangling her, even raping her. But Trueba's timely arrival breaks the mood. Years later, Alba has a similar encounter with García on her fourteenth birthday. Now a policeman, García is again in the library speaking to the senator. As he leaves, he runs into Alba, speaks to her a moment, and then abruptly kisses her on the mouth while holding her head with one hand and choking her with the other. Alba is able to push him away, and he leaves the house.

Alba does not recall these shocking encounters with Esteban García until she is an eighteen-year-old university student in love with a leftist student leader named Miguel. Alba, Miguel, and other student protesters have occupied a university building to demonstrate solidarity with a workers' strike. The students are surrounded by tanks and police who are expected to attack at any moment. After a very tense night, Alba has severe stomach cramps and decides to go home. As she leaves the building, she recognizes García as one of the policemen monitoring the situation. Watching her, García resents Alba's self-confident, haughty attitude and momentarily considers arresting her and leaving her "to rot in a cell, bathed in her own blood, until she [gets] down on her knees and beg[s] me" (276). Alba gets in a police van and goes home to the Big House, unaware of her effect on García.

While Alba clearly cannot know what García thinks during the moment of hesitation when he wavers between letting her go and arresting her, it is remarkable that she has had at this point three telling encounters with García over a dozen years without any awareness of the danger he represents. Her odd dismissal of García is reminiscent of her grandfather's similar dismissal of Pancha, García's grandmother, decades earlier at Tres Marías. One important point dramatized by these events is that members of the ruling oligarchy are often extremely naive about the inner lives of the downtrodden masses. Regardless of their opposing political views—Trueba's contempt for peasants and laborers versus Alba's great sympathy for their cause—neither Trueba nor Alba begins to fathom the darkness in Esteban García. It is easier to deny than to confront the depth of the resentment and hatred that the most aggrieved members of the oppressed classes can harbor toward the pampered rich and privileged.

Her brief encounter with García as she leaves the university site surrounded by police provokes at least a glimmer of awareness in Alba about García's escalating aggressiveness: "The nightmare had . . . crouched inside her all those years and . . . García was still the beast waiting for her in the shadows, ready to jump" (279). Yet Alba does not become more cautious in her public political activity. After the socialist government is toppled by a right-wing military coup during which both the socialist president and Alba's uncle Jaime are killed, Alba continues her naïve behavior. Even an old friend of Clara's warns Alba of the danger, telling her that "death is at your heels" and advising her to "take a trip" across the ocean (310). But so many of her acquaintances are endangered and in need of asylum that Alba selflessly devotes herself to protecting them. Remarkably, she feels that "it almost seemed like fun" (321). When Alba finds that Jaime's car is still where he had parked it before his death, she paints "two large sunflowers on the doors with the brightest yellow she could find" (322), apparently unaware that she is drawing the police's attention to her subversive activities. She hides political refugees and even weapons in the empty rooms of the Big House, never dreaming that the house of Senator Trueba could be under police surveillance.

Inevitably, the "political police" bang on the Big House door with rifle butts in the middle of the night. They terrorize the servants, ransack the house, pile books and personal documents in the courtyard and burn them. When Trueba protests, they knock Alba to the ground and call her a whore. After a siege of several hours, the police tape Alba's eyes and carry her off in a van, physically abusing her as they drive to the prison. She is beaten as she leaves the van and passed to a person whose voice she recognizes as Esteban García's. For the next month, García will inflict unspeakable mental and physical abuse on her. Alba, whose eyes remain taped shut, will be in total darkness.

The last thing that Trueba says to Alba as the police take her away is, "Don't worry, my dear. Everything will turn out fine. They can't do anything to you. This is all a terrible mistake" (342). Alas, it is indeed a terrible mistake—*Trueba's* mistake to think that he still has the power to intervene and free his granddaughter. Alba has realized this even before she is taken away. She admits to herself that "she had supposed this moment would come . . . but she had always had the irrational hope that somehow her grandfather's influence would protect her" (341). The arrival of the police triggers Alba's flash of insight, although Trueba is plainly still denying the fact that his considerable political power has passed into the hands of the police.

Trueba does mellow somewhat during his later years. However, his tolerance and kindness are self-serving, mainly directed toward members of his family. When, for instance, he sees Blanca using her money to feed the poor who show up at the door of the Big House, he raises her monthly stipend, more likely out of sympathy for Blanca's pocketbook than out of concern for the poor, whom he has spent his life ignoring. Trueba finally accepts Blanca's undeniable love for Pedro Tercero, and he uses his waning influence to help them flee the country when the time comes. He even tolerates the fact that Alba sells many of his household goods to finance her left-wing causes and to assist people in need of food and shelter. Ultimately, in an uncharacteristic act of humility, he confesses his lack of power and his despair to Tránsito Soto, begging her to help liberate Alba from Colonel Esteban García. Perhaps these late-life concessions to reality for the benefit of his family can be seen as transforming Trueba into a "benevolent patriarch," as one critic has claimed (Rodden 35).

But there is ample evidence that, however broken he is by the violence of the coup and the loss of his power, Trueba has not at all changed his attitude toward the peasants. When the military government returns to him his previously confiscated hacienda, "without giving it a second thought he left for the countryside with half a dozen hired thugs to avenge himself to his heart's content against the peasants" (Allende 327-28). He burns the peasants' homes, kills all their animals, destroys all their possessions, and drives them away with the threat that he will kill them if they return. Even at the end of the book, Trueba takes the law into his own hands to disempower the peasants and take revenge. Only after crushing them, does Trueba feel self-disgust—the hangover after an orgy of uncontrolled revenge. His impulse toward vengeance aligns him too closely with the likes of Esteban García to regard him, in any way, as a benevolent patriarch.

During her month of incarceration, Alba endures nearly uninterrupted physical and psychological abuse by Esteban García. Finally, totally depleted and hopeless, she decides "not to breathe or move, and beg[ins] eagerly to await her death" (351). This is both her darkest moment and a major turning point in her young life. Her grandmother, Clara, who has been dead for twenty years, appears to Alba with a dual message. First, "that the point was not to die, since death came anyway, but to survive." Second, "that she write a testimony that might one day call attention to [what] she was living through." That is, her immediate goal in living is to *write*, and the goal of writing is to provide documentary evidence to a blind world that "this horror . . . was taking place parallel to the peaceful existence of those who did not want to know." This is Alba's epiphanic moment. Previously, she had been drawn into her sociopolitical activism because she loved Miguel and abstractly endorsed his goal of social justice. But her activism is no more than a game to her: it "almost seemed like fun" as she drove around in her "flower child" car. Despite her good-willed actions on behalf of the poor and powerless, she had felt little genuine empathy for the people she helped. Now she fights to live so that she may write with empathic knowledge of the poor and of women in particular. Literally and metaphorically, she now sees things to which she had once been blind.

Alba is eventually released from prison because the guards think she is dying and because García has no further use for her. Fittingly, the agent of her release is a woman, Tránsito Soto. In the epilogue, Alba follows her grandmother's suggestion and begins to write a "testimony" in a voice that is unmistakably and persistently her own.[5] She gives a brief account of how she got home, with special attention to the numerous women who gave her the strength to survive and helped her on her way. She sees these women with fresh eyes, as she sees even her own neighborhood when she enters it for the first time in a month. With its gardens and walls and ostentatious prosperity, it is "like another country," surrounded by a vast but unseen city weighted down by poverty (364).

In addition to her new, hard-earned empathetic vision, Alba now regards all of her experiences, including torture at the hands of Esteban García, as fragments of an integrated design or pattern, like a "jigsaw puzzle in which each piece ha[s] a specific place." Alba's vision is not necessarily mystical or dependent on the supernatural. It derives from a practical awareness that separate parts of reality derive from and complement each other and that the *whole* is not easy to grasp. For instance, Alba now sees that her grandfather's rape of Pancha García festered within her grandson, Esteban, into an irrepressible lust for vengeance. She concludes, "It would be very difficult for me to avenge all those who should be avenged. . . . I have to break the terrible chain" (368). Alba's noble sentiments are, of course, as old as the *Oresteia* of Aeschylus or Jesus Christ's Sermon on the Mount and as modern as the passive resistance of Gandhi or Martin Luther King, Jr. One can debate the effectiveness of such tactics as well as the preconditions they require to become effective. Alba, at twenty-two, does not delve into such debates. She only knows what her experience has taught her, that, as she puts it, "my task is life and . . . my mission is not to prolong hatred . . . while I wait for better times to come" (368). Alba leaves her readers with one last, timeless conundrum: How does one break the cycle of vengeance, and how does one ensure that "better times" really do come?

Notes

1. Julio Cortázar's *Hopscotch*, Carlos Fuentes's *The Death of Artemio Cruz*, Gabriel García Márquez's *The Evil Hour*, and Mario Vargas Llosa's *The Time of the Hero*.

2. Two other works published in this peak year were Guillermo Cabrera Infante's verbally dazzling *Three Trapped Tigers* and Carlos Fuentes's prizewinning *A Change of Skins*.

3. The five are Julio Cortázar, Carlos Fuentes, Guillermo Cabrera Infante, Gabriel

García Márquez, and Mario Vargas Llosa. Three other frequently cited writers who did much of their work *before* the Boom are Jorge Luis Borges, Juan Rulfo, and Alejo Carpentier.

4. For "magical realism," see Lois Parkinson Zamora and Wendy B. Faris, eds., *Magical Realism: Theory, History, Community* (Durham: Duke University Press, 1997). This collection of essays includes Alejo Carpentier's introduction to *The Kingdom of This World*.

5. When Clara instructs Alba to write a "testimony," she consciously chooses a genre that is common in Latin America as a literary means of advocacy for the powerless and often "voiceless." The form (*testimonio* in Spanish) is usually a first-person account of the narrator's own experiences.

Works Cited

Allende, Isabel. *The House of the Spirits*. 1985. New York: Alfred A. Knopf, 1986.
_____. "Questions and Answers." 18 Feb. 2010. http://www.isabelallende.com/curious_frame.htm.
Bell-Villada, Gene. "Eros Makes War." *New York Times Book Review* 12 July 1987: 23.
Rodden, John, ed. *Conversations with Isabel Allende*. Austin: U of Texas P, 1999.

Maryse Condé and Isabel Allende:
Family Saga Novels

María Roof

At first glance, Maryse Condé and Isabel Allende might seem un-likely writers to encompass in a critical essay: one is Caribbean and the other South American; one writes in French and the other in Spanish; one earned a doctorate in comparative literature, the other became a journalist at age seventeen; one identifies herself as a member of the African diaspora, while the other traces her heritage to "a Basque sailor [who] disembarked on the coast" of her country at the end of the last century;[1] one is from the West Indian island of Guadeloupe (no longer officially a colony, but rather an "overseas department" of France), and the other considers herself a native of the independent nation of Chile. What, then, do they share besides their gender and the fact that they are both currently publishing and finding their novels translated for read-ing publics worldwide?

The traditionally distinct lines which defined literatures according to distant origins (classical, Western, non-Western), modern political divisions (French, Spanish, Chilean), language (French, Spanish), or language and geographic area (French, Canadian francophone, Carib-bean francophone, African francophone, Peninsular Spanish, Spanish American, U.S. Hispanic) have been redrawn by new configurations marking transgeographic, transhistorical, transnational, and translan-guage affinities. In their literary trajectories, both Isabel Allende and Maryse Condé have blurred borders in the Americas with their most re-cent works. Allende placed the "gringo" protagonist of her fourth novel, *The Infinite Plan* (1991; Eng. 1993), within a Latino community of California, where she currently lives. Condé crisscrossed the Ameri-cas in *I, Tituba, Black Witch of Salem* (1986; Eng. 1992) and in *Tree of Life* (1987; Eng. 1992), before setting the action of her recent novel, *La colonie du nouveau monde* (*Colony of the New World*; 1993), on the coast of Colombia. Condé has explained the latter choice of location and voiced an opinion shared by other contemporary writers: "I purposely selected this coastal region to show that it belongs to our universe and that we must not sever Guadeloupe from this culture which extends throughout the Caribbean region and Latin America, the whole American continent, in fact" (Pfaff, 238).[2]

Maryse Condé readily acknowledges a possible commonality between writers of the Americas, as well as similarities between her work and Allende's.

> I liked *The House of the Spirits* a lot, but I wouldn't say it influenced me. A sort of brotherly, or should I say sisterly, relationship, can certainly be found between *The House of the Spirits* and *Tree of Life*. This year [1994], I experimented with a course entitled: "Do women of the Americas have a common literature?" I selected Allende . . . and of course *Tree of Life*. (Pfaff, 242)

In both these novels the authors devise multigenerational family sagas using autobiographical elements.[3] It is my theory that a close reading of the works can uncover a rich range of contact and divergence in their creation of families conditioned by the vectors of race, class, and gender. This essay examines the novels for their new and important experiments in the construction of the family as a contested site of meaning, with a new subject positioning of women.

In interviews, neither author denies the importance of the family in the life of individuals; the family is meaningful, but it is a flawed institution. When questioned about the prevalence of the theme of filiation in both Latin American and Caribbean writers, and the possible need to reconstruct a heritage through fiction, Maryse Condé replied:

> Perhaps. I also believe that the family remains the essential element in our societies and social fabric. Whatever you do, you are still someone's daughter; you are always defined by a particular genealogy. . . . It's true that a number of writers in the Americas engage in a symbolic search for the real-

ity that existed before the rape of slavery. But I believe that more important are the preeminence of the family nucleus and the constant need to define yourself in terms of that nucleus. (Pfaff, 243)

Isabel Allende's position, expressed during the same year (1994), reflects a similar valorization, in contrast to her perception of families in the United States.

One of the characteristics of North American culture is that you can always start again. . . . You leave behind guilt, past traditions, memories. . . . For most people in the world, that is totally impossible. We carry with us the sense that we belong to a group, a clan, a tribe, an extended family, especially a country. Whatever happens to you happens to the collective group, and you can never leave behind the past. What you have done in your life will always be with you. So, for us, we have the burden of this sort of fate, of destiny, that you don't. (Baldock and Bernstein, 8)

Both authors, however, reject inherited paradigms of "family" as negative for individuals and groups, and they both advocate, each within the specificities of her culture, an ampler, more inclusive definition of family, which can hold in diverse elements in play. Both consider the family intersected by limitations based on class and race that no longer correspond to the modern world.[4]

The ancestor in *Tree of Life*, Albert-the-forebear, starts with nothing. His flight from sugarcane-plantation exploitation on Guadeloupe leads him into a form of self-exile to Panama during the construction of the canal. He manages to create a business which is successful until he is forced by racism-engendered violence into self-exile again, as he seeks entry into bourgeois respectability elsewhere, this time following the very American myth of El Dorado to the golden land of opportunity, San Francisco.

The family fortunes are gradually increased through classic capitalist exploitation of the poorest workers, who live in tenements owned by the Louis family. Albert's attempts to join the Marcus Garvey movement are frustrated, apparently because he holds in tension within himself contradictory positions related to class and race—a philosophical commitment to love and support the beauty of the black race, even as he subjects the blacks in his tenements to filthy, subhuman conditions.

As the family gains in financial security, the only sense of deterioration portrayed is nostalgia for the old family unity, illustrated in the photograph albums of family rituals shared in common and a knowledge of the family history which the text attempts to reconstruct, because, as the narrator explains: "The time was coming when none would be able to recount the family's past for lack of knowledge. When the living would no longer issue forth endowed with an ancient genetic heritage after interminable pregnancies in one belly or another. When the present would be nothing but the present. And the individual nothing but the individual!" (363-64).

Since it is the family which gives meaning, the recuperation of the family memory involves the construction (through fiction?) of the histories of the missing members. In *Tree of Life* Condé posits the need to create family origins in order to hold a sense of identity. The narrator, Coco, is the illegitimate daughter of Albert's daughter's liaison with a "mulatto from Senegal" (180). Abandoned by her mother for ten years after her birth in France, she remained an unschooled "mixed blood," as she was called, until she began to explore her own story and research the rest of family, especially the missing elements.

The gaps in the family history involve an anti-white, color-determined bias which is seen as historically passé, a reaction to French colonialism. The two forgotten family members were the first to marry white women, and the decision by the patriarch Albert henceforth to exclude them from the family in effect kills them by abandoning them to their individual selves and their individual suicides. *Tree of Life* overtly questions premises regarding color-based unity and disunity when, for example, Jacob repeats the oft-quoted lament that in Guadeloupe they don't want Negroes to succeed, and his granddaughter observes that Negroes who "walk all over their fellow man to succeed" are hardly unified (344).

Even more explicitly, one of the younger characters ends up repeating the "sin" of defying the family's color line by marrying a French white woman. He interprets the initial family reaction to the "massive invasion of whites into the heart of the family" (318) as class, not race, prejudice—an erroneous idea around which his parents and grandparents had mobilized. If the first white (European woman) who married into the family "had not been a factory worker, the world as we know it would have been different!" (349).

The old Guadeloupe described in the novel was a three-part country divided racially, in which whites, mulattoes, and blacks hated one another (317). But this no longer serves Guadeloupe, which must, as Coco has done with her narrative, present a history of the country that denies no particular element, proscribes no particular episodes, yet rejects an imposed heritage ("Our ancestors, the Gauls") to replace it with "My forebear Albert Louis" (3).

If the family is no longer homogeneous, "one blood, united under a single skin" (359), Coco reflects pride in claiming and proclaiming the truth of her diverse origins: "I, I was no longer ashamed. I had planted my flag on the island" (351). In an inversion of the traditional search by Americans for ancestors in Europe, even those family members born in France long for a sense of identity with Guadeloupe, for surely, as another seeker of her Louis family origins implies, racist France provides no home for them.

Tree of Life also deconstructs the broader pan-Africanist perception of Africa as the "motherland" to the children of the diaspora who seek self-definition in African roots. Coco does not follow in the footsteps of Veronica, the protagonist in Condé's first novel, *Heremakhonon* (1976; Eng. 1982), who travels to Africa in search of a "nigger [who] has ancestors!" (24). As the critic A. James Arnold observes, Veronica "can usefully be seen as a negative of Alex Haley in that she finds in

Africa lots of sex but no roots" (711). *Tree of Life* constructs a family which is "meaning-full" only when it proceeds from an American ancestor, Albert-the-forebear. Given the historical silence regarding their origins in the "History" written by the colonizers, members of the diaspora need to create families, lineages in American terms, and anchor their roots in a Caribbean, not an African-based, identity. In *Tree of Life* the family serves as a site for creating these new meanings.

* * *

Isabel Allende's *House of the Spirits* also posits a redefinition of family which requires the reintegration of excluded members, though the personal quest for identity is given less importance. In this novel, exclusion pits family members against one another and creates avoidable violence. Here too, the justification for exclusion resides in socially approved divisions based on class and race.

The House of the Spirits designates as one of the family's early progenitors Esteban Trueba, who builds his fortune in mining and land, the two potential sources of wealth in Chile at the turn of the century. Both are acquired through privileged means: inheritance or loans secured on the basis of his mother's family's "good name." Trueba is successful in bringing to life an abandoned family hacienda, on which he rules in a manner not unlike that of notoriously abusive slaveholders.

The definition of "family" is constructed along traditional oligarchical lines to exclude children sired by the patron with indigenous women. The broader social implications of this meaning of family are signaled from the very beginning of the novel, when a priest rages from the pulpit against those social personages of the early 1900s who were like the "Pharisees, who had tried to legalize bastards and civil marriage, thereby dismembering the family, the fatherland, private property, and the Church, and putting women on an equal footing with men—this in open defiance of the law of God, which was most explicit on this issue" (3).

This exclusion of unrecognized "mestizo" children drives the narrative action, though it is slow to appear in these terms. Trueba populates the countryside with children of whom he does not consider himself the father, because for a person in his position, having children—that is to say, establishing a family which includes children—involves more than mere procreation.

He figured that when he was ready, he would find a woman of his own class, with the blessings of the Church, because the only ones who really counted were the ones who bore their father's surname; the others might just as well not have been born. And he would have none of that monstrous talk about everyone being born with the same rights and inheriting equally, because if that happened everybody would go to hell and civilization would be thrown back to the Stone Age. (66)

The intersection of class and race prejudice is clearly implied, since the women producing the "others" are like his first rape victim, Pancha García, with "dark legs . . . and an Indian face, with broad features, dark skin" (56) and "straight, dark hair" (58). "Pancha's humble origin" does not prevent Trueba from performing his triply violent act: the rape of a virgin, of an indigenous person, and of a poor worker. The act replicates and reproduces traditional social relations: "Before her, her mother—and before her, her grandmother—had suffered the same animal fate" (57). And all had been servants in the "main house."

In time, Trueba's cruelty and his apparent right to fornicate at will evoke "jealous admiration among the men of his class" (63), even as it produces "the instrument of a tragedy that would befall [the] family" (190). This instrument is Trueba's grandson Esteban García, first presented in the novel driving a nail through a chicken's eye. Trueba had discarded the child's grandmother, Pancha García, as soon as she became pregnant, out of respect for his socially approved definition of family. But this exclusion ensured that Pancha "had managed before she died to poison [her grandson's] childhood with the story that if only his father had been born in place of Blanca, Jaime, or Nicolás [Trueba's legal children], he would have inherited Tres Marías and could even have been President of the Republic if he wanted" (189). When the defiant Blanca "slept with her head resting on the smooth brown stomach of her lover" (198) and became pregnant, Trueba "knew that the scandal would be the same whether she gave birth to a bastard child or married the son of a peasant: society would condemn her in either case" (213).

The nonrecognition of family members procreated out of wedlock produces a resentment hatred which expands as it becomes legacy: Trueba's grandson Esteban García "hated Esteban Trueba, his seduced grandmother, his bastard father, and his own inexorable peasant fate," but he watched his grandfather from afar in order to "imitate his gestures and speech" (189). The medieval droits de seigneur arrogated by the upper classes, when shifted to the military in the novel, are turned against the very class that used to benefit from them, the oligarchy. Trueba supports the military, gets his illegitimate grandson into the police academy, and calls on the armed forces to overthrow the elected socialist president, only to find that he is ultimately powerless to save his legitimate granddaughter Alba from arrest. From a legalized position of power, Esteban, now Colonel Esteban García, tortures Alba, ostensibly for information about guerrilla leaders; she understands, however, that he "was not trying to learn Miguel's true whereabouts but to avenge himself for injuries that had been inflicted on him from birth" (411). An image of his childhood appears to García: Alba at the hacienda in her pretty dresses, walking hand in hand with her grandfather, while he, "barefoot in the mud swore that one day he would make her pay for her arrogance and avenge himself for his cursed bastard fate" (413).

Like *Tree of Life*, which Condé has called her "forgotten novel" because it "raises too many embarrassing questions" ("The Role of the Writer," 698), *The House of the Spirits* uses family as a site to raise social issues metaphorically. At the end of the novel Alba recognizes that Esteban García was part of the grand design that included her life, the chain of events of which she is a part and from which she derives meaning. But she, the only surviving member of the family left in her country, must break the cycle of revenge, rooted in family exclusion, and redefine the family—that is, absorb all the disparate elements that tear against the national fabric: "I have to break that terrible chain. I want to think that . . . my mission is not to prolong hatred . . . while I carry this child in my womb, the daughter of so many rapes or perhaps of Miguel, but above all, my own daughter" (432).

* * *

Maryse Condé and Isabel Allende use the trope of the family to define a key subject position for women in altering the direction of their societies. Their narrators are gendered characters, females who must interpret family history from bits and pieces of incomplete histories and propose a new, more inclusive definition of family to promote unity and heal the wounds of the past. Allende emphasizes that women are in a position to effect changes because they have a natural sense of common identity. Alba finds that prisoners at the concentration camp for women care for one another and even, in sharp contrast to traditional Western definitions of family, tend to the children of others. She is rescued from a garbage dump by a woman described as

> one of those stoical, practical women of our country, the kind of woman who has a child with every man who passes through her life and, on top of that, takes in other people's abandoned children . . . the kind of woman who's the pillar of many other lives. . . . I told her she had run an enormous risk rescuing me, and she smiled. It was then I understood that the days of Colonel García and all those like him are numbered, because they have not been able to destroy the spirit of these women. (429)

Condé and Allende suggest that, because they are marginalized from power and therefore less encumbered, women can break the cycle of damaging traditions, and indeed have the moral imperative to do so. Otherwise, history becomes the circular repetition of old errors. All races, all classes, all genders, people born everywhere must be included in the modern multicultural, diversified concept of family.

The critic Adalaide Morris has posited that the family, as a site to proclaim women's agency, "offers a number of advantages to novelists interested in cultural change" (18).

> To novelists who wish to disrupt the status quo, the fact that the family is the site where values and behaviors are reproduced generation after generation is not a liability but an advantage, for there are no more crucial circuits to reconfigure than those of the primary power supply. And, finally, for novelists interested in extending the definition of 'family' beyond its familiar white, middle-class, heterosexual configuration, the range of possible familial associations is limited only by the invention and variety of the people who compose them. (19)

These novels reflect not the existential angst of solitary individuals, but the creation of an encompassing collective memory in support of solidarity.[5] Women become agents in the redefinition of identity, which is no longer restricted to one's own family, race, or class. In breaking down separations caused by socially defined difference, *Tree of Life* and *The House of the Spirits* inscribe their stories within a discourse of coalition, a "site where disparate subjectivities collide, converge, and continue to exist" (Morris, 17).[6] Both propose a reworking of the past, by women, in order to go forward.

From *World Literature Today* 70, no. 2 (1996): 283-288. Copyright © 1996 by *World Literature Today*. Reprinted with permission of *World Literature Today*.

Notes

1. Allende, *Paula*, p. 3.

2. This quote appears in a new chapter in the English version of Françoise Pfaff's *Entretiens avec Maryse Condé* an English edition of which (*Conversations with Maryse Condé*) is to be published by the University of Nebraska Press in 1996. My

thanks to the author for allowing me to consult the manuscript in English, to which the page numbers refer.

3. For correlations between biography and fiction, see especially Pfaff's *Conversations with Maryse Condé*, Condé's essay "The Role of the Writer," and the Ann Armstrong Scarboro interview included as an afterword to *I, Tituba, Black Witch of Salem*, in which Condé states that *Tree of Life* "is my own story and my family's story with, of course, the distortion of fiction" (211). For Allende, her latest nonfiction work, *Paula*, discloses the autobiography behind *The House of the Spirits*.

4. I use the term *family* here in a sociological sense, while recognizing Djelal Kadir's creative metaphor of the family as "a genealogy of literary texts" (3) in his *Questing Fictions: Latin America's Family Romance*.

5. See my study of reconfigurations of solidarities in Allende's first three novels, "Isabel Allende: Modelos de la solidaridad."

6. Cf. A. James Arnold's hypothesis that *Tree of Life* is a truly multicultural novel in other senses as well.

Works Cited

Allende, Isabel. *The House of the Spirits*. Magda Bogin, tr. New York. Bantam. 1986.

_____. *The Infinite Plan*. Margaret Sayers Peden, tr. New York. HarperCollins. 1993.

_____. *Paula*. Margaret Sayers Peden, tr. New York. HarperCollins. 1995.

Arnold, A. James. "The Novelist as Critic." *World Literature Today* 67:4 (Autumn 1993), pp. 711-16.

Baldock, Bob, and Dennis Bernstein. "Isabel." Interview originally published in *Mother Jones*; reprinted in the *Colorado Springs Independent*, 2:49 (14-21 December 1994), p. 8.

Condé, Maryse. *La colonie du nouveau monde*. Paris. Laffont. 1993.

_____. *Heremakhonon*. Richard Philcox, tr. Washington, D.C. Three Continents. 1982.

_____. *I, Tituba, Black Witch of Salem*. Richard Philcox, tr. Charlottesville. University Press of Virginia. 1992.

_____. "The Role of the Writer." Speech given on 25 March 1993 at the University of Oklahoma. *World Literature Today* 67:4 (Autumn 1993), pp. 697-99.

_____. *Tree of Life: A Novel of the Caribbean*. Victoria Reiter, tr. New York. Ballantine. 1992.

Kadir, Djelal. *Questing Fictions: Latin America's Family Romance*. Minneapolis. University of Minnesota Press. 1986.

Morris, Adalaide. "First Persons Plural in Contemporary Feminist Fiction." *Tulsa Studies in Women's Literature*, 11:1 (1992), pp. 11-29.

Pfaff, Françoise. *Conversations with Maryse Condé*. Lincoln. University of Nebraska Press. Forthcoming [1996].

Roof, María. "Isabel Allende: Modelos de la solidaridad." *Studies in Modern and Classical Languages and Literatures*. Volume 4. Winter Park, Fl. Rollins College. 1992. Pp. 127-32.

Scarboro, Ann Armstrong. Afterword to Maryse Condé's *I, Tituba, Black Witch of Salem*. Pp. 187-225.

Voices from the Political Abyss:

Isabel Allende's *The House of the Spirits* and the Reconstruction and Preservation of History and Memory in 1970s Chile and Beyond _____

Carrie Sheffield

In this highly political and media-constructed world, it is all too often the case that history becomes "spun" with a good dose of bias. Take, for example, the current crises and conflicts between Israel and Palestine. While rational thinking should not allow one to perceive one side as thoroughly "good" and the other as thoroughly "evil," it seems the American media seeks precisely that type of limited thinking. All too often presenting Israel (and even the United States) blameless and Palestine as the evil scourge of the Gaza strip, most news channels appear to cater primarily to American political ties. Of course, the story could easily be reversed. However, the point here is not to take one side in the debate. The point is only to make note of the fact that in the media's telling of the story, multiple voices are unheard, leaving gaps in the tale.

Too often it is not just media bias that is responsible for the elimination and reconstruction of memory, history, and identity. In many cases, the governments themselves participate in the free play of erasure and editing of political events in order to either hide or glorify their participation in them. And in this regard, the United States is no political saint. The United States participated in one of the most horrific and bloody political events in history: the 1973 coup d'etat in Chile.

On September 4, 1970, Salvador Allende was elected Chile's first democratically elected Marxist president. The United States' reaction was predictable. Long an opponent of Marxism, the United States government was, to say the least, not pleased with the results of the Chilean election. In *The Last Two Years of Salvador Allende*, Nathaniel Davis (a former U.S. ambassador to Chile) offers a snapshot of the U.S.

reaction to the success of Allende. He quotes Thomas Powers's account of "a meeting between President Nixon and Ambassador Korry: . . . 'Nixon then commenced a monologue that he was going to smash Allende'" (Davis 1985, 6).

The United States acted out an "anti-Allende" campaign and the CIA held "covert programs to neutralize communist influence" among the people (Sobel 1974, 121-122). CIA covert operations were implemented in order to cause national strife; they aided in instigating truck-driver strikes that depleted food supplies, provided arms for the violent coup d'etat, and interfered as much as possible with civilian and government life. The CIA "cabled their head of station in Santiago, advising him the main objective was to 'prevent Allende from taking office'" (O'Brien 1976, 172). Nixon's desire to "smash Allende" fits with the standard feelings of the U.S. government at the time—and makes the United States' cover-up and Chile's suppression of memory predictable. In *The House of the Spirits*, Isabel Allende writes of Chilean history leading up to and beyond the Chilean coup of the early 1970s; the novel is a direct response to the political elimination of people, memory, and history that occurred before and after the coup.

Allende's novel combats the ruling ideological history that, having been taught in schools over the last thirty years, becomes what Roland Barthes terms a naturalized myth: "What the world supplies to myth is an historical reality, defined . . . by the way in which men have produced or used it; and what myth gives in return is a *natural* image of this reality" (1994, 142). When written as a means of controlling and dictating identities and memories, history takes on the role of myth—appearing as natural because it is taught and dictated as natural. Barthes asserts that "myth is depoliticized speech" (143); history then, as a form of myth, is depoliticized not in the sense that it is apolitical but that it has become so entrenched in our culture as to *seem* apolitical. Naturalization is the power source behind myth; the more a myth presents itself as "natural," the more it seems to be inherent in an entire culture, and the more the general population will be ready to embrace it. Because of its guise of naturalness, myth remains a tool for the ob-fuscation of truth and oppression of dominated people.

Through its multiple voices and alternative visions of history, *The House of the Spirits* escapes the production of myth altogether. It seeks not to conceal history, identity, and memory under one all-encompassing image but to make them readily available to all. The constant political voice of *The House of the Spirits* guarantees its separation from myth; unlike myth, *The House of the Spirits* is both inherently and overtly po-litical. While myth tries to conceal its political nature, hiding behind the guise of the natural, *The House of the Spirits* places the political at the forefront; it seeks to subvert an ideology that denies (the impor-tance of) its existence.

The nonlinear and achronological structure of the novel encapsu-lates its inherent political nature. Allende's focus on what have tradi-tionally been considered unimportant, ahistorical stories (namely sto-ries of women), and her refusal to structure the novel along traditional historical lines, is a subversion of that linear tradition. While there is a general sense of forward-movement through time, there is no concrete, chronological, forward-thrusting time line in the novel: "everything [happens] simultaneously" (Allende 1993, 432). Time is reliant upon a memory that focuses on events rather than dates, and as such, the novel makes free with our preconceived and patriarchal concepts of time, moving us through the narrator's recollection of events. For example, in the space of a few pages, we are moved back in time approximately seven months. Within the space of a few chapters, we see the Trueba household days before Blanca's return and Alba's birth, we are pre-sented with Blanca, two months pregnant in the home of Count Jean de Satigny, and we are returned to the moments in time when Alba is born. The structure is presented "according to events and not in chronologi-cal order" (433) and allows for a more intense focus on the "relation-ship between events" (432) and the memories of those events.

The two narrators, Alba and Trueba, provide the reader with a view of both the dominant history taught in schools and the subversive women's memories in the novel. The difference in their narrative voices serves to highlight the single-minded linear view held by Trueba, and others within the dominant group, as a negative and repressive one. Through Alba's abundant vision and memory, and Trueba's tendency toward narrow-mindedness, we catch a glimpse of two distinct worlds, and through those worlds, we are offered a re-vision of history.

Alba's position as the voice of the text is twofold: throughout most of the novel, she maintains the role of third-person narrator, only rarely inserting a secondary, unobtrusive "I" into the line of the text but, overall, maintaining such a degree of separation from it that we are unaware that she is the narrator until her first-person epilogue. The benefit of this documentary-like, external position is that it gives an amount of credibility to her story; by not claiming the story as her own and by avoiding what would be a capitalistic appropriation/ownership of story, Alba provides an objective/subjective accounting of events. The objective/subjective position allows for the deeply personal accounts of individual people, memories, and stories in the novel while preventing the appearance of personal bias. "[T]he unnamed 'I'," as Robert Antoni suggests, "surfaces from the collective-feminine omniscient viewpoint to transport the reader for the instant to the present moment of writing" (1988, 21). The weaving of the narration from various moments and memories in the past to the present and back again serves to further obliterate the construct of a single, linear history.

Allende presents a revised cultural history, identity, and memory through Alba's narration. Through the subsequent generations of women, she revises the culturally accepted, Latin-American role of woman—that of mother-wife-daughter alone—and presents it in its true light—as revolutionary-feminist-independent woman as well as mother-wife-daughter. This movement toward independence is focused in Alba's ability to rewrite the text of history; through the rewriting, memories that history ignores are preserved and given voice.

Where the dominant history eliminates all possibilities save one, Allende's revision of history endeavors to represent and preserve all possible histories, memories, and identities. In her essay, "The Spirits Were Willing," Allende explains:

> I had the thought that if I set down in writing what I wanted to rescue from oblivion, I could reconstruct that lost world [Chile], revive the dead, unite the dispersed, capture the memories forever, and make them mine. Then no one could ever take them away from me. (1988, 241)

The concept of preservation of memories is integral to the text and is represented in Clara's "notebooks which bear witness to life" (1993, 115). Memories provide substance to history, and their preservation is necessary because the political turmoil in Chile led to an excessive loss of history and memory. Indeed, in "Payback Time for Pinochetistas," *The Nation* contributing editor Marc Cooper comments on the erasure of memory and history in Chile:

> Since Pinochet ceded power to civilian rule in 1990, two successive elected governments have tried—in the name of growth and globalization—to anesthetize the country and impose a collective amnesia about the horrors of the recent past. (1998, 24)

The House of the Spirits is a direct response to this type of political-historical annihilation, which began as soon as the Pinochet regime took power.

Esteban Trueba, the novel's "patriarch," in his role of intransigent ideologue symbolizes the government of Chile. Trueba's truth is the ideology of patriarchy, capitalism, dominance, and politically dictated history and memory; he only begins to realize it is a falsehood after his granddaughter, Alba, returns from the government torture camp and tells him her story. The same holds true of the Chilean oligarchic government of the novel; they believe the myth that Marxism is an inherently evil system and, as a result, plot with the United States to overthrow the democratically elected Marxist government. They too realize that their truths are falsehoods when the fascist Pinochet regime is installed in the Marxists' place; Trueba narrates the leaden realization:

> we thought the military was a necessary step for the return to a healthy democracy. . . . It was clear then that they didn't have the slightest intention of reopening the doors of Congress, as we all expected . . . things weren't turning out the way we had planned. (Allende 1993, 374-375)

In narrating Trueba's story, Alba shares and contextualizes more than Trueba is willing. For example, in the "Three Marías" chapter, Trueba does not share the stories of his rapes of peasant women; Alba does by writing from within the memories of those women and Trueba:

> Esteban did not remove his clothes. He attacked her savagely, thrusting himself into her without preamble, with unnecessary brutality. He realized too late, from the blood spattered on her dress, that the young girl was a virgin, but neither Pancha's humble origin nor the pressing demands of his desire allowed him to reconsider. (57)

Without Alba's explication, Trueba would eliminate memories of such things as his rapes of peasant girls, his stockpiling of arms, and his position in aiding the coup d'etat that overthrew the Marxist government because to him, and the dominant political machine, those things are insignificant.

An integral part of *The House of the Spirits* is the preservation of women's memories and histories within the severely patriarchal landscape of Latin America via what Robert Antoni terms the "feminine collective" (1988, 23). *The House of the Spirits* is divided into three main sections, one for each—Clara, Blanca, and Alba. Luce Irigaray suggests, in *Thinking the Difference*, that writers like Allende begin "to redress women's individual and collective loss of identity" by providing a historical voice that "will help them [and their memories move] from the private sphere to the public, from the family to the society in which they live" (1994, 10). This is not to say that the feminine collective eventually leads completely outward and away from the sphere of women; rather, it takes their histories and memories to the social sphere. *The House of the Spirits*, by unifying female stories into a firm network through familial and maternal bonds, takes female history and memory into the social sphere by placing it on the same plane of importance as male history.

Each section provides insights not only into the political evolution of Chile but also into the growth and continuation of feminine bonds. Clara's section begins the recording of the family history and provides for the prevention of the loss of memory and history through her notebooks; Blanca's section reveals how identity is created through love; and Alba's section prevents the loss of history, identity, and memory through the collection and presentation of the feminine collective in written form. Norma Helsper, in "Binding the Wounds of the Body Politic: Nation as Family in *La casa de los espíritus*," discusses Allende's use of the Trueba family as a signifier of Chile:

> Ultimately, Esteban and Alba are able to bridge the gap of political differences because of their loving familial ties; and Alba, through her recognition that her torturer is also her kin, proposes the family as a model for her divided country: members of this family have oppressed, wounded, and tortured each other, but they are the same ones who now heal one another. The family she posits is all of Chile. (1991, 55-56)

Similarly, the memories Alba preserves are not merely her own; they belong to all of Chile and, therefore, must be preserved.

Clara's notebooks are a means to preserve a memory that would be erased by the dominant political power. As power shifts hands, new political groups seek to construct lines of history that claim "this was the way it happened." All other alternative stories are obliterated through erasure, censure, or transformation into fairy-tale. Clara's notebooks, which tell of a time that is marked by three-legged tables, ghosts in the corners, and predictions that almost always come true, contain the type of stories often relegated to that back corner of the literary world labeled *fairy-tale*. However, by writing things down as they happened, Clara gives testimony to their truthfulness and avoids "the mists of forgetfulness" (Allende 1993, 75).

As reclaimer of history, identity, and memory, Alba is faced with the daunting task of knowing the memories of those who were born before her. Through Clara's notebooks, Alba has the opportunity to see the links between people and events:

> I write, she wrote, that memory is fragile and the space of a single life is brief, passing so quickly that we never get a chance to see the relationship between events; we cannot gauge the consequences of our acts, and we believe in the fiction of the past, present, and future. . . . (432)

The feminine collective exists to eliminate the difficulties of a short life span; through shared memories and histories, the women in the future collective (Alba and her daughters) are able to know the past and see the possibilities of the future. Shared memories and the feminine collective subvert the construct of linear history by making stories, memories, and events simultaneously available.

Blanca's chapters offer a third of those shared memories; through them we witness a mini-history of pre-revolutionary Chile and what the dominant history leaves out—he lives of those involved in shaping Chile's political identity. We see not only the relationship between events but also the relationships between people and how the political turmoil of a country can tear families apart. Blanca's section, more so than Clara's, provides the *personal* histories of individuals—the histories that are a component of identity—that the dominant history ignores. In the dominant world, it is the events that matter—who took charge and when, what country had the most money, and so on. In *The*

House of the Spirits, political events such as the 1973 coup d'etat take place as but a chapter of the history; Allende focuses the novel instead upon the lives and memories of the people involved and what causes them to make the decisions they do.

Alba's section *revises* and *re-presents* the main political event in the novel that is included in traditional linear histories. We are presented with the years immediately leading to the coup d'etat and its chaotic, fascist results. Alba gives voice to the United States' role in the coup as well as the fascist dictatorship's perpetration of torture and mass murder. As a result of the United States' involvement in the events leading up to the coup, the Chilean national economy under Salvador Allende crumbled; stores ran out of food, supplies ran low, and a black market burgeoned. Alba provides a personalized view of the crash of the Chilean economy:

> the right . . . controlled the influential mass media and possessed nearly limitless financial resources, as well as the support of the gringos [U.S. CIA operatives] who had allocated secret funds for the program of sabotage . . . stores were nearly empty. Shortages of goods, which was soon to be a collective nightmare, had begun. Women woke at dawn to stand in endless lines where they could purchase an emaciated chicken, half a dozen diapers, or a roll of toilet paper. . . . The black market flourished. (347)

Alba's narration of her memory of the "gringos'" involvement speaks to the United States' denial of most of its involvement in Chilean politics. While it has given up many documents regarding its involvement with the coup, the U.S. has refused to declassify other documents that would further prove its involvement and human rights violations made in an attempt to maintain control of history (Kornbluh 1998, 15). Alba's narration negates that control through her presentation of how the United States' involvement *directly* influenced the lives of the Chilean people:

With a stroke of the pen the military changed world history, erasing every incident, ideology, and historical figure of which the regime disapproved. They adjusted the maps . . . and appropriated distant countries in the geography books, leaping borders with impunity. . . . Censorship, which at first covered only the mass media, was soon extended to textbooks, song lyrics, movie scripts, and even private conversation. (1993, 383)

Some people, like Allende's Alba, have spoken out about the involvement of the U.S. in an attempt to prevent history and memory from being too drastically altered in favor of the dominant group. In *The House of the Spirits*, Alba's testimony gives witness to "the enormous wooden crates [of weapons] unloaded in the courtyard of her house in the middle of the night and their contents silently stored . . . in the unused back rooms of the house" (351). Parallel that to the fact that, after Salvador Allende gained office, the CIA continued its aid to the Chilean political right, contributing money and guns (O'Brien 1976). A few people involved in the coup have come forward with their stories and lend factual credence to Allende's "fiction." Genaro Arriagada, of the Christian Democratic parry in Chile, states: "the CIA made twenty-one contacts with key military and police officers. It also delivered submachine guns . . ." (1988, 5).

Alba's section also brings out the underlying stories of torture, disappearance, and governmental corruption behind the coup. It is in the concentration camp itself that the setting for the feminine collective comes to fruition. While in the "doghouse" (a small box designed to isolate and terrorize those in the camp), Alba is visited by Clara's spirit, who tells her to mentally inscribe her memories of the tragedies that have occurred:

[Clara] suggested that she write a testimony that might one day call attention to the terrible secret she was living through, so that the world would know about this horror that was taking place parallel to the peaceful existence of those who didn't want to know. . . . (Allende 1993, 414)

The written testimony Alba creates is integral to the preservation of memories. Without it, Alba's memory of Clara, Blanca, and the women in the concentration camp would fade, and there would be little left for her to pass on to her daughter. So, like Clara, Alba "bears witness to life" so that others may remember and know and so that the erasure of memories—and people—will one day stop. Isabel Allende, in "The Spirits Were Willing," notes that the reason she wrote the novel was to bring back a record of what happened and to prevent the history from being erased from the minds of the people (1988, 241).

The women in the concentration camp, like Clara, know that the writing and preservation of memory is integral for healing of mental and physical wounds. They put the notebooks in front of Alba and tell her to write because it is the only way they and their stories will be remembered. The feminine collective provides the support Alba needs to present the revision of history present in the novel; it is the chorus of women's voices following behind her that gives Alba the ability to write and preserve their (and her) testimonies.

Because of her ties to the feminine collective, Alba is able to represent strong and straightforward accounts of torture and mass murder. The descriptions of torture are blunt and forceful, and they give voice to what would otherwise be erased. For example, Alba narrates her brother Jaime's execution dryly and bluntly:

> They held him down by the arms. The first blow was to the stomach. After that they picked him up and smashed him down on a table. He felt them remove his clothes. . . . He was held captive with several other political prisoners, and the [police] tied their hands and feet with barbed wire and threw them on their faces in the stalls. There Jaime and the others spent two days without food or water, rotting in their own excrement, blood, and fear, until they were all driven by truck to an area near the airport. In an empty lot they were shot on the ground, because they could no longer stand, and then their bodies were dynamited. (Allende 1993, 371)

Alba relates her own torture no less bluntly nor distantly:

> They stripped her violently, pulling off her slacks despite her kicking. . . .
> Two hands lifted her up, and four laid her on a cold, hard metal cot with
> springs that hurt her back, and bound her wrists and ankles with leather
> thongs. . . . Then she felt the atrocious pain that coursed through her body,
> filling it completely, and that she would never forget as long as she lived.
> She sank into darkness. (409)

Alba's blunt characterization of events avoids the problem of excessive emotionality and is, therefore, more believable. Rather than appearing to be a sob-story, Alba's distant and third-person narration gives credence to memory. Through Alba, Allende gives testimony to the atrocities perpetrated in the wake of 1970s Chilean politics: torture, rape, and the erasure of history and memory.

The ability to dictate history, and therefore memory and identity, becomes a tool for social power—history becomes an Althusserian Ideological State Apparatus that functions "predominantly *by ideology*, but . . . also function[s] secondarily by repression" (Althusser 1971, 145). The proclamation that there is but one historical truth allows dominant powers to eliminate the possibility for other voices and stories. Constructed dominant truth allows for the total power of but one group; for example the United States government's elimination of the Chilean coup from its history by writing it out of existence allows the U.S. to retain its idealistic "good guy" image regardless of the legality of its actions. The U.S. government's elimination of its participation in the coup is an example of the dominant control and manipulation of history on two levels. On the one hand, the U.S. has attempted to deceive its citizens into believing in its constructed role of "global protector," and on the other, the U.S. and Chile have endeavored to eradicate and negate the cultural histories, memories, and identities of Chilean "radicals" in an attempt to maintain the illusion of political ethics/ righteousness.

Allende's revision of history is a denial of the dominant myth. Through her varied narration, use of the feminine collective, and attention to the needs of the Chilean collective, she has provided a refined revision of Chilean cultural history, identity, and memory. Her novel focuses not on any one particular event but on all factors that come into play in causing the creation of the current Chilean society. Through her nonlinear representation of events, people, and stories, Allende "reclaim[s] the past" (1993, 433) and speaks to the one-sided telling of history. Unfortunately, in order to publish within the dominant ideological systems that govern discourse, writers like Allende must shroud their voices within the cloak of "fiction." But in many cases, the genre of fiction is merely a vehicle for the telling of erased memories and histories.

In this highly politicized time, there is little doubt that more writers will come forward with seemingly fictional accounts of political and historical events. However, these voices should not be easily tossed aside. Rather, they should be read with several questions in mind: What is missing in the dominant-written "true" story? Who penned that story? Why? What alternatives does the "fiction" offer? Whose voices does it speak with? To whom does it speak? Who seeks to gain from the telling of the story? Readers must recognize the often political nature of literature, be prepared to hear voices that shout from the political abyss, and try to discern, apart from the deafening media presence, which stories are worthy of listening to.

From *Proteus: A Journal of Ideas* 19, no. 2 (2002): 33-38. Copyright © 2002 by Shippensburg University. Reprinted with permission of Shippensburg University.

Works Cited

Allende, Isabel. "The Spirits Were Willing." Trans. J. A. Engelbert. In *Lives on the Line: The Testimony of Latin American Authors*. Ed. D. Meyer, 237-242. Berkeley: Univ. of California Press, 1988.

_____. *The House of the Spirits*. New York: Bantam, 1993.

Althusser, Louis. "Ideology and the State." In *Lenin and Philosophy and Other Essays*. Trans. B. Brewster. New York: Monthly Review Press, 1971.

Antoni, Robert. "Parody or Piracy: The Relationship of *The House of the Spirits* to *One Hundred Years of Solitude*." *Latin American Literary Review* 32 (1988): 16-28.

Arriagada, Genaro. *Pinochet: Politics of Power*. Trans. N. Morris. Boston: Unwin Hyman, 1988.

Barthes, Roland. *Mythologies*. Trans. A. Lavers. New York: Hill and Wang, 1994.

Cooper, Marc. "Payback Time for Pinochetistas." *The Nation* (December 1998): 24-26.

Davis, Nathaniel. *The Last Two Years of Salvador Allende*. Ithaca: Cornell UP, 1985.

Helsper, Norma. "Binding the Wounds of the Body Politic: Nation as Family in *La casa de los espíritus*." *Critical Approaches to Isabel Allende's Novels*. Ed. S. R. Rojas & E. A. Rehbein, 49-58. New York: Peter Lang, 1991.

Irigaray, Luce. *Thinking the Difference*. Trans. K. Montin. New York: Routledge, 1994.

Kornbluh, Peter. "Prisoner Pinochet: The Dictator and the Quest for Justice." *The Nation* (December 1988): 11-24.

O'Brien, Philip. *Allende's Chile*. New York: Praeger, 1976.

Sobel, Lester A., ed. *Chile and Allende*. New York: Facts On File, 1974.

CRITICAL
READINGS

Family Systems and National Subversion in Isabel Allende's *The House of the Spirits*_____

Sara E. Cooper

The entrance of Isabel Allende into mainstream U.S. popular culture (and novelistic historiography) with works like *Daughter of Fortune* (1999) and *Portrait in Sepia* (2000) is both a logical continuation of and a divergence from her original literary path, begun with the political and magical realist novel *The House of the Spirits* (originally *La casa de los espíritus*, 1982). Allende's most recent novels are set at least partially in the United States and increasingly have gained an audience that is not Spanish-speaking nor academic. On the contrary, *The House of the Spirits*—the focus of this study—is distinctly Chilean and was discovered in the United States by scholars of Latin American literature; arguably this first novel still may be her work of greatest political and literary import. Some portion of the novel's authenticity lies in the fact that Isabel Allende is the niece of the former socialist President of Chile Salvador Allende, who was deposed and killed in the military *coup d'etat* that would eventually bring Augusto Pinochet to power. This political and personal positionality informs her first novel—the saga of one family's blend of continuity and change during this bloody time in Chilean history. In many ways the convoluted family dynamic delineated in *The House of the Spirits* reflects the complex political reality of the time; in essence, both the Trueba family and Chilean politics are shown to be systems in which each event or action requires a change or reaction from within the system. Such reactions often attempt to reestablish the systems' equilibrium, in a manner of speaking to protect them from mutating, while other reactions strive to further some break in tradition. This societal and familial dynamic follows certain patterns, and Allende's narrative configures the Trueba family dynamic not only as a reflection of what is happening on a grander scale socially, but also as inherently connected to this larger social system. This essay will explore the interconnections between the dynamic of conformity, resistance, silence, and oppression in Allende's representation of family and social systems.

Allende's *The House of the Spirits* has often been compared (and not always favorably) to Gabriel García Márquez's *One Hundred Years of Solitude* (1967).[1] Some argue that Allende's main contribution is to bring a woman's perspective and voice to the Latin American Literary Boom, and that without Márquez's model to follow Allende never would have come on to the literary scene.[2] On the other hand, Elizabeth Sklodowska maintains that Allende's work is definitely not merely a feminine rewriting of Márquez; rather, her distortion and modification of the masculinist text is an act of irony and transcendence (38). Without having to answer definitively questions of what Allende may owe to Márquez, one may see easily that the Chilean novel—like the Colombian one—narrates the magical and violent psychological connection between family and nation. Allende explains her original perception of this association as adversarial:

> My theory is that in my continent the state is generally my enemy. . . . You can only hope for repression, taxes, corruption, and inefficiency. Where is your protection, your security? In your family, and to the extent that you have your tribe around you, you're safe. (García Pinto 35-36)

Over time, and perhaps through the writing of the novel, Allende came to understand that the systemic connection between family and nation is incredibly complicated, because each relationship encompasses such a wide range of emotions. As a result of this realization, Allende was able to outline very precisely the conflictive and emotionally charged relationship of her own family, as well as between her family and her nation during the Pinochet regime.[3] Karen Castellucci Cox suggests that in the novel "family relationships [are] the foundation of a society that has become the victim of its own political missteps" (40), and in the same vein Cristina Dupláa calls *The House of the Spirits* the history of a fall—of a family and a nation (19). More than that, the novel shows the back and forth wobble of a society whose eventuality is impossible to predict. The political and social unrest in the 1970s causes tensions and rifts within families, as within the nation as a whole, with each set of pressures building on the other. I am most interested in Allende's development of this parallel struggle in the microcosm of the del Valle-Trueba clan, a family problematic that is exacerbated by the slowly growing national crisis. As both the family and social systems teeter on the brink of radical change, some characters cling desperately to a vision of the past, while others clamber to adapt to the emerging order. This inevitably leads to conflict and confrontation, which can manifest in overt brutality, covert passive-aggressive behavior, or anything in between.

The Family System

Cherie Meacham categorizes *The House of the Spirits* as a "feminist family romance," a genre that according to Marianne Hirsch's *The Mother/Daughter Plot*, privileges female connectedness as the basis for new feminist thought, strong female identity formation, and empowerment for direct action (94). Although Meacham's (like Hirsch's) critical work is not bounded strictly by psychoanalysis, she does employ certain Freudian concepts to read the novel, such as her interpreting the world of Allende's female protagonists as "pre-Oedipal" or "pre-paternal" (94). While Meacham sees male presence as interruption or "disturbing incursion" into a primarily female realm, an appealing reading that she pursues quite fruitfully, I am more interested in an alternative analysis that looks rather at the power dynamics and communication patterns among all members (male and female) of the family system. Such an approach is facilitated greatly by the incorporation of family systems literary criticism.

Therefore, before advancing into the specifics of the discussion of the Trueba family dynamic, it will be helpful to take a moment to introduce a few fundamental concepts that will inform this family systems analysis. In order to understand the underlying motivations of the characters—as members of a tight-knit and psychologically enmeshed family—as well as to comprehend the inevitable systemic responses to their actions, we turn to the contemporary theories of Family Systems.[4] Virginia Satir's ideas on communication apply the art of discourse analysis specifically to the realm of the family, providing a terminology and methodological framework for elucidating both dialogue and interior monologues in the novel. One easily makes the case that in the political and social upheavals that mark the novel's setting, and within the rigid family systems that Allende narrates, for some characters it feels too dangerous or foreign to communicate directly or overtly, so instead they have been taught or indirectly influenced to communicate via contradictory and incongruent, or even incoherent messages. According to Satir, "difficulty in communication is closely linked to an individual's self-concept, that is, his self-image and self-esteem" (94); if she views any hint of differentness in others as threatening her identity and existence, then communication will be treated as a war zone where she must constantly be on the attack or on the defense. Communication as a war zone is a concept that becomes immediately relevant, as within the first pages of the novel Clara (still a little girl) stops talking at all.

More than anyone, Murray Bowen has adapted Bertalanffy's observations on general systems for use in understanding the family. Bowen makes clear that in any system, be it a galaxy, a community, or a family, change in one part will always necessitate reactions in the other parts. In a system made up of people, dynamics of power are inextricably connected to the way those reactions will manifest; when the power structure is threatened, violence and oppression are often utilized to restore the balance. This maintenance of the same hierarchy and dynamics is called homeostasis, a phenomenon that is equally observable in the family system and the political arena. Don D. Jackson theorizes that families, like any system, attempt to sustain a balance in relationships, which he calls homeostasis; the first reaction to change will be an instinct to try vigorously to preserve the status quo. Failing that, the family will reach toward a new perceived (and relatively) comfortable balance. The maintenance of homeostasis occasions both overt and covert action on the part of family members, which can be manifested in attempts to close off the family system from outside influence or closely control any such interaction. While this can lend too much rigidity to a system and its constituent roles, the opposite phenomenon, in which the family is so open as to hold no boundaries between itself and its encompassing social system, can be equally prohibitive to the development of self and functional relationships inside or outside of the family (79-90). In contrast, paradoxically the family system is defined as well by its capacity for transformation (Palazzoli et al. 56). Such a capacity will allow for both gradual and abrupt changes within the family dynamic, ethics, composition, and relationship to other institutions in the larger social system. As mentioned above, *The House of the Spirits* shows the Trueba/del Valle family in a constant struggle between homeostasis and transformation, a battle that occurs over several generations. Homeostasis versus capacity for transformation, the effect of the family dynamic on psychological development, and the analysis of patterns of communication are just a few of the tenets of Family Systems that have immediate relevance to *The House of the Spirits*.

When it comes to literary criticism, what is particularly helpful about the theories of Family Systems is the focus on language and metalanguage, on interpreting the observable, without ever forgetting that the family system is in turn imbedded in a larger cultural and political system. Family therapists Watzlawick, Beavin and Jackson explain:

> If a person exhibiting disturbed behavior is studied in isolation, then the inquiry must be concerned with the nature of the condition and, in a wider sense, with the nature of the human mind. If the limits of the inquiry are ex-

tended to include the effects of this behavior on others, their reactions to it, and the context in which this all takes place, the focus shifts from the artificially isolated monad to the relationship between the parts of a wider system. The observer of human behavior then turns from an inferential study of the mind to the study of the observable manifestations [i.e. communication] of relationship. (21)

As readers, we are given the tools to accurately interpret the subtleties of family interactions and the suggested implications at the broader social level.

The reader intuitively senses that Allende's *The House of the Spirits* is narrating the systemicity of family. Sascha notes the "ever-repeated and ever-changing" cycle of destiny that marks the Trueba family, in which we see a chain reaction of "love and hate, passion and revenge, *chance and choice* between servitude or freedom, revolt or obedience" (310, emphasis added). The critic's idea that "*chance and choice*" will determine the sequence of events does not take into account the psychological forces involved in the family (and any systemic) dynamic. While elements of chance may intervene to shake up the family balance, more often than not the family members will respond with familiar, or learned behavior (pun intended), thus incorporating the outside influence into the regular family process. Teresa Huerta also notes the "proceso de acción y reacción" [process of action and reaction] that inevitably culminates in violence (61). This is utterly and inescapably the case. Yet, the implication here is that the reactivity is somehow automatic and emotional, perhaps even irrational, and not necessarily subject to rigorous analysis and interpretation. On the contrary, the actions taken by the various characters—Nívea, Esteban, Clara, Blanca, Alba, and the others—stem from a set of circumstances that include the political and cultural reality of the period as well as the precise makeup of their family. A family systems reading of the novel can bring a startling clarity to the seemingly murky situations that arise over the decades of the family saga. The family members seem completely caught up in the need to find some level of stability that can counterbalance the inexplicable and uncontrollable forces at work around them. However magical or strange the family may seem, and however corrupt or decadent the social system in Chile may appear, both systems are caught up in the same battle to preserve things as they are. The seemingly insoluble clashes between family and nation are only a mirror of the conflicts within the family itself. Paradoxically, the two systems are both symbiotically dependent upon each other and ideologically at odds.[5] As Salvador Minuchin argues, a family's functioning is in a sense reflective of and accountable to both its members and its community, the latter comprising the larger system to which the family belongs. Because of these complex and precarious dependencies, the homeostasis of both family and nation will be endangered repeatedly, just as each system will endanger the other, often with tragic results. One only hopes that the seeds of radical and systemic change, or morphogenesis, will transcend tragedy and prove to be a saving grace.

The Kernel of Resistance

The novel begins with a vignette that shows the disastrous effects of political machinations on the del Valle-Trueba clan. The pressures to conform to the social and political status quo are intense, and the consequences of resistance are fatal; the story emphasizes how this shapes the family ethics. Severo and Nívea del Valle are the proud parents of eleven children, but as Clara narrates, she and her older sister Rosa are the ones who most stand out—Rosa for her perfect beauty and distraction, and Clara for her mystical mental powers. The del Valles have learned to adapt to all of the girls' oddities, although they clearly fall outside of the parameters of social normality. The family at first protects Rosa from the dangers of her own loveliness and confusion and Clara from the suspicions of the neighbors and clergy. At the dinner table Nívea pulls on her daughter's braids to get her to stop making the salt shaker dance in front of guests, and everyone has become used to Clara's convenient predictions of natural disasters such as earthquakes. No one even talks about her powers any more, until they become a potential source of gossip and thus an obstacle to her father's political aspirations. At that point, Severo determines that his daughter's abnormalities will be maintained a family secret at all costs, kept hidden to protect his good name and future in politics. As a matrix of identity, this family will maintain a dynamic that continues to influence all the members to consider social ramifications as more important than clear communication or the full expression of self. The situation is reminiscent of the verbal "war zone" described by Satir, as each family member struggles to cope with the dilemma of finding truth in the rampant disparities of contradictory or absent communication. Despite our comprehension of this family dysfunction, we also clearly see that the imposition of silence and secrecy is consonant with cultural norms; moreover, here it is further linked to the sneaky and immoral practices of the governing elite.

From the beginning of the work, the narrator intimates that the ruling political system is corrupt as well as conservative. Severo, the patriarch of Clara's family, has been trying for years to enter Congress, and when he is offered a nomination by the challenging Liberal Party to represent a province he has never even seen, he turns his entire energies to achieving that end. When Rosa drinks some poison meant for Severo, a lethal warning to not rock the boat, Severo acknowledges that he should have known that he was flirting with danger:

El era el culpable, por ambicioso y fanfarrón, que nadie lo había mandado a meterse en política, que estaba mucho mejor cuando era un sencillo abogado y padre de familia, que renunciaba en ese instante y para siempre a la maldita candidatura, al Partido Liberal, a sus pompas y sus obras, que esperaba que ninguno de sus descendientes volviera a mezclarse en política, que ése era un negocio de matarifes y bandidos.

[He was at fault, for being ambitious and a show-off, that no one had told him to get into politics, that everything was much better when he was a simple lawyer and family man, that right then and there he renounced the candidacy, the Liberal Party, its pomp and its programs, and he hoped that none of his descendants would ever get mixed up in politics, which was a business made up of killers and bandits.] (40; *all translations by the author*)

Even though Severo had adopted the political expediency of secrecy and repression, even though he was prepared to clamp down on resistance within his own family for political ends, the fact that he aligns himself with the Liberal Party is a threatening divergence from political homeostasis. Significantly, when he tries to enter the political arena to effect change, an anonymous force (assumed to be connected with the political opposition) destroys his plans by rupturing his family. Although this incident serves to prepare the reader for a narrative that will link the repressive forces of politics with the intimate dynamics of the family system, it also suggests the complexity of the relationship. Severo's response to the tragedy, giving up politics and recommitting himself to a family life that he had mostly ignored for some time, shows his adaptability and the underlying openness of his nuclear family system. This is not to say that Severo is a model, or much less progressive, husband and father; on the contrary, he is the one determined that his daughters be prepared for matrimony by learning household chores (16). Nonetheless, he listens to and respects the opinion of his wife, with whom he shares the power in the domestic sphere. The power of the female voice, embodied in Nívea's influence and Clara's visionary abilities, as well as Severo's final ability to accept them, are the kernels of subversion that will surface over and over in the del Valle-Trueba saga.

Family and Political Violence

The family that is formed when Clara marries Esteban Trueba (Rosa's former fiancé) is a different animal completely, and it is this familial dynamic that will more directly represent the political climate in Chile. On the one hand, Clara remains true to her family influence, and as such maintains a locus of resistance that will exist throughout her family history; to wit, it is her stacks of diaries that eventually will prompt the telling of the family saga. On the other hand, Esteban comes to embody the oppressive and violent patriarch that rules his family and all of his domain with an iron fist, just as a long line of conservative leaders will rule the country. Antoni asserts that "Trueba is the novel's hyperbolic macho—dictator in his home, patron and rapist on his estate, and bastion of 'democracy' in government" (20). Indeed, by the end of the novel when the military Junta and Pinochet (never referred to by name) are in power, the similarities between the dictator and the family patriarch are unmistakable. Among other critics, Huerta notes the mimetic nature of Esteban Trueba, especially in his tendency toward violent domination:

La mayor parte de los juicios que pueda formarse el lector al calificar hechos de violencia, giran en torno a cierta tendencia política magistralmente ejemplificada en Esteban Trueba quien, junto con el resto de los de su clase, crea las condiciones político-sociales que serán la causa precisa del golpe de estado y subsiguiente terror político.

[The greater part of judgments that the reader makes about the violent acts revolve around a certain political tendency magnificently exemplified in Esteban Trueba who, together with the rest of his class, creates the sociopolitical conditions that will be the precise cause of the coup and the subsequent political terror.] (59-60)[6]

By this time the aging Esteban Trueba is mentally and physically devastated by years of loss, and he has moments of clarity in which he realizes that, despite the pleasures of vengeance, he has been "como un padre que ha castigado a sus hijos con demasiada severidad [like a father who punished his children too severely]" (406). In other words, he recognizes that his own efforts to maintain control have caused harm and suffering to his whole extended family. One might say that he begins to comprehend his place in the family system, at least in this limited sphere. However, he can't fathom that his country is suffering from a similar brand of injustice, on a larger scale; he stays blind to the political system's chosen methods of maintaining homeostasis. He has always maintained that Chile was "un país diferente, una verdadera república, tenemos orgullo cívico, . . . no es como esas dictaduras regionales donde se matan unos a otros, mientras los gringos se llevan todas las materias primas [a different sort of country, a real republic, we have civic pride, . . . it's not like those regional dictatorships where they kill each other and the gringos carry off all the natural resources]" (81). To be sure, Chile's political stability was relatively exemplary prior to 1973, but Esteban (like most men of his class) accepted class and ethnic oppression as consistent with "una verdadera república." Now, in the face of the cruelties perpetrated by the military junta, Esteban complains:

> Fui el primero en tirar plumas de gallinas a los cadetes y en propiciar el Golpe, antes que los demás tuvieran la idea en la cabeza, fui el primero en aplaudirlo, estuve presente en el Te Deum de la catedral, y por lo mismo no puedo aceptar que estén ocurriendo estas cosas en mi patria, que desaparezca la gente, que saquen a mi nieta de la casa a viva fuerza y yo no pueda impedirlo . . .

> [I was the first to encourage the cadets and incite the coup, I was the first to applaud it, before anybody else even had the idea in their head, I was there for the *Te Deum* in the cathedral, and it is exactly for that reason that I can not accept that these things are happening in my country, that people disappear, that they take my granddaughter away by force and I can't even stop them . . .] (440)

We see, thus, Esteban's ability to compartmentalize segments of information, denying or ignoring those parts that do not conform to the truth he wishes to see. This is his own form of communicational warfare, a verbal and psychological inconsistency that allows him to justify his government's violations of civil rights even at the end of his life when he questions his own past behavior.

Of course, the family patriarch has been utilizing just this sort of violent force from the time he takes charge of the Tres Marías plantation, long before his marriage to Clara. He physically and emotionallyexplodes after years in a family system where he had to show his gratitude for his sister Férula's continual self-sacrificing by in turn sacrificing his own life and will to provide for her and his mother. Esteban's later behavior is more comprehensible given the family context provided in the novel; over the years Férula has rejected two offers of marriage to care for her sick mother, and spoils her baby brother, reveling in how "parecía tan perfecta que llegó a tener fama de santa" [she seemed so perfect, she ended up reputed as a saint] (53).

> Sentía gusto en la humillación y en las labores abyectas, creía que iba a obtener el cielo por el medio terrible de sufrir iniquidades. . . . Y tanto como se odiaba a sí misma por esos tortuosos e inconfesables placeres, odiaba a su madre por servirle de instrumento. La atendía sin quejarse, pero procuraba sutilmente hacerle pagar el precio de su invalidez . . . [A Esteban] lo había cuidado y servido como ahora lo hacía con la madre y también a él lo envolvió en la red invisible de la culpabilidad y de las deudas de gratitud impagables.

> [She felt pleasure in the humiliation and her abject labors, believing that she would get to heaven by the suffering of such iniquities. . . . And just as she hated herself for those torturous and inadmissible pleasures, she hated her mother for being the instrument of them. She cared for her without complaint, but found subtle ways to make her pay the price of her illness. . . .

She had cared for and served [Esteban] as she now did her mother, and thus she involved him in the invisible web of guilt and the debts of unpaid gratitude.] (53-54)

Férula plays the part of the perfect daughter (and surrogate mother to Esteban) as narrated in the national rhetoric, and she exacts the price she believes is due to her. When young Esteban becomes aware of the dynamic and pulls away, Férula turns her barely contained rage and resentment upon him. He responds with scorn and emotional cutoff and, as soon as he is able, leaves for Tres Marías. A psychological reading that did not take into account even this fragment of the family system that is portrayed in the novel (such as a purely psychoanalytical reading) would fail to offer a full understanding of Trueba's motivations and behavior. One might be tempted to interpret his actions as the result of an interrupted developmental state in his infancy, which is supported by absolutely no evidence in the text whatsoever. In contrast, a family systems reading that is based on the observable (narrated) interactions between the siblings sheds light on Esteban's impulse to take all the power when he marries and establishes a new family subsystem. His behavior as an adult is not simple *machismo*, if such a thing exists. Once at the dilapidated ranch, Esteban immediately sets up a new family dynamic in which he believes himself to be the benevolent father to his workers (63), while in truth he becomes a volatile and despotic ruler who admits no contradictions and expects to be given anything he wants (74). Recognizing the family dynamic that spurs him to act in such a manner does not exonerate him, but it certainly does explain why he so fully embraces the power play of his patriarchal heritage.

Unsurprisingly Esteban Trueba has taken up the part of the father figure exemplified in Chilean family propaganda—the same role played by the leaders of the Conservative Party. He inspires fear and hate as well as obedience in his ranch hands (72), so that when he begins to carry off and rape an endless line of adolescent ranch girls, starting with Pancha García (68), very few even question his right to do so. Those who do so end up dead, a circumstance to which the authorities turn a blind eye. Any suggestion of workers' rights are "degenerate ideas . . . Bolshevik ideas. . . . They don't realize that these folk have no culture or education, they can't handle responsibility, they are children. . . . With these poor devils you have to have a firm hand, it's the only language they understand." (75). As suggested by Philip Swanson, Trueba's "discourse . . . is replete with the language of order," in contrast to his view of the workers as uncivilized and primitive (219).[7] Swanson elaborates, making a link between Allende and feminists Toril Moi and Simone de Beauvoir:

> The main strategy in this programme [sic] of marginalization . . . is the creation of an illusion of a unified individual and collective self, a given universal world order in which male, white, middle-class, heterosexual experience passes itself off as "nature." (219)

Through language and action, Esteban Trueba contentedly establishes himself as a powerful and successful feudal lord, ignoring any sign of social or political change that occurs beyond his property lines: "En realidad, la guerra, los inventos de la ciencia, el progreso de la industria, el precio del oro y las extravagancias de la moda, lo tenían sin cuidado" [In reality, the war, scientific inventions, the progress of industry, the price of gold and the extravagances of fashion didn't move him in the least] (72). As a secondary narrator, Esteban's "authoritative discourse" attempts to justify and explain the need to maintain the status quo. As put by Sharon Magnarelli, Trueba is "an ironic center of gravity: the entire novelistic universe, plot and structure, seems to revolve around him. And, as might be expected, he does everything in his discursive power to maintain himself in that position" (46). Throughout the novel, Esteban's conformity to a traditional political and family system, in which man rules by force and intimidation, will be synonymous with the efforts of the Chilean conservative elite to block social and political progress. In particular his discourse closely mirrors that of the state, in that they both attempt to justify an imposed and artificial order (Dupláa 20).

Indeed, the rural areas show little sign whatever of positive change, despite the beginnings of a revolutionary movement proselytized by traveling men dressed as clergy (79). Pointing to the disjunct between city and country, the narrator acknowledges the stirrings of social and political unrest that plague Chile throughout the twentieth century.

El país despertaba. La oleada de descontento que agitaba al pueblo estaba golpeando la sólida estructura de aquella sociedad oligárquica. En los campos hubo de todo: sequía, caracol, fiebre aftosa. En el Norte había cesantía y en la capital se sentía el efecto de la guerra lejana. Fue un año de miseria en el que lo único que faltó para rematar el desastre fue un terremoto. La clase alta, sin embargo, dueña del poder y de la riqueza, no se dio cuenta del peligro que amenazaba el frágil equilibrio de su posición.

[The country was awakening. The wave of discontent that agitated the people was beating at the solid structure of the oligarchic system. In the country there was a little of everything: drought, snails, hoof and mouth disease. In the north there was unemployment and in the capital they were feeling the effects of the far-off war. It was a year of abject misery in which the only thing missing for a complete disaster was earthquake. The upper class, however, owner of power and riches, didn't realize the danger that was threatening the fragile equilibrium of their position]. (78)

Between the Charleston, golf, the Model T, and the borrowed passion of "unas cumbias de negros que eran una maravillosa indecencia" [some negro *cumbias* that were marvelously indecent] (78), the privileged few convince themselves that their nation is enjoying a golden age that vindicates continued manipulation of the polls and control of the masses. Such a perspective can be understood as a myth of harmony, in which members of a system work together to ignore negative elements and romanticize (even invent) a completely positive portrait of the system in a particular era (Simon, Stierlin and Wynne, qtd. in Knapp and Womack, *Reading* 20).

In this same era, political rabble-rousers advocate women's right to vote, workers' right to form unions, and even the rights of children born out of wedlock. True to his conservative stance, Esteban Trueba never acknowledges the numerous Tres Marías children who bear him a striking resemblance, and when he decides he needs an heir he chooses a woman of his own class to marry—Clara (77). At the beginning of their courtship, Esteban admires and respects both Clara's history of silence, which he takes to be a virtue, and her directness, which mirrors his own (100-01). However, during their honeymoon he realizes that Clara does not love him "as he needed to be loved"; in other words, she does not belong to him, nor is she completely under his power like his workers (108). The distance between them widens upon their return, when Férula (who has come to live with them) begins doting obsessively on both Clara and her newly-born daughter, Blanca. As Férula confesses to her priest, she does everything in her power to keep the husband and wife apart, dreams about getting into bed with her sister-in-law, and spies on the couple in their marriage bed (111-12). In this way the family tensions increase, as both Esteban and Férula try to win the affection of Clara and control over the household, while Clara retreats ever more into a realm populated only by herself, her daughter, and spirits from the other world. The brother and sister desperately attempt to maintain a family system that conforms with their memory of the past, while Clara's quiet revolution irrepressibly gathers steam.

Tres Marías, the very bastion of conservatism, is ironically where "civilization" and "barbarism" become blurred, allowing the political and social insurrection to take form. When Esteban Trueba arrives at Tres Marías, his refined ways degenerate into slovenly dress and manners, until he ironically finds a "civilizing" influence through his relationship with the supposedly ignorant and childlike Pancha García. Much later, it is at the ranch that Clara—ignoring her husband's rages—begins to teach hygiene and women's rights to the female population of the ranch. Here too Blanca meets and falls in love with Pedro Tercero García,who begins his career as an activist and singer whose words will inspire a nation. At the same time, it is at Tres Marías where Trueba's obsession with a European cultured aesthetic allows Frenchman Jean de Satigny access to the family ranch, giving rise to the satiric portrayal of the foreigner, by which means the narrative mocks and undermines any true privileging of imported "civilized" culture. The debonair and allegedly rich Count Satigny proposes to start a chinchilla farm on the Trueba property, begins to court Blanca, and finally discovers Blanca's prohibited affair with Pedro Tercero. After learning that his daughter is pregnant, Esteban runs Pedro Tercero out of town and forces Blanca's marriage to the Count. Blanca's intuitive comprehension of the Count's falsity and superficiality, coupled with her determination to love a man who is of another class and political ideology, places her in direct opposition to her father's stubborn (and blind) conventionality.

Be it in the rural or urban sphere, the narrative's subversion of the patriarchal family system is most concentrated in the female protagonists. Swanson points out that in the first Trueba abode, which Esteban builds for his incipient family, the man of the house "wants his house to be 'un reflejo de él' [a reflection of him], with 'un aspecto de orden y concierto' [an aspect of order and harmony], though under the influence of Clara it becomes 'un laberinto encantado imposible de limpiar, que desafiaba numerosas leyes urbanisticas y municipales'" [an enchanted labyrinth impossible to clean, which flouted numerous urban and municipal codes] (221).[8] In other words, Esteban wishes the house to conform to his own vision of class stability and social order, while Clara is comfortable moving within the fluidity of difference and liminality of existence. In an apparently different reading, Cristina Dupláa interprets Trueba's plans for the house as symbolic of modernity and progress, and Clara's ultimate control over the structure as symbolic of tradition (22). If we understand magic as a tradition predating the political conservatism of early twentieth-century Chile, we resolve the seeming contradiction of Dupláa's commentary and recognize the ambiguity of the terms themselves. Here Esteban Trueba's "tradition" and "conformity" necessarily refer to the sociopolitical reality of the moment, and what the establishment has imposed as a supposedly solid, impermeable status quo. When Clara and the other Trueba women resist or transgress the borders of the imposed tradition, they symbolize both an age-old culture of magic and a new progressive politics. Significantly, neither this early architectural subversion of Clara's nor the later love affair of Blanca's are conscious rebellions against Esteban personally, nor do they constitute an organized resistance to conformity. Rather, the Trueba women simply follow their heart and spirit, which are more expansive and flexible than that of the family patriarch.[9] However, as they consistently come up against Esteban Trueba's disapproval, wrath, and attempts at dominance, they also begin to react on a number of levels, always sharing emotional support and understanding of one another in the face of a common obstacle. Their tactics range from the practical to the fantastic and show continuity throughout generations of conflict.

Clara's strategy for dealing with emotional stress is developed years previously, when (as mentioned above) she decides to stop talking completely after her sister's Rosa's death. It takes her family three months to notice her silence (45). When neither pills nor hypnosis nor threats nor starvation, or even frights provoked by her nanny will "curarle" [cure her] of her ill (85-86), the family adapts to her new state. Her mother especially decides to leave her in peace and "amarla sin condiciones y aceptarla tal cual era" [love her unconditionally and accept her just as she was] (89), maintaining their intimate mother-daughter connection by telling her tales of their family history. This model of acceptance and tolerance will serve the family well. For many years Clara survives her husband's tirades, she offers her children unconditional love, and she teaches them to resist passively the emotional onslaughts that mark life in the Trueba family. In most cases she reacts to Esteban's rage by emotionally detaching herself and defusing the tension with seeming non sequitur responses, a technique to be repeated and refined by various members of the family.[10] For instance, faced with his father's shouts and slamming of doors, because Esteban was "harto de vivir entre puros locos . . . Jaime no discutía con su padre. Pasaba por la casa como una sombra, daba un beso distraído a su madre cuando la veía y se dirigía directamente a la cocina, comía de pie las sobras de los demás y luego se encerraba en su habitación" [fed up of living in the midst of a bunch of crazies . . . Jaime didn't argue with his father. He would pass through the house like a shadow, giving his mother a distracted kiss when he saw her and he would go right in to the kitchen where he would eat leftovers standing up and then go shut himself up in his room] (235). Here Jaime repeats his mother's silent retreat as a reaction to the violence and domination of his father, a tool that will be passed down to Alba to survive her experience as a political prisoner. Theorist Murray Bowen posits that this sort of repetition is anything but singular; rather, it is a regular product of the multi-generational emotional process, by which one generation transmits through relationships its own levels of anxiety, self-differentiation, and ability to deal with change or difference (271). Bowen's theory of self-differentiation elucidates that a higher level of self-differentiation allows more flexibility and less symptom development in times of crisis within a relationship—such as Jaime's relatively mild retreat into his room (71, 79), whereas lower levels of self-differentiation in a family are manifested in quicker emotional perception of threat, more intense accompanying anxiety, and more extreme emotional measures to counteract the threat and anxiety (79).[11] Throughout the novel we see Esteban's emotional distress and extreme verbal and physical reactions to be indicative of his relative inability to self-differentiate, while Clara, Blanca, Alba, and here Jaime demonstrate the opposite with their more creative and less disruptive strategies for coping with emotional difficulties.

Clara's ultimate use of this withdrawal occurs years later as a reprisal against her husband's violence. Her silence paradoxically mirrors society's cowed silence in the face of systematic rape and repression of women and the lower classes; at the same time it forms a site of resistance to the oppression. When she does not speak out to Esteban, because she already has discovered the uselessness of her words, she mutely rebels by withholding her approval, her companionship, and her complicity in his actions by stubbornly refusing all his entreaties. Her silence is thus both voluntary (a conscious tactic to combat an oppressor) and involuntary (self-censorship as the only way to escape further violence). While she does not verbally interact with Esteban, she still continues to write, like the rest of the women in her line. It is this subversive narrative that provides the connecting thread of the novel as well as the underlying strength of rebellion. Marjorie Agosín calls Clara's active choice an "aesthetic of silence."

> En primer lugar, el silencio de Clara existe como una decisión, un acto consciente de enmudecer. Pero la mudez no queda rezagada a la incomunicación, sino que postula la comunicación de escribir, para dar testimonio e inaugurar una tradición que podrá ser rescatable. La segunda metáfora relativa a esta estética del silencio indicaría que mientras Clara enmudece, ella escribe y lee, desafiando el silencio exterior, que es el silencio impuesto por una sociedad poco tolerante de las anomalías.

> [In the first place, Clara's silence exists like a decision, a conscious act of becoming dumb. But her muteness doesn't fall into a lack of communication, but rather postulates written communication, in order to give her testimony and inaugurate a tradition that may be rescued. The second metaphor relative to this aesthetic of silence would indicate that as Clara becomes mute, she writes and reads, challenges the exterior silence, which is the silence imposed by a society with little tolerance of anomalies.] (450)

Clara's vocal silence, a silence that masks a potent agency and allows a flow of the hidden and written word, is more effective than direct communication in this family and political system. Here feminine silence is the tool that bleeds out the law of the father.

Antoni suggests that "Trueba's machismo is slowly subdued under the influence of the novel's three heroines . . . [as his] authoritative discourse is subdued by the internally persuasive discourse of the feminine-collective focalization" (24). Allende consciously develops this "feminine-collective" by intertwining the voices of Clara, Blanca, and Alba, all names with a primary definition or strong connotation of "white." Allende states, "I wanted to symbolize a state of purity. Not the purity that means virginity, normally assigned to women, but the purity of facing the world with new eyes, free from contamination, without prejudice, open and tolerant, having a soul capable of being moved by the world's colors" (García Pinto 30). In other words, the three women of the Trueba family share an openness to change, a resistance to the social and political stagnation that require blindness to diversity, to suffering and injustice. Perhaps this kernel of revolution is inherent to the literary genre of the magical realist novel. According to Gloria Bautista, magical realism "produce el asombro que produciría el presenciar una nueva genesis. Visto con ojos nuevos a la luz de una nueva mañana, el mundo es, si no maravilloso, al menos perturbador" [produces the shock that would come from witnessing a new genesis. Seen with new eyes by the light of a new day, the world is, if not marvelous, at least perturbing] (301). Again, the metaphor of "new eyes" accurately represents the distinction shared by Clara, Blanca and Alba: they see spirits from the world beyond, they see beyond class and color divisions, and they envision a future that differs radically from the present.

In *The House of the Spirits*, the disturbing magical and feminine narrative provides resistance to the drive toward conformity desired by Esteban Trueba, the ruling elite, and the institutions where this authoritative discourse resides (family, home, military, university, government, and society). The powers that be utilize every form of force at hand, direct or indirect, legitimate or illicit, to maintain a homeostasis in which they continue as the voice of authority. All band together to combat threats against any single entity, one example being the students' insurrection at the university. The government shuts off all services on campus (including water, electricity, but not phone) and calls out the armed guard, which arrives with numerous troops, tanks, and semi-automatic weapons. Society—in this case even the neighborhood of the university—mostly ignores the uprising as well as the promise of an armed response, letting the children go out and play on the street as soon as the sun comes out (339). Family, represented by Esteban Trueba, denounces the rebellion as communist and commands his daughter to come home immediately, as she obviously is not one of them (338). Significantly, and despite the powerful combined efforts to squelch any sort of rebellion, resistance seeps into each and every locus of domination and conformity. In the university, Alba joins the students and one professor in their solidarity with a workers' strike. All of the Trueba women, as well as Clara's sons Nicolás and Jaime, resist at the level of social and political action. Maureen Shea sees this as an example of Latin American women writers' growing awareness of sexual oppression and an empowering "female bonding created to struggle against [patriarchal] abuse in specific socio-historic moments" (53). Allende's novel goes even further, suggesting the possibility of a bonding across genders as well as generations and class divisions that can effectively resist the systemized abuses of patriarchy.[12] The nameless President (representing Salvador Allende) is elected on a platform of social justice and economic equality. Even the prostitute Tránsito Soto turns her whorehouse into a cooperative for a time. The solidarity of the group of women political prisoners will literally save Alba's life, as well as demonstrate to her the power of a committed community. The enormous and well-planned Trueba house that Esteban builds for Clara slowly becomes a labyrinth as she adds on staircases, rooms, doors, and cabinets without recourse to building permits or linear thought. And of course, Clara, Blanca, and Alba continuously foment resistance to the patriarchal system that Esteban wishes to impose on his family.

At the end of the novel, the Trueba family is in full-out crisis as a direct result of the military coup and subsequent rule of fear. While Esteban always predicted that the communists would be the downfall of the country and his family, instead it is the reaction to a communist victory that proves to be the most damaging to everything he loves. The essence of revolution, embodied by Clara's escape to the spirit world, the election of Salvador Allende, Miguel and Alba's guerilla warfare, Blanca's refusal to remarry after the failure of her marriage with the Count, the verses of Pedro Tercero and the Poet, and the feminist/ progressive narrative of the novel, finally provokes such violent reprisals that the system is irrevocably changed. The conservatives, together with Senator Trueba, begin a "campaña del terror" [campaign of terror] to undermine the Allende government (352), then the military overthrows the government and institutes censorship, a curfew, and a special military branch that kidnaps, tortures, and kills "subversives." Family members are pitted against each other, and the entire nation is ensconced in a voluntary muteness and blindness that barely maintains the appearance of normality while thousands of people disappear. The Trueba house is by now in complete decay, Jaime has been killed in the coup, and Nicolás has emigrated to the United States, leaving the remaining bunch in a house full of spirits, the most visible of which is Clara. However, the family symbol of the complete political turn-around is Alba's capture, torture, rape and imprisonment by Esteban García, illegitimate grandson of the family patriarch. It is in this moment that Esteban Trueba realizes both his own impotence and the horror of the violent power that he had once wielded.

When Alba returns home, she and her grandfather try to reinstate the appearance of normalcy, cleaning and refurbishing the old house, apparently ignoring Pinochet's continuing reign (451). The new family homeostasis again mirrors the political reality of Chile in the 1970s and 80s, in that the polished exterior hides a turbulent and conflicted interior. The novel ends with two contradictory images and narratives. First, Alba comes to terms with the cycle of violence and violation, and the child growing in her womb, "hija de tantas violaciones, o tal vez hija de Miguel pero sobre todo hija mía" [daughter of so many rapes, or maybe Miguel's daughter, but above all my own], believing it all part of a history predestined to repeat itself (452-53). Nonetheless, she takes up her pen and begins to order and write the narrative of revolution begun by Clara's diaries, written "para que me sirvieran ahora para rescatar las cosas del pasado y sobrevivir a mi propio espanto" [so that they would function now to help me rescue the things of the past and survive my own fear] (454). Margarita Saona points out that although Allende continues to situate women in the traditional bourgeois family roles, she imbues them with power to overcome and to bring the truth to light by virtue of their place in a matriarchal line that is as strong as, if not stronger than, the allegedly dominant patriarchy (218-19). In a manner of speaking, the family system in the largest sense—as an institution inextricably interwoven into the social and political fabric of the nation—has facilitated the development of complementary roles that will assure the eventual establishment of a lasting familial and national homeostasis.

Susan R. Frick notes that "As she remembers her foremothers, Alba perpetuates a cyclical repetition of the human experience, one which prevents time from becoming simply a linear progression of events and ensures a connection between herself and her predecessors across all spatial and temporal boundaries" (27). From a family systems perspective, she simply is following in the multigenerational emotional process that connects her to Clara, Blanca, and Nívea (and indeed the entire family in which she was raised). She has found a method of communication that allows her—and the family—to emerge from a century of silence, inconsistency, and confusion and directly engage with truth and memory. The transgenerational repetition of the female narrative voice emerges as a healing force, the power contained in the memory of the Trueba/del Valle women.[13] Thus, both realistically and magically, the family system finds a new balance between the violence and power, conformity and resistance, to hand down to the next generation.

From *Interdisciplinary Literary Studies: A Journal of Criticism and Theory* 10, no. 1 (2008): 16-37. Copyright © 2008 by *Interdisciplinary Literary Studies*. Reprinted with permission of *Interdisciplinary Literary Studies*.

Notes

1. Robert Antoni, for example, explores the relationship between the two novels, finding similarities between the two works, including "language, technique (e.g. extensive foreshadowing and flashbacks), characters, and events" (18). The major differences that Antoni underlines are the narrator (feminine and first person—replaced at times by a masculine first person), a more historical than mythical localization of the narrative, a subversive feminine agenda, and a tragic tone rather than comic. Antoni ultimately decides that Allende's work is "unconscious parody," rather than "piracy," and thus a legitimate contribution to the genre of the magical realist novel (16). Michael Handelsman notes that "tal vez por no estar acostumbrados a semejantes éxitos logrados por las mujeres, algunos críticos han cuestionado el talento artístico de Allende, insistiendo más bien en su parentesco con Salvador Allende, y a la vez, sugiriendo que su apellido resonante en estos tiempos tan críticos y difíciles para Chile ha sido la principal causa de su fama. También, para que no hubiera lugar a dudas, algunos comentaristas han minimizado la importancia y la originalidad de *La casa de los espíritus* al resaltar los aspectos demasiado parecidos a *Cien años de soledad*. Típica de estas insinuaciones es la noción de que Isabel Allende es poco más que la invención publicitaria de alguna que otra editorial metropolitana" (57). Significantly, the critic Sascha Talmor compares Allende's work not only to that of García Márquez, but rather to a variety of world classics, including: Thomas Mann's *Buddenbrooks*, Albert Camus' *The Plague*, Orwell's *1984*, Graham Greene's *The Ministry of Fear*, and T. S. Eliot's *The Four Quartets*. Writing from Israel for an English journal, Sascha lends a global literary perspective that is perhaps difficult to achieve for critics in the American continent.

2. Important to note is a small body of criticism, best exemplified by Gabriela Mora's study of woman as citizen in Allende's novels, which insists that they do not truly embody a feminist ethic. Mora finds various elements objectionable, but more than any other she decries the protagonists' limited political commitment and activism, as well as a too lenient treatment of the figure of Esteban Trueba. In one comment especially relevant to the current study, Mora notes: "En el esquema de conciliación de fuerzas opositoras en que se asienta *La casa de los espíritus* tanto el perdón como el amor, sin la justicia, recuerdan riesgosamente la propaganda del gobierno de Pinochet que, como defensor de los sagrados principios de la familia cristiana, habla de amor y perdón en palabras vacías, traicionados por los hechos" (56).

3. It is this focus on the systemicity of family that most links *La casa de los espíritus* to Allende's later novels set in the United States, which could prove a fruitful focus for further study.

4. For a more complete discussion of systems theory, see L. von Bertalanffy's *General Systems Theory: Foundations, Development, Applications* (Braziller, 1968). For a fully developed application of family systems theory to literary criticism, see John V. Knapp's *Striking at the Joints: Contemporary Psychology and Literary Criticism* (University Press of America, 1996). Two critical anthologies exist that bring together essays with a family systems approach: *Reading the Family Dance: Family Systems Therapy and the Literary Study*, Eds. John V. Knapp and Kenneth Womack (U of Delaware, 2003) and Sara Cooper's *The Ties That Bind: Questioning Family Dynamics and Family Discourse in Hispanic Literature and Film* (University Press of America, 2003).

5. The survival of the Trueba family absolutely depends on both the continuity and the change of the political system. Especially the more rebellious members of the family receive conflicting messages they are not able to ignore, setting up a double-bind situation, which Bowen has linked to the condition of schizophrenia. In other words, when a person (especially a child) hears from one source that in order to survive she must act in one way, then hears the opposite message from another authority, she is caught between a rock and a hard place. As a result, some children lose the ability to distinguish fact from fiction, or to effectively engage in communication; some create mental compartments into which they shuttle conflicting messages. In a way, they do not relate the two pieces of information with each other, thereby escaping the bind of feeling constant fear and threat. On the outside, this may look as if they have lost touch with reality, and of course this is close to the truth. To some extent, the characters' thoughts and actions in the novel represent the psychological reality that an individual's brain must at times be exceedingly inventive to make sense out of nonsense.

6. Huerta argues that violence and horror play an ambivalent role in *The House of the Spirits*, on the one hand catering to an audience avid for the macabre, and on the other hand serving as cathartic for the reader, by means of identification with the heroines and anti-identification with the antagonists (62).

7. Dupláa aptly recognizes that Esteban's discourse of order is actually "un simulacro de orden, poco establecido, poco sólido, en definitiva . . . un orden impuesto y antinatural," a fact which is revealed by its subsequent undermining (20).

8. Agosín notes that Clara assumes the same power to metamorphose Las Tres Marías through her magical, independent and volatile spirit (452). In essence, no space—physical or symbolic—is left untouched or unmoved by the feminine transformative powers of the Trueba/del Valle women.

9. Handelsman posits that Blanca's love affair with Pedro Tercero García represents a sexual liberation and spontaneity that contrasts with her parents' "matrimonio incompleto" and her own "matrimonio forzado y falso" (61). Despite Blanca's enjoyment of and empowerment in the relationship, it would be naive to call their affair complete or easy. To find rips in the relational fabric, one only has to note the forced separations of the two lovers, the necessary schism that opens in the family because of it, and Pedro Tercero's need to repeatedly turn to meaningless love affairs.

10. As in the case of Clara's utterance of non sequiturs or her voluntary silence, the novel offers numerous examples of the power of language to communicate on many levels—even in its suppression—and to paradoxically conceal or twist meaning with

apparently transparent language. Sharon Magnarelli asserts that "the point of [the novel] is that not all discourse is used to clarify or to communicate clearly and directly. As the authors dramatically demonstrate, discourse, even historical discourse, can be used to distract and obscure" (54).

11. Bowen marks the contrast between basic and functional differentiation. The former is more individual, passed on through generations, and subject to little variation, whereas the latter depends on the person's relationship system and may be influenced to rise or fall quickly by any number of factors, be they social, physical, situational, etc. The reciprocal element of relationships may induce one family member to temporarily "give up" some of their functioning ability, which seems to be "borrowed" by other members, making it even more difficult to gauge any person's basic or functional differentiation in a limited time frame. The higher the basic level of differentiation, the less volatile or subject to wide fluctuations is the functional differentiation (97-99).

12. Norma Helsper suggests that Allende "'steals back' the notion of family" from the political right by "forg[ing] a new model family which will include Chileans of all social classes and political tendencies. This family is the Utopian image which anchors the novel" (50, 54).

13. Alino Camacho-Gingerich suggests that the recreation of the lives of female antecedents that forms the basis of the narration is characteristic of the neofeminist novel's preoccupation in creating "imágenes de trascendencia y autenticidad para la mujer" (15).

Works Cited

Agosín, Marjorie. "Isabel Allende: *La casa de los espíritus*." *Revista Interamericana de Bibliografía* 35 (1985): 448-58.

Allende, Isabel. *La casa de los espíritus*. New York: Edición Rayo (HarperCollins), 2001.

Antoni, Robert. "Parody or Piracy: The Relationship of *The House of the Spirits* to *One Hundred Years of Solitude*." *Latin American Literary Review* 16.32 (1988): 16-28.

Bautista, Gloria. "El realismo mágico en *La casa de los espíritus*." *Discurso literario: Revista de temas hispánicos* (Paraguay) 6.2 (Spring 1989): 299-310.

Bertalanffy, L. von. *General Systems Theory: Foundations, Development, Applications*. New York: Braziller, 1968.

Bowen, Murray. *Family Therapy in Clinical Practice*. New York: Jason Aronson, 1978.

Camacho-Gingerich, Alina. "La mujer ante la dictadura en las dos primeras novelas de Isabel Allende." *Discurso: Revista de estudios iberamericanos* 9.2 (1992): 13-25.

Cox, Karen Castellucci. *Isabel Allende: A Critical Companion*. Westport, CT: Greenwood, 2003.

Dupláa, Cristina. "La voz femenina frente al discurso patriarcal en *La casa de los espíritus.*" *Foro literario* (Montevideo) 17 (1987): 19-27.

Frick, Susan R. "Memory and Retelling: The Role of Women in *La casa de los espíritus.*" *Journal of Iberian and Latin American Studies* 7.1 (2001): 27-41.

García Márquez, Gabriel. *Cien años de soledad.* Buenos Aires: Ed. Sudamericana, 1967.

García Pinto, Magdalena. *Women Writers of Latin America.* Austin: U of Texas P, 1991.

Handelsman, Michael H. "*La casa de los espíritus* y la evolución de la mujer moderna." *Letras femeninas* 14.1-2 (1988): 57-63.

Helsper, Norma. "Binding the Wounds of the Body Politic: Nation as Family in *La casa de los espíritus.*" *Critical Approaches to Isabel Allende's Novels.* New York: Peter Lang, 1991. 49-58.

Huerta, Teresa. "La ambivalencia de la violencia y el horror en *La casa de los espíritus* de Isabel Allende." *Chasqui* 19.1 (1990): 56-63.

Jackson, Don D. "The Question of Family Homeostasis." *Psychiatric Quarterly Supplement* 31 (1957): 79-90.

Knapp, John, and Kenneth Womack, eds. *Reading the Family Dance: Family Systems Therapy and Literary Study.* Newark: U of Delaware P, 2003.

Magnarelli, Sharon. "Framing Power in Luisa Valenzuela's *Cola de lagarta* [*The Lizard's Tail*] and Isabel Allende's *La casa de los espíritus* [*The House of the Spirits*]." *Splintering Darkness: Latin American Women Writers in Search of Themselves.* Ed. Lucia Guerra Cunningham. Pittsburgh: Latin American Literary Review P, 1990.

Meacham, Cherie. "The Metaphysics of Mother/Daughter Renewal in *La casa de los espíritus* and *Paula.*" *Hispanófila* 131 (2001): 93-108.

Minuchin, Salvador. *Family Kaleidoscope.* Cambridge: Harvard UP, 1984.

Mora, Gabriela. "Las novelas de Isabel Allende y el papel de la mujer como ciudadana." *Ideologies & Literature* 2.1 (1987): 53-61.

Palazzoli, Mara Selvini, et al. *Paradox and Counterparadox: A New Model in the Therapy of the Family in Schizophrenic Transaction.* New York: Jason Aronson, 1978.

Saona, Margarita. "Do We Still Need the Family to Imagine the Nation? National Family Romances by Latin American Women Writers." *Disciplines on the Line: Feminist Research on Spanish, Latin American, and U.S. Latina Women.* Eds. Anne J. Cruz, Rosilie Hernández-Pecoraro, and Joyce Tolliver. Newark, DE: Juan de la Cuesta, 2003.

Satir, Virginia. *Conjoint Family Therapy.* Palo Alto: Science and Behavior Books, 1964.

Shea, Maureen. "A Growing Awareness of Sexual Oppression in the Novels of Contemporary Latin American Women Writers." *Confluencia* 4.1 (1988): 53-59.

Simon, Fritz B., Helm Stierlin, and Lyman C. Wynne. *The Language of Family Therapy: A Systemic Vocabulary and Sourcebook.* New York: Family Process, 1985.

Sklodowska, Elzbieta. *"Ardiente paciencia* y *La casa de los espíritus*: Traición y tradición en el discurso del post-boom." *Discurso: Revista de Estudios Iberoamericanos* 9.1 (1991): 33-40.

Swanson, Philip. "Tyrants and Trash: Sex, Class and Culture in *La casa de los espíritus." Bulletin of Hispanic Studies* 71.1 (1994): 217-37.

Talmor, Sascha. "The House of the Truebas." (Review) *The Durham University Journal* 81.2 (1989): 309-12.

Watzlawick, Paul, Janet Beavin, and Don Jackson. *Pragmatics of Human Communication: A Study of Interactional Patterns, Pathologies, and Paradoxes.* New York: Norton, 1967.

Magical Places in Isabel Allende's
Eva Luna and *Cuentos de Eva Luna*_____

Barbara Foley Buedel

Widely recognized as a major contributor to Latin American litera-
ture, Isabel Allende holds a preeminent place in Latin American liter-
ary history. In *The Post-Boom in Spanish American Fiction* (1998),
Donald Shaw writes: "Without question the major literary event in
Spanish America during the early eighties was the publication in 1982
of Isabel Allende's runaway success *La Casa de los Espíritus*" (53).
Similarly, in his recent book, *Literature of Latin America* (2004),
Rafael Ocasio identifies Allende as "the woman writer from Latin
America with the greatest international readership," noting also that
"she has a significant influence on an increasingly popular, worldwide
literature written by women" (168). Linda Gould Levine in her Twayne
book (2002) succinctly assesses the author's status: "Isabel Allende is
the most acclaimed woman writer of Latin America" (ix).

Shaw maintains that the "emergence of strong female characters" is
what made Allende's first work a "genuinely 'inaugural' novel" (59,
58). This feminist perspective continues throughout her fiction and is
especially apparent in her third novel, *Eva Luna* (1987). As numerous
critics observe, this work displays aspects of the picaresque tradition: a
pseudo-autobiography with an episodic structure, Eva's marginalized
status as an orphan and domestic servant who serves a series of oftentimes unkind masters, a streetwise survival instinct promoted by her
friendship with Huberto Naranjo, a variety of experiences in different
economic classes during which she experiences both hunger and abun-
dance, and frequent demands for her to be self-reliant and inventive.[1] Yet acts of kindness are more numerous than acts of cruelty, and
benevolent mother and father figures often replace tyrannical masters. By the end of the novel, the protagonist is a successful writer, a
political activist who has participated in a guerrilla raid and escaped
without harm, and the lover of an intelligent journalist. Overall, the

tone is optimistic, a characteristic of other Post-Boom narratives that contrasts with the negative visions typically developed in Boom novels (Shaw 10, 65). Levine views the novel as a "female bildungsroman, a novel of a young woman's psychological, intellectual and moral development" (60), and Shaw describes it as "a feminist . . . quest for selfhood" (64). Above all, *Eva Luna* is a "celebratory novel that bears tribute to the power of words and the imagination, the joys of sensuality and friendship, the ability of human beings to overcome social barriers, and the re-creation of reality through the lens of fiction" (Levine 55).

The present study will analyze five magical places that appear in *Eva Luna* and in the collection of short stories that followed two years later, *Cuentos de Eva Luna* (1989). Four are named places: El Palacio de los Pobres, Calle República, Agua Santa, and La Colonia, and all but the first receive extensive development in the novel and reappear frequently in the stories.[2] Spanning multiple works, these fictional places recall García Márquez's Macondo and Faulkner's Yoknapatawpha County.[3] A fifth magical place is the *lugar ameno*, the safe haven where the act of writing takes place. This space is specified in only one story—"Cartas de amor traicionado"—but is emblematic of the novel and of many of the stories which center on storytelling, writing, and the dialectic between art and life. An overview of these magical places will enrich our understanding of Allende's documented focus in her early fiction on the themes of love, social activism, and storytelling (Jehenson 100-101; Levine 55-56; Shaw 59). In addition, my reading of these spaces will allow us to consider ways in which Allende's fiction may be more complex than its commercial success leads some critics to surmise.[4] In particular, it will be demonstrated that although Allende's fiction in these two works is grounded in human emotions arising from the drama of everyday life, it is simplistic to label her work as melodrama as some critics have done (Jehenson 100; Invernizzi [1991], cited in Shaw 58).

Of the five magical places, the summer estate known as El Palacio de los Pobres in the novel and El Palacio de Verano in the short story "El palacio imaginado" is the most ostensibly marvelous. Eva Luna records that it was built by El Benefactor (a code name for General Juan Vicente Gómez, the Venezuelan dictator who was in power from 1908 to 1935) and that upon his death, it was reclaimed by the natives and the jungle: "No pudieron expulsar a los ocupantes, porque el palacio y todo lo que había dentro se hizo invisible al ojo humano, entró en otra dimensión en la cual siguió existiendo sin perturbaciones" (*EL* 131). The night that Eva Luna travels to Agua Santa with Riad Halabí, she sees the enchanted palace for the first time and recounts that experience as follows: "El viaje duró toda la noche a través de un paraje oscuro, donde las únicas luces eran las alcabalas de La Guardia, los camiones en su ruta hacia los campos petroleros y el Palacio de los Pobres, que se materializó por treinta segundos al borde del camino, como una visión alucinante" (*EL* 130). The second time Eva witnesses the magical apparition is the day she returns by bus to the capital after participating in a guerrilla raid near Agua Santa: "En un recodo de la ruta, la vegetación se abrió de súbito en un abanico de verdes imposibles y la luz del día se tornó blanca, para dar paso a la ilusión perfecta del Palacio de los Pobres, flotando a quince centímetros del humus que cubría el suelo" (*EL* 267-68). Strikingly similar is the description that closes "El palacio imaginado": "Dicen los viajeros que a veces, después de una tormenta, cuando el aire está húmedo y cargado de electricidad, surge de pronto junto al camino un blanco palacio de mármol, que por breves instantes permanece suspendido a cierta altura, como un espejismo, y luego desaparece sin ruido" (*CEL* 234-35).

These depictions of an enchanted palace that materializes briefly and floats above the ground are undoubtedly several instances where the marvelous is most obvious, yet they are not without ambiguity. For example, the fortress appears "como una visión alucinante" and "como un espejismo"; does it "truly" materialize or only in Eva's imagination? Similarly, the second time Eva "sees" the palace she calls it "la ilusión perfecta del Palacio de los Pobres." In addition, the multiple meanings of "imaginado" in the short story's title also contribute to the sense of wonder that elicits the following question: within the world of fiction, is the apparition a dream, an illusion, or does it magically "appear"?

In analyzing the tradition of magical realism in *La casa de los espíritus*, Laurie Clancy notes a real tension between realism and fantasy and questions whether or not Allende is somewhat ambivalent about its use: "Are we to believe in 'hidden forces' or the laws of science? Sometimes Allende hedges her bets: Rosa, for instance does not actually float but *seems* to float; she *seems* to be a mermaid but is not finally, as she lacks a scaly tail" (40). In *Eva Luna* and "El palacio imaginado," the narration of the construction of the summer palace and its subsequent transformation blends social realism with the extraordinary in order to highlight a sociopolitical truth: marginalized indigenous people are able to retake their land only when the invaders (or their descendants) abandon it. Allende underscores this idea in *Eva Luna* when her narrator explains why the Indians help the guerrilla fighters:

Pero a los indios no les interesaba la revolución ni ninguna otra cosa proveniente de esa raza execrable, ni siquiera podían repetir esa palabra tan larga. No compartían los ideales de los guerrilleros, no creían sus promesas ni entendían sus razones y si aceptaron ayudarlos en ese proyecto cuyo alcance no eran capaces de medir, fue porque los militares eran sus enemigos y eso les permitía vengar algunos de los múltiples agravios padecidos a lo largo de los años. El jefe de la tribu . . . [c]olaboraría con esos barbudos silenciosos, que al menos no robaban sus alimentos ni manoseaban a sus hijas, y luego escaparía. Con varias semanas de anticipación decidió la ruta a seguir, siempre adentrándose en el follaje, con la esperanza de que la impenetrable vegetación detuviera el avance del Ejército y los protegiera por un tiempo más. Así había sido durante quinientos años: persecución y exterminio. (*EL* 264-65)

In this passage, the plight of indigenous cultures is established via didactic summary. In the same way, "El palacio imaginado" begins with a didactic introduction of the social injustices suffered by indigenous cultures and then employs magical realism, a blend of social realism and the extraordinary, to narrate the origin and outcome of the summer palace.[5]

Whereas El Palacio de los Pobres (El Palacio de Verano) epitomizes the historical reality of indigenous cultures in Latin America, Calle República functions as a microcosm of the cultural institution known as the red-light district.[6] It is magical not in the sense of the extraordinary or the supernatural but because of its allure as a site of transgression where houses of prostitution traffic in sex and cabaret nightclubs present shows of a risqué nature. Although Eva is not a "working girl" of the neighborhood, she lives there twice: once briefly when she is about thirteen and later during her twenties.

When Eva Luna rebels from one of her last masters, a government official on whose head she deliberately overturns the chamber pot she has been summoned to empty, she finds herself alone, hungry, and in the street once again. But her childhood friend Huberto Naranjo, local gang leader and petty thief, takes her to reside in an establishment run by La Señora on Calle República. Telling everyone that Eva is his sister, Huberto pays for her lodging and meals and instructs La Señora to insulate her from the sordid aspects of the brothel. In turn, he confirms that Eva will be a delightful young companion who will use her talent for storytelling to amuse her guardian. The arrangement works well for several months. Eva is adopted and cared for by La Señora and her best friend, Melesio, a transgendered man who by day is an Italian teacher and by night the best artist in the cross-dressing cabaret theatre. Business runs smoothly and peacefully on Calle República due to the cooperation of local police officials who collect their weekly commissions from the establishments, but when a new police sergeant takes over and creates trouble for the residents, their response forces the Chief of Police and the Minister of the Interior to intervene. Calle República becomes a war zone which the press names "Guerra al Hampa" and which the locals rename "Revuelta de las Putas" (*EL* 126). La Señora barely escapes, Melesio is imprisoned, and Eva finds herself in the street once again.

Rescued by an Arab merchant, Riad Halabí, Eva spends the next five years of her adolescence in Agua Santa, a third magical place. She describes it as "uno de esos pueblos adormilados por la modorra de la provincia" (*EL* 131); "una aldea modesta, con casas de adobe, madera y caña amarga, construida al borde de la carretera y defendida a machetazos contra una vegetación salvaje que en cualquier descuido podía devorarla" (*EL* 138). In general, the inhabitants seem kind and pleasures are simple in this "pueblo olvidado" and "perdido" (*EL* 149, 197) "donde nadie se queda y cuyo nombre los viajeros rara vez recuerdan" (*CEL* 68). In this almost idyllic town unscathed by modern inventions, isolated from political upheavals that characterize the capital, and joined to the rest of the world by only one phone line and a curvy road, Eva is protected and nurtured by the most respected inhabitant of the town: Riad Halabí, her Turkish-born father figure.[7] Through his intervention, Eva acquires two things that will be invaluable in the future: a fraudulent but legal birth certificate and literacy.

Taught to read and write by the schoolteacher Inés, Eva can now complement her oral storytelling with the written word. Though her daytime hours are spent reading,[8] working in the successful merchant's store, and attending his infirm wife, Eva devotes most nights to writing her stories, an activity that she later recalls as "mis mejores horas" (*EL* 177). Routine and tranquility thus characterize life in Agua Santa where "las ventanas no tenían vidrios y las puertas estaban siempre abiertas y era costumbre visitarse, pasar delante de las casas saludando, entrar a tomar un café o un jugo de fruta, todos se conocían, nadie podía quejarse de soledad o de abandono" (*EL* 144). The only exception occurs on Saturdays when the guards from the nearby prison known as the Penal de Santa María visit the local brothel and when the Indians from a nearby settlement enter town to beg for alms. Eva lives in Agua Santa until gossip unfairly implicates her in the suicide of Riad Halabí's wife. Before she leaves, the merchant, who has already given her the tool (literacy) to become a writer, also introduces her to her own sensuality.

When Eva returns to the neighborhood surrounding Calle República, she goes to work in a factory and shares an apartment with the transsexual Mimí, the former Melesio. She also reunites with Huberto Naranjo, now Comandante Rogelio and leader of the guerrillas, and for a while, the friends become lovers. Eventually, however, their relationship moves full circle, and they end as friends. Meanwhile, with Mimí's support and encouragement, Eva leaves the factory to devote herself to her writing.[9] She also meets Rolf Carlé, and the final chapters of the narrative focus on their social activism and budding romance. The novel closes with a celebration of their union, a conclusion that is set in motion in chapter 2 when the narration of Rolf's life story begins.[10] The narrative makes clear that while Eva lives a portion of her childhood on Calle República and all of her teenage years in Agua Santa, La Colonia is the town where Rolf Carlé spends his adolescence after emigrating from Austria.

Eva Luna identifies this fourth magical place as a "pueblo de fantasía" originally founded by a rich South American landowner with utopian goals who, in the mid nineteenth century went to Europe to secure a group of eighty impoverished families who were willing to move half way around the world with the express purpose of creating "una sociedad perfecta donde reinara la paz y la prosperidad" (EL 85). Distant cousins of Rolf Carlé's mother moved to La Colonia to escape the war in Europe, and it was to them that Rolf was sent as a teenager. Although during his adulthood, La Colonia would become a fashionable Sunday afternoon getaway for capital residents with cars, when Rolf arrived, it was a town "preservado en una burbuja donde el tiempo se había detenido y la geografía había sido burlada. Allí la vida transcurría como en los Alpes durante el siglo diecinueve" (EL 85). A safe harbor, La Colonia offers Eva and Rolf temporary asylum after they help Huberto Naranjo free nine guerrilla prisoners from the prison near Agua Santa.[11]

Turning to the last magical place analyzed in this study, it is emblematic of the storytelling motif extensively treated in *Eva Luna* and *Cuentos de Eva Luna*. For example, as narrator of her pseudo-autobiography (the novel) and as author of a television script entitled *Bolero* and based on her life, Eva Luna is the consummate storyteller.[12] She reprises this role in *Cuentos de Eva Luna*, a collection of short narratives that purport to be her response to Rolf Carlé's request that she tell him a story. In addition, a number of the female protagonists in this collection are storytellers or writers. Belisa Crepusculario of "Dos palabras" epitomizes the teller of tales who has learned the power of words. Elena Mejías of "Niña perversa" invents stories and attributes them to the guests who lodge in her mother's boarding house. Maurizia Rugieri of "Tosca" tries to live life as the fictional heroine of an opera. Abigal McGovern of "Con todo el respeto debido," along with her husband, invents a fantastic story of kidnapping and ransom as a strategy to climb the social ladder. And, finally, Analía Torres of "Cartas de amor traicionado" retreats to a special place to invent stories, read, and write.

Raised in a convent due to her parents' death, Analía finds quiet refuge in the attic. Unlike the attic and upstairs room that imprison, respectively, Bertha Mason Rochester of *Jane Eyre* and the narrator-protagonist of Charlotte Perkins Gilman's "The Yellow Wallpaper," the attic in "Cartas de amor traicionado" recalls Emily Dickinson's upstairs bedroom as a place to which the female writer voluntarily retreats in order to cultivate her imagination. In Allende's story, Analía repeats the journey of Eva Luna and Belisa Crepusculario, who first begin as storytellers in the oral tradition and later become readers and writers. As a child, Analía relishes the solitude that the attic affords her, escaping there to amuse herself with invented stories. But as an adolescent, she returns to her *lugar ameno* to savor the epistles she receives from her cousin and to enter into a clandestine relationship of amorous letter writing:

Se escondía en el desván, no ya a inventar cuentos improbables, sino a releer con avidez las notas enviadas por su primo hasta conocer de memoria la inclinación de las letras y la textura del papel. Al principio no las contestaba, pero al poco tiempo no pudo dejar de hacerlo. El contenido de las cartas se fue haciendo cada vez más útil para burlar la censura de la Madre Superiora, que abría la correspondencia. Creció la intimidad entre los dos y pronto lograron ponerse de acuerdo en un código secreto con el cual empezaron a hablar de amor. (*CEL* 213-14)

Analía's enjoyment of the multiple layers of meaning made possible by words recalls a crucial lesson on the magical nature of words that Eva Luna learns from her mother: "Ella sembró en mi cabeza la idea de que la realidad no es sólo cómo se percibe en la superficie, también tiene una dimensión mágica y, si a uno se le antoja, es legítimo exagerarla y ponerle color para que el tránsito por esta vida no resulte tan aburrido" (*EL* 28). Thus, the attic is a magical place, a sacred space, where the writer uses her imagination to celebrate and cultivate the creative possibilities of language.

This reading of magical places in *Eva Luna* and *Cuentos de Eva Luna* has identified four named places as well as a generic space. El Palacio de los Pobres (El Palacio de Verano), Calle República, Agua Santa, and La Colonia span multiple works and function, respectively, as microcosms of a historical condition (the plight of the indigenous), a cultural institution (prostitution), and the Latin American town geographically isolated from the political battles waged in the capital and other large cities. Magical realism is the predominant mode used to portray the four named places although the marvelous is most obvious in the narration of the enchanted palace. The fifth place—the attic— serves as a safe haven for the artist who retreats there to celebrate the magic of words. These special places are essential in the portrayal of three major themes: love and friendship, social activism and politics, including social satire, and storytelling and writing.

As a way of conclusion, I would like us to consider how three of these magical places undermine the charge that Allende's fiction is based on melodrama. Classic melodrama creates a simplified moral universe in which the conflict between good and evil is embodied in stock characters and operates according to a series of conventions: the villain poses a threat, the hero or heroine escapes, and the work has a happy ending (Rios-Font 10, 19-49).[13] With Allende's focus on storytelling, both her third novel and her collection of short stories display characteristics frequently associated with melodrama: plot centeredness, highly dramatic incidents, and strong emotionalism. In addition, El Palacio de los Pobres clearly reflects the polarization between good and evil: reclaimed by the Indians and the jungle, the enchanted palace returns to its rightful owners, and justice is served. Calle República, La Colonia, and Agua Santa, however, are more complicated.

Although Huberto Naranjo wants to insulate Eva Luna from the illicit world of prostitution located on and around Calle República, it is the community he knows, and he places her there in the care of La Señora. The inhabitants of the neighborhood foster a sense of community that allows them to survive and at times to prosper. The polarization between good and evil blurs because the narrative does not rigorously censor their activities. In fact, La Señora's entrepreneurial skills are celebrated:

> Inventó unos estrafalarios juguetes con los cuales pensaba invadir el Mercado, pero no consiguió a nadie dispuesto a financiarlos. Por falta de visión comercial en el país, esa idea—como tantas otras—fue arrebatada por los norteamericanos, que ahora tienen las patentes y venden sus modelos por todo el orbe. El pene telescópico a manivela, el dedo a pilas y el seno inflable con pezones de caramelo, fueron creaciones suyas y si le pagaran el porcentaje al cual en justicia tiene derecho, sería millonaria. (*EL* 118)

The true objects of satire are the "banqueros, magnates y encumbradas personalidades del Gobierno" who pay for her services with "fondos públicos" (*EL* 119) and the police who receive weekly payoffs. Furthermore, Mimí's response to the neighborhood is ironic. In spite of being a marginalized individual who finds social acceptance on Calle República, Mimí views the neighborhood as flawed: as soon as she and Eva can afford to move, Mimí finds them a house in the most prestigious neighborhood of the capital city. Her decision to leave the neighborhood depicts the extent to which she is affected by traditional bourgeois values and prejudice.

Rolf Carlé's adolescent home, La Colonia, is consistently portrayed as a utopia of refuge from the political and social evils of the outside world. Nevertheless, La Colonia's fairy-tale existence as a safe harbor is undermined by its self-isolation. It is "a place where no one speaks Spanish, and where many of the children have defects because of inbreeding, another reference, perhaps, to the Nazi policy of the 'pure race'" (Diamond-Nigh 37). Thus, whereas in the context of El Palacio de los Pobres magical realism honors the rights of indigenous cultures, in the case of La Colonia it portrays outsiders (Europeans) with a fantastic desire to live in a cultural bubble intended to marginalize Latin America. In short, the representation of La Colonia as a utopia is subverted by satire.

The polarization between good and evil also blurs in Agua Santa. Although it appears to be an idyllic community that integrates Hispanic, Arabic, and indigenous cultures, it is characterized by a number of social flaws. First, most of its inhabitants are illiterate, a condition that contrasts sharply with the importance Eva attributes to her own ability to read and write. Some humor is created at the expense of these simple townspeople when in the story "Tosca" they cannot distinguish between art (the opera that Maurizia is performing) and life (Maurizia's real situation). Second, the townspeople are not always charitable: founded on the mistaken belief that Eva contributed to the death of Riad Halabí's wife, gossip forces Eva to leave town. Third, patriarchal traditions such as domestic abuse are sanctioned in Agua Santa. In the short story entitled "El oro de Tomás Vargas" we read:

"En Agua Santa se podía tolerar que un hombre maltratara a su familia, fuera haragán, bochinchero y no devolviera el dinero prestado, pero las deudas del juego eran sagradas" (*CEL* 61).

Finally, Allende's characters, or at least many of them, are not the one-dimensional stock characters of melodrama. Eva's memory portrays Riad Halabí as an incredibly generous and nurturing father figure, but at the same time he sleeps with her on the eve of her departure from Agua Santa. In addition, when Eva begs him to allow her to stay, he says he cannot marry someone as young as she. Yet when she secretly visits Agua Santa several years later, Eva discovers that his second wife is even younger than Eva.

The schoolteacher Inés is beloved by all her former pupils. Together with Riad Halabí, she generously helps a number of needy children in *Eva Luna* and "El oro de Tomás Vargas," and in "El huésped de la maestra" she is described as "la matrona más respetada de Agua Santa" (*CEL* 163). Nevertheless, when the schoolteacher avenges her son's death by killing the man who accidentally shot her boy twenty years ago, the whole community, led by Riad Halabí, joins together to help her dispose of the body. Halabí enjoys significant prestige in Agua Santa and is known as a fair man, but the system of justice operating in the town clearly reflects old laws (and for some readers, outdated traditions), as Inés notes when she defends her own actions and seeks Halabí's approval: "Ojo por ojo, diente por diente, turco. ¿No dice así tu religión?" (*CEL* 165).

"La mujer del juez" portrays both Casilda, the protagonist, and Nicolás Vidal, the violent outlaw, as multifaceted characters. Although a criminal, Vidal is also a victim of birth and circumstance: "no conocía la intimidad, la ternura, la risa secreta, la fiesta de los sentidos, el alegre gozo de los amantes" (*CEL* 147). His crimes are not condoned, but his psychological make-up cultivates the reader's sympathy. Similarly, in spite of the story's title that minimizes the protagonist as subject and insinuates she is merely an extension of her husband, Casilda's actions depict her as an intelligent individual with a strong will.[14] Both

Vidal and the townspeople are initially deceived by the demure and soft-spoken exterior that masks her inner strength. She courageously opposes her husband when he abuses his civil power, and she protects her children by willingly participating in an act of sexual violence that is simultaneously portrayed as violent rape and passionate love-making. Ironically, the encounter seems to redeem the outlaw by highlighting his human nature, his emotions, yet it also defeats him by awarding Casilda the time she seeks in order to be rescued. Helene Weldt-Basson holds that the story's final paragraph "is predicated on a romantic hyperbole: Casilda's sexual gratification is so great that she forgets her revenge on Vidal and urges him to flee, while he corresponds in kind by sacrificing his life for the privilege of a last kiss and final few moments in her arms" (189). "[H]ighly implausible," these reactions parody the romantic stereotype in which the woman falls in love with her rapist (190). The outlaw who initially appears more cunning and powerful loses his life at the end of the story to a woman who is stronger and smarter than he. Traditional stereotypes are subverted in favor of more complex characters.

Although justice is served in El Palacio de los Pobres and the attic is celebrated as the writer's *lugar ameno*, three magical places—Calle República, La Colonia, and Agua Santa—blur the polarization between good and evil. In addition, many of Allende's characters are far more complicated than the one-dimensional stock characters of melodrama. Thus, while Allende's fiction, as represented by *Eva Luna* and *Cuentos de Eva Luna* is indeed accessible, a close examination of its magical places and their inhabitants demonstrates a complexity that may not be readily apparent.

From *West Virginia University Philological Papers* 53 (2006): 108-117. Copyright © 2006 by West Virginia University. Reprinted with permission of West Virginia University.

Notes

1. One of the earliest to note the picaresque tradition in *Eva Luna* is Patricia Hart's *Narrative Magic in the Fiction of Isabel Allende* (164). About the same time there appeared a number of studies devoted exclusively to Allende's adaptation of the picaresque: Haydée Borowski de Llanos, Silvia Ferrari de Zink, and Mercedes García Saraví de Miranda; Peter Earle; Carmen Galarce; Gloria Gálvez-Carlisle; and Pilar Rotella. Both Gálvez-Carlisle (166-67) and Rotella (130) signal that unlike traditional picaresque narratives, the protagonist of Allende's work shares significant narrative space with Rolf Carlé and other secondary characters (Huberto Naranjo and Melesio/Mimí). Rotella observes also that Eva is frequently rescued or aided by another character and suggests that Eva's successes mark her story as a blend of the picaresque and the romance (133).

2. El Palacio de los Pobres in *Eva Luna* is renamed El Palacio de Verano in "El palacio imaginado." The protagonist of "María la boba" works on Calle República, and there Eva Luna meets the protagonist of "Clarisa." Agua Santa is the location for "El oro de Tomás Vargas," "Si me tocaras el corazón," "Tosca," and "El huésped de la maestra." La Colonia is home for "El pequeño Heidelberg" and one of the settings in "Vida interminable." My study will cite examples from a number of stories, but it will treat more extensively the novel and two stories, "El palacio imaginado" and "Cartas de amor traicionado."

3. Although Macondo is likely the best-known mythical place of those which populate Latin American literature, María-Elena Angulo locates three others in Ecuadorian novels of "realismo maravilloso" (xi). One is La Hondura, the microcosm of the Ecuadorian lowland tropic, which serves as the geographic focus of José de la Cuadra's *Los Sangurimas* (1934) (55). Another is Santorontón, the representation in Demetrio Aguilera Malta's *Siete lunas y siete serpientes* (1970) of the remote Latin American village whose natives "believe in God, the devil, wizards, and in zoomorphic and magical transformations of the human being" (76). The third mythical place is located in Alicia Yánez Cossío's *Bruna, soroche y los tíos* (1972) and is known as La ciudad dormida, the stagnated town of Bruna's ancestors where social mores and religious laws remain intact from the seventeenth to the twentieth centuries (92-93).

4. Allende's artistry has been both questioned and defended. For example, Raymond L. Williams acknowledges that the "most widely recognized and celebrated woman writer from 1968 to 1990 was Isabel Allende." Yet he mitigates her critical importance by referring to her "commercial success" and names fourteen women writers who are "generally taken more seriously than Allende" (177). Similarly, David Buehrer questions the feminism of Allende's protagonists and suggests that in *Cuentos de Eva Luna*, the fantastic has "regressed to the mere fairy tale" with "often stereotypical, fairy-tale characters and motifs" (104). Philip Swanson, however, defends Allende from two critics who charge that some of the female characters in her first novel either perpetuate gender stereotypes or undermine the political impact. Swanson holds that Allende's popularity and public persona have "tarnished her image in certain academic circles" and argues that the terms "popular" and "serious" are not mutually exclusive (146-47). In the most comprehensive analysis to date on *Cuentos de Eva Luna*, Samuel

Amago maintains that critics have tended to emphasize "social rather than literary aspects" of Allende's fiction. He therefore focuses on her narrative technique, arguing convincingly that her stories are "bound together by formal similarities and an overall thematic and structural frame based upon the *Thousand and One Nights*" (47).

5. The story recounts in detail the construction of the edifice, its brief occupation by El Benefactor, and its gradual transformation into an enchanted palace that is reclaimed by the Indians and the jungle. The story also narrates El Benefactor's abduction of Marcia Lieberman, wife of the Austrian ambassador. Marcia willingly leaves her traditional and unfulfilling marriage to be the dictator's mistress for a time, although she eventually finds happiness living alone among the spirits of the invisible Indians who inhabit the enchanted fortress.

6. See Patricia Hart's "Magic Feminism in Isabel Allende's *The Stories of Eva Luna*" in which the critic upholds that the feminist focus of Allende's fiction "differentiates it sharply from that of her male predecessors. In stark contrast to the recurring male fantasy of the hooker with the heart of gold so beloved of Vargas Llosa and others, Allende treats prostitution with emotional reality" (107).

7. In her discussion of myth and the mythic consciousness in *Eva Luna*, Lynne Diamond-Nigh observes that gender differences disappear in the mythic world-view, and she makes an interesting case for considering Riad Halabí as the fusion of the father and the mother. She notes also that the narrative "focuses on his sensitivity, gentleness, and emotional life, a focus most usually reserved for feminine characters" (35). See her "*Eva Luna*: Writing as History."

8. Eva credits a four-volume set of *A Thousand and One Tales of the Arabian Nights* with introducing her to eroticism and the world of imagination, and quotations from this text serves as epigraphs both for *Eva Luna* and *Cuentos de Eva Luna*. The latter also includes a postscript from the Arabic text. Allende records that her first encounter with *The Arabian Nights* was a transformational experience (Levine 58), and many critics have noted that like Scheherazade, Allende and Eva Luna believe in the transformational power of words and stories. Amago underscores a significant difference in the motivation behind Scheherazade's and Eva Luna's storytelling: the former tells stories to save herself whereas the latter tells stories (*Cuentos de Eva Luna*) to save Rolf from the burden of his tortured memories (55).

9. Eva recalls that this decision was momentous: "Desperté de madrugada. Era un miércoles suave y algo lluvioso, en nada diferente de otros en mi vida, pero éste lo atesoro como un día único reservado sólo para mí. Desde que la maestra Inés me enseñó el alfabeto, escribía casi todas las noches, pero sentí que ésta era una ocasión diferente, algo que podría cambiar mi rumbo. . . . Creí que esa página me esperaba desde hacía veintitantos años, que yo había vivido sólo para ese instante, y quise que a partir de ese momento mi único oficio fuera atrapar las historias suspendidas en el aire más delgado, para hacerlas mías" (*EL* 234).

10. Eva narrates her life-story in chapters 1, 3, 5, 6, and 8 and switches to an omniscient third-person to summarize Rolf's early life in chapters 2, 4, and 7. Chapter 9 includes sections on both characters, and Eva and Rolf meet in chapter 10. In the remainder of the novel (chapter 11 and a conclusion entitled "A Final Word"), their stories fully merge into one narrative, a linguistic mirroring of their personal relationship.

Wolfgang Karrer points out that the "alternating chapter device" (155) is a generic borrowing from the soap operas whose form Eva first learns while listening to the radio in Elvira's kitchen.

11. In a similar fashion, in "Vida interminable" La Colonia offers Roberto and Ana Blaum "un lugar apartado donde refugiarse . . . una extraña aldea incrustada en un cerro tropical, réplica de algún villorrio bávaro del siglo diecinueve, un desvarío arquitectónico de casas de madera pintada, relojes de cucú, macetas de geranios y avisos con letras góticas, habitada por una raza de gente rubia con los mismos trajes tiroleses y mejillas rubicundas que sus bisabuelos trajeron al emigrar de la Selva Negra" (*CEL* 185).

12. Shaw writes: "the way in which, as almost every critic has noticed, Eva's autobiographical narrative merges with her *telenovela* script is more than just a gimmick. It is a strategy for attempting to resolve what we have seen is the Post-Boom's worst dilemma: the difficulty of expressing the real while at the same time retaining an awareness that all expressions of reality are fictions" (67). In "¿Una Scheherazada hispanoamericana?", Susana Reisz understands Eva Luna's successes—"todo se le acomoda demasiado bien al final" (120)—as logical outcomes of the soap opera formula that is both cultivated and parodied in *Eva Luna*. See also Susan de Carvalho's "*Escrituras y escritoras*: The Artist-Protagonists of Isabel Allende" and Eliana S. Rivero's "Scheherazade Liberated: *Eva Luna* and Women Storytellers."

13. Eva Luna provides two endings for her pseudo-autobiography: one in which she and Rolf Carlé remain lovers and one in which their relationship is spent. The majority of the short stories have closed endings in which some sort of justice is secured; however, the "happy ending" of some is problematic: "El huesped de la maestra" and "Una venganza" are two examples. "Vida interminable" is also exceptional because it displays an open ending in which Roberto Blaum despairs over his role in the euthanasia of his terminally ill wife and his subsequent inability to carry out the suicide he had planned.

14. See Tony Spanos's "Isabel Allende's 'The Judge's Wife': Heroine or Female Stereotype?" for a thought-provoking and open-ended discussion of Casilda.

Works Cited

Allende, Isabel. *Cuentos de Eva Luna*. New York: Rayo, 2002.

_____. *Eva Luna*. New York: Rayo, 2001.

Amago, Samuel. "Isabel Allende and the Postmodern Literary Tradition: A Reconsideration of *Cuentos de Eva Luna*." *Latin American Literary Review* 28.56 (2000): 43-60.

Angulo, María-Elena. *Magic Realism: Social Context and Discourse*. New York: Garland, 1995.

Borowski de Llanos, Haydée, Silvia Ferrari de Zink, and Mercedes García Saraví de Miranda, "'Lázaro,' 'Gardelito' y 'Eva': Tres nombres y una tradición." *Actas del III Congreso Argentino de Hispanistas 'España en América y América en España,' Buenos Aires, 19-23 May 1992*. Ed. Luis Martínez Cuitiño and

Elida Lois. Buenos Aires: Inst. De Filol. y Lits. Hispánicas, Fac. de Filos. y Letras, U de Buenos Aires, 1993. 340-47.

Buehrer, David. "From Magical Realism to Fairy Tale: Isabel Allende's *The Stories of Eva Luna.*" *West Virginia University Philological Papers* 42-43 (1997-98): 103-07.

Carvalho, Susan de. "Escrituras y escritoras: The Artist-Protagonists of Isabel Allende." *Discurso Literario* 10.1 (1992): 59-67.

Clancy, Laurie. "Isabel Allende's Dialogue with García Márquez." *Antípodas* 6-7 (1994-95): 29-43.

Diamond-Nigh, Lynne. "*Eva Luna*: Writing as History." *Studies in 20th Century Literature* 19.1 (1995): 29-42.

Earle, Peter G. "De Lazarillo a Eva Luna: Metamorfosis de la picaresca." *Nueva Revista de Filología Hispánica* 36.2 (1988): 987-96.

Galarce, Carmen J. "El discurso picaresco en *Eva Luna.*" *Signos: Estudios de Lengua y Literatura* 24 (1991): 27-31.

Gálvez-Carlisle, Gloria. "El sabor picaresco en *Eva Luna.*" *Critical Approaches to Eva Luna.* Ed. Sonia Riquelme Rojas and Edna Aguirre Rehbein. New York: Peter Lang, 1991. 165-77.

Hart, Patricia. "Magic Feminism in Isabel Allende's *The Stories of Eva Luna.*" *Multicultural Literatures through Feminist/Poststructuralist Lenses.* Ed. Barbara Frey Waxman. Knoxville: U of Tennessee P, 1993. 103-36.

_____. *Narrative Magic in the Fiction of Isabel Allende.* London: Associated UP, 1989.

Invernizzi, Virginia. "The Novels of Isabel Allende: A Reevaluation of Genre." Diss. U of Virginia, 1991.

Jehenson, Myriam Yvonne. *Latin American Women Writers: Class, Race, and Gender.* Buffalo: State U of New York P, 1995.

Karrer, Wolfgang. "Transformation and Transvestism in *Eva Luna.*" *Critical Approaches to Isabel Allende's Novels.* Ed. Sonia Riquelme Rojas and Edna Aguirre Rehbein. New York: Peter Lang, 1991. 151-64.

Levine, Linda Gould. *Isabel Allende.* New York: Twayne, 2002.

Ocasio, Rafael. *Literature of Latin America.* Westport, CT: Greenwood P, 2004.

Reisz, Susana. "¿Una Scheherazada hispanoamericana? Sobre Isabel Allende y Eva Luna." *Mester* 20.2 (1991): 107-26.

Rios-Font, Wadda C. *Rewriting Melodrama: The Hidden Paradigm in Modern Spanish Theater.* Lewisburg, PA: Bucknell UP, 1997.

Rivero, Eliana S. "Scheherazade Liberated: Eva Luna and Women Storytellers." *Splintering Darkness: Latin American Women Writers in Search of Themselves.* Ed. Lucía Guerra Cunningham. Pittsburgh: Latin American Literary Review P, 1990. 143-56.

Rotella, Pilar V. "Allende's *Eva Luna* and the Picaresque Tradition." *Critical Approaches to Isabel Allende's Novels.* Ed. Sonia Riquelme Rojas and Edna Aguirre Rehbein. New York: Peter Lang, 1991. 125-37.

Shaw, Donald. *The Post-Boom in Spanish American Fiction.* Albany: State U of New York P, 1998.

Spanos, Tony. "Isabel Allende's 'The Judge's Wife': Heroine or Stereotype?" *Encyclia* 67 (1990): 163-72.

Swanson, Philip. *The New Novel in Latin America: Politics and Popular Culture after the Boom*. Manchester: Manchester UP, 1995.

Weldt-Basson, Helene C. "Irony as Silent Subversive Strategy in Isabel Allende's *Cuentos de Eva Luna*." *Revista de Estudios Hispánicos* (U de Puerto Rico), 31.1 (2004): 183-98.

Williams, Raymond L. *The Twentieth-Century Spanish American Novel*. Austin: U of Texas P, 2003.

Mourning Becomes *Paula*:
The Writing Process as Therapy
for Isabel Allende_____

Linda S. Maier

Isabel Allende's *Paula* (1994) is a moving tribute to her late daughter. What began as an anguished letter written at the hospital bedside of her comatose daughter developed into a memoir, and the writing process converted the author's grief into a celebration of life. Reviewers have pointed out that the book contains two narrative threads which ultimately coalesce: 1) the autobiographical account of Allende's tumultuous life, and 2) the chronicle of Paula's illness and death (December 1991-December 1992) (Hornblower, Ruta). When he declined to be interviewed by Allende, poet Pablo Neruda hit the mark, saying that she puts herself at the center of everything she writes (qtd. in Allende, *Paula* 202). Be that as it may, Puerto Rican writer Rosario Ferré maintains that all writing is essentially autobiographical and motivated by a desire for self-creation (144, 137-38). This inquiry into female self-identity marks Allende's and other Spanish American Post-Boom women writers' works and, at least in her writing, is linked to the restorative nature of motherhood and mother-daughter relationships, whether fictional—as in the Trueba/del Valle families of *La casa de los espíritus*—or real—namely, her own relationship with her daughter Paula (Frenk 68, 73; Lindsay 141, 144; Meyer 360-61). As one reviewer has noted, with its "unusual combination of self-affirmation and loss," this book could easily have been titled *Isabel* since it only nominally centers on Paula (Ruta; also Cortínez 63).

Allende's impulse to take over the spotlight may here be attributed to her parental role and grief and to her quest for creative empowerment in the face of bereavement. The therapeutic release offered by writing helped her recover from loss, as she has explained: "I had a choice. . . . Was I going to commit suicide? Sue the hospital? Or was I going to write a book that would heal me?" (qtd. in Hornblower). In fact, Allende's literary debut in 1982 was likewise prompted by deep-seated emotions and an optimistic belief in the healing power of literature: "Escribí *La casa de los espíritus* como una forma de secarme las lágrimas que llevaba por dentro y darle cuerpo al dolor, para hacerlo mi prisionero. Le atribuí a la escritura el poder de resucitar a los muertos, reunir a los dispersos, reconstruir un mundo perdido" (Allende, "El canto" 276). This article will explore Allende's writing in relation to the stages of grief outlined by Elisabeth Kübler-Ross and other thanatologists—denial and isolation, anger, bargaining, depression, and acceptance. It will also place special emphasis on issues of parental bereavement depicted in the book and examine the transformation of human tragedy into one of Allende's best works and a prime example of Spanish American Post-Boom literature (Correas Zapata 121; Ruta).

Allende has acknowledged her inurement to loss and separation (for example, loss of country, family members, and personal roots), but describes Paula's death as "la última y más grave separación de [su] vida" (qtd. in Álvarez-Rubio 1064). In fact, grief is a type of separation reaction in which the bereaved individual mourns the loss of a loved person or abstraction (Freud 243; Knight and Herter 197). Parental bereavement often parallels pathological grief, which according to some experts sets it apart from other forms of loss (Rando 46). The death of a child, whether in infancy or adulthood, is considered "the most significant and traumatic death of a family member" (Clayton 169; Clayton qtd. in Rando 48). Because the child represents an extension of the parent, "the loss of a child is more of a personal loss of self than any other loss" (Rando 49). Consequently, her daughter's death precipitates Allende's struggle to maintain her own individuality in the face of personal loss. As Ferré has noted, writing—a product of autobiographical experience and imagination—is an act of self-creation that in turn generates a sense of usefulness and pleasure. To defer the pain of watching her daughter's gradual decline, Allende seeks the personal gratification of storytelling, and like the protagonist of her third novel *Eva Luna*

(1987) "invents her stories—her life—to survive the reality of her existence" (Laurila 185). Anticipatory mourning, or gradual detachment of emotional investment, may take place during a prolonged illness such as Paula's and prepares the bereaved parent for the eventual loss (Blank 206; Knight and Herter 199). Like a dying patient informed of a fatal prognosis, parents and family members adjust to impending death by stages that at times may coexist and overlap (Kübler-Ross 149, 236).

The unexpected news of Paula's sudden collapse and hospitalization due to porphyria cut short Allende's speaking tour to promote the Spanish publication of her novel *El plan infinito* in December 1991. The author immediately rushed to Madrid, and for the next year mother and daughter existed in a state of unreality and suspended time: "Desde ese momento la vida se detuvo para ti y también para mí, las dos cruzamos un misterioso umbral y entramos a la zona más oscura" (*Paula* 29). The shock numbed Allende's sense of the passage of time, and her life history seemed like a Mexican mural painting in which all events occur simultaneously, "como si mi vida entera fuera una sola imagen ininteligible" (*Paula* 29). Retracing her autobiography is a way to preserve her connection with her child. Inadvertently, Paula provides her mother with a rare opportunity for self-exploration: "La experiencia de explorar la propia vida es muy interesante, supongo que por eso hay tantos adictos al psicoanálisis. Son raras las oportunidades—excepto en terapia o en un confesionario—en que disponemos de tiempo y permiso para observarnos, revisar el pasado, trazar los mapas del camino ya recorrido y descubrir cómo somos" (Correa Zapata 14-15).

This personal crisis gives rise to Allende's aesthetic fusion of autobiographical and confessional elements in *Paula*. Seated at her daughter's hospital bedside, Allende appears as a solitary middle-aged woman unburdening her past to a young female listener, an image that both mirrors and inverts the concept of religious confession. Like the heroine of a confessional novel, she retraces her past life and experiences deep internal pain and suffering in a search for meaning and self-understanding (Axthelm 6-12). At the same time, she presents a self-aware, autobiographical account of her own life story with a forward-looking sense that she will ultimately surmount any setback: "[B]y writing, the author is creating [her]self in terms of [her] past experiences *as [she] sees them from the present*" (Porter 148).

Even though Paula was in critical condition in the intensive care unit and later suffered irreversible brain damage, Allende refused to believe that her twenty-eight-year-old daughter would be taken from her (*Paula* 257-58). She rejected the neurologist's diagnosis: "'Aquí hay un error. . . . Usted no sabe lo que está diciendo'" (*Paula* 228). She describes a recurring dream that illustrates her denial of Paula's imminent death in which she tries to prevent her daughter's ascension to heaven (*Paula* 84-85, 365-66).

After the initial outpouring of family sympathy, Allende remained in Madrid to look after her sick child. She checked into a hotel and abandoned all other obligations to watch over Paula. At first, Paula's husband Ernesto and Allende's mother accompanied her at the sickbed, but eventually mother and daughter lived together in virtual isolation. Toward the end, Paula essentially reverted to a state of infancy, as her mother describes: "Paula depende de mí para sobrevivir, ha vuelto a pertenecerme, está otra vez en mis brazos como un recién nacido" (*Paula* 299). This intimate communion is reinforced through her writing, which originated as a letter, and as usual, she shares her work in progress with only her mother or in this case, Paula (Allende, "Conversando" 193). Furthermore, this bond evinces the Post-Boom tendency "for the writer to be much closer emotionally to his or her principal characters than was usual in the Boom" (Shaw 64).

Face to face with death, an individual generally experiences a chaotic range of emotions that may include anger, guilt, fear, envy, and resentment (Kübler-Ross 44). Allende is no different. She is filled with rage at the possibility of Paula's passing, but stubbornly ignored it, as she has stated: "After they told me, I went on writing because I could not stop. I could not let anger destroy me" (qtd. in Hornblower). Allende also feels guilty for entrusting her daughter to the care of hospital personnel (*Paula* 30-31). At one point she confesses her overwhelming fear of death: "Estoy asustada. Algunas veces antes tuve mucho miedo, pero siempre había una salida de escape. . . . Ahora estoy en un callejón ciego, no hay puertas a la esperanza y no sé qué hacer con tanto miedo" (*Paula* 182). Writing becomes an act of hope to combat the "paralyzing feeling" of despair ("Writing As an Act of Hope" 48, 50).

Out of desperation, the afflicted individual engages in bargaining to obtain more time and postpone the inevitable loss (Kübler-Ross 72-74). Paula's mother is not the only one who offers to switch places with her daughter. An elderly patient in the intensive care unit, Don Manuel, volunteers to die in exchange for Paula's life as does Allende's seventy-year-old mother: "Mi madre sigue regateando con Dios, ahora le ofrece su vida por la tuya, dice que de todos modos setenta años son mucho tiempo, mucho cansancio y muchas penas. También yo quisiera ocupar tu lugar, pero no existen recursos de ilusionista para estos trueques . . ." (*Paula* 84, 93, 108). One day Paula nearly died in the hospital but was revived not by medical expertise but by her mother's and grand-mother's silent pleas:

El tiempo se detuvo en los relojes, las curvas y picos verdes en las pantallas de las máquinas se convirtieron en líneas rectas y un zumbido de consternación reemplazó el chillido de las alarmas. Alguien dijo no hay más que hacer . . . y otra voz agregó ha muerto, la gente se apartó, algunos se alejaron y pudimos verte inerte y pálida, como una niña de mármol. Entonces sentí la mano de mi madre en la mía impulsándome hacia adelante y dimos unos pasos al frente acercándonos a la orilla de tu cama y sin una lágrima te ofrecimos la reserva completa de nuestro vigor, toda la salud y fortaleza de nuestros más recónditos genes de navegantes vascos y de indómitos indios americanos, y en silencio invocamos a los dioses conocidos y por conocer y a los espíritus benéficos de nuestros ante-pasados y a las fuerzas más formidables de la vida, para que corrieran a tu rescate. Fue tan intenso el clamor que a cincuenta kilómetros de distancia Ernesto sintió el llamado con la claridad de un campanazo, supo que rodabas hacia un abismo y echó a correr en dirección al hospital. Entretanto en torno a tu cama se helaba el aire y se confundía el tiempo y cuando los relojes marcaron de nuevo los segundos, ya era tarde para la muerte. Los médicos vencidos se habían retirado y las enfermeras se preparaban para desconectar los tubos y cubrirte con una sábana, cuando una de las pantallas mágicas dio un suspiro y la caprichosa línea verde empezó a ondular señalando tu retorno a la vida. ¡Paula! te llamamos mi madre y yo en una sola voz y las enfermeras repitieron el grito y la sala se llenó con tu nombre. (*Paula* 107)

After this reprieve, Allende clutches at straws to defer Paula's death; like many families in similar circumstances, she turns to fortune-tellers, faith healers and alternative medicine (Kübler-Ross 149). Almost from the outset of Paula's illness, Allende contemplates removing her daughter from the hospital to prolong her existence and improve her quality of life. Contrary to general public opinion, medical experts have suggested that a dying patient often receives superior care at home where she occupies a central position. The direct care of a loved one also helps to soften the future blow (Rees 209). Allende eventually makes elaborate arrangements to transport Paula from Madrid to San Francisco and then to nearby San Rafael. She furnishes her home with the necessary medical equipment and hires several attendants, and Paula occupies the ground floor television room where her niece Andrea had been born not long before.

Depression is a normal response to the imminent loss of a loved one. This condition is characterized by an inability to concentrate and loss of interest in the outside world, insomnia, tearfulness, and feelings of extreme sadness and hopelessness (Blank 204; Clayton 168; Freud 244). Kübler-Ross defines two types of depression: 1) reactive depression, which usually involves much verbal interaction, and 2) preparatory depression, which is usually an unspoken accommodation to the final parting. In effect, Allende's writing allows her to tacitly express her unutterable grief: "Ahora estoy obligada a permanecer quieta y callada; por mucho que corra no llego a ninguna parte, si grito nadie me oye. Me has dado silencio para examinar mi paso por este mundo, Paula, para retornar al pasado verdadero y al pasado fantástico, recuperar las memorias que otros han olvidado, recordar lo que nunca sucedió y lo que tal vez sucederá. Ausente, muda y paralizada, tú eres mi guía" (*Paula* 181).

In an attempt to cope with Paula's medical emergency, Allende begins to exhibit many of the symptoms of depression. The tremendous emotional and physical stress bring about weight loss and aging; in fact, the author hardly recognizes a photo of her former self: "No reconozco a esa mujer, en cuatro semanas el dolor me ha transformado" (*Paula* 27). At first, exhaustion and insomnia induce her to take sedatives in order to sleep:

> Los peores presagios me asaltan de noche, cuando siento pasar las horas una a una hasta que empiezan los ruidos del amanecer mucho antes del primer atisbo de luz y recién entonces me duermo tan profundamente como si hubiera muerto. . . . Las primeras semanas tomaba unas pastillas azules, otro de los muchos remedios misteriosos que mi madre receta a su criterio y extrae generosamente de una gran bolsa, donde acumula medicamentos desde tiempos inmemoriales. . . . Las píldoras azules me sumían en un sopor confuso, despertaba con los ojos cruzados, y tardaba media mañana en adquirir cierta lucidez. Después descubrí en una callejuela cercana, una farmacia del tamaño de un armario atendida por una boticaria larga y seca, toda vestida de negro y abotonada hasta la barbilla, a quien le conté mis pesares. Me vendió valeriana en un frasco de vidrio oscuro y ahora sueño siempre lo mismo, con pocas variaciones. Sueño que soy tú, Paula. . . . (*Paula* 140)

She later stops taking sleeping pills and makes up her mind to do without antidepressants: "También la doctora Forrester me recetó algo para la depresión, guardo el frasco cerrado en la cesta de las cartas de mi madre, escondido junto con las píldoras para dormir, porque he decidido no aliviarme con drogas; éste es un camino que debo recorrer sangrando" (*Paula* 324). Allende's husband, attorney William Gordon, becomes alarmed at her deteriorating health and preoccupation with her daughter: "'Estás obsesionada, sólo hablas de ella, no puedes pensar en nada más, vas rodando por un abismo con tanto impulso que no puedes detenerte. No me dejas ayudarte, no quieres oírme. . . . Debes poner algo de distancia emocional entre ustedes dos o te volverás loca. Si tú te enfermas ¿quién se hará cargo de tu hija?'" (*Paula* 176).

Previous experience in the management of adversity often enables individuals to develop creative strategies to respond to anticipated loss (Nighswonger 274). In fact, Kübler-Ross even compares a terminal patient to a teacher from whom much can be learned about the nature of death and dying (xi). Similarly, Allende views the ordeal as a life lesson with Paula as the teacher: "Se me ocurre que tu enfermedad es una prueba, como las que tuvo que soportar aquel infeliz [Job]. Es mucha soberbia de mi parte imaginar que yaces en esta cama para que nosotros, los que aguardamos en el corredor de los pasos perdidos, aprendamos algunas lecciones, pero la verdad es que así lo creo a ratos. ¿Qué quieres enseñarnos, Paula?" (*Paula* 85-86). According to the writer, suffering may be a source of aesthetic inspiration (Álvarez-Rubio 1064). In fact, Allende's entire career as a writer may be traced to her practice of writing personal letters. In 1967, editor Delia Vergara happened to read part of a letter Allende had written to her mother and asked her to contribute to the Chilean women's magazine, *Paula*. Subsequently, her grandfather's approaching death motivated her to write a letter, which became her first novel, *La casa de los espíritus* (1982). It is only natural for Allende to record her impressions in writing, and this book is simply one in a series of her psychotherapeutic exercises.

Resolution of grief continues long after the death of a loved one (Kübler-Ross 158). The process is especially lengthy and intense for a bereaved mother who simultaneously endeavors to retain the memory of her dead child and disengage herself. Recovery includes sharing her story with others, as Barbara D. Schatz explains:

It is vital to the health and healing of a bereaved mother that she be allowed to repeatedly tell her story. . . . [Her] story will include her unique relationship with her child, the meaning she attributed to that child's life, the circumstances surrounding the death of the child, a description of the child, anecdotes about the child, and the details of her emotional struggles as she learns to live without her child. The healing of a bereaved mother's grief is dependent upon the willingness . . . to listen as the "story" of a bereaved mother unfolds. (304-05, 313)

Like Allende, other women, such as author Anne Morrow Lindbergh, have found solace in writing after the death of a child (McCracken and Semel).

After working through the previously-described stages, a bereaved individual comes to accept loss. Gradual adjustment to eventual separation leads to the realization that death is an intrinsic part of life (Kübler-Ross 125). This task is more easily accomplished if some meaning can be derived from the experience (Nighswonger 274). Acceptance implies the recognition that bereaved parents will live the rest of their lives without the child (Schatz 313). Successful recovery from mourning involves the withdrawal of emotional energy and reinvestment in another relationship (Rando 47).

Paula's slow decline allowed Allende to accede by degrees to her daughter's death. She and Ernesto improvised a ceremony of farewell, "un breve rito de adiós" (*Paula* 322). Yet Paula's death was embedded in the larger circle of life. In the very same room several months earlier Allende's granddaughter Andrea had been born to her son Nicolás and his wife Celia; the following year her third grandchild was delivered in the same place: "Paula's dying and my grandchildren growing up are tied together in an organic way. . . . I finally understood what life is about" (qtd. in Hornblower). Allende recalls holding Paula both at the moment of her birth and death (Cheever 36); she welcomed her into the world and witnessed her parting: "Then one day, you are holding your daughter because she's dying. You hold her, and you hug her, you spend the day and the night with her, and she dies, very peacefully, and you realize that you have not died, that you are there. And the fear is gone, the fear of pain, and the fear of death" (qtd. in interview with Baldock and Bernstein). Allende discovered that the moment of death is, as described by Kübler-Ross, "neither frightening nor painful, but a peaceful cessation of the functioning of the body" (246). One moment Paula is alive; the next she's gone: "Adiós, Paula, mujer. Bienvenida, Paula, espíritu" (*Paula* 366). Personal salvation and spiritual resurrection are often mentioned by Allende as the impetus of her writing: "In the process of writing the anecdotes of the past, and recalling the emotions and pains of my fate, and telling part of the history of my country, I found that life became more comprehensible and the world more tolerable. I felt that my roots had been recovered and that during that patient exercise of daily writing I had also recovered my own soul" ("Writing As an Act of Hope" 43).

To heal the wound left by the loss of that part of herself embodied in her daughter, Allende inadvertently undertook the therapeutic activity of writing about her bereavement. Her creative talent empowered her to resolve her own individual grief and achieve a greater sense of inner strength and confidence; at the same time, her work transcends private sorrow (Bess and Bartlett 317-18; Schatz 314). By sharing her story, Allende both speaks "for those who have no voice and for those who are kept in silence[,] [f]or my children and my future grandchildren" (in other words, Paula) and also capitalizes on her ambition to produce enduring literature (Allende, "Writing As an Act of Hope" 51, 62). In one fell swoop she fulfilled a fortune-teller's prophecy that Paula would one day become famous as well as earned a level of critical respect that her previous writing never elicited (*Paula* 186). In a sense, *Paula* immortalizes them both (Correas Zapata 141; Dulfano 4).

As Allende underwent the five stages of grief, she plunged into a new writing project which became the book *Paula*. Though at first glance the title may seem incongruous, the author's role as a bereaved parent attempting to detach herself from her offspring explains her compulsion to reclaim her own past. The writing process served as her means of coping with personal tragedy and loss: "The book helped me to go through mourning and survive. Word by word, and tear after tear, I retraced every step of that horrible year. And by doing so, I retraced every step of my life. And I was able to put everything together in these pages in such a way that I could then see a light at the end of a very dark tunnel. [. . .] And while it was painful, it was also joyful because I was [. . .] I was [. . .] walking. I was not stuck, paralyzed in the pain. I was walking through the pain" (Rodden 447). As Danish author Isak Dinesen once said, "All sorrows can be borne if you put them into a story or tell a story about them" (qtd. in Ruta). In fact, Allende's story-telling not only promoted the mourning process but also renewed her faith in life. Paula's death thus marks both a personal as well as a liter-ary renaissance for Isabel Allende.

In a supreme act of displacement through aesthetic creation, Isabel Allende's *Paula* both helped the author overcome personal tragedy and secured her position in the Spanish American Post-Boom. Her blend-ing of multiple generic discourses and traditions—such as family ro-mance, soap opera, melodrama, history, (auto)biography, elegy, con-fession, testimonial, etc.—and especially the incorporation of "popular" elements into "higher" forms of fiction typify Post-Boom writing (Frenk 67, 83; Lindsay 135-139, 145; Meyer 364; Moody 39, 42; Perricone 42; Marcos and Méndez-Faith 291; Shaw 71). Moreover, Allende's engagement with such familiar narratives and psychological processes contributes to the Post-Boom reader-friendliness of her work and consequently to her phenomenal commercial success (Frenk 83; Shaw 72). Her representation of strong female characters, such as Paula and herself, lends her work a sense of gender empowerment, which along with her buoyant optimism, mark the Post-Boom genera-tion. Faced with the incomprehensibility of her daughter's impending death, Allende turned to writing to regain a sense of order and in the hope that reality can be understood after all (Shaw 58, 59, 71-72).

Works Cited

Allende, Isabel. "El canto de todos." *Evaluación de la literatura femenina de Latinoamérica*, Siglo XX: *Il Simposio Internacional de Literatura*. Vol. 1. Ed. Juana Alcira Arancibia. San José: Editorial Universitaria Centroamericana, 1985. 271-77.

_____. "Conversando con Isabel Allende." *Critical Approaches to Isabel Allende's Novels*. Eds. Sonia Riquelme Rojas and Edna Aguirre Rehbein. New York: Lang, 1991. 191-97.

_____. Interview. With Bob Baldock and Dennis Bernstein. *Mother Jones* 19 (1994): 21-22+.

_____. *Paula*. Barcelona: Plaza & Janés, 1994.

_____. "Writing As an Act of Hope." *Paths of Resistance: The Art and Craft of the Political Novel*. Ed. William Zinsser. Boston: Houghton Mifflin, 1989. 39-63, 156-57.

Álvarez-Rubio, Pilar. "Una conversación con Isabel Allende." *Revista Iberoamericana* 60 (1994): 1063-71.

Axthelm, Peter M. *The Modern Confessional Novel*. New Haven and London: Yale UP, 1967.

Bess, Joseph, and Gene E. Bartlett. "Creative Grief." Kutscher 317-18.

Blank, H. Robert. "Mourning." Kutscher 204-06.

Cheever, Susan. "Portrait: Isabel Allende. The Author's Own House of the Spirits in Northern California." *Architectural Digest* 52 (1994): 32, 36, 38-39.

Clayton, Paula J. "Evidences of Normal Grief." Kutscher 168-73.

Correas Zapata, Celia. *Isabel Allende: Vida y espíritus*. Barcelona: Plaza & Janés, 1998.

Cortínez, Verónica. "Paula: Memorias en silencio." *Antípodas: Journal of Hispanic Studies of the University of Auckland and La Trobe University* 6-7 (1994-95): 63-75.

Dulfano, Isabel. "Autobiography and Fiction: Isabel Allende in/and *Paula*." Fifth Annual Conference on Ibero-American Culture and Society: Latin American Women Writers—Discourse on/of the Feminine. University of New Mexico, Albuquerque. 9 Feb. 1996.

Ferré, Rosario. "La cocina de la escritura." *La sartén por el mango: Encuentro de escritoras latinoamericanas*. Ed. Patricia Elena González and Eliana Ortega. Río Piedras, Puerto Rico: Ediciones Huracán, 1984. 137-54.

Frenk, Susan. "The Wandering Text: Situating the Narratives of Isabel Allende."

Latin American Women's Writing: Feminist Readings in Theory and Crisis. Ed. Anny Brooksbank Jones and Catherine Davies. Oxford: Clarendon, 1996. 66-84.

Freud, Sigmund. "Mourning and Melancholia." *The Standard Edition of the Complete Psychological Works of Sigmund Freud.* Ed. James Strachey. Vol. 14. London: Hogarth, 1964. 237-60.

Hornblower, Margot. "Grief and Rebirth." Rev. of *Paula,* by Isabel Allende. *Time* 10 July 1995: 65.

Knight, James A., and Frederic Herter. "Anticipatory Grief." Kutscher 196-201.

Kübler-Ross, Elisabeth. *On Death and Dying.* New York: Macmillan, 1969.

Kutscher, Austin H., ed. *Death and Bereavement.* Springfield, IL: Thomas, 1969.

Laurila, Marketta. "Isabel Allende and the Discourse of Exile." *International Women's Writing: New Landscapes of Identity.* Ed. Anne E. Brown and Marjanne E. Goozé. Westport, CT: Greenwood, 1995. 177-86.

Lindsay, Claire. "Re-reading the Romance: Genre and Gender in Isabel Allende's 'Niña perversa.'" *Romance Studies* 19 (2001): 135-47.

McCracken, Anne, and Mary Semel, eds. *A Broken Heart Still Beats: After Your Child Dies.* Center City, MD: Hazelden Information & Educational Services, 2000.

Marcos, Juan Manuel, and Teresa Méndez-Faith. "Multiplicidad, dialéctica y reconciliación del discurso en *La casa de los espíritus.*" *Evaluación de la literatura femenina de Latinoamérica,* Siglo XX: *Il Simposio Internacional de Literatura.* Vol. 1. Ed. Juana Alcira Arancibia. San José: Editorial Universitaria Centroamericana. 1985. 287-98.

Meyer, Doris. "'Parenting the Text': Female Creativity and Dialogic Relationships in Isabel Allende's *La casa de los espíritus.*" *Hispania* 73.2 (1990): 360-65.

Moody, Michael. "Isabel Allende and the Testimonial Novel." *Confluencia: Revista Hispánica de Cultura y Literatura* 2 (1986): 39-43.

Nighswonger, Carl A. "The Vectors and Vital Signs in Grief Synchronization." Schoenberg 267-75.

Perricone, Catherine R. "Genre and Metarealism in Allende's *Paula.*" *Hispania* 81.1 (1998): 42-49.

Porter, Laurence M. "Autobiography Versus Confessional Novel: Gide's *L'immoraliste* and *Si le grain ne meurt.*" *Symposium* 30 (1976): 144-59.

Rando, Therese A. "Parental Bereavement: An Exception to the General Conceptualizations of Mourning." Rando 45-58.

_____, ed. *Parental Loss of a Child.* Champaign, IL: Research Press, 1986.

Rees, W. Dewi. "Bereavement." Kutscher 207-09.

Rodden, John, ed. *Conversations with Isabel Allende.* Austin: U of Texas P, 1999.

Ruta, Suzanne. Rev. of *Paula,* by Isabel Allende. *The New York Times Book Review* 21 May 1995: 11.

Schatz, Barbara D. "Grief of Mothers." Rando 303-14.

Schoenberg, Bernard, et al. *Anticipatory Grief.* New York: Columbia UP, 1974.

Shaw, Donald L. *The Post-Boom in Spanish American Fiction.* Albany: SUNY P, 1998.

The Metaphysics of Mother/Daughter Renewal in *La casa de los espíritus* and *Paula*_____

Cherie Meacham

> Until a strong line of life, confirmation, and example stretches from mother to daughter, from woman to woman across the generations, women will still be wandering in the wilderness.
>
> —Adrienne Rich 246

The quality of mother/daughter bonding has been the subject of considerable comment on Allende's first novel. Doris Meyer writes about *La casa de los espíritus*: "Allende creates a feminocentric novel that—in the tradition of the self-conscious text—represents through discourse two empowering and transforming female experiences associated with renewal: giving birth and being born" (300). While Meyer focusses on the dialogic quality of the female voice that is empowered through generational solidarity, Mary Gómez Parnam emphasizes the socializing function of matrilineage in the novel, which privileges the maternal role as nurturer, protector and teacher. For Susan Lucas Dobrian, the genealogy of women presented in *La casa* offers a historically specific account of female experience that negates the reductive and repetitive stereotypes of women within androcentric myth. For Pamela Moore, however, a mythical pattern of cycles governs the lives of the Trueba women and is capable of initiating a new ethical, or "religious" order: "Allende's women are moral representatives. Their domestic, magical, and political feats are accomplished in the name of a more maternal, nurturing world" (97). Expanding upon Moore's conjoining of myth, maternity and morality, this study takes a broadly comparative view of the reciprocal renewal achieved by mothers and daughters in *La casa de los espíritus* and Allende's recent autobiographical work, *Paula*. Within these two texts, the over-arching presence of pre-Christian imagery, particularly the Greek myth of Demeter and Persephone, is explored in the context of its ancient metaphysical promise as well the psychosocial dimensions outlined in contemporary feminist inquiry.

One recent critical study, *The Mother/Daughter Plot* by Marianne Hirsch, categorizes fiction by North American and European women according to their portrayal of mother/daughter relationships. The category that might best be used to describe Allende's work is the "feminist family romance" of the late seventies and early eighties. Basing her analysis largely upon the theories of female development offered by Nancy Chodorow and Adrienne Rich, Hirsch describes the period as characterized by a quest for a new "psychic geography of feminist consciousness" pursued through a "passionate embrace of female allegiance as the basis both of female plotting and of female subject formation" (129).

With an emphasis on the pre-Oedipal or pre-paternal stage of development, feminist family romances share a series of characteristics that seem applicable to the two texts in question. Initially, they are embedded in a historical context of the cataclysmic failure of patriarchal culture—the apocalyptic threat of war and nuclear holocaust in North America, which was paralleled by the terrorism of right wing dictatorial regimes in Latin America. Viewing female experience as marginalized from power structures, Hirsch contends that women writers offer "a fantasy of cultural survival through the dissemination of traditional feminine values into the public world" (135). Within such a paradigm, female presence is associated with plenitude rather than lack, the male is relegated to secondary status in the family, and adult personality is viewed as embedded in relationship and empathy rather than autonomy and domination.

A significant element of this transformational agenda is spirituality. In "The Metaphysics of Matrilinearism in Women's Autobiography," Stephanie Demetrakopoulos describes the crucial role played by maternal relationships as women attempt to reestablish the "sacrality of feminine experience." Demetrakopoulos claims that "Women derive a sense of feminine godhead from their biological connections with one another" (181). She believes the myth of Demeter and Persephone best inscribes this experience with its story of the initial idyllic dyad of mother and daughter, a disturbing male incursion that separates them, the consequential searching and mourning of the mother for the daughter, and the final joyous reunion of the two signifying human victory over adversity. Demetrakopoulos quotes Carl Jung to emphasize the metaphysical dimension of the myth, which "gives the individual a place and a meaning in the life of the generations, so that all unnecessary obstacles are cleared out of the way of the life-stream that is to flow through her" (181). This study will seek points of commonality and difference in the use of the myth in *La casa de los espíritus* and *Paula*.

Allende creates the space for her construction of a resistant spirituality by immediately displacing Catholic dogma in *La casa de los espíritus*. Here, the reader is introduced to its central character, Clara del Valle, as a child publicly challenging the authority of the Catholic Church. Clara's small voice announces clearly the disaffiliation with Christian practice that Allende expresses throughout her work: "— ¡Pst! ¡Padre Restrepo! Si el cuento del infierno fuera pura mentira, nos chingamos todos" (*Casa* 14). Father Restrepo's response is to denounce and excommunicate Clara as a witch, which definitively divorces her from the influence of the patriarchal theology he espouses.

In its stead, Allende introduces an alternative image of female divinity associated with nature through the presence of Clara's sister, Rosa la Bella. Many of Rosa's characteristics disassociate her from Christian tradition. Allende depicts her as "la criatura más hermosa que había nacido en la tierra desde los tiempos del pecado original" (*Casa* 12). Rosa also seems distractedly absent and oblivious to the concerns of most mortals. Her apparent self-containment coincides with Esther Harding's description of an ancient and pre-Christian concept of virginity: "The (young woman's) right to dispose of her own person until she marries is part of the primitive concept of liberty." Harding continues, "She is not related to any god as wife or 'counterpart' but is her own mistress, virgin, one-in-herself" (103-5). Possessing a similar virginal autonomy, Rosa resembles Persephone, the maiden, before her rape by Hades and her descent to the underworld.

Although Rosa remains the maiden, a series of aquatic images signal her capacity to become the Great Mother, creatrix and source of life. Rosa is closely identified with nature and fertility through the peculiar greenish tinge of her hair (Boschetto 527). Her slow movements and silent character manifest a "gracia marítima" that resembles the movement of "un habitante del agua" (*Casa* 12). In his analysis of the Great Mother archetype, Erich Neumann associates water imagery with the "primordial womb of life, from which innumerable myths of life are born" (47). Esther Harding concurs that goddesses were regarded by the ancients as "guardians of the waters, rivers, brooks, and streams, . . . probably because they so aptly symbolize that invisible hidden power of 'bringing forth from within,' which is the peculiar characteristic of feminine creation" (111). Rosa's potential for creating an Edenic world is expressed artistically in the exuberant tapestry she weaves. However, long before the maiden's identity merges with that of the mother, Rosa dies as the innocent victim of an assassination attempt directed at her father. This unremediable patriarchal incursion is parodied in the grotesque image of the autopsy that despoils her virginal womb. Rosa remains an abstract motif of truncated feminine creativity whose presence foreshadows the travails of the women who follow her. The shock of observing Rosa's autopsy through a kitchen window forces Clara into a silence that further disconnects her from all influences outside the intimate circle of her family and doting mother.

Unlike most of the goddesses of the Greek pantheon, "Persephone is the maiden who has a mother" (Downing 38). The myth describes her childhood as idyllic in the perfect union of the mother-daughter dyad. Contemporary feminists like Adrienne Rich underline the power and resilience that is implicit in the maternal bond: "The cathexis between mother and daughter—essential, distorted, misused—is the great unwritten story. Probably there is nothing in human nature more resonant with charges than the flow of energy between two biologically alike bodies, one of whom has lain in amniotic bliss inside the other, one of which has labored to give birth to the other" (225-26). Allende's descriptions of Clara's joyful childhood spent at her mother's side reflects this unique intimacy:

> La relación con su madre era alegre e íntima, y Nívea, a pesar de haber tenido quince hijos, la trataba como si fuera la única, estableciendo un vínculo tan fuerte, que se prolongó en las generaciones posteriores como una tradición familiar. (*Casa* 78)

At nineteen, Clara breaks her silence to announce her decision to marry Esteban Trueba, Rosa's bereaved suitor. As she enters the realm of male experience, Clara defies traditional acculturation to the roles of wife and mother within Hispanic society, described by Julia de Foor Jay as an apprenticeship for servitude and submission to husbands and sons (95). Clara insulates herself from menial household tasks by inhabiting a self-enclosed world of magical spirits and sensuous fantasy. A series of water images connect Clara with her mythical sister Rosa and a forgotten world of feminine power. Sensual pleasure is associated with water in descriptions of Clara's distracted intimacy with Esteban, described as sailing a ship "en el agua mansa de la seda azul" and the baths lovingly administered by her sister-in-law, Férula (*Casa* 113). Water is also associated with her potential for creation through the fluids of birth and lactation that create and sustain the lives of her three children. In a circle of maternal fluids, Clara maintains contact with her own mother, which she extends to a "jouissance" of experience derived from her own body and its connection with yet another generation. A parody of mother/daughter reunion is played out when Clara retrieves her mother's severed head, which, like a benevolent Medusa, witnesses the natural birth of Clara's healthy twins, Jaime and Nicolás.

Like Persephone, who returns from marriage without having completely lost the innocence of her maidenhood, Clara maintains a "virginal" authenticity and self-containment throughout her life. Christine Downing has observed that "being mother does not, after all, have to mean not being the maiden." She continues, "Persephone and Demeter are distinguished in the myth and the rite, but precisely in order to insist on their unity." The union of the two females transcends the "either/or" of bipolar thinking by demonstrating that "one can be experienced and innocent, turned toward other and in-oneself" (41). Clara's power through all of life's stages depends upon her refusal to be corrupted or made cynical by the vicissitudes of experience.

Clara's unwillingness to abandon sensual pleasure in her role of wife and mother is continued and expanded in the experience of her daughter, Blanca. Repeating the "green world" imagery identified with her aunt Rosa, Blanca spends her summers enjoying the freedom of nature on the family estate. Like other defiant heroines, she becomes "part of it and its eternal rhythms" (Pratt 19). As an adult, Blanca takes Clara's example of private resistance one step further; she challenges the power of the patriarchal father in her love affair with Pedro García, the son of a laborer. Ironically underscored by the virginal purity associated with her name, Blanca removes her clothing to walk bathed in the moonlight to frenzied encounters with Pedro in a grove of trees by the side of the river. The presence of the moon, long identified with feminine divinity, the water, darkness and the unbridled passion of the lovers informs the scenes with a pagan sensibility. The episode reflects the orgiastic dimension of ancient female rituals that "provided an outlet for women to celebrate their eroticism, power, pride and joy" (Pratt 173).

By conjoining female sexuality with pre-Christian images of spirituality, Allende aligns herself with other post-colonial writers who posit with Catholic dogma a primary role in shaping an oppressive ideology of mothering. Julia de Foor Jay, in depicting the long shadow that the Catholic Church exerts over the bodies and psyches of women, quotes Yvonne Yarbro-Bejarano: "Catholicism in its institutionalized form . . . inculcates in women the need to sublimate the body and its desires" (100-101). Linda Feyder concurs stating, "It is a faith that has placed taboos on female sexuality making the Hispanic woman ashamed of her own body" (107). Kimberly Joyce Pollock compares the unrealistic standards imposed by the virgin birth story with the deformation of female circumcision: "The only 'good' mother is the one who has suffered the pain of childbirth, yet has not experienced the joys of sexual satisfaction. 'Good' women do not experience pleasure; they only suffer and sacrifice their children for the glory of God" (49). For these feminists, and for Allende, the linkage of sexuality and religion in an ideology that distorts female development mandates a similar linkage in any strategy that strives towards full liberation.

By such standards, Blanca's transgression against this patriarchal order is threefold: she exercises a woman's right to erotic expression, she gives away her own virginity and decreases her value as a commodity of patriarchal exchange, and she defies class boundaries by loving the son of a peasant family. Having raised Blanca to be true to herself rather than conform to societal expectations, Clara sides with the daughter against the enraged father. The gravity of the triple challenge is underscored by Esteban's singular act of violence against his beloved wife; he inflicts a powerful blow that knocks out her front teeth, profiling a pattern in which female rebellion is met with violent and unavoidable retribution.

The incident returns Clara to a world of silence and again puts into motion the mythical structure that governs the seasons in the Eleusinian mysteries. Repeating Persephone's abduction to the underworld by Hades, Esteban forces Blanca into a loveless marriage. Clara becomes disoriented and distracted, mourning the separation like Demeter who weepingly searches the earth for her lost child. A Chilean metaphor for Hades' underworld is constructed through Blanca's semi-conscious state in the oppressive heat of the Atacama desert, the omnipresence of ancient Incan artifacts, and her husband's bizarre fascination with Incan mummies. Like Persephone, Blanca eventually escapes the hellish place to be rejoined with her mother for the birth of her daughter, Alba. As Pamela Moore comments: "If the women's lives are circular, it is because they are the foundation of new life" (99).

Myth merges with history in the final scenes of the novel, which contain a thinly disguised portrayal of the terrorism of the Pinochet dictatorship (Earle 547). Paralleling accounts given by thousands of women who harbored or simply were acquainted with dissidents (Bunster-Burroto), Alba is arrested by the dictatorial regime. She quite literally enters the hell-like underworld of military terrorism; she is brutally interrogated, raped, tortured, and thrown into solitary confinement in a small tomb-like box. As Alba approaches the limits of her endurance, she finds salvation not in God but in communion with other women. Clara's spiritual intervention defeats death with her insistence that Alba record the details of the ordeal in her mind so that others could know the truth. Reciprocally, Alba will use her grandmother's diaries to bring Clara to life in the memory of the readers. Alba's identity merges with that of her foremothers' not only in the text of the novel but also in her approaching role as a mother. The love she experiences for the unborn child, probably a product of her incarceration, demonstrates that her spirit has survived the physical ordeal. She has resisted the temptation to hate and thus become the image of her tormentors. Adrienne Rich comments on the relevancy of Demeter and Persephone's transformation for women of all eras:

> Each daughter, even in the millennia before Christ, must have longed for a mother whose love for her and whose power were so great as to undo rape and bring her back from death. And every mother must have longed for the power of Demeter, the efficacy of her anger, the reconciliation with lost self. (240)

Although Alba is able to use the violence committed against her as an agent for self-renewal and affirmation, the sacrificial element of the story remains. Not in historic reality, in the novel, nor in the myth, do women have the power to abolish the horrors of the underworld. Their experience manifests a view of life that is cyclically related to death, "with a valuing of the alternating rhythms and waxing and waning, growth and decay, waking and sleeping, activity and receptivity, extroversion and introversion" (Downing 16). With Alba's mitigated victory, Allende elevates the figure of a vulnerable young women to the status of the tragic hero who carries the dignity, the burden, and the hope of humanity.

A close similarity in thematic and structural patterns connects Allende's first novel with her recent autobiographical work, *Paula*. Rather than targeting a political and historical context, the resistant power of the mother-daughter dyad in *Paula* functions as a strategy to complete a more personal and existential quest. The emphasis of the narrative changes from daughter to mother as Demeter's ancient sorrow and struggle to recover Persephone from the dark underworld is echoed in Allende's account of the bittersweet year spent by the side of her unconscious daughter. Allende's personal tragedy parallels that of las madres de la Plaza de Mayo and thousands of other Latin American women whose cruel historical moment was marked by the loss of sons and daughters in the civil strife that swept the continent in the seventies and eighties. In lecturing on the topic and within the text itself, Allende acknowledges the frequency with which mothers lose children to the conditions of poverty and injustice in all parts of the world.

On one hand, the image of the "mater dolorosa" unites women across lines of race, class, and ethnicity and historical period. However, the shift in voice to the seldom-heard perspective of the mother contradicts essentialist images of maternity. Marianne Hirsch contends that such a voice transgresses psychoanalytical views by presenting the mother as subject and not mere object of infantile desire, as artistically creative rather than biologically passive, and as possessing the capacity for fantasies that transcend or contradict the needs of children. Hirsch, who has found feminism and maternalism at times to be mutually exclusive, claims, "Until feminists can find ways to speak as mothers, feminism as a social and intellectual movement will be unable to account for important experiential differences among women" (196). In *Paula*, the myth of Demeter and Persephone serves as a point of departure for a story of maternal foibles and desires that never enter the idealized realm of Clara, "clarividente."

Reflecting the intensity and persistence of Clara's bond with both Nívea and then Blanca, Allende immediately privileges the mother/daughter relationship in *Paula*. She describes an intimacy that transcends generations and reduces males to a peripheral role by referring to her mother as "es el amor más largo de mi vida." Allende continues, "comenzó el día de mi gestación y dura medio siglo, además es el único realmente incondicional, ni los hijos ni los más ardientes enamorados aman así" (*Paula* 60). Similarly, as Paula's mother, Allende claims that "ese tiempo que estuviste dentro de mí fue de felicidad perfecta, no he vuelto a sentirme tan bien acompañada" (*Paula* 132). After years of adulthood and separation, the circle is tragically closed again by illness: "Has regresado al lugar de la inocencia total, has vuelto a las aguas de mi vientre, como el pez que eras antes de nacer" (*Paula* 44). Through the comings and goings of other loved ones, Isabel is the most constant attendant at her daughter's side. She is the fiercest defendant of Paula's dignity and comfort and is the last one to give up hope for her recovery. Finally, Paula dies where she entered the world, in the arms of her mother.

Beyond this physical proximity, Isabel fights to maintain an intense emotional connection with her unconscious daughter through her literary imagination. On the written page she converses with Paula long after her daughter is incapable of verbal communication. Through this text, the author will always have access to the most specific details of the final precious months with Paula. Most importantly, within the text Paula's short life has a place on the continuum of four generations of women. Allende's descriptions of her daughter provide an image of womanhood developed to the fullness of intellectual, emotional and spiritual potential that is the culmination, not the severing, of mother/daughter ties.

Rather than an explicitly violent political system, the male agent that disrupts mother/daughter unity appears implicitly in the abstract presence of the medical/science complex, which repeatedly makes grave errors in the treatment of Paula's porphyria. Allende admits that such incompetence probably caused her daughter's death ("imaginar cómo habría sido si hubieras caído en mejores manos, si no te hubieran aturdido con drogas . . ." ([*Paula* 30]). Allende also criticizes the sterile and dehumanizing conditions within that system, which deals with patients as biological specimens rather than complex human beings. Paula's specialist is described as "distraído y apurado," "más interesado en hilvanar las estadísticas de su computadora y las fórmulas de su laboratorio que en tu cuerpo crucificado sobre esta cama" (*Paula* 16). As Paula falls more deeply into the dark underworld of unconsciousness, Isabel fights to hold her close within a cyclical pattern of mother/daughter solidarity that is capable of transcending even the most extreme conditions of separation.

Echoing Clara's open challenge to Padre Restrepo, Allende begins to distance herself from formal religion in the early pages of her "letter" by quoting one of Paula's last statements: "Ando buscando a Dios y se me escapa, mamá" (*Paula* 27). While Allende never openly challenges her daughter's religious beliefs, the juxtaposition of Paula's tragic circumstances with the generosity, innocence and good works of her short life precludes the possibility of divine justice. As though having been abandoned by God, Paula descends into the darkness with only her mother as guide and protector: "las dos cruzamos un misterioso umbral y entramos a la zona más oscura" (*Paula* 29).

Allende further undermines claims of Christian salvation with a series of descriptions that document her disillusion with formal religion. She states in the early pages of the text: "Tu abuela ruega por ti a su dios cristiano y yo lo hago a veces a una diosa pagana y sonriente que derrama bienes, una diosa que no sabe de castigos, sino de perdones" (*Paula* 87). She confesses, "Dios te mira a los ojos y dice tu nombre, así te escoge, pero a mí me apuntó con el dedo para llenarme de dudas"

(*Paula* 93). With comical anecdotes, like one in which her veil myste-riously falls off during her first communion, as well as more serious discussions of sin and ritual, Allende describes the pervasive influence of the church in her life "como una piedra de molino" (*Paula* 129). The substituting metaphysical structure—the periodic waning and waxing pattern of female relationships—appears in the epic structure of *La casa de los espíritus* as a major transforming event in each generation. In *Paula*, more personally and psychologically oriented, the pattern re-peats itself often within the experience of each individual. Like Clara, Isabel's grandmother La Memé transcends death by communicating spiritually with family members in times of need. Her hand mirror, which passes first to Isabel and later to Paula, symbolizes the merging identities of women over generations. Isabel's relationship with her own mother demonstrates a similar pattern. The arrival of Tío Ramón initially removes the children from their mother's bed and later ex-pands that separation with the frequent and prolonged trips required by his position in the diplomatic core. Allende expresses initial distress over these separations but eventually finds ways to transcend them through daily correspondences and phone conversations. Later, her mother willingly disrupts her life with Ramón to return to her daugh-ter's side in vigil over Paula, first in Madrid and then in California.

The same pattern becomes visible in the narration of the year Isabel spends at Paula's bedside. Paralleling the seasons of Demeter's quest, mother and daughter are separated in the winter when Paula initially loses consciousness. In midwinter, Paula nearly dies but seems to be pulled back by the joint wills of her mother and grandmother, "en silencio invocamos a los dioses conocidos y por conocer y a los espíritus benéficos de nuestros antepasados y las fuerzas más formidables de la vida" (*Paula* 107). Moving toward spring, Allende feels Paula is re-turning to her when she is able to breathe without the respirator and is transferred out of intensive care. In the regular ward, Isabel herself takes over much of her daughter's daily care.

The second part of the story embarks where hope for recovery ends.

Again increasing distance is implied when Allende ceases writing in the direct and intimate "tú" form and begins writing about Paula in the third person, "Ya no escribo para que cuando mi hija se despierte no esté perdida, porque no despertará." She then quotes the inescapable reality of the specialist's diagnosis: "Paula tiene daño severo, no hay nada que hacer, su mente está destruída" (*Paula* 227). Yet the almost superhuman efforts of the mother again rescue the daughter when, disregarding all medical advice, Isabel makes the hazardous journey from Madrid to San Francisco to install Paula in a clinic near her home and family. As the two arrive, Isabel comments on the incomparable beauty of the spring day (*Paula* 239).

While a similar plot structure certainly connects *Paula*, *La casa de los espíritus* and the myth, the three also share thematic considerations that revise traditional images of mothering. One central theme deals with the correlation between maternity and creative expression, as evidenced in *La casa de los espíritus* by Rosa's tapestry, Clara's writing, Blanca's sculpture, Alba's drawings and the creation of the text itself. Commenting on "Writing and Motherhood," Susan Suleiman describes two central and contradictory views on the topic to be "opposition and integration, motherhood as an obstacle or source of conflict and motherhood as source of connection to work and world" (362). Exploring the latter argument, she quotes Julia Kristeva, who believes that motherhood, in and of itself, can favor artistic creation "to the extent that it lifts fixations, makes passions circulate between life and death, self and other, culture and nature" (366).

Allende clearly posits her literary efforts between her mother and her daughter in *Paula*. Like Clara, Allende attributes her first exposure to storytelling and family histories to the bedtime tales told by her mother, "nos contaba anécdotas de sus antepasados y cuentos fantásticos salpicados de humor negro, nos hablaba de un mundo imaginario donde todos éramos felices" (*Paula* 42). Her mother encourages her first efforts to write by giving her "un cuaderno para anotar la vida" (*Paula* 67). Early and regular separations between Isabel and her mother initiate a daily letter writing habit, "el registro de nuestras vidas" (*Paula* 101). Her mother becomes her primary editor and prompts her to publish her first novel. Allende even describes her completed project with maternal imagery: "esa pila de hojas amarradas con una cinta era para mí como un hijo recién nacido" (*Paula* 304).

Life and art merge as Allende begins the long and complex biographical and autobiographical narrative of her family as an effort to guide Paula back to life (*Paula* 11). Yet her daughter's prolonged illness also gives the author the time and incentive to seek to order and design in her own life, which initially appears to be "una sola imagen ininteligible" (*Paula* 31). Allende commits herself to exposing honestly the most intimate details of her life as a unique gift to Paula, stating, "Hasta ahora no he compartido mi pasado, es mi último jardín, allí donde ni el amante más intruso se ha asomado" (*Paula* 32). Later she notes the transformation the project has brought about in her: "ya no soy la misma mujer, mi hija me ha dado la oportunidad de mirar dentro de mí y descubrir esos espacios interiores, vacíos, oscuros y extrañamente apacibles, donde nunca antes había explorado" (*Paula* 300). As in *La casa*, the act of writing also takes on the spiritual dimensions of personal redemption, which is a significant element of the myth: "Me vuelco en estas páginas en un intento irracional de vencer mí terror, se me ocurre que si doy forma a esta devastación podré ayudarte y ayudarme, el meticuloso ejercicio de la escritura puede ser nuestra salvación" (*Paula* 17).

Although love between men and women is not the central issue in these works, it is a prominent and necessary one that establishes the parameters of mothering and self expression. While not a violent incursion, romantic love does serve a disrupting function in *Paula*. Its entrance is often abrupt and stubborn; at times it betrays the women, and other times it provides them with the necessary assistance to survive in a sexist world. Maintaining mother/daughter solidarity as constant, Allende demonstrates the changing dynamics of romantic love to be an unstable product of the historical era. She challenges machistic tradition with the content of these generational accounts, which serve to reveal a movement toward greater authenticity and reciprocity in male-female relationships.

Since Allende admits that her grandmother, la Memé, inspired her creation of Clara Trueba (*Paula* 37), it is not surprising that the portrayals of their marriages are similar. While no physical conflict appears in the biographical narrative, Allende observes, "Creo que vivían en mundos irreconciliables y se amaron en encuentros fugaces con una ternura dolorosa y una pasión secreta" (*Paula* 37). Allende's grandfather, El Tata, lived by a standard of strength and self-denial that was required by the demands of a more unruly time and his status as landowner. He does become more flexible as he houses his daughter and watches her struggle to support her family. According to Isabel, he eventually accepts her arguments in defense of women's rights. In *Paula*, El Tata is a benevolent patriarch who dutifully loves and protects his family from the injustices of the very system he himself represents.

Isabel's mother, who originally is as naive as she is beautiful, enters into marriage with a charming scoundrel who abandons her and her three small children in Peru. When she falls in love again, she totally defies convention by choosing to live with a married man who is one of the ugliest men her daughter had ever seen (*Paula* 59). The partnership that Isabel's mother strikes with Tío Ramón provides a model of deep commitment and a stable family environment that had been absent from the previous church-sanctioned marriage.

Allende's own difficulties with romantic love are related to the same social and religious pressures that are targeted in *La casa de los espíritus*. Like her mother and grandmother, Isabel is denied access to information about sexuality when she is growing up. She characterizes her English schooling as puritanical, "que exaltaba el trabajo y no admitía las necesidades básicas del cuerpo ni los relámpagos de la imaginación" (83). She laments the repression and frustration that characterized her long courtship with her first husband, described as a double bind of standards that first denies the existence of a woman's sexual desires and also threatens condemnation for her loss of chastity or an unwanted pregnancy. Allende concludes, "A pesar de mi rebeldía, el temor de las consecuencias me paralizaba" (*Paula* 117).

Isabel contrasts her own repression with the sexual freedom exhibited by her daughter, who insists upon having access to birth control pills at the age of sixteen. It is significant that Paula obtains her psychological specialty in sexual therapy, precisely the area of development that was most taboo and unobtainable to the women in generations before her. Although providing comic relief when they appear in the chagrined mother's bag at a customs desk, the paraphernalia of sexual pleasure used by Paula in her work in no way impinge on her virtue. Like Blanca in *La casa de los espíritus*, Paula represents a fully developed image of female personhood in which innocence and purity coexist with sexuality. Allende's views seem to parallel those of the authors of *The Mother Daughter Revolution*, for whom sensual expression is seen as intrinsic to "our (very) capacity to live and feel fully . . . the touchstone for every aspect of our lives both in our relationships and our work" (Debold 207).

Rather than attempting to restrain Paula, Allende accepts the generational change and uses the information for her own growth. Perhaps emboldened by her daughter's example, Allende challenges the cultural stereotype of mature women and mothers as asexual by exploring her own sexual potential in middle age. Her experience demonstrates the reciprocal growth and renewal that is present in the ancient myth and is observed by contemporary feminists: "A young daughter's knowledge and love can help a mother to remember and find the wellspring of her own resistance, which is essential for courageous change" (Debold 94).

In an episode related to the theme of sexuality, Allende describes an incident that occurs during her first marriage. It is a curious confessional that makes no excuses and states no regrets. With her life uprooted by self-exile to Venezuela, her children entering adolescence and her youth fading, she succumbs to the need for physical and emotional intimacy in an affair with an Argentine musician. Tortured in the conflict this creates between her own needs and those of her family, she deserts her husband and children to live for a while with her lover in Madrid. She eventually returns, but remains curiously "furiosa sin saber por qué" (*Paula* 284). She later describes the extent of her pain over the episode: "Esa relación frustrada fue una herida abierta durante más de dos años; estuve literalmente enferma de amor, pero no lo supo nadie" (289). Marianne Hirsch views such a split loyalty to self and others as a common theme in maternal narratives: "A mother cannot articulate anger *as a mother*; to do so she must step out of a culturally circumscribed role which commands mothers to be caring and nurturing to others, even at the expense of themselves" (170).

The account has a central position in the narrative and is fraught with tension. From the perspective of the mother, it explicitly signifies unrecognized pain and sacrifice; from the perspective of the daughter, the reader imagines what could have been a sense of abandonment and resentment. These two positions imply a conversation that will never take place and hangs like unfinished business to interrupt the idealized portrayal of mother-daughter solidarity.

Having established her alienation from social and religious conventions, Allende turns to her own experience as a woman and a mother to find guidance and strength in final stages of her vigil over Paula. She summarizes the impact of generational solidarity among the women in her family: "Pienso en mi bisabuela, en mi abuela clarividente, en mi madre, en ti y en mi nieta que nacerá en mayo, una firme cadena femenina que se remonta hasta la primera mujer, la madre universal. Debo movilizar esas fuerzas nutritivas para tu salvación" (*Paula* 87). During the most difficult moments of Paula's decline, Isabel is rejuvenated by the birth of her granddaughter. Her attendance to her dying daughter is thus offset with the contact and care of new and promising life.

According to scholars, the most significant part of the Demeter/Persephone legend is Demeter's gift of the ceremonies at Eleusis. For two thousand years, those rites were practiced as the most sacred of all rituals by men and women who believed that "those who partake of the rite have fairer hopes concerning the end of life" (Harrison 51-52). Adrienne Rich quotes the Roman Cicero on the profound significance of the Mysteries: "We have been given a reason not only to live in joy but also to die with better hope." For Rich, the myth offers a female-centered alternative to the Father God:

> The role played by the Mysteries of Eleusis in ancient spirituality has been compared to that of the passion and resurrection of Christ. But in the resurrection celebrated by the Mysteries, it is the mother whose wrath catalyzes the miracle, a daughter who rises from the underworld. (239)

As spring moves to summer and summer to fall, Isabel slowly makes her peace with what she now perceives to be her daughter's imminent death. Yet, as Paula's physical state deteriorates, Isabel feels that her spiritual presence intensifies. She moves Paula into a room in her home and tenderly provides for her daily care. One night she has the vivid sensation that Paula enters her dreams and speaks clearly of her needs. This intimacy climaxes when Isabel reads the letter that Paula had written long before her illness: "No quiero permanecer atrapada en mi cuerpo. Liberada de él podré acompañar de más cerca a los que amo" (*Paula* 355). Isabel writes, "El invierno ha vuelto, no deja de llover, hacer frío y día a día tú decaes" (*Paula* 356). She now returns to the direct and intimate form of "tú" to finish the narration.

Approaching the final stage of Paula's descent, Allende experiences a profound catharsis in which she, for the first time, fully abandons herself to Demeter's ritual of maternal mourning. Again, water imagery connects individuals to the transcending mystery of natural maternal forces. Alone in the mountains, her tears merge with the rain of a torrential downpour. Rosa's identification with the earth goddess associated with green nature and water is repeated as Isabel covers her body with wet mud and cries out, "Tierra, acoge a mi hija, recíbela, envuélvela, diosa madre tierra, ayúdenos" (*Paula* 358). She thus commits their fate to the cycles of nature inscribed in Demeter's story with its timeless pattern of winter and spring, life and death, solitude and intimacy, loss and renewal. These polarities, which remain diametrically opposed in patriarchal thought, are intricately intertwined in the daughter's journey to sustain a dialectic of hope and transformation for those who remain.

Just as Isabel feels the presence of her own grandmother La Memé as a spiritual guide in times of difficulty, so does the spiritual presence of la Granny and Tía Abuela preside over the scene of Paula's death. As Allende closes the memoir with the words, "Adiós, Paula, mujer. Bienvenida, Paula, espíritu" (*Paula* 366), she echoes views of those who, like Christine Downing, see in Persephone's descent into the underworld not an end, but a new journey of acceptance, discovery and transformation through a realm of the souls. Paula's death occurs ironically during the Christmas season, sacred time for the birth of hope in the Christian world.

In *La casa de los espíritus* and *Paula* readers are taken outside 2,000 years of Western and Christian ideology through the cyclical structure of union, painful separation and joyful reunion of mothers and daughters modeled in the female-centered myth of Demeter and Persephone. In offering a pattern of ritualized mourning that also evokes renewal on many levels, Allende's portrayal of mother/daughter relationships in these two works counterpoints a legacy of betrayal in which mothers socialize daughters into subservience and self-denial. In a broad sense, Allende reflects Latin America's past and recent history in centering motherhood as the most crucial element in shaping its future. As she states in *Paula*, "Lo imperdonable es que son las madres quienes se encargan de perpetuar y reforzar el sistema, criando hijos arrogantes e hijas serviciales; si se pusieran de acuerdo para hacerlo de otro modo podrían terminar con el machismo en una generación" (157).

Some readers might reject reference to the biological image of the maternal body as an essentialist concession to patriarchy's imprisonment of women within the gendered maternal role. It is important to emphasize that the existence of such a model need not imply that it is the only one nor that it should be imposed oppressively on all women. However, like other post-colonial writers, Allende's use of the myth of Demeter and Persephone emphasizes the mother-daughter relationship as a particular target of patriarchal assault, "for dividing mother from daughter severs woman from herself" (Lee Yongue 75). Rather than capitulating to patriarchal ideology and abandoning this core experience that binds many women, Allende works to liberate the maternal, to creatively revitalize its associated imagery and to restore the powerful mystery that it once transported to the personal, social, historical and metaphysical reality of women. Having established the soothing rhythms of mother/daughter solidarity in the fictional world of *La casa de los espíritus*, Allende demonstrates in *Paula* its efficacy in helping women to survive one of life's most dreaded adversities, the death of a child.

From *Hispanófila*, no. 131 (January 2001): 93-108. Copyright © 2001 by the University of North Carolina. Reprinted with permission of the University of North Carolina.

Works Cited

Allende, Isabel. *La casa de los espíritus*. Mexico: Edivisión, 1987. References to the novel within the text are made with the abbreviation "Casa."
_____. *Paula*. Mexico: Plaza y Janés, 1994.
Boschetto, Sandra M. "Dialéctica metatextual y sexual en *La casa de los espíritus* de Isabel Allende." *Hispania* September 1989: 526-32.
Brown-Guillory, Elizabeth, ed. *Women of Color: Mother-Daughter Relationships in 20th Century Literature*. Austin: U of Texas P, 1996.
Bunster-Burroto, Ximena. "Surviving Beyond Fear: Women and Torture in Latin America." *Women and Change in Latin America*. Ed. June Nash and Helen Safa. Massachusetts: Bergin and Garvey, 1986. 297-325.
De Foor Jay, Julia. "(Re)claiming the Race of the Mother." Brown-Guillory 95-116.
Debold, Elizabeth, Marie Wilson, and Idelisse Malave, eds. *Mother Daughter Revolution: From Good Girls to Great Women*. New York: Bantam Books, 1994.
Demetrakopoulos, Stephanie E. "The Metaphysics of Matrilinearism in Woman's Autobiography." *Women's Autobiography: Essays in Criticism*. Ed. Estelle C. Jelinek. Bloomington: Indiana UP, 1980. 180-205.

Downing, Christine. *The Goddess: Mythological Images of the Feminine.* New York: Crossword, 1989.

Earle, Peter G. "Literature as Survival: Allende's *The House of the Spirits.*" *Contemporary Literature* 1987: 543-554.

Feyder, Linda, ed. Introduction. *Shattering the Myth: Plays by Hispanic Women.* Houston: Arte Público, 1992. 5-8.

Gómez Parnam, Mary. "Isabel Allende's *La casa de los espíritus* and the Literature of Matrilineage." *Discurso* Fall 1988: 193-201.

Harding, Esther. *Women's Mysteries Ancient and Modern: A Psychological Interpretation of the Feminine Principle as Portrayed in Myth, Story and Dreams.* New York: Harper Colophon Books, 1971.

Harrison, Jane Ellison. *The Religion of Ancient Greece.* London: Archibald Constable & Co. Ltd., 1905.

Hirsch, Marianne. *The Mother/Daughter Plot: Narrative, Psychoanalysis, Feminism.* Bloomington: Indiana UP, 1989.

Lee Yongue, Patricia. "My Mother Is Here: Buchi Emecheta's Love Child." Brown-Guillory 74-94.

Lucas Dobrian, Susan. "El mito y la magia femenina en *La casa de los espíritus.*" *Hispanic Journal* Fall 1991: 305-325.

Meyer, Doris. "Parenting the Text: Female Creativity and Dialogic Relationships in Isabel Allende's *La casa de los espíritus.*" *Hispania* May 1990: 360-365.

Moore, Pamela L. "Testing the Terms: 'Woman' in *The House of the Spirits* and *One Hundred Years of Solitude.*" *The Comparatist* May 1994: 90-100.

Neumann, Erich. *The Great Mother: An Analysis of the Archetype.* Trans. Ralph Manheim. Bollingen Series XLV. Princeton: Princeton UP. 2nd ed. 1963.

Pollock, Kimberly Joyce. "A Continuum of Pain." Brown-Guillory 38-55.

Pratt, Annis. *Archetypal Patterns in Women's Fiction.* Bloomington: Indiana UP, 1981.

Rich, Adrienne. *Of Woman Born: Motherhood as an Experience and an Institution.* New York: W. W. Norton, 1976.

Suleiman, Susan Rubin. "Writing and Motherhood" *The (M)other Tongue: Essays in Feminist Psychoanalytic Interpretation.* Eds. Shirley Nelson Garner, Claire Kahone, Madelon Sprengnether. Ithaca: Cornell UP, 1985. 352-57.

Isabel Allende, Fortune's Daughter_____

John Rodden

Since the death of her twenty-seven-year-old daughter, Paula Frías, in December 1992, Isabel Allende has frequently stated that she is a "changed" woman. Evidently, the struggle to save Paula—who suddenly fell ill in 1991, slipped into a coma, and died twelve months later from a rare immune deficiency disease (porphyria)—deepened Allende.

My own interviews with Allende before and after Paula's death confirm this perception. I have found her a noticeably different woman— more reflective, less goal-directed, more self-revealing, less guarded— from the writer I knew when we taught together at the University of Virginia in the late 1980s. She also told me in a May 1995 interview that her grief over Paula's death was so paralyzing that she might never write again—at least, not fiction. She had just published *Paula*, her memoir about the agony of watching Paula die. Writing that book had not only led to Allende's spiritual transformation but altered her experience of writing. Suddenly it was far more enjoyable—and yet it seemed not to matter so much. Allende found herself savoring the activity of writing more and worrying less about the literary "product." As she told one interviewer:

> Before, I always wanted *to get things done*. Fast and well. I always wanted a finished book. I wanted to come to the end and to have something. Now I enjoy the process far more. I've discovered in a much deeper way the joys of writing itself. I've really learned to enjoy writing, which means to enjoy living and being present to it. . . . Rather than focus on the finished product, I'm enjoying each moment in the process. . . .
>
> Nothing will ever be more significant than this loss. And now I know: I could die tomorrow.

Nonetheless, the capacity to craft her writing into a readable product did return. In the last three years Allende has produced two books—a

---

lighthearted cookbook, *Aphrodite: A Memoir of the Senses* (1998), and a novel, *Daughter of Fortune* (1999), Allende's first work of fiction in eight years.

Allende's literary rebirth has coincided with—and is apparently indebted to—her mystical turn, which has resulted in her discovery of a new House of the Spirits. With that discovery have come existential "lessons" that Allende has drawn from the harrowing year of Paula's sickness and death: the words *destiny, trust, acceptance,* and *openness* come up again and again in her interviews after Paula's death. Indeed, the whole cast of her conversation has shifted to the spiritual realm. As she told one interviewer:

> Life is like a very short passage in the long journey of the soul. It is just an experience that we have to go through, because the body has to experience certain things that are important for the soul. But we shouldn't cling to life and the world so much: we shouldn't cling to the material aspects of the world, because you can't take them with you. You will lose them no matter what.

Since the mid-1990s Allende has repeatedly spoken of learning to "let go." As she put it in another interview: "When I said *dead*, [Paula's death] became real and I could deal with it."

Elsewhere Allende has spoken of another, more mundane death, or form of clinging, with which she still copes: literary ambition. "Ambition is like a bottomless pit," she says. After the publication of *The House of the Spirits*, she "had the sensation that I had done something in my life and I could now die in peace," but soon the hydra-headed monster returned to haunt her: "One becomes ambitious and wants more and more."

Asked in other interviews to sum up what she has learned as a result of Paula's death, Allende makes her spiritual discovery even more explicit:

Your approach to the world is different. . . . You become more detached. . . . You gain a sort of spiritual dimension that opens up completely your world.

I've asked myself countless times: Why her? Why her and not me? If I pray, maybe it will happen to me and not her—that's sometimes what I thought. I asked, Why didn't she die at the beginning? Why did she stay for a year in a coma?

It was tragic, but I learned a lot in that time. It would have been much easier if she hadn't had the coma. The pain was much greater because she stayed a year.

Because Paula stayed, I learned a lesson. My destiny was to lose a child. . . . I did all I could to save Paula, and I could not protect her from her condition and from the world. I believe we are not just body and mind. We are spiritual too. . . .

I'm less passionate now. . . . I've already changed a great deal. I'm letting things happen more, not forcing them. I'm not as goal-oriented as before. . . . I used to live a great deal in the future, with plans and dreams and goals. But I came to realize that life is now.

On another occasion Allende explained: "I finally understood what life is about; it is about losing everything. Losing the baby that becomes a child, the child who becomes an adult, like the trees lose their leaves. So every morning we must celebrate what we have."

Allende is speaking of learning a different kind of exile—a taking leave of the temporal world. And she now seems to be approaching the sense of peace and acceptance implied in a statement made to Eva Luna, the autobiographical TV journalist-heroine of the earlier works of Allende's fiction. As Eva is told just moments after the death of her mother, "Everyone dies, it's not so important."

For Allende, the death of Paula eventually became both all-important and "not so important." The contradiction is only apparent: it is a paradox resolved by surrender and acceptance. Allende closes *Paula* on a note of affirmation: "Godspeed, Paula, woman. Welcome, Paula, spirit." Paula Frías has merely gone to her spiritual home, joining those intrepid women who govern the Trueba mansion—or, even better, those beneficent ghosts that watch over them.

* * *

And yet: an emotional Armageddon still awaited Allende. Plunged in depression and rage during the mid- and late 1990s, she struggled through conflicts within both her family and herself. She was trying to cope with the overwhelming burden of two family tragedies: not only did she and her husband, William Gordon, have to face Paula's passing, but they also had to deal with the horrible death of Gordon's teenage daughter from a drug overdose. Their marriage—Allende had wed Gordon in 1988 and had permanently relocated to his home in San Rafael, California—was on rocky ground for a while; they entered therapy and slowly worked together to confront their demons.

By the time the Spanish edition of *Aphrodite* had come out, in November 1997, Allende no longer felt "stuck in the loss" of Paula. Although she had feared that she might never write again, the act of composing *Aphrodite*, as Allende explained during her U.S. book tour in the spring of 1998, helped her rediscover the capacity to live in the present. Allende had written her memoir of her daughter's death; now she would write a celebration of life, a "memoir of the senses."

Aphrodite is, Allende has said, her "healthy reaction to mourning and writer's block" that followed Paula's death. Her struggle to emerge from her "long tunnel" of grief is a prominent theme in *Aphrodite*: "After the death of my daughter, I spent three years trying to exorcise my sadness with futile rituals. Those years were three centuries filled with the sensation that the world had lost its color and that a universal greyness had spread inexorably over every surface. I cannot pinpoint the moment when I saw the first brush strokes of color, but when my dreams about food began, I knew that I was reaching the end of a long tunnel of mourning and finally coming out the other end, into the light, with a tremendous desire to eat and cuddle once again."

By her own account, Allende recovered her artistic powers and her feeling for the sensuality of language by immersing herself joyously in the world of amour and appetite. Revive the senses and the imagination, she counsels, and you will revive the spirit, too. So Allende affirmed life by relishing two of its earthiest desires—sex and food—and in a light, delicate, feminine, playfully poetic way. "When I wrote *Paula*, about her death, I cried every day," Allende discloses. "Now, when I was putting together *Aphrodite*, I finally laughed. A lot." *Aphrodite* connects Allende's love of writing to the primal drives that create and perpetuate life and make it pleasurable—and thereby reconnects the author to her deepest wellspring as a storyteller.

In literary terms, *Aphrodite* is virtually unclassifiable. Viewed biographically, however, this lavishly illustrated cookbook clearly served as an aphrodisiac for Allende's dormant literary powers. Here we witness the woman known to her fans as "the Chilean Scheherazade" assuming the persona of the Greek goddess of love and beauty. Indeed, the book is the author-grandmother's personal recipe for summoning the love goddess within, a self-help book on how to recover a keen taste for life's sweetness—and bittersweetness.

As in her earlier books, Allende credits her family—and her familial House of the Spirits—with helping her complete the new book (most of the recipes were developed by her mother, Panchita Llona). They have also, she insists, guided her through the "tunnel of mourning" into "the light": "I don't believe in ghosts. But I do believe in memory. When I say somebody's spirit helps me, I mean that when I need poetic inspiration, I think of my grandmother and the crazy character she was. When I need something to be from the heart, I think of Paula, who had such generosity. When I need courage, my grandfather, this stubborn Basque, carries me through. I have photographs of them, all over."

Memory, of course, is the memoirist's prize resource. It is significant that Allende's two books in the mid-1990s, *Paula* (1994) and *Aphrodite* (1997), were memoirs—indeed, that she chose to write another

work of nonfiction after *Paula*. Although Allende's memory had returned, aided by her family spirits, the imaginative powers through
which her novels emerged still had not. As she admitted to one interviewer, throughout the mid-1990s she simply could not write fiction:
"Fiction, for me, just happens. I let the story unfold itself. I don't think
of a plot, an outline, characters. I allow them to appear before me. After
Paula died, it just wouldn't come like that. So I did nonfiction: first I
wrote about her illness and her death. And now, this [*Aphrodite*]."

Allende has always maintained that, while her nonfiction—like her
journalism—is an act of will, her fiction arrives unbidden and on its
own schedule, a gift from beyond. The gift of fiction had been absent
from her life for a long time. Eventually, however, it returned. In October 1999, having entered "the light," Allende published her sixth
novel, *Daughter of Fortune*.

* * *

How Allende skillfully drew on her own fortunes—which were inextricably bound up with her daughter's fate—is one of the new
novel's fascinations for the informed reader. *Daughter of Fortune* represents an advanced stage in Allende's remarkable program of writing
as self-therapy. Allende looked forward to the new millennium and renewed her life by looking back to the nineteenth century and writing a
bildungsroman about a Victorian maiden—and also by looking back
on her own life: the novel's autobiographical resonances are manifold.
In fact, despite the obvious differences between the heroine's fortunes
and Allende's own, *Daughter of Fortune* is essentially another memoir, this time in the form of a historical romance that broadly reinvents Allende's youth. Certain parallels between Allende and Eliza
Sommers, her heroine, are quite explicit; in one interview Allende specifically compares her own upbringing and subservient feminine habits in her first marriage with those of Eliza, who lavishes her Chinese
paramour with attention:

My mother and I were the only females, along with the maidservants who were females and who were serving everybody else. That was the model I had—but I was extremely rebellious and I never accepted the situation. . . . I worked, I had several jobs, and I never used [my first husband's] name as a married woman. But I would serve him like a geisha. I would take his clothes every night, and hang them on a chair. If we were at a party, and there was a buffet, for example, I would serve his plate. Now I look back and I can't believe it—I would cut his nails and hair.

Allende also compares her empty despair and sexual numbness in the wake of Paula's illness with Eliza's identity crisis following her exile from Chile and her miscarriage:

Eliza has to run away from home and all her life changes. She loses her center completely, and I think there's an emotional and physical reaction to that—she closes down. And I felt that way when my daughter fell sick. The very moment that I saw her in intensive care I was menstruating then, and I went into menopause—I thought. It was very sudden and my body closed down and remained closed for three or four years until I forced myself to come back.

Daughter of Fortune may be read as the fictional counterpart to *Paula*, since they traverse the same physical space and a comparable social and emotional terrain. *Daughter of Fortune* is also a logical successor to Allende's novel *The Infinite Plan* (1991), also set in California; whereas the latter recasts the life history of her second husband, William Gordon, the former reimagines Allende's own life. One notable result is that dark-haired Eliza is a recognizable portrayal of Allende herself. A tempestuous, headstrong, adventuresome, upper-class, adopted girl, Eliza too emigrates from Chile to California as she follows the man she loves. In one interview Allende talks about her own exile experience in ways that illuminate and enrich our understanding both of Eliza's character and of Allende's empathy for the struggles of today's immigrant poor from Latin America:

> They come because they're desperate, so I feel their situation mirrors a little bit what I experienced when I went to Venezuela. Of course, I wasn't as poor as these people are, and I was more educated, but . . . I was running away from something. So I can relate to their situation.
>
> [But I relocated to the United States] because I fell in love. . . . I did not come in despair. I came because I wanted to be with a man. But I still had to adapt. I had to learn a new language, learn another way of life, and I also had very difficult stepchildren who were into drugs—a very messed-up family. . . . His daughter was a drug addict, and she died of an overdose.

The immigration motif in *Daughter of Fortune* lends the novel a gripping contemporary relevance: the book is a study in borderlands and border culture. Allende challenges her readers to ponder the complexities of temporal as well as geographic borders: the countless parallels between the lives of young Latinas in the nineteenth and twenty-first centuries. The novel's opening scenes are set in the Chilean port of Valparaíso in the 1840s. Eliza, a foundling, is taken in by an English clergyman and his spinster sister. She is brought up to be a proper, virtuous English lady, corseted and subjected to strict piano practice (with a rod in her back to keep it straight). Eliza's independent spirit chafes at the formalities and rigidness of British club life in Valparaíso, and she escapes whenever possible to share the warm, easygoing company of the superstitious Indian cook, who tells Eliza of the legends and traditions of Chilean culture.

At sixteen Eliza falls in love with Joaquín Andieta, a passionate intellectual from the Chilean working class. When California gold fever spreads to Chile, Eliza's lover emigrates, hoping to send back enough money to take care of his poverty-stricken mother—and leaving the pregnant girl behind. Going in search of Joaquín, she conceals herself in the hold of a ship, falls ill, loses her baby, and is saved by a Chinese healer, Tao Chi'en. In California, against the colorful Wild West backdrop of bandits, madams, and prostitutes, a second love story develops between Eliza and Tao Chi'en.

Rushing from one dramatic scene to the next, heedless of improbabilities, *Daughter of Fortune* is a high-spirited romp in the picaresque tradition beloved of Spanish writers from Cervantes to Pérez Galdós. Unashamedly, indeed insouciantly and effusively, Allende trots out all the stereotypical conventions of popular romances and Golden Age dramas: the foundling Eliza discovers that she is really the illegitimate daughter of the clergyman's sea captain brother; the clergyman's sister hides her scandalous affair with a married man years earlier; the crossdressing Eliza conceals her female identity during her manhunt for Joaquín, even touring with an acting company and playing a male stage role; she is befriended by a bighearted peasant woman and by tarts with hearts of gold; and it all leads to a Dickensian happy-end marriage to the good doctor who saved her life and has patiently awaited her.

And in good Victorian tradition, Allende does not shrink from investing her characters with names that are richly allusive and transparently symbolic: the heroine's name evokes both Bernard Shaw's rags-to-riches Eliza Doolittle and Jane Austen's prim Esther Summerson, and the Chinese healer's name implies balanced energy and dynamic serenity, making him a perfect foil to the impetuous revolutionary Joaquín.

Allende also packs her epic with the social history of the tumultuous decade from 1843 to 1853: British expatriate life "in the colonies," Mapuche Indian customs in midcentury Chile, the American immigrant experience and the California gold rush of 1849, Tao Chi'en's youth in Hong Kong in the aftermath of the Opium Wars, and much more. Sometimes the novel's historical allusions are quite specific; for instance, Joaquín Andieta is obviously the Chilean freedom fighter Joaquín Murieta, who roamed the California valleys and staged Robin Hood-style robberies.

Reviewers on both sides of the Atlantic greeted *Daughter of For-*

tune as evidence that Allende's fictional powers had fully returned. "One of the great writers of our time," *Hispanic* hailed her. "A rich adventure story set against the emergence of the American nation," trumpeted Great Britain's *New Statesman*. "It may well be her best novel yet."

By January 2000 *Daughter of Fortune* had climbed the best-seller lists of most European as well as North and Latin American nations. But the "gold rush fever" for the novel was still to come. On 17 February it was named the March selection for Oprah's Book Club. Oprah Winfrey's vast TV audience began snapping up the novel, which shot to the top of the Amazon.com bookseller list within eight hours and rose that week to the number-one position on the *New York Times* best-seller list. (Allende's Web site, www.isabelAllende.com, received more than half a million hits on the day of Oprah's announcement.) More than a million copies of the American edition alone sold during February and March.

On 28 March, Allende appeared on the Oprah Winfrey Show and discussed *Daughter of Fortune*. At Oprah's traditional televised dinner with fans of her club's author of the month—the four guest fans of Allende were a North Carolina graduate student, a Panamanian housewife, an a cappella singer, and a young businesswoman and mother of three—she shared what she had "learned in the course of losing Paula" and the rituals through which she "remembers her daughter's spirit every day." A few weeks later, when asked to comment on the record-breaking sales of her novel, Allende replied in two words: "Thank Oprah."

* * *

In truth, as Allende well knew, she had her faith in herself—and in her family and in destiny—to thank chiefly for her phenomenal literary and publishing triumph. Just as Eliza Sommers reinvents herself numerous times and creates a new life for herself in the San Francisco

Bay Area, so too has Allende. Like Eliza, she is a "daughter of fortune," blessed with the courage to grow through her crises. Author and heroine each possess the strength of what Allende describes—referring both to the mystery of sex and to Eliza's wonder at the adventure of life—as "an honest desire to decipher enigmas." What she once said of Eva Luna aptly sums up the latest phase of her own life quest: "Eliza Sommers, soy yo."

In a strange way, Allende—long known as the embodiment of Eva Luna—is her own newest heroine, too. In the aftermath of Paula's death, Allende, like Eliza during her own journey to California, has lost her goal-directed focus yet not her spirit or impetus. One recalls Tao Chi'en's words to Eliza: "You don't go anywhere in life, Eliza, you just keep walking."

So what might be the next milestone in Allende's passionate pilgrimage? "I want to make a few changes," she has told one interviewer. "I want more privacy. More silence. I have been doing too much out in the world." But Allende vows to keep writing. Indeed, her creative rebirth and newly reconstructed House of the Spirits continue to flourish: she is reportedly already more than halfway through her seventh novel.

From *Hopscotch: A Cultural Review* 2, no. 4 (2001): 32-39. Copyright © 2001 by Duke University Press. All rights reserved. Used by permission of the publisher.

La hija de la fortuna:
Cross-Dressing, Travel,
and Gendering the Self_____

Nadia Avendaño

The search for identity oftentimes has been linked to the act of travel because it necessarily brings about change. Travelers may find their sense of self sharpened by the journey. Although travel writers, to some degree, construct their own persona, the process of travel constructs them in return. It is for this reason that travel literature currently enjoys a position of privilege among contemporary literary critics as it has proven to be a rich vehicle for the exploration of cultural and individual identity. The travel may take the form of quest narrative, initiatic journey or Bildungsroman, picaresque encounters, spiritual search or self-actualization, or any number of other configurations of the "journey" structure.

Despite the change in historical circumstances from one epoch to another, men have generally been associated with adventurous movement and women with domestic stasis. In recent decades, literary critics have begun to look at female travel narratives as rich sources for the exploration of female identity. According to Marilyn C. Wesley in her introduction to *Secret Journeys: The Trope of Women's Travel in American Literature*, the trope of women's travel in fiction and non-fiction functions as a structure for the expression of difference. Wesley posits that the female journey narrative is an innovative and dynamic response to the tension between "imposed ideological stasis and gendered freedom" (xiv). Karen Lawrence maintains that "the trope of travel . . . provides a particularly fertile imaginative field for narrative representations of women's historical and personal agency" (20). According to Susan Carvalho, travel by women may thus be studied as a specific motif or sub-genre of women's writing. The act of travel itself implies female agency and self-determination "in those texts where the woman articulates her own journey rather than serving as accompaniment to the male traveler" (28). It is for this reason that women's narratives of travel are such rich sources for explorations of identity and representation.

The following pages will analyze the exploration of gender and identity in Isabel Allende's *La hija de la fortuna* (1999). In this novel, the representation of the woman traveler is a central and subversive attribute and serves as a metaphor of female agency. Through the narrative enactment of the journey, I will examine how the protagonist deconstructs and reconstructs the conventional female self, thus achieving a more self-constructed identity. This text displays a postmodern sensibility where identity is a performance which is fluid, not fixed. In traveling through spaces, the protagonist travels through identity. In Allende's novel the protagonist travels to California in the midnineteenth century to avenge her honor and must live for several years dressed as a man. I will show how the protagonist's act of traveling and cross-dressing serves as tools for the exploration of identity.

Isabel Allende's novel *La hija de la fortuna* (1999) falls under the general category of travel literature, a genre that has proven to be a rich vehicle for the exploration of cultural and individual identity, and therefore favored among contemporary literary critics. In this text, the protagonist undergoes a series of adventures or experiences that trace a path of character development and questions and rewrites prescribed conventions of gender. This travel narrative concentrates on deconstructing female stereotypes through the creation of a disorderly female protagonist who questions the patriarchal conventions. It is a tale about the crossing and transgressing of boundaries, in every sense—boundaries of gender, sexuality, class, and physical space. Allende creates a protagonist that deconstructs the notion of the woman as stagnant and bound to the home. The protagonist transgresses society's norms and its imposed expectations in search of the space in which to create her own destiny.

Allende's novel, set from 1843 through 1853, is about Eliza Sommers, the adopted child of a socially elite British family in Valparaíso, Chile. Eliza falls in love with Joaquín Andieta, who deserts her in hopes of finding instant wealth and status in the California gold rush.

The sixteen year old, discovering she is pregnant, decides to recover her lost honor and travel to California where she must dress in men's clothing. Throughout the novel, Eliza embarks on an emotional, psychological, and physical journey, which shapes her development and results in self-discovery and self-realization and at the same time transgresses society's norms and its imposed expectations.

Eliza's impetus for travel is due to the lack of options afforded to women. Eliza knows what future awaits a single pregnant woman:

> "Estaba atrapada y apenas empezara a notarse su condición, no habría esperanza ni perdón para ella. Nadie podría entender su falta; no había manera alguna de recuperar la honra perdida." (149)

There is a defiance of patriarchy implied by Eliza's act of traveling. Eliza now leaves the traditionally configured private, enclosed, domestic female space and enters the public, open, male-controlled space definitively and with the understanding that she will not be able to return to Chile. Marilyn Wesley points out that the woman traveler challenges the historical notion of male movement versus female anchoring. Wesley continues on to say that the woman traveler refuses society's conventions of a woman's place in the world and thus becomes a "transgressor" of these conventions (xviii). By traveling, Eliza is the deviser of her own destiny. She is rebelling against patriarchal norms and acting on her own terms.

Allende wishes to shed light on the difficulty a woman encounters in overcoming restrictive nineteenth century Chilean norms and her need to break away from this enclosed space. Marcelo Coddou reiterates this idea:

> Eliza . . . emprende sus viajes iniciáticos que la conducirán al final encuentro de sí misma, conseguido gracias al abandono y alejamiento del hogar, espacio-claustro que le habría significado una muy probable sumisión a restrictas normativas de vida. (37-38)

Her journey towards the construction of self is a success because the growth experiences generated by the journey help her achieve self-confidence, independence, and allow her to achieve a self-constructed identity, from "la hija de nadie" to "la hija de la fortuna."

Because women traveling alone in the nineteenth century is a rare occurrence (with the exception of prostitutes) Eliza is forced to dress as a man. At the end of the pivotal chapter appropriately titled "Despe-dida," the narrator comments on Eliza's rebirth, as she removes her re-strictive nineteenth-century female clothing and trades them for loose men's clothing on the night of her departure to California:

> A medida que sus atuendos de niña inglesa se amontonaban en el suelo, iba perdiendo uno a uno los contactos con la realidad conocida y entrando inexorablemente en la extraña ilusión que sería su vida en los próximos años. Tuvo claramente la sensación de empezar otra historia en la que ella era protagonista y narradora a la vez. (168)

As Eliza sheds her traditional upper-class female garments she is con-scious that she is entering a new phase of her life, one in which she is the subject and the creator. Eliza will map out her life from this mo-ment forward, and in the process arrive at greater self-discovery and self-definition tracing a road to freedom. Eliza crosses over gender, race, and national boundaries by dressing like a Chinese boy then later like a Chilean boy, changing her name to Elias. Her male disguise lends her social agency because it acts as a mask or a shield that she can hide behind thus allowing her the freedom to move about undisturbed. This experience proves crucial because it provides her a life unencumbered by the social codes and constraints a woman endures (Martínez 56). It is interesting to note that by dressing as a male, Eliza takes the first step in her journey towards self-discovery.

Eliza's cross-dressing allows the novel to explore multiple ques-tions of the female construction of gender. It supports Judith Butler's theory that gender is a cultural and social construction and therefore performative (xv). It also underscores Simone de Beauvoir's theory that woman is not an essential or universal category that depends on a biological state but rather it is learned through culture. Allende deconstructs and subverts essentialist definitions of both female and male identity and opens up new spaces and new possibilities for the construction of self.

Eliza discovers that dressing like a male allows her a freedom never before experienced as a woman, that of invisibility, which affords her the luxury of looking for Joaquín Andieta without harassment: "la ropa de hombre le daba una libertad desconocida, nunca se había sentido tan invisible" (241). Researchers have documented that the rarity of women in California during the early years of the gold rush created a heightened interest in the female sex (Gould Levine 139). Within this context, it is evident why Eliza is obligated to disguise her sex.[1] The narrator comments on Eliza's relative success at maintaining this invisibility in her travels: "No había afinado la puntería, pero sí su talento para volverse invisible. Podía entrar a los pueblos sin llamar la atención, mezclándose con los grupos de latinos, donde un muchacho con su aspecto pasaba desapercibido" (293).

Eliza, dressed as a male, finds freedom in not being the object of the masculine gaze or the object of masculine desire. Thus, women's appropriation of the male costume protects them from the ambivalent contradictory position women hold in a patriarchal society where they are invisible in terms of active autonomous subjects but visible in terms of objects of desire. As Carvalho explains: "They are at once doubly marked and erased: hypervisible as spectacles or as decoration, but invisible in terms of autonomy and power" (32). The crossing over into a male space provides women a unique opportunity to transcend economic, social, and sexual restrictions (André 80).

Eliza becomes aware of this contradictory situation as a woman and is able to escape this restrictive, confining cultural bind by binding her breasts and clothing herself as a male. Consequently, she is freed from the male gaze and acquires the power and autonomy to map out her own future without the cultural baggage and restrictions imposed on women, which make it virtually impossible for a woman in the nineteenth century to chart her own future. Among these restrictions are social norms, female codes of conduct mentioned previously, confining clothing, and danger of male violence.[2]

Eliza is not only freed socially by male clothing but she also expresses feeling naked in these new clothes in contrast to the figure-shaping (figure-distorting) female clothing of her adolescence. The traditional nineteenth-century clothing for women included:

> un corsé tieso mediante huesos ballena y tan apretado que no podía respirar a fondo ni levantar los brazos por encima de los hombros; tampoco podía vestirse sola ni doblarse porque se quebraban las ballenas y se le clavaban como agujas en el cuerpo. (34)

By shedding these female clothes, Eliza feels like she can breathe more deeply and she delights in the newfound liberation of her body through the loose-fitting, unrestrictive male clothing. The shedding of her clothes symbolizes the first step to the shedding of cultural baggage, everything that society imposes on women in order to subjugate them. The narrator states that: "Una vez que se repuso de la impresión de estar desnuda, pudo disfrutar de la brisa metiéndose por las mangas de la blusa y por los pantalones. Acostumbrada a la prisión de las enaguas, ahora respiraba a todo pulmón" (241). It is interesting that Eliza finds it natural to wear men's clothing because had she been discovered, it would be deemed "unnatural" to social codes of femininity. Allende wishes to destroy the definitions of what is natural and unnatural for women as well as criticize and condemn the restrictive, figure-distorting female clothes of the nineteenth century.

Eliza's costuming questions gender roles because it allows Eliza to realize the grave discomfort she experienced with her former clothes and thus question the need for restrictive female clothing. However, the male costume never requires Eliza to question her sexual identity.

Eliza is always certain of her sexual identity and never "feels" like a man. She never has, nor desires, a male consciousness. The narrator refers to the protagonist as Eliza and not Elias and is described with adjectives in the feminine. She is not a cross-dresser either because she does not derive erotic pleasure from dressing or passing as a man. Rather, she is what critic Chris Straayer calls a "temporary transvestite," one who adopts male clothing as a matter of circumstantial necessity or convenience (36).

In Allende's novel, the protagonist's male disguise serves not only as a vehicle for the questioning of gender roles but also as a vehicle of self-discovery. Though dressed as a man, Eliza remains a woman. As mentioned earlier, she never acquires a male consciousness. In fact, the temporary adoption of a masculine identity not only fails to hinder her quest for a unique female identity, but it facilitates her developmental process (Carvalho 34). According to Marjorie Garber, cross-dressing helps to define gender categories:

> Paradoxically, it is to transsexuals and transvestites that we need to look if we want to understand what gender categories mean. For transsexuals and transvestites are *more* concerned with maleness and femaleness than persons who are neither transvestite nor transsexual. They are emphatically not interested in 'unisex' or 'androgyny' as erotic styles, but rather in gender-marked and gender-coded identity structures. (110)[3]

Eliza's alter ego, Elias, magnifies and intensifies her consciousness of womanhood in terms of traditional personality characteristics because it is by pretending to be male that she becomes so acutely aware of her femaleness. For example, as Elias she becomes a cook and a piano player, she demonstrates maternal tenderness for the orphaned Tom sin Tribu, she finds solidarity and comfort in the company of women, and she writes and adorns the letters of passion and of farewell that illiterate frontiersmen send to their wives and families back home.

Though it seems as if Eliza falls into traditional gender roles, her situation is different because she chooses which traditional female roles she wishes to keep and which ones she wishes to discard. Thus her disguise allows her developmental process to progress naturally without society imposing their social norms of conduct on Eliza. That is to say that she does not have to perform according to her gender, rather, she is able to acquire a self-constructed identity and not a culturally imposed one. She recognizes that all gender roles rigorously enforced and codified stifle individual growth, and she chooses those that will further her growth and independence.

Through her male disguise, Eliza also learns the roles that men have to perform and comments to Tao Chi'en in a letter how tedious these gender constructions are: "En mi papel de hombre me cuido mucho de lo que digo. Ando con el ceño fruncido, para que me crean bien macho. Es un fastidio ser hombre, pero ser mujer es un fastidio peor" (298). Therefore, in the same way that travel can be a catalyst to self-development and self-discovery, the adoption of a male identity in this case is seen as an intermediary step for her journey towards self-discovery.

Along with discovering greater female consciousness as said earlier, Eliza discovers freedom and "se enamoró de la libertad" (296). This discovery results in the awareness of freedom as liberation from the social conventions, constraints, and fears that have held her captive all her life. She realizes that what hinders women from achieving self-autonomy and self-empowerment is fear. The narrator explains Eliza's realization as follows:

El miedo había sido su compañero: miedo a Dios y su impredecible justicia, a la autoridad, a sus padres adoptivos, a la enfermedad y la maledicencia, a lo desconocido y lo diferente, a salir de la protección de la casa y enfrentar los peligros de la calle; miedo de su propia fragilidad femenina, la deshonra y la verdad. La suya había sido una realidad almibarada, hecha de omisiones, silencios corteses, secretos bien guardados, orden y disciplina. (296)

This fear has been deeply socialized in Eliza from an early age and thus she has not been aware of its power over her until she is able to discover freedom by dressing as a man. This demonstrates that the manner in which women are socialized is directly linked to their submissive and passive qualities. It also shows how this fear is not inherent in females but rather socialized. Allende destroys social myths that attribute fear as an inherent quality in women. The author demonstrates that the first step to destroying these myths is to acknowledge their existence.

Dressed as a boy, freed from societal norms, Eliza is able to "grow up" by discovering freedom. This journey leads her to a feeling of empowerment never before experienced. This newly acquired sense of freedom culminates one morning when she feels for the first time happiness never before felt: "la invadió una dicha atávica jamás antes experimentada" (297). Eliza leaves Chile with the sole purpose to find Joaquín and become his slave for life but "ya no se sentía capaz de renunciar a esas alas nuevas que comenzaban a crecerle en los hombros" (296). Eliza not only crosses over boundaries and undermines conventions but she acquires the metaphoric wings that allow her to continue on her journey through life. When she became pregnant, Eliza had written in her journal that she was not deserving of happiness, however, in the last few months riding on horseback through California, "sintió que volaba como un condor" (297). The protagonist is happy to have found this freedom to move through space uninhibited and without the restrictions imposed upon women by society. Eliza is conscious of her gradual transformation from a submissive woman to a self-empowered one.

Along her journey, many established truths are destroyed, much to Eliza's surprise. For example, she had been socialized to believe that a woman could not survive without the protection of a man: "Sin un hombre que la proteja y la mantenga, una mujer está perdida, le había machacado Miss Rose, pero descubrió que no siempre era así" (302). Eliza discovers that there are jobs that a woman can do that are not valued in Chile but are appreciated in California. For example, she is able to set up her own business. "Ella organizó un negocio de *empanadas* para vender a precio de oro" (264). She was also hired to play the piano and she read and wrote letters for the illiterate. These abilities traditionally reserved for women, such as cooking, in Eliza's case do not signify submissiveness rather they offer her the possibility for survival, something that she utilizes for her own benefit. Allende redefines and validates these traditionally devalued tasks relegated to women.

Eliza's strength of character continues to be challenged throughout the novel. Her bravery is put to the test in many instances. Eliza is the only "man" who volunteers to amputate a man's fingers that have developed gangrene. Babalú is filled with admiration and respect towards Eliza/Elias, claiming, "Eres todo un hombre, Chilenito" (331). On another occasion, when a fire breaks out in her home, she risks her own life to save the boy inside. These heroic deeds demythify the established truths propagated by patriarchal society that women are the weaker sex and are incapable of surviving without a man (Guerra-Cunningham "Algunas reflexiones . . ." 35).

In open defiance of the restrictions that had structured her childhood and had determined her early youth, Eliza manages to adapt to the rough living conditions and constant danger experienced by the male adventurers involved in the Gold Rush. The more she is confronted with challenges, the more courageous she becomes: "le había perdido el miedo al miedo" (297). In one of her many letters to Tao Chi'en, Eliza explains her process of transformation:

> Estoy encontrando nuevas fuerzas en mí, que tal vez siempre tuve, pero no conocía porque hasta ahora no había necesitado ejercerlas . . . todos [los aventureros californianos] se sienten dueños de sus destinos, de la tierra que pisan, del futuro, de su propia irrevocable dignidad. Después de conocerlos no puedo volver a ser una señorita como Miss Rose pretendía. (297-98)

It is important to note that Eliza believes she may have always had the strength inside her but as a woman was never required to utilize or develop this quality. Allende wishes to suggest that women are taught to repress certain characteristics, such as strength of character, bravery, and courage. Because Eliza is given the opportunity to live as a man for a period of time, she is now capacitated to claim control of her own destiny and never wishes to return to the constricted and repressive life of a "lady." Eliza transgresses the realm of propriety for females by acting outside of the rules and by desiring completion and freedom for herself. This quote also underscores Eliza's growing understanding of what it is to be female.

In her letters to Tao Chi'en Eliza describes her emotional as well as psychological changes and her aspiration to retain the rights only men enjoyed, those of embracing the spirit of adventure and forging their own destiny.

> No sé en qué vuelta del camino se me perdió la persona que yo antes era, Tao. Ahora soy uno más de los incontables aventureros. . . . Son hombres orgullosos . . . que no se inclinan ante nadie porque están inventando la igualdad. Y yo quiero ser uno de ellos. (297)

Eliza makes the distinction of the person she used to be and the person she is now. She is conscious that she has reinvented herself and identifies herself as an adventurer. She wishes to become one of the many pioneers during the Gold Rush that enjoyed freedom.

Eliza writes her experiences, her thoughts, and the observations of her journey. This act of writing is seen as an ideal vehicle for the exploration of the constructed gender identity. It is seen as an aid to her process of assessment and growth. The text as exploration and expression is a recurrent motif throughout *Hija de la fortuna*, beginning with Eliza's simultaneous discovery of maps and books: "En el cuarto de los trastos, donde se acumulaban vejestorios, encontró mapas, libros de viajes y documentos de navegación de su tío John, que le sirvieron para

---

precisar los contornos del mundo" (54). The most significant texts within the novel are Eliza's diaries and her written correspondence with Tao Chi'en. Her letters to her friend are in a way another kind of diary because Eliza is never sure if Tao Chi'en receives the letters, and they are never answered. Consequently, they function more as articulation for her than as communication with him. Eliza is able to put her thoughts down on paper and delve into self-analysis. The act of writing in her diary begins as a way of remembering: "Eliza solo escribía para recordar" (122). It then shifts to a way of knowing, of processing and comprehending her own physical and spiritual journey: "Escribía incansable en su diario con la esperanza de que al hacerlo las imágenes adquirieran algún significado" (335).

As Eliza writes, both in her diary as well as in her letters, she constructs her own female identity. She writes not what she has learned but what she is in the process of experiencing and learning. These diary entries and letters to Tao Chi'en document her day-to-day process of self-development and self-awareness. These texts demonstrate work in progress, the discovery of uncharted social and spiritual territory, and the process of the journey. At the end of the novel, Eliza achieves her quest as she constructs her own identity, which subsequently leads her back to the repossession of her body and femininity when she finds it essential to cast off her masculine attire. However, it is important to note that she never again wears a corset.

Eliza's journey begins with her search for Joaquín, but ends with her discovery of self. She decides to remain with Tao Chi'en to help him rescue enslaved Chinese prostitutes. This choice is made only after she reaches a position of empowerment, after she has acquired agency and autonomy. She has constructed an identity for herself and at the end of the novel begins this new phase of her life with Tao Chi'en.

Eliza's evolving identity is mirrored by California's emerging identity, in its extraordinary variety, instability, fluidity, and potential explosiveness. In a letter to Tao, Eliza comments on her capacity to create her own identity: "para mí este pais es una hoja en blanco, aquí puedo escribir mi nueva vida, convertirme en quien desee, nadie me conoce salvo tú, nadie sabe mi pasado, puedo volver a nacer" (301). This statement supports the idea that Eliza's journey has been one of re-birth and has served as a catalyst for the construction of self. As Eliza states, this unsettled, unmarked country affords her the anonymity to rewrite herself into history, with a new female identity. Because it is a frontier, it is a place where traditional concepts of gender and class can be challenged and it functions well as a device for the exploration of categories, of class and race as well as gender, for it represents a society in formation, a natural crossroads where traditional distinctions are blurred and where all are seeking fortunes, carving out their own space and inventing new roles.

In conclusion, Eliza's journey allows her to discover new possibilities for her gender. Through her explorations, experiences, and adventures she transcends the traditional limitations of her assigned gender and creates alternative choices for the female subject. At the same time she demythifies traditional gender representations of women. Eliza transgresses social conduct codes by abandoning the secure private world of the home or convent and entering the unsafe, dangerous public world. Allende's protagonist constructs her identity at the same time that she realizes her own dreams and takes on her own projects, making her own decisions and building her own future. Eliza's insurgent conduct subverts female expectations of social conduct by breaking away from the status quo. This woman embodies the notions of contemporary feminism in a historical past represented in fiction. This narrative creates a female subject no longer measured by matrimony or motherhood, but by her strength in creating her own place of resistance where she can nurture her own needs and evolve according to her own rules.

Notes

1. During this time, the racial prejudice towards ethnic minorities had begun to escalate. (Almquist, Alan F. and Heizer Robert F. *The Other Californians: Prejudice and Discrimination Under Spain, Mexico, and the United States to 1920*. Berkeley: U of California P, 1971.) Because Eliza chooses a minority identity, as long as she is careful to immerse herself solely with other minority groups such as the Chinese and the Latino populations, she is able to travel unnoticed. For further studies that discuss the deep-seated racial prejudice inflicted on minorities during these times see: Daniels, Roger and Spencer C. Colin, Jr. *Racism in California: A Reader in the History of Oppression*. New York: Macmillan Company, 1972 and DeWitt, Howard A. *The Fragmented Dream: Multicultural California*. Iowa: Kendall/Hunt Publishing Company, 1996.

2. It should be added that the minority male figure also suffers from a contradictory position in that he is visible as a scapegoat, one to be persecuted and targeted by the dominant society, but invisible in terms of autonomy and power. In fact, throughout the novel, Allende comments on the overt discrimination minority groups had to endure.

3. Garber offers an in depth study on female transvestism. For female transvestism in Spain, see especially Bravo Villasante, Carmen. *La mujer vestida de hombre en el teatro español: siglos XVI-XVII*. Madrid: Sociedad General Española de Librería, 1976 and Melveena McKendrick. *Women and Society in the Spanish Drama of the Golden Age: A Study of the Mujer Varonil*. London: Cambridge UP, 1974.

Works Cited

Allende, Isabel. *La hija de la fortuna*. New York: Perennial, 1999.

André, Maria Claudia. "Breaking Through the Maze: Feminist Configurations of the Heroic Quest in Isabel Allende's *Daughter of Fortune* and *Portrait in Sepia*." *Latin American Literary Review* 30.60 (2002): 74-90.

Butler, Judith. *Gender Trouble*. New York: Routledge, 1999.

Carvalho, Susan. "Transgressions of Space and Gender in Allende's *Hija de la Fortuna*." *Letras Femeninas* 27.2 (2001): 24-41.

Coddou, Marcelo. *Isabel Allende: Hija de la fortuna: re diagramación fronteriza del saber histórico*. Valparaíso: U de Playa Ancha, 2001.

Garber, Marjorie. *Vested Interests: Cross-Dressing and Cultural Anxiety*. New York: HarperCollins, 1992.

Gould Levine, Linda. *Isabel Allende*. New York: Twayne Publishers, 2002.

Guerra-Cunningham, Lucía. "Algunas reflexiones teóricas sobre la novela femenina." *Hispamérica* 28 (1981): 29-39.

Lawrence, Karen R. *Penelope Voyages: Women and Travel in the British Literary Tradition*. Ithaca: Cornell UP, 1994.

Martínez, Z. Nelly. "Isabel Allende's Fictional World: Roads to Freedom." *Latin American Literary Review* 30.60 (2002): 51-73.

Straayer, Chris. "Redressing the 'Natural': The Temporary Transvestite Film." *Wide Angle* 14.1 (1992): 36-55.

Wesley, Marilyn C. *Secret Journeys: The Trope of Women's Travel in American Literature*. Albany: State U of New York P, 1999.

Self-Portrait in Sepia?
Isabel Allende's Technicolored Life _____
John Rodden

The appearance in mid-2001 of Isabel Allende's newest novel, *Portrait in Sepia*, closed out the trilogy that began with *House of the Spirits* (1982) and marked the publication of Allende's ninth book. It became a top bestseller, as in the case of all her fiction. Indeed, Allende's books have topped the bestseller lists in Europe, Latin America, and the United States, selling an estimated eleven million copies in thirty languages including pirated editions in Turkish, Vietnamese, and Chinese. The last decade has witnessed her meteoric rise to the status of the leading female literary voice from Latin America and the bestselling female writer in the world.

This essay focuses on Allende's work since the publication of *Paula* in 1995, the story of her only daughter's short life and tragic death. *Paula* is a mother's heart-rending memoir about her daughter Paula, who died at the age of 29 in December 1992 of a rare metabolic disorder. The Chilean-born Allende, who was the goddaughter and cousin of assassinated Chilean president Salvador Allende, wrote the book—which also deals with her own past and was her first work of nonfiction—partly to assist other families who have suffered similar overwhelming losses. She regards the sharing of herself in the book and in her public engagements as a chance to aid her readers. As we shall see, Allende's own story culminates in a dramatic comeback that refutes, as it were, F. Scott Fitzgerald's infamous claim that there are "no second acts" in American fiction. Our discussion also furnishes insight into the reception and impact of Allende's recent work, thereby illuminating the nature of her extraordinary literary celebrity.

The story of Allende's last decade runs briefly as follows: In 1995 a new Isabel Allende began to emerge from the excruciating pain and trauma of the previous three years. When Allende returned from her book tours for *Paula* to her San Rafael home, she struggled to cope with the enormous loss of her daughter's death. Allende felt paralyzed. She feared that she might never write again—or, at least, never write fiction again. Ultimately, she recaptured her lust for life and regained her literary gifts by writing another work of nonfiction, *Afrodita: Cuentos, recetas y otros afrodisíacos* (1997, published in English as *Aphrodite: A Memoir of the Senses* a year later). Its bawdy mix of food and sex whetted her creative appetites. But still the "comeback," as of early 1999, was not a full one: Allende had written no work of fiction in more than eight years.

Aphrodite enabled Allende to break through her writer's block and write a swashbuckling epic in the form of a nineteenth-century historical romance, *Daughter of Fortune* (1999), which immediately became another bestseller. Allende's recovery was complete when the novel was selected by TV host Oprah Winfrey as the March 2000 selection for Oprah's Book Club. Allende quickly followed it up with the third and final epic novel in the "Spirits" trilogy, *Portrait in Sepia*, whose success incontrovertibly established Allende's re-arrival as a major international literary figure. Indeed Allende has been awarded national book prizes in Germany, Chile, Switzerland and Mexico, including Chevalier dans l'Ordre des Arts et des Lettres in France. In the United States alone, Allende has received honorary doctorates from Bates College, Dominican College, New York State University, and Columbia College. And so, within three decades of the 1973 coup of Marxist leader Salvador Allende, when she was a TV interviewer in Santiago, Isabel Allende had fully reinvented herself as a serious novelist and celebrity—and in a new country and a new language, no less. This is a feat in the literature of exile that has few rivals in contemporary American letters.

On December 8, 1991, while attending a Barcelona book party for the publication in Spain of *El plan infinito* [*The Infinite Plan*], Isabel Allende received word of a cataclysmic event that would alter her life abruptly: her 27-year-old daughter, Paula, who had fallen sick on December 6 and entered a Madrid hospital, had slipped into a coma. Paula would die precisely one year later to the day. Like Alba in *The House of the Spirits*—who followed the advice of the spirit of her grandmother Clara, and wrote to "survive" the ordeal of her rape and her family's anguish—Allende coped with Paula's death by heeding the counsel of her mother, who told her: "If you don't write, you'll die." Allende explains of the note-taking that led to *Paula*: "I was not thinking of publishing. . . . My only goal was to survive; that is the only time that I have written something without thinking of a reader."

In the mid-1990s, readers of Allende gained through *Paula* a deeper understanding of the paradoxical woman behind the work: a woman who, though private, likes to be seen and noticed; who luxuriates in solitude yet possesses a flamboyant, extroverted sensibility and lives life intensely; who is a careful planner yet glories in the moment; who has a steadiness and an iron will dedicated to work, and yet also a spontaneous emotional life and a tendency to act on impulse; who has a shrewd pragmatism and keen sense of responsibility, and yet is ruled by passion and does not wait for Life to happen but rather provokes her Destiny.

Writing the story of her confrontation with Paula's death also led ultimately to Allende's spiritual transformation. Nonetheless, Allende struggled through the mid-1990s with the overwhelming burden of two family tragedies: not only did she and her husband, retired lawyer William Gordon, have to cope with Paula's death, but also with the horrible death of Gordon's teenage daughter (from a drug overdose). These events put a great strain on Allende's recent marriage to Gordon; she had married Gordon and settled in California in 1987 (after meeting him during a book tour). Their marriage was on rocky ground for awhile; Allende and Gordon entered therapy and slowly worked together to confront their demons.

By the time of the appearance of the Spanish edition of *Aphrodite* in 1997, Allende no longer felt "stuck in the loss" of Paula's horribly tragic death. The act of composing *Aphrodite*, as Allende explained during her U.S. book tour in the spring of 1998, helped her rediscover a capacity to live in the present. She had written her memoir of her daughter's death; now she would write a celebration of life: a "memoir of the senses." *Aphrodite* is, she said in one interview, her "healthy reaction to mourning and writer's block" that followed Paula's death.

Memory, of course, is the memoirist's prize resource. And it is significant that Allende's two books in the mid-1990s were memoirs, i.e., that Allende wrote another work of nonfiction—rather than fiction—after *Paula*. While memory had returned, aided by her family spirits, the imaginative powers through which her novels emerged still had not. Indeed, as Allende admitted to one interviewer, throughout the mid-1990s she simply could not write fiction, because "it just wouldn't come. Fiction, for me, just happens, I let the story unfold itself. I don't think of a plot, an outline, characters. I allow them to appear before me. After Paula died, it just wouldn't come like that. So I did nonfiction: first I wrote about her illness and her death. And now, this [*Aphrodite*]."

Allende has always maintained that while her nonfiction—like her journalism—is an act of will, her fiction "just comes," arriving unbidden and on its own schedule, a gift from beyond. The gift of fiction had been absent from Allende's life for a long time. Eventually, however, it did "just come." In October 1999, having entered "the light," Allende completed her sixth novel, *Daughter of Fortune*.

How Allende skillfully drew on her own fortunes—which were inextricably bound up with the tragic fate of her daughter's death—was one of the chief attractions of *Daughter of Fortune* for the informed reader. Indeed the novel represented an advanced stage in Allende's remarkable program of writing as self-therapy. Allende looked forward to the new millennium and renewed her life by looking backward to the nineteenth century and writing a *Bildungsroman* about a Victorian maiden—and also by looking backward on her own life: the autobiographical resonances of the new novel are manifold. In fact, despite the obvious plot differences between the fortunes of the novel's heroine and Allende's own, it is no exaggeration to call *Daughter of*

Fortune another memoir, this time in the form of an historical romance that broadly reinvents Allende's own youth. Some of the parallels between Allende and Eliza Sommers, the novel's heroine, are quite explicit.

Daughter of Fortune may thus be read as the fictional counterpart to *Paula*, both of which traverse the same physical space and a comparable social and emotional terrain. And the new work is also a logical successor to her previous novel, *The Infinite Plan* (1991), also set in California. Whereas that book imaginatively recast the life history of her husband William Gordon, the new novel re-imagines Allende's own life. The result is that dark-haired Eliza Sommers is a recognizable fictionalized ancestor of Allende herself. A tempestuous, headstrong, adventuresome, upper-class adopted girl, Eliza too emigrates from Chile to California as she follows the man she loves.

Daughter of Fortune is, in one sense, a study in border culture, challenging readers to ponder the complexities of temporal as well as geographical borders: how the life of a young Latina possesses countless parallels in the nineteenth and twenty-first centuries. The novel's opening scenes are set in the Chilean port of Valparaíso in the 1840s. Eliza is a foundling, taken in by an English clergyman and his spinster sister. She is brought up to be a proper and virtuous English lady, complete with corsets and strict piano practice (with a rod in her back to keep it straight). Eliza's independent spirit chafes at the formalities and rigidities of British club life in Valparaíso, and she escapes whenever possible to enjoy the warm, easygoing company of the superstitious Indian cook, who tells Eliza stories of the legends and traditions of Chilean culture. At 16, Eliza falls in love with Joaquín Andieta, a passionate intellectual from the Chilean working class. When California "gold fever" spreads to Chile, Eliza's lover emigrates, hoping to send back enough money to take care of his poverty-stricken mother—and leaves the pregnant girl behind. She goes in search of Joaquín, concealing herself in the hold of a ship, falls ill, loses her baby, and is saved by a Chinese healer, Tao Chi'en. In California, against the colorful backdrop of the bandits and madams and call girls of the Wild West, a second love story eventually develops between Eliza and Tao Chi'en.

Reviewers on both sides of the Atlantic greeted *Daughter of Fortune* as evidence that Allende's fictional powers had fully returned. But the "gold rush fever" for the novel, incited by media celebrity, came in February 2000, when Oprah Winfrey, the most popular talk show host in the United States, chose *Daughter of Fortune* as the March selection for Oprah's Book Club. Oprah's vast TV audience soon began snapping up Allende's new novel, which rose that week to the No. 1 position on the *New York Times* bestseller list (and shot to the top of the Internet's Amazon. com bookseller list within eight hours). A few weeks later, asked to comment on the record-breaking sales of her new novel, Isabel replied in two words: "Thank Oprah."

In truth, however, as Isabel Allende well knew, she had her faith in herself—and in her family and in Destiny—to thank first and foremost for her phenomenal literary and publishing triumph. Just as Eliza Sommers reinvented herself numerous times and established a new life in the San Francisco Bay area, so too had Isabel Allende. Like Eliza, Allende had become a fortunate daughter of fortune, blessed with the courage to grow through her crises.

In the aftermath of Paula's death, Allende's journey, like Eliza's own to California, has lost its goal-directed focus yet not its spirit and drive. One recalls the words of Tao Chi'en to Eliza: "You don't go anywhere in life, Eliza, you just keep walking." Or perhaps galloping. Almost without pausing for breath after her appearance on the Oprah Winfrey Show, Allende began writing a new novel, whose origin partly owes to Allende's experience with Oprah's Book Club. Many readers, including Oprah herself, had told Allende that they wanted more closure to *Daughter of Fortune*. That desire gave impetus to thoughts already taking shape in Allende's imagination.

Such was the context in which *Portrait in Sepia* was conceived. On January 8, 2000—even before the phone call from Oprah—Allende began writing what would become *Portrait in Sepia*. It was completed in less than a year and appeared in Spanish in May 2001 under the title *Retrato en Sepia*, and then in November in English from Harper-Collins. This sequel to *Daughter of Fortune* is also a prequel to her first novel. *Portrait in Sepia* is the middle saga in a trilogy spanning several generations and three continents.The people portrayed in the novel are the grandparents of those in *The House of the Spirits* and the grandchildren of those in her previous book, *Daughter of Fortune*.

Portrait in Sepia thus completes the story that began with *The House of the Spirits*. It picks up with Eliza Sommers and Tao Chi'en's love affair, tracing the lives of their children, Lucky and Lynn Sommers, and Lynn's daughter, Aurora del Valle. But *Portrait in Sepia* is chiefly the tale of Aurora, also known by her Chinese name of Mai Ling, a photographer who travels the coast from her native San Francisco to the Straits of Magellan in the late 19th and early 20th centuries. A successor to the clairvoyant Clara of *The House of the Spirits* and Eliza in *Daughter of Fortune*, Aurora is named after a new dawn in a New World. Like Eliza, Aurora too is a daughter of fortune, raised amid Santiago's wealthy class. Set largely in San Francisco and Chile between 1862 and 1910, the novel spans the first thirty years of the life of Aurora, a woman of mixed race—part Chilean, part Chinese, part English—who tries to unravel her past. Born in San Francisco in 1880, Aurora tells her story three decades later from Chile, to which she was taken as a small girl.

The novel opens with the death of Aurora's mother during her birth. Aurora is raised by her maternal grandmother, Eliza Sommers, until she is five, then by her paternal grandmother, Paulina del Valle, who conspires to conceal from the child the unusual circumstances of her birth. (Paulina withholds important details of Aurora's family from her, such as the true identity of her father.) At the age of five, Aurora suffers a trauma when her grandfather, Tao Chi'en, is assassinated by a Chinese secret society. She is delivered over to the Chilean aristocracy and undertakes a journey of self-discovery to southern Chile, where she is unhappily married. Aurora experiences various wars—the War of the Pacific (1879-84), when Chile invaded Peru and Bolivia and wrested important territory from them, and the civil war that followed. Seeking the source of her anxiety against a backdrop of the civil war, Aurora retraces her origins to San Francisco's Chinatown. (The scenes of life under the dictatorial president Balcameda seek to remind readers, as the dust jacket points out, of General Pinochet's authoritarian regime.)

Aurora is given a camera at age 13 and immediately becomes a dedicated photographer, an erstwhile feminist committed to her professional passion, and a model career woman who lets nothing stop her. Aurora, the narrator, seeks to understand the trauma of her first five years by using her camera to decipher her nightmares. "Each of us chooses the tone for telling his or her own story; I would like to choose the durable clarity of a platinum print, but nothing in my destiny possesses that luminosity. I live among diffuse shadings, veiled mysteries, uncertainties; the tone for telling my life is closer to that of a portrait in sepia."

The Kodak camera is the key tool in Aurora's reconstruction of her life. The camera is her mechanism for discovery, exemplifying the power of images to capture the truth of a moment. In photography, Aurora discovers that "Everything is related. What at first view seems to be a tangle of coincidences is in the precise eye of the camera revealed in all its perfect symmetry." She reflects: "Through photography and the written word, I try desperately to conquer the transitory nature of my existence, to trap moments before they evanesce, to untangle the confusion of my past." We see here that Aurora is a vocational and spiritual ancestor to Eva Luna, working with still images rather than the motion pictures of television.

It is only by reviewing the images she has captured that Aurora can comprehend her own history. In the process of developing these images, the true identity of the subjects is revealed, from their secret origins to their marital infidelities. Aurora thus becomes a photographer dedicated to capturing "the multi-faceted and tormented face of Chile, a country with a bad memory." Her ethos is summed up in the attitude of her teacher, Don Juan Ribero: "He believes in photography as a personal testimony, a way of seeing the world, and that way must be honest, using technology as a medium for capturing reality, not distorting it."

When *Portrait in Sepia* appeared in English in October 2001, it became another bestseller and received warm reviews. *The New York Times* wrote: "Isabel Allende makes it look easy. It is a book about transformation—of people and nations and of the rights of women." In the *Washington Post*, Jonathan Yardley called *Portrait in Sepia* "the best book Allende has published in the United States since her splendid first novel of nearly two decades ago." *The Times* (London) concluded: "You could say that the author is pioneering a new genre, not magical realism and certainly not naturalism, but a kind of hyperfiction: a highly colored turbocharged version of possible truths." *The Weekend Australian* raved, "Isabel Allende is an absolute dyed-in-the-wool hussy of a storyteller. She is the undisputed queen of Latin American writers, a peppery tease. She flaunts love and delight, grief and loss, death and violence with the ease of a seasoned, yarning jezebel."

But there were some loud demurrals from this chorus. *The Rocky Mountain News* asked, "Can there be a feminist bodice ripper?" It answered, "Probably not," and gave Allende's novel a grade of C+. *The Independent* (London) bemoaned: "The story never really lifts off the page. The living image in *Portrait in Sepia* fails to emerge from the shadows." Nonetheless, the New York *Daily News* pronounced Allende "the romance queen of the literary novel. The book is languorous, sweet-toothed, voluptuous, and a little trashy."

Not everyone is happy with Allende's productivity. Her publisher's new headline—"top-selling female writer in the world"—invites charges (tinged perhaps with envy) that she panders to her public. For instance, *The Rocky Mountain News* concluded: "She seems to be cranking them out at a pace similar to that enjoyed by many romance novelists. One wishes she would take a breath."

Already she has taken steps to enrich her personal life. According to her husband, William Gordon, "When we lived in our other house, we didn't entertain very much. Isabel sort of stuck to her room. Now she's opened up. She really entertains her friends and it's wonderful to see. She's begun to enjoy life a little bit, which is not easy for her."

Her day is well-ordered and includes a rich family life. Her son Nicolás and his children live just five minutes away from her. She conducts interviews and other business out of her Sausalito office, which once housed the town's first brothel, then was a chocolate chip cookie factory, and next a church before becoming her home base. "It's going down in the social scale," she jokes.

Allende turned 60 in August 2002. On that occasion, she had mused, "It's a time for reflection. You have a chunk of life behind you. All the interesting things have already happened. From now on, I can sit on my laurels and crush them. If I die tomorrow, it's fine because I've done everything I came to do."

Perhaps so—but her readers hope not.

From *Society* 42, no. 3 (March/April 2005): 62-65. Copyright © 2005 by Springer New York. Reprinted with kind permission of Springer Science and Business Media.

Isabel Allende in Context:
The Erasure of Boundaries_____

Linda Gould Levine

In a 1994 interview on immigration and integration in the United States, Isabel Allende pointedly remarked, "The borders are there to be violated permanently" ("Immigration" 380-81). At a time when the topic of borders invites countless—and heated—debates over national security and immigration policy, Isabel Allende's life is marked by the erasure of borders and her fiction by traversals of the boundaries that have traditionally separated people. Her comment provides a telling metaphor for her narrative world, in which her characters cross not only geographical borders but also the borders separating gender, social class, ethnicity, religious beliefs, and ingrained views of national identity. As a result, the terrains of her novels are fluid and, occasionally, utopian, giving life to Allende's profound belief that human destiny is not fixed or determined by absolute categories but open to multiple possibilities.

The driving force behind Allende's belief are the particular circumstances of her life, which she has taken great care to document in interviews, speaking engagements, and, most notably, her memoirs *Paula* (1994) and *My Invented Country* (*Mi país inventado*, 2003). In fact, just as she explores her characters' origins in great depth in her novels, Allende similarly re-creates and offers her readers the story of her own origins and her own childhood in an unusual household, where "countless skeletons" hidden from view "planted the seeds of literature" in her life (*Invented* 90). Yet, just as she erases the boundaries that circumscribe the lives of her characters, she similarly blurs the boundary between truth and fiction, or the real and the imaginary, in the narration of her own life. Hence, her memoirs are filled with comments that warn her reader to not believe everything she writes. Clearly distancing herself from the process of reproducing the "truth" of her life and offering her readers a textured view of "writing the self" that is similarly reflected in her fiction, she observes, "I selected some memories, altered some events, exaggerated or ignored others" (165).

On a broader level, by implicitly negating the notion of an "essential" self that becomes fixed or reproduced on the written page, Allende suggests that identity and selfhood are intimately related to a process of self-construction or performance—be it the acts of writing, narrating, or inscribing in images, or dressing oneself in masculine or feminine clothing. The "truth" of the self ultimately becomes merged, then, with the "truth" of self-inscription. As she states in *My Imagined Country*, "Word by word I have created the person I am" (198), a conscious agenda that she further describes by noting, "I have tried to polish the details and create my private legend" (180). This sense of the role of art in enlarging life and making it immune to the passage of time is, in turn, transferred to her characters, who engage in similar quests for self-creation and transcendence in specific moments of history. In *Portrait in Sepia* (2000), Aurora del Valle resorts to both photography and writing as a means to "create [her] own legend" in early-twentieth-century Chile (304); in *Zorro* (2005), Zorro erects himself as legend through three literal and metaphorical "strokes of his sword" (205) in early-nineteenth-century Spain; and these strokes are equivalent to the words Eva Luna inscribes "on a clear white piece of paper" (251) as she tells the story of her life in twentieth-century Venezuela in *Eva Luna* (1987). Eliza Sommers of *Daughter of Fortune* (*Hija de la fortuna*, 1999) fuses her quest for independence with the newly created terrain of the nineteenth-century California gold rush and remarks, "This land is a blank page; here I can start life anew and become the person I want" (280), and Inés Suárez of *Inés of My Soul* (*Inés del alma mía*, 2006) authorizes herself as her own chronicler in sixteenth-century Chile, yet she also casts doubt on her objectivity by remarking, "I suppose that as life passes we embellish some memories and try to forget others" (96). Likewise, Violette Boisier uses clothing and cosmetics to fashion herself as courtesan and legend in late-eighteenth-century Saint-Domingue (Haiti) in *Island Beneath the Sea* (*La isla bajo el mar*, 2009).

At the same time that Allende suggests that the practice of enhancing some memories and forgetting others is fruitful for fiction writing or the project of self-creation, she indicates that it is dangerous when imposed on the realms of history and politics. An ardent critic of the Pinochet dictatorship, she uses the pages of *The House of the Spirits* (*La casa de los espíritus*, 1982) to denounce how "with a stroke of the pen the military changed world history, erasing every incident, ideology, and historical figure of which the regime disapproved" (325). In a similar vein and with similar language, she critiques in *Daughter of Fortune* the xenophobic practices of "Americans" on the California frontier and the "thought that a stroke of the pen could erase a long history of Indians, Mexicans, and Californians" (339). This engagement with history is a central aspect of Allende's writing and one of the factors underlying her continual erasure of boundaries.

Symbolically and literally, the origin of this engagement as well as the crossing of borders can be traced to her early travels with her mother and surrogate father, Tío Ramón, when she was eleven years old. If, as a young girl, she lived for two years in Bolivia and three years in Lebanon and gleaned while crossing the borders of South America her "first hint of the vastness of the world" (*Invented* 78), her subsequent exile to Venezuela in 1975 and move to the United States in 1987 gave her a transnational perspective that continues to imbue her vision of culture and history. Having fled Chile and emigrated to the United States, experiences that incite in her concomitant nostalgia and hope for the future, she sees herself inhabiting an all-inclusive terrain that brings together North and South America. This geographical traversal is transferred, in turn, to her fiction and enjoys great prominence in *Daughter of Fortune* and *Portrait in Sepia*, two novels that are joined by *The House of the Spirits* to create a tight universe of recurring characters and narrative scenarios that clearly stands as a crisscrossing of literary boundaries within Allende's vast body of work.

Allende's implicit rejection of the equation of identity with nationhood—which, in its most extreme fashion, has led to ethnic cleansing and the destruction of minority cultures and religions—has led her to seek new configurations of home and belonging, ones found not only in two continents and two countries but also in the terrain of literature, the homeland of other writers. Her pointed declaration, "I don't belong to one land, but to several, or perhaps only to the ambit of the fiction I write" (*Invented* 178), similarly evokes Henry James's affirmation that "his true country, his home, was that of the imagination" (Nafisi 216). This nomadic subjectivity, tinged with the contours of literature and transferred to her characters, reveals how Allende's cultural and historical sensitivity operates simultaneously on several different levels. Within this context, special meaning is added to her interrogation of cultural norms on the other side of the Pacific in *The Infinite Plan* (*El plan infinito*, 1991), the first novel she wrote after moving to California in 1987. Based on the life of her husband, the San Francisco lawyer (and now writer) William Gordon, the novel is submerged in the social and political history of Allende's adopted country. Weaving together a compelling narrative in the third and first person, Allende describes the life of Gregory Reeves as he grows up as an Anglo in a Los Angeles barrio in the 1940s and 1950s, traverses such diverse landscapes as Berkeley and Vietnam in the 1960s and early 1970s, and defines himself in corporate America and private practice in San Francisco in the 1970s and 1980s.

Through Gregory Reeves's uneven odyssey and his "problematic blend between rootedness and fluidity" (Swanson, "California" 64), Allende demonstrates how boundaries can be inverted, erased, reinstated, and problematized. Reeves indeed inhabits what the writer Gloria Anzaldúa has called the "borderlands" that "are physically present wherever two or more cultures edge each other, where people of different races occupy the same territory" (vii). It is precisely this awareness of what it means to be both white and a minority on one side of the borderland and white and a majority on the other that gives Reeves a vantage point from which to judge cultural and historical production. If his friend Carmen Morales helps him to cross the "invisible frontier" that separates different neighborhoods in Los Angeles (88), and if his mentor, Cyrus, guides him across intellectual borders, he summons their examples during his stay in a small village in Vietnam, where "he stopped seeing himself as a white giant, he forgot differences in size, culture, race, language, and goals, and allowed himself the pleasure of being like everyone else" (201). While this experience of union—paradoxically achieved during a war that split American society—is not sustainable upon his return to California and his integration into a corporate world that values white giants, Reeves's ultimate act of self-healing involves a return to the erasure of boundaries as he forges an ethics of pragmatic idealism that enables him to use his law practice to assist illegal immigrants and the disenfranchised.

A characteristic trademark of Allende's fiction is thus given special prominence in *The Infinite Plan*. At the same time that she records, in an almost journalistic fashion, the contours and external realities of four decades of twentieth-century America, she implicitly juxtaposes codes of exclusion and oppression with a profound sense of hope and optimism. Although the lives of her many characters and their individual histories often become fused with collective history—such as the conquest of Peru and Chile in the sixteenth century or the Haitian slave revolt at the end of the eighteenth century and the exodus of white landowners to Louisiana—they still maintain a sense of autonomy that enables them to transcend barriers of class, race, and gender. This is most particularly true of her many female protagonists, who erase the boundaries of gender to create a sense of identity outside the strictures of convention and who implicitly imitate their creator by authorizing their own first-person narratives. Allende's narrators' self-inscription bears tribute to the author's ability to reconfigure from a female perspective the contours of the "metaphorical penis," as critics Sandra Gilbert and Susan Gubar have aptly named the writer's pen (3).

This sense of the rejection or erasure of gender norms also emerges as a dominant theme in Allende's biography. By her own account, she has been aware of gender bias since she was five years old (*Paula* 142).

More desirous of imitating her imposing grandfather than following the path of her mother, who was abandoned by her husband, Tomás Allende—Salvador Allende's cousin—when Isabel is three, prior to her exile in 1975 Allende showed a strong desire for independence but also a strong adherence to gender norms in her role as wife and mother (146). Her concerted attempt to present in fiction the shedding of the symbolic and literal corset constraining female behavior that she herself lived in is most apparent in two of the novels that she wrote since her immigration to the States and her marriage to Gordon: *Daughter of Fortune* and *Inés of My Soul*. Despite obvious differences between these two novels, situated respectively during the California gold rush and the conquest of Chile, their textured presentation of the crossing of geographic, ethnic, and gender boundaries during foundational moments of history when national and individual identities are being forged carry notable similarities that crystallize in great measure Allende's view of the shifting terrain of gender formation. If, as Homi Bhabha has theorized, "'in-between' spaces provide the terrain for elaborating strategies of selfhood—singular or communal—that initiate new signs of identity" (1), the psychological and cultural border zones that Allende fictionalizes in Eliza Sommers' voyage from Valparaíso, Chile, to California and Inés Suárez's journey from Palencia, Spain to Peru, and Chile give rise to new signs of female identity— the postulation of a "nomadic subject" (Martínez 55) and cultural hybridity.

Precisely because the gold rush was a period when the boundaries between male and female were subject to blurring and women dressed like men and often successfully hid their true identities until their deaths, Eliza Sommers disguises herself and survives in a rugged California while she seeks her lover, Joaquín Andieta. That is, at the same time that Eliza engages in a quest firmly rooted in a heightened romanticism that defines Allende's female characters, she subverts the culture of "corset, routines, social norms, and fear" in which she was raised (275) by disguising herself as a male and internalizing the trappings that male garb implies. If feminists have long argued that women do not have "penis envy" but rather envy of the privileges implied by the male organ, Eliza experiences in her role as Chile Boy—or Elías Andieta, half brother of Joaquín—a sense of freedom of movement that allows her to reflect, "I go about with a scowl so people will think I'm tough. It is tedious to be a man, but being a woman is worse still" (277). She is so good at banishing her fear that when she performs the difficult surgery of amputating two fingers from the hand of the bandit Jack she is rewarded with the ultimate affirmation of her successful crossing of genders—"You're a real man," one of her companions tells her (308). Implicitly illustrating Judith Butler's theorization of gender as "performative" or intricately related to "the various acts that constitute its reality" (136), Allende provides in Eliza Sommers a case study for the creation of gender, in a specific time and place, that is fluid and mobile and subject to reevaluation and change.

Yet, despite the "blank page" that California appears to offer for self-inscription, Allende does not simplify the gender fusion and confusion that overcome Eliza as she describes to Tao Chi'en the disconcertment her role as an "ingénue" in an itinerant theater production caused her: "I didn't know whether I was a woman dressed as a man, a man dressed as a woman, or an aberration of nature" (274). Situated in the "in-between spaces" of gender norms, Eliza, after living for four years as a man, returns at the novel's close to her female identity—and female dress—but performs or refashions them from the perspective of a woman who has lived a series of "deterritorializing flights" (Martínez 55) that impede her from conforming again to the literal and symbolic corsets of her past. At the same time that Allende reconfigures gender, she also provides a crossing of cultural boundaries in the union of Eliza and Tao Chi'en, whose "similarities had erased differences of race" in the midst of an increasingly xenophobic society in which Eliza is viewed as a "greaser" and Tao Chi'en as a "revolting Chinese pagan" (363). By erasing the boundaries of cultural and ethnic difference and offering a textured view of "unhomely" individuals who can make a home "anywhere in the world" (Martínez 65), Allende's novel celebrates new ways of configuring identity and notions of belonging.

The trajectory of Inés Suárez is presented in a similar way in *Inés of My Soul*. Here, too, as in *Daughter of Fortune*, it must be noted that Allende interrupts or suspends female biological determinism to allow her protagonist to engage in ventures antithetical to her sex. Like Eliza Sommers, who aborts on the boat to California and thus arrives on land unimpeded in her search for Joaquín, the infertile Inés Suárez is given a freedom of movement unavailable to mothers of her social class and nationality. Hence, her role in the founding of Chile and her assimilation of masculine codes of behavior are unimpeded by biology, although enhanced by her "female" skills as seamstress and *empanada* maker galore. Not limited, however, by these skills, Inés transgresses the boundaries prescribed to women in two notable ways. Firstly, she dresses like a conquistador, fights like a conquistador, and even saves the lives of her fellow Spaniards by decapitating Mapuche prisoners and flinging their heads "through the air as if they were stones" (204). Secondly, she assumes the right of male inscription by telling her own story of the founding of Chile and proudly proclaiming, "And I can speak with authority" (64). With each of these episodes, Allende further erases boundaries as she blends the historical with the fictitious.

Allende has documented with great care the role that research played in her construction of the life of Inés Suárez. Ever aware that she might be accused of giving free rein to her "pathological imagination," she tells her readers in the bibliographical note included at the end of the novel that it took her four years to research the events of the novel and that "many episodes from the life of Inés Suárez and from the conquest of Chile seem beyond belief, and I want to demonstrate that they are historical fact" (319). While there were other Spanish women who dressed like men and fought in the conquest of the New World—among them Catalina de Erauso, also known as the "Lieutenant Nun"—they were certainly few and far between. Their scarcity justifies Allende's concern that the historical basis of her narrative and of

Inés's role in the founding of Chile be clear. As protagonist and chronicler, acutely aware that she will no doubt be written out of history, despite the fact that together with Valdivia, she "conquered a kingdom" (85), Inés learns to read and write and painstakingly imprints her own legend on that of Chile. The immediate recipient of her tale is Isabel, the *mestiza* daughter of her second husband, Rodrigo de Quiroga, to whom she writes:

> This is my story, and that of a man, Don Pedro de Valdivia, whose heroic feats were recorded by chroniclers in rigorous detail; his exploits will endure in those pages till the end of time. However, I know Valdivia in a way history could never know him: what he feared and what he loved. (99)

Imprinting "herstory" as well as "history," Inés writes herself out of the anonymity that Valdivia himself consigned her to and thus crosses the border that separates the visible from the invisible, or the male from the female.

As Inés narrates in her memoirs deeds that circumscribe her activities to the realm of the feminine—cooking, sewing, healing, cultivating herbs as beauty aids—and to the masculine—her participation in battles and key role in finding water while crossing the desert—she specifically highlights the date of her most courageous act in battle: September 11, 1541. The reader may well wonder if the decapitation of the Mapuche caciques and subsequent saving of Santiago de la Nueva Extremadura on this date—the same date as the Chilean military coup in 1973 and the attack on the Twin Towers in New York in 2001—is actually true or mere "coincidence" (Galehouse 19). Or if it instead reflects Allende's belief that the past and the present are united by "greed and power," with the end of "extending 'values'" used to justify "torture, imperialism, conquest, invasion and occupation of another land" ("Chile" 6). This blurring or erosion of the boundaries between crucial moments in history is further underscored when Inés, implicitly reflecting Allende's belief, writes in her chronicle: "Violence . . . exists everywhere, and has throughout the ages. Nothing changes; we humans repeat the same sins over and over, eternally" (245). If Allende believes that women can easily assimilate the violence around them, she also tempers this view with a note of magical realism that reveals an additional erasure of boundaries. Unable to explain the origin of her trancelike decapitation of the prisoners, Inés relates that the "bloody ghost" of her dead husband, Juan de Málaga, inspired her and aided her in battle (200). Curiously, this explanation, ensconced in the framework of an historical novel, is consistent with the presence of Inés's husband's ghost throughout much of the novel and with Inés's increasing realization that "the veil that separates this world from the next grows thinner with age" (229).

Allende's entire body of work is similarly permeated by a profound belief in "the power of the spirit," a feeling she has articulated with particular passion since her daughter Paula's death in 1992 ("Love" 23). She has also stressed the strong influence of her maternal grandmother, Isabel Barros Moreira, in guiding her toward an all-inclusive view of life and spirituality, specifically noting in *My Invented Country*:

I did not inherit my grandmother's psychic powers, but she opened my mind to the mysteries of the world. I accept that anything is possible. She maintained that there are multiple dimensions to reality, and that it isn't prudent to trust solely in reason and in our limited senses in trying to understand life; other tools of perception exist, such as instinct, imagination, dreams, emotions, and intuition. She introduced me to magical realism long before the so-called Boom in Latin American literature made it fashionable. . . . My grandmother claimed that space is filled with presences, the dead and the living all mixed together. It's a fabulous idea. (69-70)

Allende's first novel, *The House of the Spirits*, provides ample claims for this view of life and pays tribute to her grandmother, Isabel—whose telepathic abilities are transferred in turn to Clara del

Valle—as well as to her grandfather, Agustín Llona Cuevas, the model for the family patriarch, Esteban Trueba. In a broader context, *The House of the Spirits* offers a highly suggestive model of Allende's first endeavor to erase boundaries as she presents a view of gender, class structure, magical realism, and history in a complex narrative structure that similarly reveals her ability to fuse together such different literary models as the family saga, historical fiction, and magical realism. In particular, her use of magical realism—premised on the juxtaposition of the real and the magical, the "unexpected alteration of reality," and the "expansion of the . . . categories of reality" (Carpentier 53)—well surpasses Clara's telekinetic feats—like "playing Chopin with the lid of the piano shut" (123) and wandering through the house after her death—and Pedro García's supernatural ability to lead the ants away from Esteban Trueba's estate. Allende's magical realism functions simultaneously as part of the legacy of Latin American literature, most notably Gabriel García Márquez's *One Hundred Years of Solitude*; as a tribute to her family history and, most specifically, her grandmother's legacy; and, more significantly, as a metaphor for the fissures in conventional reality and the blurring of fixed categories that characterize the novel as a whole. The very fact that the narration of a family saga imbued with historical significance is presented almost in its entirety through the voice of a woman, Alba, who identifies herself in the novel's epilogue as narrator and implicit "author" of the work, not only reverses the male-authored model of García Márquez's novel but also highlights the multiple acts of creative fusion performed by the del Valle/Trueba women. In this regard, the term "magical feminism," coined by critic Patricia Hart and defined as "magical realism employed in a femino-centric work" (29-30), captures the unique blend of feminism and magical realism, each of which is steeped in literary tradition, that Allende employs.

Thus we read that Rosa embroiders tablecloths filled with "creatures that were half bird and half mammal" (6) and that Blanca recreates for Alba her own versions of classic fairy tales, having a prince sleep for one hundred years and a wolf disemboweled by a little girl dressed in red. Alba grows up in a house filled with such eccentricity that she passes into adolescence "completely ignorant of the boundary between the human and the divine, the possible and the impossible" (255), and this fusion of opposites and these creative renditions of myth, folktale, and adolescence are imposed, in turn, onto the social context of the novel. Allende clearly suggests the erasure of the boundaries separating class through the union of the *patrón*'s daughter, Blanca, and the foreman's son, Pedro Tercero García. She also underscores the erasure of the boundaries separating male and female through the various ways the luminous women of the family—Nívea, Clara, Blanca, and Alba—challenge patriarchal authority, be it by chopping down the foreboding family tree, using silence to gain power, or harboring victims of the military coup.

Despite these acts of subversion, however, Allende's novel does not celebrate a utopian view of the reconfiguration of gender or power. As magical realism gradually cedes to the forces of historical reality that implicitly reflect Chilean politics during the Salvador Allende presidency and subsequent military coup by General Augusto Pinochet, *The House of the Spirits* painfully reveals that the boundaries that cannot be erased are those separating the political agenda of the socialist Allende from its implementation in a country characterized by a sinister union of the forces of the Right, the upper class, the military, and United States economic interests. But at the same time that Allende's concluding chapters reproduce "the conspiracy" and "the terror" that destroy a national vision for social change, she also portrays individual and collective acts of transcendence—most notably Alba's attempt to understand Colonel García's existence—that suggest a model for breaking the "terrible chain" of violence and revenge (368) and the possibility of freedom from the prolongation of hatred.

Precisely because the theme of freedom is such a compelling force in Allende's life and fiction, she finds a particular challenge in presenting to her readers the dream of liberation that encompasses an entire nation. *Island Beneath the Sea*, set in a country that was devastated by an earthquake the same month the English translation of the novel was published, has particular relevance not only because of its complex treatment of slavery and freedom in the eighteenth and nineteenth centuries but also because of the relationship it suggests between historical struggles of the past and the present reconstruction of Haiti. Like other Allende novels—*Daughter of Fortune, Portrait in Sepia, Zorro, Inés of My Soul*— *Island Beneath the Sea* is a "wandering text" (Frenk 66) that traverses continents and boundaries—not only the geographical ones that separate Haiti, Cuba, and the United States but also those that separate races and the enslaved and the free.

Though other Allende novels—such as *Eva Luna,* in which Eva is the offspring of a European mother and a South American father of the Luna tribe—have treated the issue of *mestizaje*, or racial blending, the issue becomes even more problematized in *Island Beneath the Sea*. Faithful to the countless gradations of race and blackness recognized in Saint-Domingue (present-day Haiti) and Louisiana at the end of the eighteenth century and the beginning of the nineteenth century, Allende's portrayals of identity formation and hybrid identities are complex, as is her depiction of the pernicious and devastating legacy of colonialism. While *Inés of My Soul* presents the chronicle of the colonizer, albeit a female one, *Island Beneath the Sea* offers a third-person narration accompanied by the first-person account of a colonized subject, the slave and mulatta, Zarité, who travels with her French master, Toulouse Valmorain, from Haiti to Louisiana, where she is finally given freedom. Indeed, this is the first time that a subaltern or colonized subject has been given such narrative authority in one of Allende's novels.

As in *The House of the Spirits*, in which Estaban Trueba's rape of the peasant Pancha García initiates the chain of violence that dramatically shapes the narrative of his family, Toulouse Valmorain's rape of Zarité and other countless acts of forced coupling similarly unleash a well of resentment in his descendants, legitimate and illegitimate, that not only affect his family history but are also ensconced in the broader narrative of the struggle for freedom by people of color in Haiti and Louisiana. While presenting the social stratification in Saint-Domingue—where the erasure of boundaries, even within the realm of fiction, is severely impeded by the class and racial hatred that exists among the *grands blancs*, or rich white plantation owners; the *petits blancs*, or poor whites; the *affranchis*, or free mulattoes; and the black slaves—Allende brings life to these codifications by revealing different models of transgression and the intersection of ideology and romance.

What is particularly interesting in this context is the discrepancy between the public and the private, or the facade of conventionality that certain white male characters are forced to observe as they forge romances with women of color. If Captain Etienne Relais lives his professional life in full support of French colonialist ideology, in his private life, he lives the anticolonialist dream of a passionate love affair with the courtesan beauty of mixed blood; if Dr. Parmentier's respect for cultural differences extends to his desire to cross the boundary separating Western medicine and the practices of Tante Rose, the *mambo* or black priestess and healer, he is unable to fully erase these boundaries in his private life and maintains a separate residence from Adele, his mulatta lover and the mother of his children.

Allende clearly reserves for the offspring of Valmorain—the quadroon Rosette, daughter of Toulouse and Zarité, and the white heir Maurice, son of Toulouse and his Spanish wife, Eugenia—the utopian agenda of forging a union of racial equality in North America. Rosette and Maurice's wedding ceremony on the sea circumvents the prohibition on land against the marriage of two siblings. The gracious toast offered them by Zacharie, ex-slave and husband of Zarité, celebrates "this symbolic couple of the future, when races will be mixed and all human beings will be free and equal under the law" (432). And Maurice's teacher, Harrison Cobb, plans to make Maurice and Rosette the signature couple of his abolitionist agenda. Ceding, however, to the exigencies of a historical moment and social climate that prevent the reconciliation of family differences, Allende thwarts her characters' happiness. In this regard, her portrayal of Rosette is particularly compelling and captures the clashing components of gender and race formation in New Orleans. Acutely aware of her status as a quadroon with fewer rights than her half brother, Maurice, and sorely embarrassed by her mother, Zarité, Rosette nonetheless possesses the sense of entitlement and dignity of a beautiful young woman who grows up in a white household with a rich white father. Within this contradictory framework and mind-set, she is prepared to follow the custom of the *plaçage* available to light-skinned women and offer herself as Maurice's lover. When he protests this economic and sexual arrangement in the name of racial equality and instead marries her, Rosette's sense of self-worth leads her to defend her honor against the calumny of her father's second wife, the *créole* Hortense Guizot. This act of self-defense tragically helps the white woman to win legal immunity and condemns Rosette both to prison and, after her release from prison, to death during childbirth.

Yet, juxtaposed to this individual story of tragic romance—which is unusual in Allende's fiction—and the impossibility of erasing boundaries in a colonialist society is the broader narrative of the slave rebellion in Haiti and the founding of the black Republic of Haiti in 1803. Carefully integrating into the fabric of her novel her trademark interests in historical facts and diverse cultural practices, Allende re-creates a foundational moment in Haitian history in which the religious and spiritual beliefs of an African legacy are highlighted both for their singularities and for their similarities to Catholicism. As the Spanish priest, Père Antoine, tells Zarité: "My God is the same as your Papa Bondye, but with a different name. Your *loas* are like my saints. There is room in the human heart for all the divinities" (277). The very title of the novel—an evocation of the paradisiacal homeland of Guinea that the revolutionary Gambo remembers and longs for—bears further tribute to the belief of many Haitians that the souls of the dead remain connected to the living and inhabit another space, the island beneath the sea, where they await reunion with family and loved ones. This erasure of the boundary between life and death, a theme that has been present in Allende's fiction since *The House of the Spirits* and that is articulated most eloquently in the novel by Gambo, thus comes full circle in *Island Beneath the Sea*.

The novel also contains additional echoes of many of Allende's previous texts, expanding upon her tightly knit literary universe, in which deep and tangential connections link together various parts of her fiction and erase the boundaries between each of her works. Thus, we note that the sharing of knowledge between Dr. Parmentier and Tante Rose evokes in great measure the relationship between Dr. Ebanizer Hobbs and Tao Chi'en in *Daughter of Fortune*. The teachings that Maurice Valmorain internalizes from Harrison Cobb and the inspiration he receives to eradicate slavery recall multiple narrative scenarios in Allende's fiction, among them the challenge to authority and defense of equality that the adolescent Zorro learns from Captain Santiago de León on his journey to Spain; the invaluable mentoring the bibliophile and communist activist, Cyrus, offers Gregory Reeves in *The Infinite Plan*; the gifts of sexual knowledge and literacy that Eva Luna receives from Riad Halabí in *Eva Luna*; and the multifaceted instruction that Aurora del Valle receives from the agnostic feminist and socialist, Matilde Pineda, her photography teacher, Don Juan Ribero, and her friend and relative, Nívea del Valle.

Similarly, the confrontation between Maurice Valmorain and his father parallels a confrontation between Clara and Esteban Trueba. Both Clara and Maurice challenge the hypocrisy of the two masters, who indulge in countless sexual pursuits with peasant women and women of color but impede their offspring, Maurice and Blanca, from doing the same out of love. Further, the assistance Père Antoine gives Zarité in her quest for freedom is similar to the help Padre Mendoza offers the *mestiza* warrior, Toypurnia, in *Zorro*; and the healing skills Zarité learns through her work with both Tante Rose and Leanne Owen recall the healing skills that Eliza and Inés acquire through their respective contact with Tao Chi'en and Catalina. Similarly, the spirit of the legendary Gambo, who inspires blacks to continue their struggle against Napoleon's forces in Haiti, cannot help but evoke the spirit of *Inés of My Soul*'s Lautaro, who inspires the Mapuche to continue their resistance against the Spaniards. Finally, the novel's many examples of linguistic hybridity, which place at center stage voodoo and French terms, also bring to mind the integration of Chinese in *Daughter of Fortune*, Native American concepts in *Zorro*, and words from the Mapuche language, Mapudungu, in *Inés of My Soul*.

By blurring together narrative scenarios throughout her vast body of fiction, Allende underscores her belief that the struggle between oppression and freedom is manifested in similar patterns of violence and hope. To break down the barriers that separate cultures and individuals and that perpetuate these patterns, she suggests, people need mentoring, healing skills, acts of solidarity, shared knowledge, and "boundary-dissolving notions like love and understanding" (Swanson, "Z/Z" 266). One might even argue that much of Allende's success as a writer is related to her belief that the boundary separating author and reader must also be erased to achieve the kind of intimate and highly personalized relationship she seeks with her public. In this context, the structure of *Eva Luna* is particularly illustrative. If in this work Allende creates a hybrid narrative that simultaneously resembles the picaresque novel, the female-centered bildungsroman, the tale of romance, and the author's own personal refashioning of the *Thousand and One Nights*, one passage in particular crystallizes the union Allende seeks between author and reader, or narrator and recipient. Eva shares with Rolf Carlé a tale about a storyteller who is asked to sell a past to a warrior whose life "is filled with blood and lamentation" (281). The storyteller not only tells the warrior a story but also gives him her own past and her own memory and thus fuses both their lives "into a single thread" and "a single story" (281). Like Eva Luna, Allende, too, seeks to impart her particular vision of the world to her readers and erase the boundaries that separate distant moments in history from contemporary reality. By creating tales that captivate the reader's interest and draw on universal experiences, she transcends borders and traverses cultural divides, creating along the way tantalizing bridges that her readers may also cross.

Works Cited

Allende, Isabel. "Chile, Conquest, Courage and Love." Interview with Bethany Latham. *Historical Novels Review* 39 (2007): 5-6.

_____. *Daughter of Fortune.* Trans. Margaret Sayers Peden. New York: HarperCollins, 1999.

_____. *Eva Luna.* 1988. Trans. Margaret Sayers Peden. New York: Bantam Books, 1989.

_____. *The House of the Spirits.* Trans. Magda Bogin. New York: Alfred A. Knopf, 1985.

_____. "Immigration, Integration, and Blending Cultures." Interview with Bob Baldack and Dennis Bernstein. *Conversations with Isabel Allende.* Ed. John Rodden. Austin: U of Texas P, 1999. 379-82.

_____. *Inés of My Soul.* 2006. Trans. Margaret Sayers Peden. New York: HarperPerennial, 2007.

_____. *The Infinite Plan.* 1993. Trans. Margaret Sayers Peden. New York: HarperPerennial, 1994.

_____. *La isla bajo el mar.* Barcelona: Plaza & Janés, 2009.

_____. *Island Beneath the Sea.* New York: HarperCollins, 2010.

_____. "Love, Life, and Art in a Time of Turmoil: An Interview with Isabel Allende." Interview with Margaret Munro-Clark. *Antípodas: Journal of Hispanic and Galician Studies* 6-7 (1994-1995): 15-27.

_____. *My Invented Country: A Memoir.* 2003. Trans. Margaret Sayers Peden. New York: HarperPerennial, 2004.

_____. *Paula.* 1995. Trans. Margaret Sayers Peden. New York: HarperPerennial, 1996.

_____. *Portrait in Sepia.* Trans. Margaret Sayers Peden. New York: HarperCollins, 2001.

_____. *Zorro.* 2005. Trans. Margaret Sayers Peden. New York: HarperPerennial, 2006.

Anzaldúa, Gloria. *Borderlands/La Frontera: The New Mestiza.* San Francisco: Aunt Lute Books, 1987.

Bhabha, Homi K. *The Location of Culture.* New York: Routledge, 1994.

Butler, Judith. *Gender Trouble: Feminism and the Subversion of Identity.* New York: Routledge, 1990.

Frenk, Susan. "The Wandering Text: Situating the Narratives of Isabel Allende." *Latin American Women's Writing: Feminist Readings in Theory and Crisis.* Ed.

Anny Brooksbank Jones and Catherine Davis. New York: Oxford UP, 1996. 66-84.

Galehouse, Maggie. "Conquer and Convert." Rev. of *Inés of My Soul*, by Isabel Allende. *New York Times Book Review* 14 Jan. 2007: 19.

Gilbert, Sandra M., and Susan Gubar. *The Madwoman in the Attic: The Woman Writer and the Nineteenth-Century Literary Imagination.* New Haven, CT: Yale UP, 1979.

Hart, Patricia. *Narrative Magic in the Fiction of Isabel Allende.* Cranbury, NJ: Associated University Presses, 1989.

Martínez, Z. Nelly. "Isabel Allende's Fictional World: Road to Freedom." Spec. Issue: *Isabel Allende Today. Latin American Literary Review* 30.60 (2002): 51-73.

Nafisi, Azar. *Reading Lolita in Tehran: A Memoir in Books.* New York: Random House, 2004.

Swanson, Philip. "California Dreaming: Mixture, Muddle and Meaning in Isabel Allende's North American Narratives." *Journal of Iberian and Latin American Studies* 9.9 (2003): 57-67.

_____. "Z/Z: Isabel Allende and the Mark of Zorro." *Romance Studies* 24.3 (2006): 265-77.

Archetype, Not Ideology:
Isabel Allende's Balance of Opposites_____

Vincent Kling

> The history of a writer is his search for his own subject, his myth-theme, hidden from him, but prepared for him in every hour of his life.
>
> —Thornton Wilder 657

Writers may come to love their craft over time, as Isabel Allende now does, but few have ever said that writing is easy. By nature, it is a struggle to record and convey a vision that is often initially situated in a place words cannot reach. The Austrian novelist and playwright Peter Handke points out the hard task writers face when, reflecting on his own work, he remarks that writing is generated at "precisely the moments . . . in which extreme need to communicate coincides with extreme speechlessness" (34). Allende relates a moment like this, which she experienced in 1981 when she began a letter to her dying grandfather only to watch in amazement as the communication took on a life of its own and became her first novel, *The House of the Spirits*. She was an acclaimed journalist, but now, impelled to write in a personal, intimate vein, though having no idea how, she found her voice and her vision by giving her speechlessness room to begin resounding. She listened as voices spoke through her, wrote "as if in a trance," submitted to "a long process of introspection," and undertook "a voyage toward the darkest caverns of consciousness, a long, slow meditation" (*Paula* 9).

Safety is never guaranteed on such a voyage. Allende's metaphor of caverns shows the soul of the writer in solitude, but Lawrence Ferlinghetti's description of writing as a trip across a high wire adds a necessary supplement, because by the very fact of publication writers reach out to audiences and readers—an aspect of her art to which Allende assigns great importance—committing what is deepest inside them to public scrutiny and possible misunderstanding. So they are "constantly risking absurdity," if not injury, performing a tightrope act

Allende's Balance of Opposites **239**

high in the air, itself a paradoxical feat requiring the simultaneous negotiation of opposite forces (Ferlinghetti 30). They must respond to their impulses while obeying the strictures of an overall design they might only intuit, always venturing on the next step unsure if it will bear their weight, starting out without knowing if they will complete the journey. Only through those perilous trips across the wire, however, achieved by concentrated, painstaking balance, can they find for themselves and for their audiences what Allende calls "particles of truth" (*Paula* 9).

While Ferlinghetti's image seems to catch the unease all writers pass through, it also needs to be adapted to each individual equilibrist, varied according to height, weight, center of gravity, lead foot, length of the balancing bar, speed, and thickness of the wire. If the process were uniform, every piece of writing would turn out the same. The emergence of an author's own voice through what Thornton Wilder—referring to James Joyce—calls "the search for his own subject, his myth-theme" (657) creates differences of style and structure from one literary artist to the other. David Foster Wallace could not have trimmed his elaborations without hurting the essence of his truth any more than Raymond Carver could have amplified his terseness.

Yet this generic image of balance may be the most apt one for Allende because her whole "subject," her method, her approach to form and content, and indeed her very personality, could not have developed except through her exercise of a precarious equilibrium between apparently diametrical opposites dwelling side by side, or even intertwined, each element combining with the other to produce a greater whole. When Linda Gould Levine writes that *The House of the Spirits* is marked by "the coexistence of different realms of human experience within one subject" and "the blending of characters previously located in different ideological spheres," she could also be speaking of Allende's whole artistic endeavor (35). All in all, paradox is *the* key concept for Allende, and tracing it in various configurations through her art will help us understand better a body of work often subjected to

shallow readings and then treated with faint but unmistakable condescension, halfhearted respect, or head-patting indulgence. Isabel Allende is a more sophisticated literary artist than many give her credit
for. She does not experiment with literature, because formal experimentation does not interest her, but she is a masterful practitioner of
her craft, more at home with modernist approaches and methods in fiction than at first appears. She uses paradox and diametrical oppositions
to convey a vision of truth it would not be possible to capture through
any other means, and she reaches her deepest themes by exploring
those archetypes of death and resurrection that seemingly occupy the
"darkest caverns of consciousness" in all humans (*Conversations* 106).

What novel better illustrates the balance of extreme opposites than
Allende's first, *The House of the Spirits*? Mystical visions of the spirit
world exist with rapturous physicality and sexuality; timelessness and
eternity dwell alongside urgently topical politics; the sheer gusto of
solid, realistic storytelling and the shimmering fantasy of magic are
constantly juxtaposed in a fluent narration; extremes of grief and joy
are intertwined; virtue and vice combine, sometimes in the same person; careless idealism can generate violence and violence idealism.
The Catholic Church is the institution quickest to suppress and condemn, for example, but Allende makes a study in hilarity out of the
thundering fury of a pastor who denounces a prostitute incapacitated
by arthritis. The priest's judgment is negated, rendered irrelevant by
the narrator's resort to healing comedy. And in a seeming incongruity
standard for Allende, the Church is also the institution quickest to organize soup kitchens during the reign of terror, defying tyranny to fulfill the gospel mission of feeding the hungry—though a narrator eager
to avoid wallowing in emotionalism carefully refrains from inject-
ing sentimentalism into that manifestation of courage and love. Paradox begets paradox: the more thoroughly these "Communist priests"
(*House* 324) and their helpers live out the corporal works of mercy, the
more suspicion but also grudging respect they reap from the male
power establishment the Church usually bolsters. Allende's modality

of reconciliation is always in the fore, present everywhere in her work. Clara directly challenges that furious pastor and loosens his grip on power, but she does so with all the innocence and candor of the child she is, with no hint of rancor or strife. She is the first of those women who, as Richard McCallister notes, exercise authority even though they possess no power. She is a creation of an author who knows her own mind and heart but is not doctrinaire or dogmatic, for those who learn to dwell comfortably in paradox, characters and author alike, soon learn that truth can reside equally in seeming opposites.

Allende's mode of paradox appears, in fact, to draw sustenance from a dynamic in which wisdom and healing emerge from the balancing of opposites. Her willingness to embrace dichotomies offers in itself a process of reconciliation, because both terms of the paradox turn out to be opposing elements of a profound reality that rely on that opposition to be expressed. Paradox, after all, is the time-honored mode of revealing mystery in simple but cryptic formulations. What body of spiritual wisdom has not been conveyed by paradox? Plato called the erotic impulse both a demonic and a divine force, each polarity essential, each charged by its relation to the other. The New Testament exhorts believers to be as cunning as serpents but as innocent as doves, and the teacher who said he was meek and humble of heart also said he came to bring a sword, not peace. Not surprisingly, then, Allende's anguished life experience deepened her articulation and her art over time, as she found paradox a revelation of meaning, not a clever mental construct. She closed her memoir of her daughter's illness and death, *Paula*, with the words: "Godspeed, Paula, woman. Welcome, Paula, spirit" (*Paula* 330). The contradiction here is only superficial, because Allende resolves the paradox, as John Rodden expresses it, through acceptance and surrender. That acceptance is by no means a drop-off into dull complacency nor the surrender an abject forfeiture of self, however. They are, instead, the instruments of Allende's movement toward greater joy and freedom.

The process of resolution Rodden describes for Allende represents the opposite of the Hegelian dialectic. It is not possible for dichotomies or paradoxes to remain after the Hegelian movement from thesis to antithesis to synthesis has been completed. Thesis and antithesis are subjugated—and the terminology of struggle and victory characterizes Hegel's essence—by a synthesis that is achieved through exclusion, division, and consistency admitting of no contradictions. That synthesis in turn becomes the new starting point of the process, for it is now a thesis that must be pitted against a new emerging antithesis until the terms are again made to resolve in a higher-order synthesis. It is not a coincidence that Karl Marx adapted Hegel's method for it efficiently articulates a model of material evolution, tracing a belief in progress, in onward-and-upward movement, through which weaker entities must inexorably yield to stronger ones. As a material process, Hegelian dialectic is alien to a view like Allende's, however, because Allende resolves paradox by holding the contradictory terms in harmonious, creative tension and taking their seeming contradiction intact into a yet more encompassing reality, as when she can at one and the same time grieve the passing of the mortal, physical Paula and salute the spirit Paula, now released from time and contingency into immortality. None of the terms need be relegated or excluded, as in Hegel. Allende's method fosters profusion and inclusion, the movement from torture and violence into a peace that passes all understanding, and an assertion of life in all its fecundity. Paradox cannot include ideology, which is always the monolithic assertion of a single overriding dogmatic premise with no ambiguity or nuance. Alba, the narrator of *The House of the Spirits*, has undergone physical mutilation, gang rape, beatings, imprisonment, and other extreme forms of humiliation, but these experiences have only given her greater serenity and a more loving embrace of life. It seems consistent with such a hard-won harmony that she is pregnant and will bear new life after her long tale ends. After violence, reconciliation; after death, life; after suffering, peace and forgiveness. Ideology has no place here.

Underestimations of the vibrant complexity of Allende's art of paradox and failures to trace her literary roots deep enough have at times caused her to be misread. Allende is often seen as a Marxist, for example, and so she is, but only to the extent that Marxism, with its aim of improving the lot of the destitute, offers one fragment, one segment—but a limited one in that it is unable to transcend the material plane—of a more comprehensive reality.

It is not unusual, then, for critics to misjudge Allende as grounded primarily in ideologies and isms. One analyst, for instance, draws on the work of Marcelo Coddou to note how the "females of the Trueba-del Valle family" in *The House of the Spirits* "all bear names that recall an ascendancy of light" (McCallister 24), but then he reaches the categorically false conclusion that this "progression of the dawn corresponds to the Marxist unfolding of history toward *aufgehoben*—the transcendence of history." Whiteness has associations with monarchism, not Marxism, the dawn signals a new beginning rather than the end point reached when history is finally *aufgehoben*, and history can hardly be in the process of being *aufgehoben* anyway, since Alba is carrying "this child in my womb, the daughter of so many rapes or perhaps of Miguel, but above all, my own daughter" (*House* 368) and so furthering the legacy and lineage about which she is writing. History shows every sign of continuing robustly through the new baby and no trace of coming to a close.

Another category of analysis is needed, one compatible with paradox, and the color symbolism of the women's names is one indication that matter and spirit undergo alchemical purification in the novel. Alchemy proposes a structure of nature in which the physical and the spiritual are fused together and completely interpenetrate each other. Before modern science enforced an unbridgeable separation of matter and spirit through empirical experimentation, no such dichotomy was known. Every physical reality had its exact correspondence in the metaphysical realm, all concrete objects were analogues of abstractions, and the entire process of apprehending the universe was based on complete, point-by-point correspondences between matter and spirit.

The whole aim of alchemy was to make of the body a spirit and of the spirit a body, as the scholar of wisdom traditions Titus Burckhardt says. Any resemblance between this view and the mutuality of matter and spirit in Allende is inevitable.

The universal premises of alchemy are clearly hospitable to paradox and, in fact, could not exist without it, but, more specific to Allende, the three stages of alchemical purification, with their characteristic colors in sequence, serve as an overall structure of *The House of the Spirits*. The first stage, as summed up by John Granger, is the *nigredo*, or the black, initial phase, in which the old state of being is about to be "renovated or reborn in a new form" (Abraham 135). Accordingly, black predominates in the first chapters of the novel. The dog Barrabás, the first "character" mentioned, turns out to be black once he is cleaned up. He arrives on Holy Thursday, the day before the all-black liturgy of Good Friday. Uncle Marcos arrives in a black coffin tended by men in black. As if letting the reader in on her strategy, Allende's narrator mentions that on his earlier visit Uncle Marcos had "performed alchemy experiments in the kitchen" (*House* 11). Characters are almost always introduced with some reference to their black hair or other dark coloring, and the whole García clan, from Pancha on, is described as dark skinned and black haired. When Esteban Trueba meets his grandson Esteban García, that budding figure of hatred and revenge, he sees a "dark little boy" (174), and, indicative of the boy's unregenerate brutality, never to emerge into a new form, García is a dark adult whom Alba recognizes by his voice. Blindfolded, she has an image of his dark coloring during the times he tortures her. The alchemical color symbolism alone reveals the moral nature of this character and serves as a first element in descriptions that then trace the growth of the others.

The second phase of purification is the *albedo*, the white stage of cleansing and refining. That phase is reflected, of course, in the succession of the women's names—Nívea, Clara, Blanca, and Alba—and especially in Allende's technique of emphasizing first their dark hair and eyes. The women's names, as is appropriate to agents of purification, proceed toward generally lighter color designations as the power of the men recedes and the nation enters into healing after the upheavals and atrocities of a male-driven military coup d'état. Alba, herald of the dawn and in herself the dawn as the bearer of new life, understands through the ministrations of a caregiving woman that "the days of Colonel García and all those like him are numbered, because they have not been able to destroy the spirit of these women" (365). By no means incidentally, the child Alba is carrying is a girl, and it is unthinkable that her name, which we do not learn, would not connect her to the line of the *albedo*. The power of the *albedo* enables Alba to write the book we are reading because it has reconciled opposites; it has redeemed her grandfather's autocracy, power lust, and violence to the point that it is he who urges her to write and explore the house for old photograph albums. As he "slowly lost the rage that had tormented him throughout his life," he can die peaceful and happy at last, uttering a pure "white" name, transfigured by joy in calling "Clara, clearest, clairvoyant" (367).

Three traits mark the *rubedo* or red phase, the last and highest level of alchemical purification, and we will consider them in turn. The first is the revelation that apparent contradictions and contraries dwell in a higher harmonious coexistence, exhibiting a unity that cannot become evident until the soul has undergone great suffering, which usually involves a blood sacrifice. The nature of the sacrifice is archetypal in that the maimed victim achieves the height of spiritual illumination, not in spite of, but because of acute suffering. The *rubedo* dominates *The House of the Spirits* from the first day of the coup until Alba's return to her home and the ending of the novel. Not only the bloodshed at large but also the beatings that Alba undergoes, the torture, the multiple rapes, and the sadism of Esteban García produce the opposite effect of the one intended. The brutality of the regime, for instance, only serves to reactivate the moribund Church's dedication to gospel teachings as priests set up soup kitchens.

As for Alba herself, her movement toward the *rubedo*, even before her imprisonment, is heralded by her presence among the mourners

following the grave of the poet in defiance of the regime. She is holding "a bouquet of the first carnations of the season, red as blood" (329).
The spirit of final purification through keen suffering that begins here
then carries through when Clara appears to Alba in prison, chides her
for her self-pity, and urges her to start writing. Similarly, Ana Díaz pro-
cures a notebook in the women's camp and refuses to allow Alba to use
her mangled right hand as an excuse not to write, simply pressing a
pencil into her other hand. Through the shedding of her blood, Alba
has discovered her true calling, that myth-theme hidden from her up
until then, to recall the words of Thornton Wilder, but she reaches an
even greater spiritual height in relinquishing hatred. She had been eager to avenge herself one day on Esteban García, but as time passes she
begins to understand that no event happens fortuitously; "it all corresponds to a fate laid down before my birth, and Esteban García is part
of the design" (367). Alba comes to see that her fate is part of "an un-
ending tale of sorrow, blood, and love" (367) and that if she does not
understand something, it is because of her own limitations, for all
things are connected in a harmonious whole. Contraries, those coexist-
ing terms of paradox, are not so much resolved as subsumed in a universal vision that reveals that all things linked to all others, the very opposite of monolithic ideology, which excludes, narrows the range of
reality, and rushes to judgment and condemnation. Reading the novel
through the lens of alchemy, we see, too, that Rosa's name indicates
that she is a purified soul born into a stage already beyond the *albedo*—
hence her unearthly, ageless beauty—but never able to develop fully
into the *rubedo* before her premature death. A Marxist reading furnishes no such understanding.

As with Allende's alleged Marxism, so too with her feminism. Just
as her use of alchemy reveals an attunement to archetypes, to elemental, mythic forms of narration, so, too, is her feminism of ancient lineage, more a primal expression of truth in a mythic mode than a social
or political program of liberation. True, Allende "voraciously read
feminist texts that were circulating in Chile" (Levine 5) in the early

1970s, and she readily admits her debt to Simone de Beauvoir and above all to Germaine Greer's major work, *The Female Eunuch*, which allowed her to acknowledge the "anger, impotence, and injustice" she felt "without knowing why" (*Conversations* 137). No less thoroughly than Alba in *The House of the Spirits*, however, she learned to forfeit negative emotions and turn them into acceptance. She writes "with a sense of joy, as if I were playing" (109)—not a tone ideologues are able to strike. Nor do they use humor, as Allende consistently did in her amusing but effective feminist articles in the women's magazine *Paula*, which she collected in 1974 under the title *Civilice a su troglodita* (civilize your troglodyte).

The joke comes to mind in which the question is asked, "How many feminists does it take to change a lightbulb?" and an angry woman answers, "That's not funny!" Allende would probably laugh, for her feminism is not defensive. Its wellsprings reach back to mythic roots and nourish the workings of nature itself. Hers are sagas of women who have authority without power, as McCallister notes, because they are forces of nature, earth mothers, generative bodies, earthy and earthly but also spiritual in their power to inspire, to charge the men around them with supreme need and energy, and to renew the cycle of life through their preternatural fecundity. Allende draws on the same body of matriarchal/fertility-goddess archetypes as Joyce, who produced the great yea-saying Molly Bloom in *Ulysses*, and William Faulkner, whose Eula Varner charges the whole Snopes trilogy with male yearning and erotic energy.

Allende's humor, compassion, and trust in elemental modes of narration invoke life-giving mates and mothers who would find paltry the desire to become CEOs or successors to political figures such as the Indian Prime Minister Indira Gandhi or the Israeli Prime Minister Golda Meir and thereby further the very male power structures that have led to so much exploitation and violence. "Male" values come into play, but are transformed into positives, as women acquire worldly power mainly to relinquish it. So when many of the reviews and even the jacket copy for Allende's novel *Inés of my Soul* call the first-person and real-life narrator Inés Suárez a "conquistadora," they are confusing Joan of Arc with Margaret Thatcher, as it were. Inés is a warrior as intrepid as any profiteer, a cartographer, and an explorer who helps extend Spanish rule in Chile, but her motives have nothing to do with money or power. She knows how to acknowledge the oppressed other, and she urges the men in her life to do the same. The Chilean Indians call the Spaniards "*huincas*"—liars and grabbers of land—but Inés, one of the few persons who knows their traditions and laws, returns the favor of knowledge by translating into Mapuche Alonso de Ercilla y Zúñiga's epic poem "La Araucana," which she helped inspire and which praises the indigenous people with no trace of condescension to "the noble savage." Likewise, her companion, Pedro de Valdivia, even though he has perpetrated cruelty and abuse against the Mapuche, comes to deplore the viciousness of other Spaniards who are killing them off (*Inés* 118-20). Consistent with her ability to dwell in paradox, Allende has created in Inés a character based on an actual historical figure who can fear and hate the indigenous people and respect and admire them at the same time.

Thus the women of Allende's novels, even the less than radiantly beautiful ones, have the paradoxical traits of strong sexual allure and gravity and restraint. They are at one and the same time goddesses of decorum and instantly and utterly captivating to the men around them, fulfilling the men's erotic and sexual destinies to the full, free of shame, false restraint, or calculation. Typically, for instance, Blanca, on first arriving at Tres Marías as a little girl, takes off all her clothes and immediately runs out naked to play with Pedro Tercero García, physically and spiritually entangling herself with him for life; when he runs away from her in shame and fear at the onset of their adolescence, she instinctively goes to find him and reclaim their primal union. So often are they depicted as physically intertwined, wrapped in each other's arms, tumbling on the ground together, literally inseparable, that the image arises of the two sexes originally united as one organic being and later artificially separated, as in the myth Aristophanes recounts during Plato's *Symposium*.

Seen alchemically, the union of Blanca and Pedro Tercero García represents the second trait of the *rubedo*, the "chemical wedding" (Abraham 138), a fusion of opposites that must attract because neither can be complete without the other, the same impulse that Aristophanes claims draws each sex to the other. This wedding, a culminating moment of the *rubedo*, takes place between a Red King and a White Woman. Blanca's name amply testifies to her nature, and the red qualities of Pedro Tercero García come into play when the mystic union occurs between them in their adolescence; after she finds him by the riverbank, he takes her to a secret domain of his, a locus of initiation, to face the sun, rising red over a volcano (lava is red), as they witness a reddish-brown mare give birth. The foal stumbles in its efforts to stand, but its mother "neighed a greeting to the morning sun" while "Blanca felt her breast shoot with joy, and tears came into her eyes." She then whispers to Pedro, "When I grow up, I'm going to marry you and we're going to live here in Tres Marías" (*House* 125-26). That grown-up wedding would only ratify the alchemical marriage that has occurred long before, in a fusion that bonded little boy and little girl for eternity the first second they met.

The third and last aspect of the *rubedo*, the emergence of the Philosopher's Stone, brings about a triumphant rising to new life after death, and we can approach that phase best by putting the resurrection first. At first glance, Allende's authorship of what seems like a conventional cookbook—among which it is sometimes shelved in bookstores—is jarringly incongruous with her elemental, archetypal feminism, as if a mystic earth mother had turned into a chirpy little housewife, Molly Bloom into Betty Crocker. The title *Aphrodite* should alert us, however, that these recipes have a very zestfully proclaimed purpose, that of exciting and prolonging sexual desire. Allende gleefully notes, "The road of gluttony leads straight to lust, and, if traveled a little farther, to the loss of one's soul" (*Aphrodite* 13). And she can hardly wait, for the "loss" of the soul means regaining it on a higher plane of awareness, acceptance, and integration of self. Allende has collaborated with others, including her mother, a great cook, to concoct this rebuke to restrictive Calvinist gloom; it is a celebration of the senses, a book of delicious food, delicious eroticism, delicious tales and stories. The subtitle of *Aphrodite* in English, *A Memoir of the Senses*, sounds downright tame compared to the explicit eroticism of the original subtitle: *Cuentos, recetas y otros afrodisíacos* (*Stories, recipes, and other aphrodisiacs*). Stories, food, and the sheer pleasure of company are all aphrodisiacs to be savored to the full. Lest we miss the obvious, Allende declares, "We're going to concentrate on *pleasure*" (*Aphrodite* 11, emphasis hers).

Aphrodite is even more astonishing when considered in the sequence of Allende's work, for it is the book that followed her memoir *Paula*, the harrowing story of her daughter's protracted fatal illness and death and of the numbing grief the mother underwent. *Paula* sounds the lonely, painful depths of loss and sorrow, and—like other memoirs of grief, such as C. S. Lewis's *A Grief Observed*, Joan Didion's *The Year of Magical Thinking*, and Elizabeth McCracken's *An Exact Replica of a Figment of My Imagination*—unflinchingly relives the "paralyzing sadness and pain" she felt for years after Paula's death (Levine 132) and from which only the writing of the memoir could have freed her. Allende directly links that grief to her recovery from it, however, by describing it in further detail in *Aphrodite*: "I spent three years trying to exorcise my sadness with futile rituals. Those years were filled with the sensation that the world had lost its color and that universal grayness had spread inexorably over every surface" (24-25). Yet the color returned with her appetite for food and other sensual indulgences, and so we read in the very next paragraph about "philters . . . spices, herbs, drugs" and even "candy penises offered in the marketplace" (25). From grief to exuberant sexual celebration, with no sense of contradiction—or rather with a contradiction celebrated as a paradox that can embrace the knowledge of how new life emerges out of death, how the seed must die in the ground before it can sprout, how the final meaning of the alchemical cycle has now been completed.

By this point, we almost have to conclude that the closing of the cycle, with its purifying transition from grosser to finer, from despair to acceptance, from death to new life, is at the vibrant center of both Allende's life and art. It constitutes her own myth-theme, her deepest core conviction that forgiveness and compassion, so easily mistaken as weakness or passivity, are the only possible ways of achieving wisdom and happiness. This enactment of a striving for sublime forgiveness through compassion in the face of evil, joined with acceptance of apparent losses which are in fact gains, is the pinnacle of enlightenment in any system of spirituality; it links Allende as well to her own creation, Alba, to Molly Bloom, and to all those mythic figures of heroism whose greatness finally derives from their courage to seek the embrace of reconciliation.

Returning to *The House of the Spirits* with our sense for the alchemical process heightened, we see that this whole pattern of the journey had been announced on its very first page. Or is it purely random that black Barrabás—a name associated with the passion of Jesus Christ in the first place—arrives on Holy Thursday, the first day of the *triduum*, the solemn period in which the most vivid reenactment of death and resurrection takes place throughout the Christian world?

The archetypal level on which Allende creates also helps dispel misunderstandings about magical realism as she deploys it. First comes a purely technical consideration of plot structure, though. One telling caricature of literary genres that are too often misused shows a dartboard at which the blocked writer can throw a dart to pick some arbitrary device that will relieve him of the need for skill in creating formula fiction. Under "Fabulism," Colson Whitehead spoofs shortcut magical realism: "Ladies with wings and men without mouths. Dancing trees and talkative cows. . . . This is the perfect genre for writers who may be tempted to throw out manuscript pages when they get stuck—with magic realism, you can just conjure up a flaming tornado and whisk troublesome characters away" (23). Indeed, more than one writer famous as a magical realist will sometimes cheat by substituting some outlandish, unexpected action for the next logical and consistent development in the plot. If anything at all can happen at any time, regardless of motive or agency, then there can be no plot to begin with, and magical realism is demeaned to the level of the abracadabra carnival magic act. While Allende has been moving since the early 1990s "away from magical realism to a more straightforward literary realism" (Rodden 18), she is still widely known as an adherent of the earlier method. It would be worthwhile to reread all her early work to verify that she never cheats. The magic of the events is always a correlative, clearly grounded in commonsensical character psychology, to the developments on the purely realistic plane. It is no strain at all on credulity or logic when Clara keeps reappearing in the house after her death, for it is common for the dead to remain vividly in the memories of those around them. Her scolding visit to her imprisoned granddaughter Alba, in which she chides her for trying to starve herself and confers upon her the mission of writing, is entirely consistent with the psychology of persons who rally in extremis and come to life again. Clara may be the mystic guide from near-death back to life, but no data-driven clinician involved in case studies of the dying would fail to recognize the phenomenon of the near-dead rallying with the appearance of a dead family member or close friend.

And what is magical realism, after all, but yet another strategy for allowing contraries to dwell in a paradoxical but profoundly truthful mode of understanding? In an essay titled "Modern Fiction," a novelist no less experimental or esoteric than Virginia Woolf had called for exactly this kind of precarious but exhilarating balance between the material and spiritual, marking the ways in which she strove to achieve it in her own work and pointing out the crippling restriction common to the work of H. G. Wells, Arnold Bennett, and John Galsworthy: "We should say that these three writers are materialists," who "have disappointed us" because through them "whether we call it life or spirit, truth or reality, this, the essential thing, has moved off, or on, and refuses to be contained any longer in such ill-fitting vestments as we provide" (qtd. in Lehmann 45-46). By balancing interior and exterior states, spirit and matter, outward setting with psychological states, Woolf renewed the novel in the 1920s with techniques alien to the older materialists, who were relentlessly fixed on outer detail to the exclusion of the interior life. No one would think of labeling *Mrs. Dalloway* or *To the Lighthouse* a work of magical realism, but that is more a matter of nomenclature, because Woolf is doing in those novels what Allende does, balancing the inner and outer worlds, the realms of matter and spirit, showing their interrelation by never allowing the one to rescue the other from plot problems. And when she moves toward more conventional or mainstream realism, she still holds in balance her paradoxical opposites. *The Infinite Plan*, for instance, is a virtual documentary record of the lives of her second husband and his forebears, fully grounded in actual events, and yet it proposes and works out the kinds of large cosmic designs through apparent coincidence to which no credence can be given without a set of eminently spiritual convictions. Accusations of Allende's having fallen off after *The House of the Spirits* are leveled mainly by critics who have applied to her work a label—magical realism—that was never very clearly defined anyway and that was not used by the author herself. After devising such a shallow or inaccurate category, they have taken her to task for not conforming to it.

Because Allende has negotiated polarities with skill, never cheating by creating a short circuit between magic and realism, her craft could be seen as a major influence on the generation of Latin American writers after her, just as Woolf was a model for countless novelists during and after her time. Allende's art is no trickster's indulgence, like pulling rabbits out of hats, for her discipline and control of her techniques ground the realism of the torture, the rapes, and the general violence and power mania. She chronicles these realities so firmly that her techniques can serve as a clear blueprint for emulation. Allende is not explicitly acknowledged by newer novelists whose project is to evoke the constant atrocities of Latin American politics and history with documentary precision and gruesome emotional effect at the same time—Fernando Vallejo, Laura Restrepo, Juan Gabriel Vásquez and Roberto Bolaño come to mind—but their pacing and plotting, their skill in balancing contrasts and holding opposites in equilibrium have much in common with Allende's artistic practice. Her influence appears almost palpable, for example, in Colombian Evelio Rosero's *Los ejércitos* (*The Armies*), which begins in an Eden-like garden of music, food, and sensual desire, only to move inexorably toward cruelty and horror, massacres and slaughters, with an almost unbearable graphic specificity that makes the reader begin to dread turning the page. If Allende was never so ruthlessly exact in her depiction of savagery in *The House of the Spirits* and *Of Love and Shadows*, among other works, her whole modality of balancing opposites appears to have opened up to later novelists potentialities for handling dark and light, sumptuousness and privation, pastoral and wasteland in ways that hearken back to her skill. The once-vexed question of whether Allende's early novels are imitations of Gabriel García Marquéz now seems superseded by the more likely consideration that her work has given voice to those coming after her.

Allende's use of traditional patterns rooted in the archetypal and mythic involves a backward glance but only insofar as it points a way forward. Her governance of magical realism has expanded the dimensions of contemporary fiction by reconciling the mundane with the miraculous, the supernatural with the documentary, the immanent with the workaday. Throughout the twentieth century, one of the most compelling and authentic modes of recording experience was to show how spirituality had been traduced and betrayed by a concentration on the squalor, the restriction, the emotional impoverishment of spiritual isolation. From the wasteland of T. S. Eliot to the bleak silences of Samuel Beckett, the ferocious invectives of Louis Ferdinand Céline and of

Curzio Malaparte to the universal nay-saying of Karl Kraus and the unrelenting negations of Thomas Bernhard, writers would have been considered to be lying if they had not created emotional worlds of drab, angry struggles nearly devoid of hope. This is by no means the sole modality of modern literature—much of which, like *Ulysses* or Mikhail Bulgakov's *The Master and Margarita,* has been marked by high comedy and even burlesque as an answer to despair. Still, Eliot spoke for a generation when, in *The Waste Land*, he reverted to archetypes as a way to enact defeat and offer only a very faint hope of renewal, tentative and frail. Allende, who, in her own way, returns to archetype and mythic narration, carries this chronicle through despair and beyond, asserting the linkage of body and spirit, of matter and mind, in ways that honor the truth of art, the fictional art of walking the tightrope to reenact the fullness of human experience through narrative.

Final defeat and gloom have often been considered more genuine than patterns of conflict that emerge into hope, so Allende's willingness to embrace renewal after sorrow marks another way in which she is constantly risking absurdity. The overused word "closure" well characterizes her approach to structure. The last pages of *Paula* do not bring the grieving to an end, but they also decline the open-ended, unresolved kind of grief Peter Handke records in his memoir of his mother's suicide, *A Sorrow Beyond Dreams*. By providing her works with definite endings, most with strong resolutions, Allende offends against a prevailing canon that declares that the very existence of a beginning, a middle, and an end is a betrayal of human experience. She knows that she is frequently dismissed as a mere journalist, writing "popular romance, or even kitsch," if not "literary soap operas" (*Conversations* 106), but she chooses not to rebut, confident enough in her intent and her content not to have to knock down straw figures. Allende is confident in her artistry, and this present essay will be successful if its author has understood and communicated some of the vision and the method of this extraordinary artist.

Works Cited

Abraham, Lyndy. *A Dictionary of Alchemical Imagery*. New York: Cambridge UP, 1998.

Allende, Isabel. *Aphrodite: A Memoir of the Senses*. New York: Harper, 1998.

_____. *Conversations with Isabel Allende*. 1999. Ed. John Rodden. Austin: U of Texas P, 2004.

_____. *The House of the Spirits*. New York: Knopf, 1985.

_____. *Inés of My Soul*. New York: HarperCollins, 2006.

_____. *The Infinite Plan*. New York: HarperCollins, 1993.

_____. *Paula*. 1994. New York: Harper, 1995.

_____. "Writing as an Act of Hope." *Paths of Resistance: The Art and Craft of the Political Novel*. Ed. William Zinsser. Boston: Houghton Mifflin, 1989. 39-63.

Bennett, Caroline. "The Other and the Other-Worldly: The Function of Magic in Isabel Allende's *La casa de los espíritus*." *Isabel Allende*. Ed. Harold Bloom. Philadelphia: Chelsea House, 2003. 171-82.

Burckhardt, Titus. *Mirror of the Intellect: Essays on Traditional Science and Sacred Art*. Albany: State U of New York P, 1987.

Didion, Joan. *The Year of Magical Thinking*. New York: Alfred A. Knopf, 2005.

Ferlinghetti, Lawrence. "Constantly Risking Absurdity." *A Coney Island of the Mind*. New York: New Directions, 1958. 9-46.

Granger, John. "Literary Alchemy." *Unlocking Harry Potter: Five Keys for the Serious Reader*. Wayne, PA: Zossima, 2007. 46-117.

Handke, Peter. *A Sorrow Beyond Dreams*. 1974. New York: NYRB Classics, 2002.

Hart, Patricia. *Narrative Magic in the Fiction of Isabel Allende*. Rutherford, NJ: Fairleigh Dickinson UP, 1989.

Lehmann, John. *Virginia Woolf*. London: Thames and Hudson, 1975.

Levine, Linda Gould. *Isabel Allende*. New York: Twayne, 2002.

Lewis, C. S. *A Grief Observed*. 1961. New York: Harper, 1989.

McCallister, Richard. "Nomenklatura in *La casa de los espíritus*." *Critical Approaches to Isabel Allende's Novels*. Ed. Sonia Riquelme Rojas and Edna Aguirre Rehbein. New York: Peter Lang, 1991. 21-36.

McCracken, Elizabeth. *An Exact Replica of a Figment of My Imagination*. New York: Little, Brown, 2008.

Plato. *Symposium*. Trans. Benjamin Jowett. 5 Feb. 2010. http://www.anselm.edu/homepage/dbanach/sym.htm.

Rodden, John. Introduction. *Conversations with Isabel Allende*. 1999. Ed. John Rodden. Austin: U of Texas P, 2004.

Rosero, Evelio. *The Armies*. Trans. Anne McLean. New York: New Directions, 2009.

Whitehead, Colson. "Picking a Genre." *New York Times Book Review* 11 Nov. 2009: 23.

Wilder, Thornton. *The Bridge of San Luis Rey, and Other Novels, 1926-1948*. New York: Library of America, 2009.

Z/Z:
Isabel Allende and the Mark of Zorro_____

Philip Swanson

Critical reaction to Isabel Allende's fiction often gives a sense of prevailing attitudes in Latin American literary studies. She is routinely accused of naivety, a tendency towards stereotyping that runs counter to feminism and oppositional politics, an emotional idealism that shows little understanding of the reality of social problems, and, in general, the perpetuation of bourgeois norms. She is attacked too for producing work which is seen not to be part of the literature of immediate resistance or equivalent to that of testimonial writers who have not—like Allende—moved away from Chile, for failing to represent the full range of subaltern relations and for not being radically disjunctive in formal terms. The implicit assumption underlying such positions is that what matters in Latin American fiction is politics and complexity, that is, a radical leftist politics preferably expressed through a radically subversive narrative form. Such nonsensical presumption has become something of a norm in Latin Americanist criticism, and from this narrow ideological perspective, Allende's narrative may seem far too playful or 'magical' to be associated closely with the testimonial or immediate resistance and far too readable to be compared closely with the often near-hermetic intellectual intricacy of more favoured writers. Yet the fact is that more people are going to read Allende than the work of academics or intellectuals who valorize oppositionality through formal rupture, and her work is therefore likely to have much greater impact than the self-referential theoretical discoursing of the academy and its preferred authors.[1] The importance of her first novel, *La casa de los espíritus* (1982), is precisely that it breaks with the tendency in Latin American literature towards the complex and the obscure, and channels so-called Magical Realism into a more communicative direction. For Allende, 'la magia de las palabras' '[lo que] tiene de maravilloso un libro', is it establishes 'un vínculo entre quien lo escribe y quien lo lee', allowing writers to become 'intérpretes de la realidad' and 'contribuir a un mejor destino de nuestra tierra' position is unashamedly middle-brow, as is the audience she aims at, and she specifically eschews academic validation in favour of what she calls her own 'underdeveloped' literature.[2] Indeed, Allende's seemingly mushy outlook is actually not that far in reality from that of many serious academic critics who might characterize their position as 'ethical'. The increasingly loose phenomenon of postcolonial critical practice, for instance, is now not only thoroughly mainstream but based on pretty commonplace and common-sense notions. Boiling down to the idea that any way of understanding culture involves an inevitable mixing of perspectives in which each affects the other, its emphasis on 'dynamic transformation via conflict, friction, asymmetry, translation and dialogue, [. . .] constant negotiation and diplomacy, with acute attention to the potential incommensurability of the horizons of thinking and theorizing'[3] is not really saying much that differs particularly from Allende's own narrative world in which binary oppositions are set up and then problematized or dissolved so as to create a greater sense of awareness of and respect for different positionalities. She may think and write in terms of boundary-dissolving notions like love and understanding (rather than, say, hybridity and transculturation), but this does not necessarily make her narrative stance any less powerful or meaningful.

Now, postcolonial critical practice can obviously be linked to the much touted notion of Magical Realism, also often associated with writers like Allende.[4] Magical Realism is an inevitably paradoxical term. Thus the most obvious question to ask about it is also the most fraught: how far does it reveal or obscure reality? In the study of Latin American literature, critics have been historically divided broadly between those who see the magical or fantastic dimension as underlining the essentially fictional or unknowable nature of both literature and reality, and those who see the magical or fantastic as a means of opening up imaginative new perspectives on social or political reality.

There is no doubt that political readings of Latin American literature are now in the ascendancy, but they are often far from unproblematic. For example, the famous opening of the best-known Magical Realist novel, *Cien años de soledad* (1967), in which the founding father of the town in which the tale is set introduces his children to reading creatively with the imagination and to the dazzling beauty of the most fabulous diamond on earth (actually the previously unknown substance, ice), could be read either as an incitement to freedom of thought or as the revelation of the unavoidable limitations of error-prone human understanding. Indeed, it has been argued that García Márquez's fantasy-laden allegorical approach to history creates a rich literary experience but a rather ineffective political commentary, whereas Allende's *La casa de los espíritus*—despite being derided as a pale imitation of the seminal Colombian novel—enjoys sharper political focus precisely because it systematically subverts the magical dimension in order to confront the reader with harsh reality.

Allende has recently taken this idea of linking the magical to the real a stage further via her production of a trilogy of novels for children or 'young adults' dealing with the experiences of a teenage Californian hero in the Amazon, the Himalayas and the African jungle.[5] Here Allende uses a mainstream publishing outlet to mobilize the sense of magical freedom and innocence implicit in children's fiction to convey reasonably clear centre-left liberal ideas on the postcolonial experience to a wide and often implicitly 'First-World' public. Her latest venture at the time of writing, a rip-roaring novel based on the iconic (Latin) American figure of Zorro, continues the spirit of adventure-cum-education at the heart of her youth fiction but this time aimed at all generations. Here the narrative context is clearly a colonial one, but the text as a whole elaborates what can be seen as an untheorized and not exclusively leftist postcolonial commentary on the relationship between so-called Third and First Worlds and between Europe and the Americas.

For many people, the image they have of Zorro comes from the TV series made by Disney, first aired on the ABC network in the USA between 1957 and 1959 or—even if they never saw the series—the accompanying emblematic image of the masked hero and his rearing black steed silhouetted against a lightning-charged sky. Such an image reminds us of the profoundly iconic nature of Zorro as mass popular cultural symbol. The fact that Allende chose to pen the first real Zorro novel is probably an indicator for some of her total absorption into the market and mass culture. However, Zorro—as two men in one and as a Californian straddling the worlds of 'Latin' and 'North' America—may also be the perfect culminatory embodiment of the non-binary ideal that is at the theoretical heart of much of her work. It is somehow fitting that Allende's most conspicuous incursion into the mass culture market is once more an attempt to use the popular as a means of communicating a challenging and possibly even at times transgressive message to as wide a readership as possible.

Zorro, of course, was always both a popular figure and a transgressor of norms. Moreover, the outlaw-hero/peasant-gentleman ambiguity has always been central to his construction. The roots of the Zorro legend[6] lie partly in the figure of the Mexican bandit Joaquín Murrieta, whose (real or imagined) adventures in gold-rush California have already been exploited by Allende herself in her novel *Hija de la Fortuna* (1998). Though probably no more than a greedy thug, Murrieta was progressively transformed into a Latin Robin Hood following the romanticization of his career by the part Native American writer John Rollin Ridge in his 1854 book, *The Life and Adventures of Joaquín Murieta* [*sic*], *the Celebrated California Bandit.*[7] Obvious, if muddled, echoes persist clearly into versions of Zorro, such as the 1998 blockbuster movie *The Mask of Zorro*. Here, the young apprentice Zorro is Alejandro Murrieta, whose brother Joaquín has been (effectively) killed for thieving, and who seeks revenge against the soldier Captain Love; Ridge's Murieta is also a victim of injustice, similarly motivated by the hanging of his brother for stealing a mule and eventually hunted down and killed by Harry Love. Yet accounts of Zorro's escapades are also almost certainly influenced by the antics of a distinctly non-peasant and purely fictional figure, the Scarlet Pimpernel.[8] Created by the Baroness Emmuska Orczy in 1905 (ten sequels—containing much reasonably accurate historical background—followed *The Scarlet Pimpernel*, prompting later many films, TV shows and a musical), the 'demmed elusive Pimpernel' was a brilliant swordsman who rescued aristocrats destined for the guillotine during the French Revolution. The daring hero, though, is none other than the apparently foppish Englishman Sir Percy Blakeney, in reality a man of principle and a master of disguise. The analogous yet contrasting figures of Murrieta and the Pimpernel were doubtless the inspiration for Zorro's first outing, in the 1919 serialized novel *The Curse of Capistrano* by the writer of westerns and other adventures for pulp magazines, Johnston McCulley. The series was hugely popular and some sixty-four further serials followed, in which the hero Zorro fought against injustice in California's Pueblo de los Angeles. McCulley's character was the spark for a massive pop cultural industry, especially following the masked man's transition to the silver screen in films like *The Mark of Zorro*, with idols Douglas Fairbanks in the original 1920 movie and Tyrone Power in the 1940 talkie remake. Some thirty-eight movies have been made in total (not to mention the five serial titles in the 1930s and 1940s by Republic Pictures), the latest coming in the same year as Allende's novel, 2005—the sequel to *The Mask of Zorro*, Martin Campbell's *The Legend of Zorro* starring Antonio Banderas and Catherine Zeta Jones. The television series mentioned above, starring Guy Williams as Zorro, was the biggest-budget western production of its time, and it spawned numerous imitations (real-life and animated) in the USA and abroad right into the twenty-first century—the most recent TV version at the time of writing being DIC Entertainment's *The Amazing Zorro* for Nickelodeon in 2002. Perhaps even more significantly for the development of a modern icon, the Disney TV series sparked a merchandizing craze for everything from toy swords to lunch boxes, a mania which continues to this day with collectors' sites, new exclusive toy lines (such as Playmates' in 1998) or movie tie-ins. There have even been musicals (at least eight, with a West End London musical with music by the Gipsy Kings planned by AKA Productions at the time of writing); and Italy's Caneva World Movie Studios boasts a fabulous Zorro restaurant and show set in 'a real Mexican Fazenda' (*sic*).[9]

The great anomaly of the Zorro industry, however, was—until 2005—the absence of any major literary treatment of him. The anomaly was only corrected when Isabel Allende was commissioned to write the novel of Zorro by John Gertz, owner of the rights to the Zorro character and founder of Zorro Productions (1977). Allende was at first unsure about the project, thinking it unsuitable for a 'serious writer',[10] but was persuaded when she realized she would have complete freedom of invention within the reasonable limits of fidelity to the spirit of the character. And so the idea of the novel came to be the filling in of the background to Zorro, the character's life story from birth to the assumption of his role as masked freedom fighter in Spanish California. Indeed the original working title for the book was *Los orígenes de la leyenda de Zorro* (The Origins of the Legend of Zorro), and it was expected to take the form of more than one volume. However, it was eventually published simply as *Zorro* (with the subtitle of *Una Novela*). The story—which is expected to form the basis of the third movie in Columbia Pictures' Zorro trilogy—deals, then, with a familiar theme in Allende's work: that of origins and destiny. Set in the Americas and Europe between 1790 and 1840, it tells the story of Diego de la Vega (alias Zorro), starting with his parents' love affair and ending with him, as Zorro, bringing down corrupt authorities and freeing Indian slaves in Alta California in 1815 (an epilogue dated 1840 ties up some loose ends). The novel is chock full of romantic swashbuckling antics, including sword fights, duels, dramatic rescues, attending to damsels in distress, pirate attacks and so forth. Yet Allende also includes many novel flourishes in her tale. For example, Diego is a *mestizo*, with a Native American Indian mother and a Spanish hidalgo for a father. Moreover, his education as Zorro is really conducted in Europe, more specifically Napoleonic Spain, where he is exposed to both revolutionary ideals and a patriotic code of honour, joining—at the behest of his brilliant fencing master—'La Justicia', a secret society for the promotion of fairness and dedicated to the rescuing of the unfairly imprisoned. Many of the novel's most vivid scenes are actually those which take place in Spain, a nation 'convulsed by political repression, poverty and violence': here Allende's depiction of the various social classes displays a Dickensian brio which stands comparison with a novel such as Charles Palliser's *The Quincunx* (1989). There is even a colourful interlude in Barataria on the Gulf of Mexico in which Diego comes into contact with the legendary buccaneer Jean Laffite.[11] On top of all this, the story enjoys a very intriguing and somewhat problematizing narrative perspective: the mysterious unnamed chronicler of events turns out in the epilogue to be one of the novel's characters, Isabel de Romeu, probably a secret admirer of Diego and something of a victim of unrequited love.

At the heart of the portrait of Zorro is the idea of duality. Virtually all of Isabel Allende's fiction exploits the motif of binary oppositions and their dissolution. Zorro is no exception. The key binary relationship is between Diego and his alter ego Zorro, but there are many others too: Diego and his so-called milk brother Bernardo;[12] Diego and his rival-cum-model Jean Laffite; Diego and his arch enemy Rafael Moncada; Diego's mother and father—an Indian and a Spaniard; Diego's mother herself—daughter of an Indian and a Spaniard; the twin influences of father figures in California representing the Church and (loosely) the state (or religion and the sword), Padre Mendoza and Alejandro de la Vega; the twin influences of father-like figures in Spain, representing French liberalism and Spanish honour, Tomás de Romeu and Manuel Escalante; Europe and Latin America, France and Spain, Napoleon Bonaparte and Ferdinand VII; the sisters, Juliana and Isabel de Romeu; Isabel the character and Isabel the narrator; Isabel the narrator and Isabel (Allende) the author; history and literature; fantasy and reality.

The list could go on and on. The implications of such a pervasive pattern of dualities will be considered in due course, but for the time being a useful entry point is the central organizing duality of the transformation of Diego de la Vega into Zorro.

Though Zorro is a fictional creation, Allende's narrative provides a convincing personal history and historical context for the development of such a figure. One of the pleasing aspects of the novel is the way it makes Zorro so acceptable by presenting him not as some arbitrary superhero but as a product of circumstances, influences and practical, social and moral education. The novel begins before he is born, and the love affair of his future parents—the soldier and bastion of traditional Spanish values, Alejandro de la Vega and the spiritual Indian warrior, Toypurnia—represents an important basis for their future offspring's career. Diego is inclined to a dual identity from the outset, one which straddles a wide social and cultural spectrum. From his mother and her family, he learns practical skills, knowledge of nature and the lay of the land, spiritual values, the power of instinct and a sense of solidarity with the oppressed, while from his father's side he gains access to the world of established society, reading, formal education, intellectual ideas, equestrianism, fencing and duels. His sea journey to Barcelona develops this learning process, as he learns to climb the ship's rigging and perform acrobatics on its masts, as well as to acquire the tricks of salty seamen such as magic, sleight of hand, card sharping, story-telling, and a fondness for disguise and practical jokes (sometimes involving the amusing use of a black cape and mask). In Barcelona, he has contact with high society but also makes friends with gypsies, honing his physical skills in their acrobatic circus-style performances. He studies too under the tutelage of the author of the fencing manual his father gave to him in California. But, although the Maestro Manuel Escalante runs what is called 'la Academia de Esgrima para Instrucción de Nobles y Caballeros', he also introduces Diego to the secret organization, 'La Justicia', which is dedicated to combating oppression of all kinds (in the historic context, of course, of religious fanaticism, the French occupation of Spain in the early nineteenth century, and the slave trade). Now, Diego undergoes his second initiation in the novel. The first was at the hands of the Native American Indians. This was a kind of purification ritual in which he was to make contact with the Gran Espíritu in search of a vision of his destiny. Alone in a forest wilderness, he reaches a new plane of reality and comes face to face with what is revealed to be his totemic animal, *el zorro*, the fox: as his healer grandmother, Lechuza Blanca explains, he will now learn—like the fox—to discover what cannot be seen in the dark, to disguise himself, to hide by day and act by night.[13] This primitive nature-orientated Native American initiation is complemented by the more metropolitan European one in the secret lodge in big-city Barcelona. This initiation also involves skill, physical strength and agility too as well as the rather more controlled revelation that instinct can be trained through practice and that the key to success in combat is the suppression of anger. At its conclusion, and in a marked echo of the Indian ceremony, Diego unhesitatingly assumes his new codename: Zorro, the Fox (p. 160). The point is, though, that despite the seeming differences, the Native American wisdom behind the first ritual is really not at all dissimilar to the intellectual currents of late eighteenth- and early nineteenth-century Europe that motivate the second. The Indian quest for *Okahué* is to find the basic virtues of honour, justice, respect, dignity and courage (p. 43). La Justicia's oath is to seek justice, nourish the hungry, clothe the naked, protect widows and orphans, give shelter to the stranger and never spill innocent blood (p. 156). Bernardo, Diego's Indian soulmate, cannot help but note 'cuán parecidos eran los principios de La Justicia al Okahué de su tribu' (p. 160). Thus Zorro is a kind of postcolonial hero *avant la lettre*.

Of course, the spirit of fairness has also been growing in the young Diego. He has challenged bullying at school, observed the shameful mistreatment of the Indians in California, noted the discrimination against Bernardo both in Pueblo de los Angeles and Barcelona, and witnessed religious, political and ethnic persecution in the Spain of Joseph Bonaparte and Ferdinand VII. In Barcelona, he now begins to use his masked-man disguise to promote justice, by, for example, freeing prisoners and helping the despised gypsies escape torment and death. Soon small boys are scraping the letter Z on city walls. Later, in his daring rescue of Escalante from the army barracks, Zorro himself, in a ludic impulse, traces a Z on the wall with three strokes of his sword: the authorities are enraged and a legend is born. The hunt for Zorro underscores the imperative of disguise (and therefore accentuates the sense of duality). In an obvious echo of Sir Percy Blakeney, Diego has been affecting the manner of a feeble foppish dandy. The jaunty persona of the playful caballero in a mask, so familiar from the Zorro films, is not long in appearing. The cracks in the seeming blend of identification with the nobility and the common man are becoming more difficult to discern. Yet there is a duality in the motivation for Zorro too. Though he certainly is driven by a sense of justice, there is also a strong sense that he is just as motivated by the boyish fantasy of using his antics to win the heart of the woman he thinks he loves, the beautiful Juliana de Romeu (e.g. pp. 240-47). Zorro is of course a romantic hero in the sexual sense too (and the skills he learns also include charm, musicianship and dancing). Also, as in the traditional adventure movie,[14] the hero's battle against evil becomes synecdochically focused on one man, in this case the novel's villain Rafael Moncada. Moncada goes from Spanish cad to corrupt politician as he moves to Alta California to enslave the Indians in order to make his fortune via the illegal pursuit of the trade in oyster pearls. Yet he is also Juliana's suitor and, eventually, abuser. Zorro's ultimate defeat of Moncada is thus something of an act of personal revenge (the initial motivation in *The Mask of Zorro*) and an assertion of doomed love. However, the triumph over Moncada is also the logical conclusion of Diego's destiny as charted by Allende's narrative of education. According to the narrator, 'la historia concluye cuando el héroe regresa al punto de partida, transformado por sus aventuras y por los obstáculos superados. Esto es lo habitual en las narraciones "épicas"' (p. 317). He has lost Juliana and spares Moncada's life. This is not then just a matter of love and revenge. The story of Diego is his preparation for the assumption of the classic role of Zorro as defender of the innocent peasantry of Alta California. By travelling, learning and returning, Allende's Diego de la Vega earns the mantle of the Zorro the readers all know.

So, Zorro is a hero. But he is also a rather ambiguous one. The backstory approach and the narrative perspective of an adult Isabel de Romeu allow a fuller picture than is conventionally provided of a traditional hero, the narrative here dwelling, for example, on the callowness of youth and the ravages of age. Thus Diego arrives in Barcelona as a mere stripling with protruding ears and a high-pitched voice (p. 97) and ends up in California loveless and balding (p. 381). As has been suggested, Zorro's motivation is sexual desire or love as much as justice. This problematizes the democratic credentials of the hero, who can be seen uncritically issuing 'orders' to Indians or 'instructions' to women (e.g. pp. 351).[15] It also blinds him to reality at times and reveals his vanity: as the narrator comments at one stage, 'la vanidad le impedía ver claro, como suele ser el caso de los galanes como él' (p. 311). Indeed Isabel's narrative places much emphasis on Diego's vanity and proneness to exaggeration, a particularly pathetic and comical example being his self-obsessed shopping for Zorro outfits in the style of his buccaneer rival Jean Laffite (pp. 319-20). A key moment in the dramatic development of both the plot and the identity of Zorro is the brilliant execution of the seemingly impossible rescue of Escalante from an impregnable port barracks. It is here, as we have seen, that Diego, acting on a cocky playful impulse, scratches for the first time the letter Z on the wall with three strokes of his sword. Previously the mark had only been made by juvenile admirers of the unknown masked man. Now Diego experiences a sudden realization: 'la advertencia de Bernardo de que el Zorro terminaría por apoderarse de él acudió a su mente, pero ya era tarde' (p. 205). At a crucial moment in the elaboration of the Zorro legend (the creation of the famous calling card of the mark of the letter Z), Diego effectively becomes a tragic victim of his own imagination. Moreover, this uneasy ambiguity is also at the heart of Zorro's supposedly real name, Diego. Toypurnia's seemingly surprising insistence on the name Diego for her child is shrouded in mystery (p. 36). Yet when Toypurnia eventually explains to her grown-up son that she chose to give him the name of his pro-Indian and freedom-loving Spanish grandfather, Diego responds:

> —Siempre tuve curiosidad. ¿Sabías que Diego quiere decir suplantador?
> —No. ¿Qué es eso?
> —Alguien que toma el lugar de otro—explicó Diego. (p. 337)

This enigmatic allusion is never returned to or clarified. Coming in the context of Zorro's return to California to rid its people of evil and exploitation, it casts a bizarre cloud over the legend of Zorro and leaves an uncomfortable sense of ambiguity in the air.

This ambivalence in the portrayal of the hero is complemented by a more generalized pattern of duality or ambiguity in the novel. This duality is that inherent in the notion of postcolonialism. The structuring of the narrative around the New World and the Old, and—even within the sections on the Americas—between Indian and Spanish heritage, points up the sense of dualism. Of course, as in virtually all of Allende's novels, a key dualism is once more that of Civilization and Barbarism. The colonial governor in Monterrey compares himself to the original Spanish conquistadors and 'ejercía el poder con la recóndita certeza de que era su maldito destino sacar a Alta California de la barbarie' (p. 27), longing to 'regresar a la civilización' (p. 30). The civilizing project is specifically linked to race, the process of white settlement being seen as a crucial element in bringing progress to 'esa tierra salvaje' (p. 86), echoed in the concerted attempt to turn the Indian Toypurnia—Pygmalion-style—into Regina, a model of European refinement. But the project fails. 'Progress' is ironically reduced to the erection of some public buildings, a bull ring and a brothel (p. 50); Regina abandons the farce of colonial assimilation and returns to her Indian ways; and the region in general becomes prey to the rapacious appetites of white colonizers like Moncada. Yet the correction of the myth of colonial 'civilization' is promoted via the idea of Independence. Diego learns to admire the United States for securing freedom from the English yoke and begins to dream of a similar future for the Spanish colonies. However, the *post*-colonial notion of Independence is hugely problematic and really indicates the residual inequalities of a postcolonial mentality. Diego's philosophy of Independence is forged and developed by his immersion into a precisely European school of thought and, of course, the Civilization-versus-Barbarism ethic is actually a product of Independence, reflecting the anxieties of the white creole elite seeking to establish authority in the wake of the immediate postcolonial experience. Is, therefore, Zorro's blow for independence at the novel's climax anything more than a romantic pipe dream?

In a more general sense, this apparent problematization of reality via dualisms may be basically a characteristic Allendean allusion to cultural relativism. It is interesting that one native American Indian finds it difficult to grasp the concept of the mythic land of Spain ('la España mítica') (p. 91)—an ironic inversion of conventional Eurocentric assumption about the so-called New World. And though guns are thought of as white man's magic (p. 15), the Indians are baffled by the unfathomable practice of planting flags in the illusion that one can somehow thereby possess land and by the white cult of worshipping a crucified man and the related habit of living contrary to one's inclinations in this world in order to enjoy a hypothetical well-being in another (pp. 11-12). While Allende may have played down Magical Realism and emphasized historical research in the writing of Zorro,[16] the novel is actually full of examples of the naturalistic presentation of primitive beliefs via a style of matter-of-fact realism—for example, the souls of the dead are trapped in tar deposits, dolphins are sacred creatures who swim in circles to keep the world in good order and assist in child birth, and Regina has a third eye in the back of her head that can see what others cannot (pp. 33, 35, 74). Apart from Diego's spiritual initiation with his totemic animal, the fox, the most striking and consistent examples of a Magical Realist style are the numerous deadpan descriptions of telepathic communication which litter the narrative. The effect of this stylistic feature is ostensibly to privilege, in a revisionary postcolonial manner, what might, in a different context, be called the Third-World view as much as the First-. They highlight the limited assumptions of the colonial mentality, often via ironic contrast—as, for instance, in the example of the priest Padre Mendoza's 'saving' of the boys Diego and Bernardo by furnishing them with magical talismans in the form of two St Christopher medals (p. 102). Yet this is no facile glorification of the primitive viewpoint. Magic for Allende is always a conduit to realism. So, for example, when the gypsy Amalia believes she has been saved by the miraculous power of her amulets and the timely intervention of her husband's ghost, the reader knows full well that she has actually been saved by the concrete actions of Zorro (p. 165). And while Padre Mendoza's belief system may be gently mocked for being no less supernatural than that of the Indians he seeks to evangelize, he is also a good and rational man committed to the cause of prosperity and justice for all (p. 17), as well as hugely influential on Diego. Moreover, Diego's full moral education essentially takes place in Europe and it is training, discipline and rational thought and argument that hone his intuitive skills and help him become the liberator Zorro.

Is the ambiguity at the heart of the Zorro figure, then, detrimental to the reader's acceptance of him as hero and standard-bearer for justice? The answer probably has to be no, for dualism—or, better, the dissolution of binary logic that it implies—is at the heart of Allende's notion of justice in all her novels. Western patriarchal binary logic underpins false notions of order and hierarchy and the destabilization of such a logic represents a challenge to monolithic notions of authority and truth. Though he undergoes a process of education and evolution, Diego de la Vega in Allende's novel is always both Diego and Zorro—boy and man, intuitive American and schooled European, adventurer and activist. At one stage, he says, referring to his two personae, that 'no sabía cómo era, si ninguno de los dos, o la suma de ambos' (p. 230). Most crucially, he is *mestizo*, of mixed race. This in-betweenness defines his (postcolonial before the event?) identity, as he grows up under the twin influences of his mother and father's side of the family (p. 44), ultimately revelling in being a descendant of the legendary El Cid as well as of Indian warriors (p. 74). Furthermore, the division between native instinct and foreign discipline is also fully blurred, as the rigorous training ('el severo entrenamiento') of La Justicia actually teaches him that instinct and skill ('el instinto y la destreza') are what direct one's movements (p. 229). Finally, the binary division is thoroughly undone through the image of multiplication. In a climactic near-fusion with his milk brother Bernardo and perhaps with the entire Californian peasantry, Diego asserts:

> Deseo que el Zorro sea el fundamento de mi vida, Bernardo. Me dedicaré a luchar por la justicia y te invito a que me acompañes. Juntos nos multiplicaremos por mil, confundiendo a nuestros enemigos. (p. 329)

A species of sublimation of the self to the people, this ideal of duality becoming multiplicity is an embodiment of the spirit of Zorro: democratic, pragmatic, sensitive to difference, committed to freedom for all.

As one would expect in the writings of a popular feminist like Allende, this idea of the dissolution of binarisms also includes breaching the gender division. In a dramatic moment towards the end, a third Zorro intervenes (pp. 373-75)—subsequently revealed to be Isabel de Romeu, the female narrator who is herself loosening the binary divide by acting as the nameless chronicler of the male Zorro's deeds.[17] Isabel's prologue suggests a kind of equivalence between female writer-narrator and male hero-protagonist. In an implicit comparison between the pen and the sword, she presents her writing as an adventure, 'ya que una página en blanco me intimida tanto como los sables desnudos de los hombres de Moncada' (p. 7). In the same passage she implies that she and Diego are equally idealists ('idealista') and that this is what compels her to write his adventures: that is, her role is to ensure that Zorro's actions have value precisely because she makes known the ideals behind them to a wider audience (p. 7). Yet her narrative often tends to undermine the male hero, as on one occasion when the narrator, in a strikingly self-conscious intervention that reminds us that this narrative is *her* artefact, interrupts the account of a daring display of heroism to tell the reader that she only has Zorro's word for the accuracy of her description and that he is prone to exaggerating his feats (p. 371). Moreover, in many senses Diego/Zorro comes across very much as *her* creation (which, in a literary sense, he indisputably is). At one stage, for instance, the narrator describes the young Diego as 'un proyecto a largo plazo' noting, none the less, that '[ella] contaba con buena materia prima' (p. 118). In a sense, the real drama here is the process of female literary creation and communication, in which idealistic or even utopian values are effectively conveyed to ordinary readers by the magic of writing, which, paradoxically, gives abstract ideas concrete form.

The figure of Isabel reinforces, then, Allende's notion of Magical Realism, in which 'magic' is a means of establishing a link with 'reality'. Hence the ambiguity of Isabel herself. The narrator's true identity is only revealed in the epilogue, but she has appeared throughout as a character in her own narrative. Her characterization reveals an intriguing blend of modesty and pride. There are numerous mildly deprecating references to Isabel's pedestrian and rather unfeminine looks, yet there is a marvellous moment when the über-macho Laffite, disarmed by the feisty heroine, exclaims: '*Pardieu!* Una hermosa dama . . .' (p. 276). The narrator is clearly playing some kind of cheeky game based on the withholding of her true identity, as in the scene where she claims to be puzzled about how Isabel could be aware of Diego and Juliana's nocturnal nestlings since she was always the first to fall asleep and the last to wake up (p. 249). Any simplistic binary distinction between narrator and character is being dissolved here. Indeed the very technique of drawing attention to literariness in what also presents itself as a species of both researched and eyewitness historical biography emphasizes the porous, non-binary nature of the text. Isabel makes no bones about the literary nature of her venture, happily referring to the people in the story as 'nuestros personajes' (p. 319). She chooses not to dwell on childhood because it is dull and suspenseless 'desde el punto de vista literario' (p. 97). She feels fortunate to have Moncada as a character because he is the necessary villain *par excellence* for an adventure story (p. 170). The narrator even tells us that: 'al principio me propuse escribir una crónica o biografía, pero no logro contar la leyenda del Zorro sin caer en el desprestigiado género de la novela' (p. 235). Unsurprisingly, the novel concludes on a profoundly literary note, the final period or fullstop underlining that this has all been a story or fabrication:

> Y con esto concluyo mi narración, queridos lectores. [. . .] El Zorro me tiene harta, y creo que ha llegado el momento de ponerle punto final. (p. 382)

The unstable transitional state between history-biography and fiction is, of course, a strong feature of Allende's narrative.[18] Novels like *La casa de los espíritus*, *El Plan Infinito* (1991) and *El Bosque de los Pigmeos* (2004) all allude to an Allende-like figure recreating the past to form a fiction, but one which will have relevance to the real world. The echo of Alba from *La casa de los espíritus* (herself an echo of Allende), in particular, is unmistakeable in *Zorro*'s epilogue where Isabel (also an echo of Isabel the real author?) reveals her true identity and tells us that she has reconstructed the past from her notebooks in a way that combines a sense of truth with the perspective of the interpretative filter of the observer (p. 379). She compares her notebook to the fantasy maps of Captain Santiago de León—a process of charting the world but in a way which, though unreal, is true in that it captures the essence of human desires. What she calls literary licence is something she sees as a legitimate form of lying because the process of embellishment creates a greater sense of truth in the reader (p. 235). There is an interesting parallel with the two languages shared by Toypurnia and

Diego, the intimate Indian tongue and the more formal Spanish. 'La primera lengua era para sentimientos', we are told, 'la segunda para ideas' (p. 332). This corresponds to the process identified in *La casa de los espíritus* whereby the amorphous ideal of non-binary *féminité* was channelled into a material expression of more readily comprehensible ideas conveyed by narrative. Perhaps when Isabel comments, as narrator, that clichés contain great truths (p. 287), she is suggesting that the power of popular narrative is that it can cut through the intellectual abstraction of theory and communicate broadly meaningful ideas in a more direct and therefore effective way. The casual tongue-in-cheek comment near the end that 'no hay nada tan insatisfactorio como un final con cabos sueltos, esa tendencia moderna de dejar los libros por la mitad' (p. 380), is perhaps meant as a swipe at the typical New Novel of the Boom with its overriding penchant for ambiguity and complexity (and the academic critical culture it helped spawn)—a form of fiction once emblematic of Latin American literature but now superseded by the global success of Allende, a figure sometimes ridiculed for her populism but who is able to reach audiences in a way that the male writers of the Boom could only have dreamed of. Similarly, Allende's narrative makes no self-conscious attempt to harness postcolonial or other convoluted theoretical discourses to underpin her ideas. Instead she revels in the fun of popular adventure, but with enough of a twist to engage her readers beyond the mere thrill of the ride. Addressing a mainstream and global audience,[19] she none the less gets across a sense of the real nature of the (Latin) American experience and the issues it raises to those whose own real worlds may or may not be Latin or even American, worlds, moreover, which are probably blissfully oblivious to the theoretical concerns of the academic study or conference hall that operate at some considerable remove from the arena of true action and adventure.

From *Romance Studies* 24, no. 3 (2006): 265-277. Copyright © 2006 by Maney Publishing. Reprinted with permission of Maney Publishing.

Notes

1. Philip Swanson, *Latina Americana Fiction: A Short Introduction* (Oxford: Blackwell, 2005) gives a fuller account of the issues raised here. With regard to the broad critical divide mentioned, compare, for example, Donald Shaw, *Nueva narrativa hispanoamericana* (Madrid: Cátedra, 1999); and Gerald Martin, *Journeys through the Labyrinth* (London: Verso, 1989). See also Swanson, *The New Novel in Latin America: Politics and Popular Culture after the Boom* (Manchester and New York: Manchester University Press, 1995) for a commentary on this division; and Martin, 'Alvaro Mutis and the Ends of History', *Studies in Twentieth Century Literature*, 19 (1995), 117-31, for a response. A useful survey of critical reactions to Allende is Beth Jörgensen, '"Un puñado de críticos": Navigating the Critical Readings of Isabel Allende's Work', in Rosemary G. Feal and Yvette Miller (eds), *Isabel Allende Today* (Pittsburgh: Latin American Literary Review Press, 2002), pp. 128-46. There have, of course, been many very appreciative studies of Allende's work, as the previous survey shows: among those not mentioned by Jörgensen are Marcelo Coddou (ed.), *Los libros tienen sus propios espíritus: Estudios sobre Isabel Allende* (Xalapa: Universidad Veracruzana, 1986); Sonia Riquelme Rojas and Edna Aguirre (eds), *Critical Approaches to Isabel Allende's Novel* (New York: Peter Lang, 1991); Karen Castellucci Cox, *Isabel Allende: A Critical Companion* (Westport: Greenwood Press, 2003). Jörgensen is one of those who criticize Allende. For some of the other criticisms mentioned, see, for instance, Donald L. Shaw, *The Post-Boom in Spanish American Fiction* (Albany: State University of New York Press, 1998) and Susan Frenk, 'The Wandering Text: Situating the Narratives of Isabel Allende', in Anny Brooksbank Jones and Catherine Davies (eds), *Latin American Women's Writing: Feminist Readings in Theory and Crisis* (Oxford: Clarendon Press, 1996), pp. 66-84 (Frenk also quotes from: Catherine Boyle, *Chilean Theatre 1973-1985* (Rutherford NJ, 1992)). Frenk herself is not negative and confronts precisely perceived mischaracterizations of Allende's work. The ideas in this opening paragraph are explored in: Philip Swanson, 'California Dreaming: Mixture, Muddle and Meaning in Isabel Allende's North American Narratives', *Journal of Iberian and Latin American Studies*, 9 (2003), 57-67. The reference to Z/Z in the title of this article is, of course, a play on Roland Barthes' *S/Z* as well as a small *hommage* to a chapter of Bernard McGuirk's *Latin American Literature: Symptoms, Risks & Strategies of Post-Structuralist Criticism* (London: Routledge, 1997)

2. Allende's comments are in Isabel Allende, 'La magia de las palabras', *Revista Iberoamericana*, 51 (1985), 451; John Rodden (ed.), *Conversations with Isabel Allende* (Austin: University of Texas Press, 1999), p. 309.

3. The quotation is from Mark I. Millington's excellent article, 'On Metropolitan Readings of Latin American Cultures: Ethical Questions of Postcolonial Critical Practice', in Robin Fiddian (ed.), *Postcolonial Perspectives on the Cultures of Latin America and Lusophone Africa* (Liverpool: Liverpool University Press, 2000), pp. 27-50. It is not the intention here to rehearse yet again the arguments of postcolonial criticism in detail: the focus will be on Allende's own intuitive articulation of a broadly parallel approach. Millington and Allende above are quoted in Swanson, 'California Dreaming'. For a fuller explanation and justification of Allende's break with tendencies towards

complexity in Latin American fiction, see Philip Swanson, 'Tyrants and Trash: Sex, Class and Culture in *La casa de los espíritus*', *Bulletin of Hispanic Studies*, 71 (1994). 217-37.

4. The ideas on Allende and Magical Realism in this and the next paragraph are explored in Philip Swanson, 'Magical Realism and Children's Literature: Isabel Allende's *Ciudad de las Bestias*', in Stephen M. Hart and Wen-chin Ouyang (eds), *A Companion to Magical Realism* (Woodbridge: Támesis, 2005), pp. 168-80.

5. The novels concerned are *La Ciudad de las Bestias* (2002), *El Reino del Dragón de Oro* (2003) and *El Bosque de los Pigmeos* (2004). The capitalization, unusual in Spanish titles, is correct as it stands. The use of a Californian hero raises the question of the changes in Allende's writing since her move to the USA; for more on this, see note 15 below and Swanson, 'California Dreaming' and 'Magical Realism and Children's Literature.'

6. Much of the background information here on Zorro is to be found on the website of Zorro Productions Inc. (http://www.zorro.com/) and in the book written by their Vice-President and Creative Director, Sandra Curtis: *Zorro Unmasked: The Official History* (New York: Hyperion, 1998). I am grateful to Sandra Curtis for her generous response to my queries on Zorro.

7. Joseph Jackson's introduction to the 1955 University of Oklahoma Press (Norman, Oklahoma) edition offers a useful survey of the Murrieta phenomenon. More recently, see John Boessenecker, *Gold Dust and Gunsmoke* (New York: John Wiley and Sons, 1999), dealing with a range of gold-rush outlaws. A useful source is William Mero, 'Joaquín Murrieta: Literary Fiction or Historical Fact?' (http://www.cocohistory.com/essays-murrieta.html). Note that, due to Anglicization, the outlaw is often referred to as a variation on Joaquin Murieta rather than Joaquín Murrieta.

8. The website of Blakeney Manor, the 'home of the Scarlet Pimpernel', is an amusing and useful resource (http://www.blakeneymanor.com/).

9. See http://www.canevaworld.com/ms/legend_e.php.

10. Quoted by Dan Glaister in 'Zorro and Me', *The Guardian*, G2 (18 May 2005), 6-7 (p. 6). This is a useful source, as is Aitana Beascoa, 'La marca del Zorro', *Qué leer*, 101 (2005), 56-57. Allende explained the background to the project at a launch press conference in Birmingham, Alabama, in May 2005.

11. The privateer's name is usually rendered as Lafitte (as in the English translation of Allende's book), though Laffite is the spelling he used in his signatures and the one used in the original Spanish version of Allende's novel. Another small inconsistency is that the map accompanying the HarperCollins English edition of *Zorro* spells Barataria as Barrataria.

12. So called because Bernardo's mother Ana, a neophyte from the local Mission, also nurses Diego following his mother's hugely debilitating labour.

13. Isabel Allende, *Zorro: Una Novela* (New York: HarperCollins, 2005), p. 83. All subsequent references will be incorporated into the main text.

14. The novel is actually full of subtle allusions to adventure films, most notably Westerns, James Bond movies and tales of super-heroes. The centring of *Zorro* around the backstory of the hero's growth and preparation for his future role brings to mind Quentin Tarantino's *Kill Bill* movies (2003 and 2004) and, more recently, Christopher

Nolan's masked-man epic *Batman Begins* (2005). Moreover, the filmic references reinforce the idea to be discussed later of idealistic fiction as a potent source of inspiration for real-life practices.

15. The element of command comes across much more strongly in the English version: *Zorro: The Novel*, trans. by Margaret Sayers Peden (New York: HarperCollins, 2005), pp. 351, 358. It is worth noting that Allende's novels are now usually published more or less simultaneously in English and Spanish, and that even the Spanish version of recent novels has been published in New York. This suggests that the writer is consciously addressing an audience well beyond Latin America, including specifically the Hispanic USA and the wider global market.

16. See, for example, Vanessa Thorpe, 'Hero Worship', *Books Quarterly* (Waterstone's), 17 (2005), 42-47.

17. Interestingly, Isabel, with her mixture of boyish awkwardness and adventurousness on the one hand and feminine beauty on the other, is a kind of embodiment of the non-binary ideal. At one stage the young female, whilst becoming increasingly aware of her womanliness and nascent sexuality, is described as having 'un aspecto viril' or boyish appearance and wishes she had been born a man (p. 254).

18. For more developed arguments on this aspect, see Swanson, 'Tyrants and Trash', 'California Dreaming' and 'Magical Realism and Children's Literature'.

19. See note 15 above.

Unscrambling Allende's "Dos palabras":
The Self, the Immigrant/Writer, and Social Justice_____

Luz María Umpierre

> I lost the world where I belonged. Now I don't belong anywhere.
>
> —Isabel Allende (Cheever)

This paper rose out of a "request." In 1996, for five and a half months, I worked as a resource person and teacher at Fayetteville-Manlius High School, a prestigious public school on the outskirts of Syracuse, New York. One of our Spanish teachers found out that Isabel Allende was coming to town to give a lecture. Concerned about the students' provincialism in not knowing who Isabel Allende was, she proposed that all advanced Spanish, English, Social Studies, and History classes at the school read one of Allende's short stories from *Eva Luna*, "Dos palabras," in its English translation, and that the students be encouraged to attend the lecture by Allende in a plush conference hall in downtown Syracuse at $18 a ticket.

Mind you, even in this plush neighborhood where the school is located, not too many students were eager to pay the fee to hear a woman they had never heard of. So the teacher had another "brilliant" idea: I would give a lecture to the whole school on Isabel Allende as a sort of pep rally to get them motivated to attend the lecture.

To make a long story short, the school bureaucracy intervened to explain how it was impossible for me to give a single lecture on Allende. So a scheme was set up by which I would scramble myself, or as we say at home, become a "revoltillo." I was to give the same lecture for seven out of the eight periods that comprised the school day. As it turned out, I saw over 450 students on that day, and in having to repeat myself, my jokes, my questions, over and over again, I came to realize that the story of "Dos palabras" was like one of those programs on TV for which the signal is scrambled so we cannot watch it without subscribing to that particular channel or paying our cable TV bill. Yes, I'll answer your question. Most of my papers in academia are weird and shocking, but the idea of Allende playing the part of a cable TV company is one that was clear to me in this reading. It was probably because of my reading being weird that quite a number of students decided to dish out the $18 and go see Allende in person in a hall packed with over 2,000 people from a staunch conservative, Republican city in upstate New York.

I began my "lecture/reading" by explaining that in order to understand the historical underpinnings of the stories of Allende from *Eva Luna*, one has to understand the plight of the poor and indigenous people in Chile. To exemplify this, I explained that the main character in "Dos palabras" was born into a family so miserable that until she was twelve years old, all she could do was to try to survive hunger and fatigue. I explained that there is a high mortality rate among infants in Chile (I explained that that is so in the US, too). At one time, Belisa, the main character, had to bury four of her brothers. It is precisely her fear of dying that drives her to get away and run to the coastal lands, away from her place of birth. It is there that Belisa learns that there is something called "words"—reading, writing—in the world. Belisa learns to read because, as she explains, words are not owned by any one person, as is the case with land. I explained to my young audience that if you are not a landowner in Latin America, the next best thing, if you are an upwardly mobile privileged person, is to embark on a quest for wealth, to engage in commerce.

Belisa, although not privileged, finds a second reality in learning about words: she can trade and do commerce with them. I explained to the students that in many Latin American countries, people who can read establish themselves in public places, even on the streets, ready to write a letter, a document, a love poem, for a fee. This trade has been vividly portrayed in the film *Central Station*.[1] Belisa had a tent with which she established herself at fairs to offer her services just like the main female character in the film. I began to think about all the people I had helped myself to fill out documents in this country to claim health benefits, social security, and the like. It was at this point in the lecture, when I started to feel an affinity with the text, that I noticed that Belisa's name, read unscrambled, was "Isabel." I realized that Allende's main writings had come after she migrated out of Chile where she, like Belisa, had had to run away from her place of birth for fear of death. It was in Venezuela that her writing of novels began. And it is at that time of starting to write that people in academia labeled Allende herself a rerun of Gabriel García Márquez. I even attended a conference in Costa Rica in the 1980s where Allende was accused of not being a feminist and of being a farce—a copycat.[2]

These experiences of my own had made me better realize the connection between Allende's and Belisa's realities in the story. Belisa at one point in her life read the dictionary, a book that she bought with her first savings, but she quickly threw it into the sea after realizing that she did not wish to sell "palabras envasadas"—canned words. Well, I said to myself, Allende herself had to get rid of the García Márquez "dictionary" in her life, metaphorically speaking, in order to be able to rise as a writer in her own right. By rejecting the dictionary, also, Belisa wanted to declare her independence from the commercialist enterprising world that had devastated the Chilean economy, especially the Chilean mines. Belisa does not want her trade of words to be equated with the established business class that devastated Chilean natural resources. By the same token, I thought, Allende had to disassociate herself from the main trafficker of words to whom she was being compared at that time in the 1980s in order to be taken as a bona fide writer.

In a recent CNN/*Time Magazine* interview Allende has said: "Maybe my books sound like my life." In "Dos palabras" Allende wrote about her own life as a writer/immigrant and about the power of words to achieve social justice. In the story, Belisa becomes famous as a trader of words because of the fact that she gives each client two secret words to have as their own. The ability to empower her clients with ownership is important if we take into consideration that the people

---

who seek her are illiterate and poor. Her fame becomes such that a military man, known as El Coronel in the story, kidnaps her in an attempt to have her work for him. El Coronel wishes to be elected President and for that he needs a "discourse"/speech that he can give to the people and incite them into voting. Even though she has been kidnapped for this task, she agrees to do it because she feels "el impulso de ayudarlo, porque percibió un palpitante calor en su piel" (14). Although he is an illiterate militia man, it is what she senses within him, his passion, his warmth, that drives her to write.

Allende herself is keenly aware of the importance of following passionate characters, especially those who don't follow the norm. Her cousin/uncle Salvador Allende was such a man, a man who believed in socialist ideals at a time when they were being persecuted on the American continents by the United States in light of Cuba. For his passionate ideals, he lost his life and rule of his country.

After Belisa decides to compose the "discourse"/speech for El Coronel, she says that she wanted to *descartar*, leave out, "las palabras ásperas y secas, las demasiado floridas, las que estaban destenidas por el abuso, las que ofrecían promesas improbables, las carentes de verdad y las confusas, para quedarse sólo con aquellas capaces de tocar con certeza el pensamiento de los hombres y la intuición de las mujeres" (18). In this description we see how words are being described as people. Belisa wants to leave out words that have been abused, lies, and confusing speech. In her discourse she wants to produce a statement that would make both men and women feel for what they hear out of both thought and intuition, and be touched by it.

El Coronel's campaign around the country, repeating Belisa's created speech, also resembles Salvador Allende's coming to power. El Coronel wanted to go to "los pueblos más olvidados" (19), the most forgotten places in the country. The reactions of those who listened to him resemble too the reactions given by the supporters of Salvador Allende: "estaban contagiados de su deseo tremendo de corregir los errores de la historia y alegres por primera vez en sus vidas" (19). They felt moved because they thought that the country stood its first chance to right what was wrong through socialist ideas.

Up to now we have seen how Belisa's story resembles Isabel Allende's own and the story of the ideals represented by Salvador Allende. It is at the crux of the success of El Coronel with Belisa's words, however, that we see another literary mechanism come into play.

While El Coronel had been successful, he was now coming more and more under the spell of the two words that Belisa had given to him. The words become synonymous with the feeling he had when Belisa whispered them into his ear: a feeling of raw passion. His senses become possessed with the memory of "el olor montuno, el calor de incendio, el roce terrible y el aliento de yerbabuena" (20). The description allegedly is that of Belisa, but it is inescapable to think that this is also the description of a countryside. He remembers the smell of mountains, the heat of burning, the smell and touch of the *yerbabuena* plant. In my estimation, he has fallen in love not necessarily with Belisa, something that is obvious, but rather with the country that he has now seen.

At this point in the story, El Coronel's right-hand man sees that he is becoming less of a political and military man and more of a person obsessed with words. In his fear of losing El Coronel, he seeks Belisa, who had already been waiting for this to happen. The two personal and secret words that she gave to El Coronel have changed his life. She takes with her "su tintero, . . . el lienzo": ink and paper, the tools of her trade in following El Mulato. By empowering El Coronel with words, she has made him lose his "machismo" and gain a better sense of his country and of himself. He no longer needs "los ojos carnívoros del puma"—his fierceness for battle—but rather his "quietud," his quiet understanding of the power of words as fighting tools (20). Belisa's two words and her speech have also transformed his view of the nation. When he first approached Belisa, he just wanted the "discourse"/ speech to be able to speak like a candidate, like a politician, and to be accepted and elected by popular vote. After repeating the speech around all corners of the country, acceptance is reached, the presidency is achievable, but this is no longer enough for him. He needs to have the country by him and with him, and the country for him is now symbolized by Belisa. Instilling, with magic words, the love of country through love of words has been Belisa's major achievement.

In the case of Allende, it is because of her exile from Chile to Venezuela that she herself began to feel that words could capture the country and the family she had lost. Thus, she set out to write *La casa de los espíritus* as a way of putting in a scrapbook family memoirs or, metaphorically, making a video to remember her own country.[3]

Allende had become homeless, a woman without a country. Carole Boyce Davies paraphrases June Jordan and what was said at the "Dreaming of the Homeland: African Writers in Exile Conference" and states that:

> Being homeless can also carry a privilege of the ability to move rather than being abused, oppressed or exploited. In other words, homelessness itself cannot be trivialized or essentialized into a flat, monolithic category. For some writers exile is a desired location out of which they can write. (114)

It is Belisa's exile from her home in the short story that provokes her to devote her life to writing for those who are "analfabetas." By comparison, it is Allende's exile into Venezuela that brings about her need to capture the memories of her lost home in a novel for herself and those who like herself had to flee after the coup. Belisa's exile from her home brings her closer also to the inner politics of her own country as a result of her association with El Coronel. Allende's homelessness provokes the yearning to "remember" herself to that home by using her creative powers to write her story and that of her family. Neither Belisa nor Allende, however, write straight memoirs of their lives in their state of homelessness, but rather decide to empower others through their writing. Belisa does this by helping the illiterate and El Coronel to communicate freely and to open their imaginations to the power of words and memory with the aid of the two secret words that she bestows on her clients. Allende, by fictionalizing her life and using magic realism, constructs her story as a universal "relato" for anyone remembering him or herself to the homeland.

And now a confession. Why did Allende's story affect me so profoundly when I was giving my lecture to the students at the high school, as I mentioned at the beginning of this paper? Why did I choose to submit this paper/story on exile for publication? I have personal reasons. I myself am in exile from my homeland—Puerto Rico. In "Dos palabras" Belisa ran away from her home for fear of dying of hunger. Allende herself left Chile fearing for her life because of her association with Salvador Allende at a time of persecution. I left Puerto Rico because it had become intolerable to live in my own homeland as a Lesbian.

Shortly before the incident at the high school that provoked my initial comments for this paper, I had undergone some of the most horrific experiences that any human could go through. In 1992, I was presented with false charges by SUNY Brockport in an effort to have me fired from my tenured position because of my advocacy for Gay and Lesbian rights, my open Lesbianism, and how I had risen to defend Puerto Rican students, women, the disabled, against the injustices of one of the worst university atmospheres that I have ever witnessed in my life. Suspended without pay, for years I fought a legal battle that went up to the Second Circuit Court of Appeals in the federal court system. For two of those years, having lost my home, my savings, my livelihood, I was homeless myself for a period of time—literally homeless. Thus, after reconstituting myself and regaining my lost dignity by being given a job at the high school where the ideas for this paper began, I started to engage once more in the realm of my own creative writing, my own trafficking with words, my homeland.

"Language," says Czesław Miłosz, "is our only homeland." And I knew then that laboring with Allende's short story and its deciphering, its "unscrambling," were also revealing aspects of my own exile and homelessness while I was creating my own home of words. It was after my delving into the world of Allende and Belisa that I finished my collection of poems *for Christine* in honor of those who had helped me to survive. My book has been described as proof of how the human spirit can survive in spite of uttermost humiliation. While homeless, I would go without eating and used the little money I had to rent computers for a few minutes in order to express my own pain and my ordeal in poems. In those minutes in which I wrote, I had a connection to the idea of a home: language was my shelter, my safe haven, my protector, my hope.

I will go back to a quote of Davies that I used previously: "Being homeless can also carry a privilege of the ability to move rather than being abused, oppressed or exploited" (114). I have found these words to be true in my own life. Exile from our home or homeland can allow us to stand in opposition to our own victimization. In my case, it was the rigidity of my parent/homeland towards Gays and Lesbians that provoked my initial exile, an exile that helped me speak about my own truths from abroad without the fear of becoming a victim of my own language and words. Even though speaking those truths and others about social justice caused me the persecutions at SUNY Brockport, I was able to survive because I had stood before alone in exile with only the power of my own words. And all of us—Allende, Belisa, myself, and those of you in exile—in seeing our societies from a distance, our homes from afar, and our homelands from abroad, we can regain the realm of words which returns us always to language, our ultimate home.

This essay first appeared in *MELUS: Journal of the Society for the Study of the Multi-Ethnic Literature of the United States*, issue 27.4 (Winter 2002), pages 129-136, and is reprinted by permission of the journal. Copyright © 2002 by MELUS/University of Connecticut.

Notes

To my aunt Carmen who filled my head with stories of our people and asked me to imagine worlds into which I could transcend.

1. A Brazilian film nominated for the Oscar as best foreign film in 1999 that deals with the relationship between a woman and a child. The woman sits at a central station of trains and offers her services to write letters and poems, or fill out documents for anyone who can pay her.

2. I presented a paper in 1991 on this subject at an international conference in homage to Allende at the University of Miami. I also tried to publish, between 1984 and 1991, an article unmasking the alleged "feminist" scholar who made the assertions against Allende and her lack of "feminism." Time after time my article was rejected on the grounds of being too political. However, the anti-Allende critic continued to be given a voice in newspapers like *Suplemento en Rojo* (Puerto Rico) to continue her attempt at defaming Allende.

3. It does not surprise me that her novel has been made into a film with Allende's assistance. However, Allende says that watching Meryl Streep and Jeremy Irons in *House of the Spirits*, the film, she forgot that they were playing her grandparents. In my opinion, another level of distance was established in her once she saw the "representation" of her own words and life.

Works Cited

Allende, Isabel. "Dos palabras," [in] *Cuentos de Eva Luna*. Buenos Aires: Sudamericana, 1990. 13-22.

Cheever, Susan. "Portrait: Isabel Allende." s.d.

CNN/*Time Magazine*. Interview with Isabel Allende. 20 June 1999.

Davies, Carole Boyce. *Black Women, Writing and Identity: Migrations of the Subject*. London and New York: Routledge, 1994.

Foster, Douglas. "Isabel Allende Unveiled." *Mother Jones* (December 1988): 43-49.

Miłosz, Czesław. Poetry Reading at the M.L.A. Annual Convention, 1998.

Umpierre, Luz María. *for Christine*. North Carolina: Professional P, 1995.

The Cultural Work of Magical Realism in Three Young Adult Novels_____

Don Latham

Magical realism, once associated almost exclusively with Latin American literature, can now be found in literary works from around the world, including literature for young adults. Neither fantasy nor realism, magical realism combines elements of both to present a matter-of-fact world in which the extraordinary exists side by side with the mundane realities of everyday life. That magical realism would be particularly well suited to the young adult novel is not surprising given the means by which it accomplishes its cultural work. As Lois Parkinson Zamora and Wendy B. Faris explain, magical realism transgresses boundaries; it concerns itself with "liminal territory . . . phenomenal and spiritual regions where transformation, metamorphosis, dissolution are common" (1995, pp. 5-6). In significant ways, this liminal territory mirrors the "in-betweenness" of adolescence itself—a state that is no longer childhood and not yet adulthood.

Of the numerous characteristics of magical realism outlined by Faris, five seem especially apropos to the thematic concerns of young adult fiction:

1. the unsettling disruption of otherwise realistic narratives by magical events or beings;
2. a merging of different realms;
3. a depiction of identity (as well as space and time) as fluid rather than fixed;
4. a preponderance of metamorphoses; and
5. a questioning of the established social order ("Scheherazade's Children," 1995, pp. 168-179 passim)

Taken together, these characteristics function as subversive narrative elements, serving to question and destabilize the values and as-

---

sumptions of the dominant, i.e., adult, society. In its emphasis on the fluidity of identity and the questioning of authority, magical realism proves to be a quintessentially "adolescent" mode (by which I mean to suggest that magical realism offers a liberating potential that makes it particularly well suited to young adult literature).

How then are we to understand the presence of these subversive elements within the young adult novel, whose cultural work, as Roberta Seelinger Trites has noted, is supposedly to socialize adolescents so that they will be ready to enter adult society (2000, p. 7)? The presence of magical realism within young adult novels raises questions about the cultural work of these novels as well as that of magical realism itself: (1) Can such young adult novels serve a socializing function? (2) Can magical realism function subversively within these novels? And (3) what is the relationship between these two apparently contradictory social purposes? Focusing on Francesca Lia Block's *Baby Be-Bop* (1995), David Almond's *Kit's Wilderness* (2000), and Isabel Allende's *City of the Beasts* (2002), I will argue that each novel uses the characteristics identified above to accomplish its cultural work of socialization *through* subversion.

These novels provide apt examples of both young adult fiction and magical realism. All three authors have received critical acclaim for their young adult novels, all have worked consistently (although not exclusively) within the magical realist mode, and all three have been compared to and/or acknowledged the influence of Gabriel García Márquez, the Colombian writer considered by many to be one of the greatest practitioners of magical realism.[1] The three novels discussed here share formal similarities as well: each tells a coming-of-age story, each features a grandparent who plays a pivotal role in shaping the identity of the adolescent protagonist, and each uses ghosts as a motif in its narrative presentation.

Before turning to the novels, let us consider the notion of "cultural work" and how that concept relates to the young adult novel and to magical realism. I am using the term "cultural work" in the sense that

Jane Tompkins uses it in her groundbreaking study *Sensational Designs: The Cultural Work of American Fiction 1790-1860.* According to Tompkins, cultural work is the task of "expressing and shaping the social context that produced [any given literary work]" (1985, p. 200). As such, it involves strategies that attempt "to win the belief and influence the behavior of the widest possible audience" (p. xi). What then is the cultural work of the young adult novel? According to many scholars, one function of the young adult novel is to socialize young adults and thus prepare them to take their place within adult society as productive citizens. Trites sees this developmental task as a matter not so much of becoming an adult or achieving maturity as it is of accepting one's place within society's power structures (pp. 7, 19). As she explains,

> The Young Adult novel . . . came into being as a genre precisely because it is a genre predicated on demonstrating characters' ability to grow into an acceptance of their environment. That is, the YA novel teaches adolescents how to exist within the (capitalistically bound) institutions that necessarily define teenagers' existence. (p. 19)

The cultural work of the young adult novel, then, is to delineate society's power structures and to depict the successful integration of young adults into these power structures.

By comparison, the cultural work of magical realism seems diametrically opposed to that of young adult novel, for the effect of magical realism is generally to undermine society's power structures. Maggie Ann Bowers explains that magical realism can be considered subversive "because it alternates between the real and the magical using the same narrative voice" (2004, p. 67). As a result, notions of empirical reality as being somehow distinct from magic are called into question. Magical realism might also be considered transgressive in the sense that it "crosses the borders between the magic and the real to create a further category—the magical real" (Bowers, 2004, p. 67). Whether one sees magical realism as subversive or transgressive (or both), the effect is the same: "The reader becomes aware that if the category of the real is not definite then all assumptions about truth are also at stake" (Bowers, 2004, p. 68). Because of its subversive and transgressive nature, magical realism has been the narrative mode of choice in works "written from the perspective of the politically or culturally disempowered" (Bowers, 2004, p. 33) as a way of undermining the power structures of the dominant society. For that reason, magical realism is often associated with the perspectives of certain national and ethnic groups that were at one time colonized and/or otherwise disenfranchised, such as Latin Americans, Indians, Africans, African Americans, and Native Americans. Indeed, as Faris says, through the texts of magical realist literary works, "marginal voices, submerged traditions, and emergent literatures have developed and created masterpieces" (*Ordinary Enchantments*, 2004, p. 1).

While adolescence is not normally thought of in these terms, in many ways teenagers share some of the characteristics of "the politically and culturally disempowered." Developmentally and culturally they exist in an in-between state on the boundaries between childhood and adulthood. The fact that they are in the process of fashioning their identities also means that identity seems explicitly, and sometimes frighteningly, fluid to them. And, although they constitute a powerfully seductive demographic in the eyes of marketers, teens have little real political or social power. Their behavior is highly regulated by an adult society, in which teens have essentially no political voice (at least not until the age of 18). Any real political or social power comes through a testing of boundaries, a subversion of the power structures in which they are bound. When an adolescent is also a member of a larger disempowered cultural or ethnic group, the issues become even more complex. Suffice it to say that, given the way it accomplishes its cultural work, magical realism is a particularly appropriate narrative mode for depicting the complexity of contradictions and conflicts that characterizes the young adult experience.

To be sure, magical realism is not the only narrative mode in young adult fiction that deals with identity formation, nor is it the only mode that works through subversion. Given that fashioning an identity is a foremost concern of most young adults, it is not surprising that literature written for this group reflects that concern, regardless of what other themes may be explored within individual works. But there is, I believe, a crucial difference in the *way* that identity formation is portrayed in magical realist works, which has to do with the influence of magic as a catalyst. Works of realism and works of pure fantasy may very well contain subversive elements, portraying, for example, the fluidity of identity (a particularly postmodern notion) and the corruption of adult society. But in magical realist fiction, the irreducible element of magic serves as a primary catalyst for identity formation. In realism, no supernatural element is obvious in the text although a character may profess a belief in the supernatural (in religion, for example). In pure fantasy, magic may very well be present in the text, but it is depicted as part and parcel of the alternate universe that is being portrayed; within this world magic is part of the "natural" order. In magical realism, however, the magic represents an intrusion into an otherwise realistic environment, and paradoxically it is this merging of the magical and the real that serves to socialize the young adult reader by portraying an alternative—and perhaps subversive—view of society.

A key element of magical realism is the realism, for the impact of the magic depends in large part on how convincing and realistic the context is in which that magic appears. Each of the novels under discussion here invokes realism by employing realistic settings and situations and by citing familiar modes from young adult fiction. *Baby Be-Bop* and *Kit's Wilderness* could be considered "problem" novels, a genre characterized by its supposedly realistic treatment of personal and social issues. *Baby Be-Bop*, the fifth novel in Block's Weetzie Bat series, is both a coming-of-age and a coming out story, focusing on Dirk McDonald, a gay teenager living in Los Angeles, who, after the deaths of his parents, is being raised by his unconventional grandmother. The novel depicts Dirk's developing identity and his struggle to accept his sexuality. *Kit's Wilderness* is the story of Kit Watson, a 13-year-old boy who has moved with his family to Stoneygate, an economically depressed, former coal-mining village in northern England, to take care of his dying grandfather. The novel focuses on Kit's deepening relationship with his grandfather and his developing friendships with two schoolmates, Allie Keenan and John Askew. *City of the Beasts* [the first novel in Allende's young adult trilogy that also includes *Kingdom of the Golden Dragon* (2004) and *Forest of the Pygmies* (2005)] combines elements of both the problem novel and the adventure story in telling the story of 15-year-old Alexander Cold. Elements of the problem novel can be seen in the fact that Alex's mother is battling cancer and, in fact, is so seriously ill that Alex and his sisters are sent to stay with various relatives while their mother undergoes treatment. Elements of the adventure story can be seen in the fact that Alex (minus his sisters) ends up accompanying his unconventional journalist grandmother on a trip to the jungles of South America in search of the legendary Beast. In their invocation of realism, problem novels, and adventure stories, these novels are working within well-known and popular genres.

At the same time, each novel disrupts its "familiar" narrative presentation by incorporating elements of magic. This intrusion of magic, according to Faris, causes "unsettling doubts" in the reader, but such is not the case with the characters or the narrators. And this, Amaryll Beatrice Chanady explains, is the key distinction between magical realism and the fantastic: whereas in the fantastic the supernatural "is portrayed as problematical," in magical realism it is presented "in a matter-of-fact manner" (1985, p. 24). In *Baby Be-Bop*, Block sets the stage for magic by incorporating imagery reminiscent of fairy tales. At the same time, the novel is set in the realistic and yet not quite real world of Los Angeles, a kind of "liminal territory" that Block lovingly refers to as "Shangri-L.A." Dirk and his grandmother, Fifi, live in a house described as having a "steep chocolate frosting roof," a "bird-bath held by a nymph," and "seven stone dwarfs in the garden" (Block, 1995, *Baby Be-Bop*, p. 6). Dirk also has a magic lamp, given to him by his grandmother to use as a hood ornament on his car. The lamp, she explains, is a family heirloom, to which Dirk can tell his secrets whenever he is ready. But these elements, while suggesting magic, are not themselves magical. The real magic occurs later in the novel when Dirk is visited by the ghosts of his great-grandmother and his father, and with the aid of a genie is given a vision of his future boyfriend, Duck. Admittedly, Dirk is in a semi-conscious state when he experiences these visions, after having been badly beaten by a gang of neo-Nazis. These visions could be chalked up to trauma-induced hallucinations were it not for the fact that he sees his future boyfriend. A reader of *Weetzie Bat* (1989), however, the novel to which *Baby Be-Bop* is a prequel, would recognize Dirk's vision of Duck as "true." This prophetic vision cannot be explained as mere hallucination. Moreover, as an instance of "real" magic, it suggests that the visitations by the ghosts may have been real as well.

Like *Baby Be-Bop*, *Kit's Wilderness* also contains elements of magic that cannot be accounted for through rational explanation. Kit's grandfather, for example, tells him the story of Silky, a child who many years ago was trapped in the coal mine when one of the tunnels collapsed. His body was never recovered, and, since then, he has haunted the mine, not in a menacing but rather in a mischievous kind of way. The story itself is not magical, of course, and it might be explained away as nothing more than local legend. However, the grandfather's unquestioning belief in Silky, whom he claims to have seen many times, prepares the way for Kit's own personal magical experience: Kit himself soon begins to see ghost children just at the periphery of his vision, and his perception is confirmed when he discovers that his friend Askew can see them as well. The fact that Kit and Askew see ghost children suggests that Kit's grandfather may have seen a real ghost as well. As in *Baby Be-Bop*, the irreducible element of magic allows for, we might even say encourages, a supernatural interpretation of the other possibly magical elements.

In *City of the Beasts* the magic begins almost as soon as Alex enters the jungle. Early on, he has a magical encounter with a caged jaguar that fixes him with his eyes and speaks his name: "Alexander." Afterwards, he recalls feeling as if he had entered "a different world," in which "he and the jaguar blended into a single voice" (Allende, 2002, *City of the Beasts*, p. 108). When he tells his friend Nadia about the experience, she explains that the jaguar is his totemic animal, the animal spirit that accompanies him like a soul. According to her, many people never discover their totemic animal. Alex ranks among the great warriors and shamans because he has found his "without looking" (Allende, 2002, *City of the Beasts*, p. 108). Later, while participating in the funeral rites for a chief, Alex drinks a strong potion that causes him to feel that he is being transformed into the jaguar that he saw in the cage. While this experience may be simply a chemical-induced hallucination, Alex's earlier, magical communication with the jaguar suggests that it could be real as well. Once again, the irreducible element of magic colors the way we read subsequent events and does not permit easy rational explanations.

Each of these novels depicts a world that is realistic yet contains a kind of magic that is visible to those who know how to see, and each of the protagonists has, or develops, this ability to see. As a result, each learns things about himself, including the fact that he possesses a capacity for discerning the magic that permeates the physical world. While the realism provides a credible context, the magic drives the plots and plays a major role in shaping the identities of the protagonists. Moreover, it is the incongruity between the realism and the magic that calls into question other aspects of the rational world and causes the protagonists to question the values and assumptions of the dominant society.

One such tenet called into question is the belief in a clear and stable boundary between the realms of the living and the dead. All three works feature ghosts. Dirk, for example, receives visits from his great-grandmother and his father, both deceased. They tell him their stories and, in doing so, help him to tell his own story and accept his emerging identity and sexuality. These ghosts represent Dirk's heritage, and their words attest to the power of narrative to restore what has been suppressed or lost. That these visitations may be hallucinations does not invalidate their reality for Dirk; in fact, their indeterminacy further illustrates the "near-merging" of realms that Faris identifies as a characteristic of magical realism (*Ordinary Enchantments*, 2004, p. 21). Kit also sees ghosts, in the form of the spectral children from the various mining pit disasters. These shadowy figures represent the history and tragic legacy of this former coal-mining village. Through these ghosts, and through the stories his grandfather tells, Kit comes to appreciate his own heritage and to understand more fully the rich and yet often difficult life his grandfather has led. When Kit transforms his grandfather's story of Silky into his own story as a project for school, he shows that he has internalized the past as a part of himself and in turn translated it for those of his generation. Alex encounters various ghosts and ghost-like beings in the jungles of the Amazon. One such spirit is the shaman's wife, a former slave whom the shaman mercifully liberated by killing her. In gratitude, she became his wife, and now her barely visible spirit accompanies him wherever he goes. As a former slave, this character—really more of a presence in the novel than a fully realized character—represents the culturally disempowered and marginalized and their remarkable endurance. Other ghost-like beings are the People of the Mist, an ancient community of natives, untouched by time and modern civilization. Strictly speaking, the People of the Mist are not ghosts, but they do have the ability to make themselves nearly invisible; whether this is accomplished through cunning feats of camouflage or through magic is never made clear. In any case, it is surely this trait that accounts for their having been left undisturbed for so many centuries. As members of an ancient culture and what many would call a "third-world" culture, they represent not only the marginalized, but also the ghostly persistence of the past in the present. In all three novels, the presence of ghosts attests to the unsettling permeability of supposedly fixed boundaries—between the dead and the living, the past and the present, and the marginalized and the empowered.

Further emphasizing the blurred distinctions between life and death, each of these novels features a protagonist who experiences a kind of death-in-life experience. Dirk ends up in a semi-conscious state after being beaten by a gang of neo-Nazis. After this vicious beating, Dirk wants to die—and he nearly does—but he is saved by the visitations from the ghosts of his great-grandmother and his father and the stories they tell him, as well as the vision the genie shows him of his future boyfriend. Not only do these stories give him a reason to want to go on living, but they also enable him eventually to tell his own story and in so doing accept himself for who he is. Kit Watson has a similar kind of death-in-life experience while playing the game called Death. In this "game," which is presided over by Kit's schoolmate John Askew, the participants gather in the abandoned mine pit and choose who will "die" that day. "Dying" involves entering a trance-like state, in a grim re-enactment of the multiple deaths that occurred in the mine over the years. For Kit the game is real. Unlike his friend Allie, who says that when she "died," she was just pretending, Kit insists that he did not pretend. Playing this game allows Kit to establish a connection with the Stoneygate children of the past, the ghosts of whom he first sees in the abandoned mine and then later on the edges of the wilderness. The game also allows him to symbolically confront death even as his grandfather is confronting death and to forge a connection with John Askew, whom he is able eventually to save from his own self-destructive tendencies. Alex experiences death in life during his initiation into the community of the People of the Mist. After enduring hours of this ritual, Alex begins to "[lose] his sense of time, space, and his own reality" while "sinking into a state of terror and profound fatigue" (Allende, 2002, *City of the Beasts*, p. 233). At times, he experiences searing pain and feels that he is about to lose control. At the height of the ordeal, he recalls his totemic animal, and once again he is transformed into the black jaguar. Through this magical transformation and by calling on his inner strength and courage, he is able to survive the test and become a man. Afterwards he recognizes that "he had left his childhood behind and that from that night on he would be able to look after himself" (Allende, 2002, *City of the Beasts*, p. 236).

In the process of developing an adult identity, each protagonist becomes acutely aware of the fact that identity is fluid and contingent rather than fixed, and each achieves this awareness through a series of personal metamorphoses, not all of which are directly associated with magic. Dirk loses his childhood innocence after he and his friend Pup kiss two girls. Dirk knows that this encounter has wrought an irrevocable change in his sense of himself: "Before [they] had kissed the girls they were still safe in their innocence, little Peter Pans never growing old, never having to explain" (Block, 1995, *Baby Be-Bop*, p. 26). Kissing the girl only causes Dirk to feel more strongly his love for Pup, but now that love is "rag[ing] through him bitterly" (Block, 1995, *Baby Be-Bop*, p. 26). When Pup subsequently rejects Dirk's love, saying that he "'can't handle it'" (Block, 1995, *Baby Be-Bop*, p. 31), Dirk reacts by radically altering his appearance in a symbolic attempt to alter his identity. He shaves his hair into a Mohawk, dyes it jet black, and begins to dress in black and wear buttons of punk rock bands pinned to his collar. He acknowledges, however, that his new image is merely a "disguise" (Block, 1995, *Baby Be-Bop*, p. 32), an attempt to hide the truth of his sexuality. But his actions also suggest that identity is disturbingly malleable, and that it can be manipulated to conceal as much as it reveals. The metamorphoses in Dirk's feelings and appearance are not magical, nor are they positive, but the ultimate metamorphosis he experiences is both. The visitations he receives from his great-grandmother, his father, and the genie help to transform his bitterness and self-hatred into understanding and self-acceptance. The genie explicitly identifies the power of narrative as the cause of Dirk's transformation: "'You gave your story. And you have received the story that hasn't happened yet'" (Block, 1995, *Baby Be-Bop*, p. 104). For Dirk's part, he understands the true significance of the metamorphosis he has undergone: "He was alive. He didn't hate himself now. There was love waiting; love would come" (Block, 1995, *Baby Be-Bop*, p. 105). The magic lies not only in Dirk's visions of his past and his future, but also in the transformative power of narrative. As the genie says, to "'de-story'" is to destroy; to restore is to "'re-story'" (Block, 1995, *Baby Be-Bop*, p. 104).

Kit Watson experiences a similar kind of realization, although through different means. The fluidity of identity is emphasized in Almond's novel in several ways, not all of which involve magic. Kit's friend Allie, for example, aspires to be an actress, precisely because she is thrilled by the opportunity to change her identity at will. Kit, however, rejects this way of developing his identity, as is evident in his insistence that when he "died" in the game called Death, he was not pretending. His great fear is that he may actually be, or that he has the potential to become, a figure of darkness and self-destruction like his friend John Askew. Early on, Askew tells him, "'You're like me, Kit. You think you're different, but you'll come to see that me and you is just the same'" (Almond, 1999, *Kit's Wilderness*, p. 12). Kit is both repelled by and drawn to Askew. At one point he dreams of following Askew across the wilderness, which can be read symbolically as the transitional territory of the adolescent. Kit's dream takes a turn, however, and ends violently with Askew's hands at his throat. Askew is a marginalized person in this community, partly because of his family's reputation for violence and drunkenness. Even though the Askews have lived in Stoneygate for generations, they are still outsiders of a sort. As Geraldine Brennan has observed, Askew's invention of the game called Death is a way for him "to assert the authority that he cannot acquire through a more respectable route" (2001, p. 103). Kit, then, in being both attracted to and repelled by Askew is responding in part to the boy's marginalized status. Ultimately, Kit appropriates Askew's experience for his own story while at the same time using the narrative to better understand both himself and Askew. In writing the story of

Lak, the caveboy who risks his life to save his baby sister, Kit acknowledges that he is writing the story not just for a school assignment, but also for Askew. The connection between the two boys' identities is further emphasized, and strengthened, when they work together as collaborators, with Askew drawing illustrations for Kit's stories. These elements in and of themselves are not magical, but the connection between Kit and Askew derives from their ability to perceive magic, namely the ghost children of Stoneygate. Through this shared experience, Kit and Askew experience a transformation: Kit comes to a fuller understanding of his past and of his place within this community, while Askew is drawn out of his self-destructive isolation and into the community of which he has never really been a part. Through their magical, mystical connection to each other, they are transformed in such a way that they are able to form a deeper connection with their community and, consequently, prepare to take their place as adults within this community.

Alex too experiences profound changes in his identity through his adventures in the jungles of the Amazon. To be sure, some of these changes are the result of his having been thrust into a drastically different environment from the one he is accustomed to, but others are clearly the result of magic. In many ways, the deeper he goes into the jungle, the more difficult it becomes for him—and for the reader—to separate the magical from the real. When he first arrives on his grandmother's doorstep, he appears to be a typical American teenager, or at least a typical teenager as portrayed in many young adult novels: he is a picky eater, he likes sports, he plays a musical instrument, he has a crush on the prettiest girl in school, etc. In fact, before his mother gets sick, he thinks of himself as "a pretty normal person" (Allende, 2002, *City of the Beasts*, p. 15). But during his adventure, the accoutrements of civilization are stripped away, allowing him to develop a stronger, more complex and more empathetic identity than he otherwise might have done. His finicky eating habits quickly disappear as the basic need for food takes over. He soon sheds his heavy, "civilized" clothing when it proves to be more burdensome than protective. And, as he gradually begins to recognize and accept the possibility of magic in the world, more significant changes occur. This shift in perception happens in a dramatic fashion when he gazes into the eyes of the caged jaguar. When he learns from his friend Nadia that the jaguar is his totemic animal, he begins to think about identity in a new way, and this new way of thinking changes him profoundly. Alex begins to see his innate strength, a strength that is demonstrated time and time again during his jungle adventure—during the chief's funeral rites and later during his own initiation rite. On several occasions, when he needs to draw on his inner strength, he is transformed into the jaguar. This corporeal transformation signals a sociocultural one as well, for Alex comes to realize that he "[cannot] put his trust in reason after having experienced the hazy territory of dreams, intuition, and magic" (Allende, 2002, *City of the Beasts*, p. 250). The metamorphosis in his identity is symbolized by his transformation into the jaguar, but clearly the change is even more profound than that.

In each of these works, magic serves not only as a catalyst for identity transformation, but also as a means for questioning the established social order. *Baby Be-Bop*, for example, shows the insidious and pervasive effects of homophobia on the development of gay adolescents. Dirk learns at an early age that, as a male, you are expected to be strong; difference is not tolerated: "The weak, skinny, scared boys got picked last. They got chased through the yard and had their jeans pulled up hard" (Block, 1995, *Baby Be-Bop*, p. 4). His grandmother's gay friends, Martin and Merlin, reflect the pernicious effects of homophobia in their "startled and sad" eyes. Dirk knows intuitively that "[t]hey had been hurt because of who they were" (Block, 1995, *Baby Be-Bop*, p. 6). Later, when Dirk declares his love for Pup, he is rejected, not because Pup does not return his love, but rather because Pup, having internalized homophobia, cannot accept that aspect of himself. Dirk is beaten up by the neo-Nazis partly because he insults them, but also because they know that he is gay. When they call him a "faggot," Dirk feels that, in spite of his efforts to hide it, they have discovered his "terrible secret" (Block, 1995, *Baby Be-Bop*, p. 45). Fortunately for Dirk, he survives the beating, and, with the help of his grandmother as well as the genie and the ghosts of his great-grandmother and his father, he is able to accept himself and to tell his own story. As a result of his ordeal, he comes to realize that "[o]ur stories can set us free. . . . When we set them free" (Block, 1995, *Baby Be-Bop*, p. 106). The stories become a way for Dirk to accept his sexuality and forge an adult identity in spite of the oppressive effects of heterosexual society. The magical visitations and prophetic vision, along with the ministrations of Dirk's grandmother, offer an implicit criticism of society's pervasive homophobia and in so doing help Dirk to break free from the self-loathing that such homophobia has engendered.

Similarly, Kit Watson forges an adult identity by learning about the economic oppressiveness of a post-industrial, often dehumanized, society, and it is the ghost children of Stoneygate who help to facilitate his growing awareness. The part of northern England where Kit lives is where Almond himself grew up. Almond has said that this place and its people "have historically been pretty much excluded from mainstream English culture" (Almond, 2005, "Fiction and Poetry Award Winner," p. 31). In that sense, these people have been culturally disempowered. Part of Kit's development involves his coming to understand that fact about this place and its people and his relationship to their history. In returning to Stoneygate, Kit returns to the world of his grandfather, a world that was once both nurtured by and exploited by coal mining interests. The coal mine, now depleted of its rich ore, has been abandoned, and the people who worked there forgotten. The dangerous working conditions that made this prosperity possible are emphasized repeatedly throughout the novel by numerous references to mining accidents. Shortly after Kit returns to Stoneygate, his grandfather takes him to the monument commemorating the Stoneygate pit disaster of 1821, in which one hundred and seventeen people were killed, many of them children. As Kit traces the names on the monument, he comes to that of "Christopher Watson, aged thirteen" (Almond, 1999, *Kit's Wil-*

derness, p. 21). In this moment of recognition, Kit becomes keenly aware of his innate connection with this place and its people. He also realizes that had he been born in an earlier generation he, like his grandfather, would have gone down into the pit. As his grandfather says of himself and those of his generation, "'We understood our fate. There was the strangest joy in dropping down together into the darkness that we feared'" (Almond, 1999, *Kit's Wilderness*, p. 19). Now the mine is defunct, and Kit and the other children, through the game called Death, ritually re-enact the dangers their ancestors faced. Ironically, with the closing of the mine, physical danger has been replaced with debilitating desperation. One casualty of this dehumanized economic system is Askew's abusive and alcoholic father. As Kit's grandfather explains, Askew's father is one who has been "'wasted'" because there is "'[n]o proper work for him to do, nothing to control him'" (Almond, 1999, *Kit's Wilderness*, p. 109). As a result, he is a "'bitter soul'" (Almond, 1999, *Kit's Wilderness*, p. 110) who takes out his frustration on his son. Part of Kit's identity development hinges on his coming to understand the legacy of the past, with its joys and sorrows, its dangers and harsh economic realities. Much like Dirk, Kit is able to transform these social realities into stories that help him to define his identity. Moreover, these stories help to establish his friendship with Askew—a friendship that ultimately saves Askew from both his father's abuse and his own self-destructive tendencies. But again, it is Kit's and Askew's shared ability to see the ghost children of Stoneygate that helps both of them to see their mystical connection to each other and to the past.

The insidious effect of economic exploitation is a recurrent theme in *City of the Beasts* as well. Many of the people Alex meets in the jungle are outsiders who wish to exploit the natives for their own gain, and each represents a particular societal institution. Professor Ludovic Leblanc, for instance, is presented as a caricature of the American academic. He has made a career of studying the natives of the Amazon region, yet his persistent views of them as bloodthirsty savages show that he has little real understanding of their culture or their true nature.

Mauro Carías represents the wealthy entrepreneur without a conscience. He is willing, even eager, to exploit people and resources, no matter what the cost, for his own financial gain. His corrupt comrade in arms, Captain Ariosto, is the commander of the local barracks and representative of the military establishment. Dr. Omayra Torres, an employee of the National Health Service, goes along on the expedition supposedly to vaccinate the natives against the white man's diseases, but in reality to administer viral agents intended to infect the natives and kill them off. Alex's maturation process, in part, involves his discovery that these people, these representatives of various societal institutions, are vain, dishonest, and heartless. In short, they display the characteristics that Professor Leblanc accuses the native peoples of possessing. In actuality the natives offer a contrasting model for a society based on the communal values of mutual care and support. As Alex develops his identity, he internalizes the natives' values while rejecting the values of the corrupt white officials.

It is largely Alex's acceptance of the possibility of magic—made possible by his initial encounter with the caged jaguar—that allows him, even compels him, to question his society's values. Although the novel is filled with examples of such questioning, one example in particular stands out. At one point, Alex has a vision of visiting his mother in her hospital room in Texas as she receives chemotherapy—a vision, incidentally, that his mother experiences simultaneously. This mystical vision gives his mother the strength to fight for her life. At the same time, it causes Alex to question the efficacy of medical science. Later, he works arduously to capture a few drops of the rare and precious water of health so that he can take it to his mother. He knows that "his hopes had no logical base," but he has also learned through his journey "to open his mind to the mysteries" (Allende, 2002, *City of the Beasts*, p. 318). When it is eventually revealed that Dr. Torres has been infecting the natives with a virus, Alex's mistrust of medical science and his eagerness to explore magical alternatives seem all the more well founded.

So, to return to the questions I posed in my introduction: (1) Can young adult novels that employ magical realism serve a socializing function? (2) Can magical realism function subversively within these novels? And (3) what is the relationship between these two apparently contradictory social purposes? The answer to all three questions is that magical realism in young adult novels can and does use subversive strategies to promote socialization. As we have seen, all three works under discussion here employ magical realism to question and undermine received notions about the nature of reality and the social order. However, they ultimately use this subversive technique for the purpose of socialization. All three works contain positive adult role models, especially in their portrayal of the protagonists' grandparents and their supportive, socializing role in helping shape their grandchildren's identities by fostering an appreciation for the past and a deeper understanding of their relationship to that past. Furthermore, each work depicts a protagonist undertaking a journey of self-discovery that ultimately allows him to return to society a changed and more mature person. Dirk McDonald's journey allows him to discover his family roots and to both accept and create his gay identity. Kit Watson's journey helps him discover his heritage and to integrate that heritage into his own emerging identity. Alex Cold's journey, into the jungles of the Amazon and into the recesses of his inner self, allows him to discover that he has the courage and strength to be the Jaguar. Each protagonist is changed by his experience. Each gains the potential, through creating and telling his own story, to change the society to which he returns. These three novels, in highlighting the special ability of their adolescent protagonists to see the extraordinary amid the ordinary, implicitly offer an empowering message to their adolescent readers, namely that they too have the potential to transform not only themselves, but also the communities in which they live.

Note

1. See, for example, "Isabel Allende" (2005), *Contemporary Literary Criticism*; "LJ talks to *Weetzie Bat* novelist Francesca Lia Block" (2005); and Almond (2005) personal interview.

Works Cited

Allende, I. (2002). *City of the beasts.* Trans. Margaret Sayers Peden, New York: HarperCollins.

_____. (2004). *Kingdom of the golden dragon.* Trans. Margaret Sayers Peden, New York: HarperCollins.

_____. (2005). *Forest of the pygmies.* Trans. Margaret Sayers Peden, New York: HarperCollins.

_____. (2005). In *Contemporary literary criticism.* (n.d.). *Literature Resource Center.* Gale: Florida State University, 23 Nov. 2005. http://www.galegroup.com.proxy.lib.uiowa.edu.

Almond, D. (2005). Fiction and poetry award winner. *Horn Book*, 81, 31-36.

_____. (1999). *Kit's wilderness.* London: Hodder Children's Books, 1999; New York: Delacorte, 2000.

_____. (2005). Personal interview, 22 Apr. 2005.

Block, F. L. (1995). *Baby be-bop.* New York: HarperCollins.

Bowers, M. A. (2004). *Magic(al) realism.* New York: Routledge.

Brennan, G. (2001). The game called death: Frightening fictions by David Almond, Philip Gross and Lesley Howarth. In K. Reynolds, G. Brennan, & K. McCarron (Eds.), *Frightening fiction: R. L. Stine, Robert Westall, David Almond and others* (pp. 92-107). New York: Continuum.

Chanady, A. B. (1985). *Magical realism and the fantastic: Resolved versus unresolved antinomy.* New York: Garland.

Faris, W. B. (2004). *Ordinary enchantments: Magical realism and the remystification of narrative.* Nashville, TN: U of Vanderbilt P.

_____. (1995). Scheherazade's children. In Z. L. Parkinson & W. B. Faris (Eds.), *Magical realism: Theory, history, community* (pp. 163-190). Durham, NC: Duke UP.

LJ talks to *Weetzie Bat* novelist Francesca Lia Block. LibraryJournal.com. 23 Aug. 2005, *Library Journal* 23 Nov. 2005. http://www.libraryjournal.com/article/CA6250385.html.

Tompkins, J. (1985). *Sensational designs: The cultural work of American fiction 1790-1860.* New York: Oxford UP.

Trites, R. S. (2000). *Disturbing the universe: Power and repression in adolescent literature.* Iowa City: U of Iowa P.

Zamora, L. P., & Faris, W. B. (1995). Introduction: Daiquiri birds and Flaubertian parrot(ie)s. In L. P. Zamora & W. B. Faris (Eds.), *Magical realism: Theory, history, community* (pp. 1-11). Durham, NC: Duke UP.

"I Am Inventing Myself All the Time":
Isabel Allende in Her Interviews_____

John Rodden

In September 1972, just a year before his death, Pablo Neruda invited thirty-year-old Isabel Allende, then a modest celebrity in Chile as a television and magazine reporter, to visit him at his seaside home at Isla Negra. A gracious host, Neruda praised her humorous pieces, telling her that he even photocopied them and showed them to friends. For her part, as Allende recalls in her memoir *Paula*, she "made meticulous preparations for that meeting; I bought a new recorder, wrote out lists of questions, I read two biographies and reread parts of his work—I even had the engine of my old Citroën checked so it would not fail me on such a delicate mission." Alas, unbeknownst to her, the feckless mission was doomed from the start:

> After lunch it began to rain; the room darkened. . . . I realized then that the poet was weary, that the wine had gone to my head, and that I must hurry.
>
> "If you like, we can do the interview now," I suggested.
>
> "Interview?"
>
> "Well, that's why I'm here, isn't it?"
>
> "Interview *me*? I'd never put myself through that," he laughed. "My dear child, you must be the worst journalist in the country. You are incapable of being objective, you place yourself at the center of everything you do, I suspect you're not beyond fibbing, and when you don't have news, you invent it. Why don't you write novels instead? In literature, those defects are virtues."[1]

Indeed they are. And fortunately, Isabel Allende ultimately followed Neruda's advice: A decade later, she turned from journalism to fiction, and since then has acknowledged her meeting with Neruda as "a turning point" in her life (see interview no. 11 in this volume). Equally fortunate for her readers—and especially pertinent to the contents of *Conversations with Isabel Allende*—she has "put [her] self through" hundreds of interviews in the last dozen years, a period that has witnessed her meteoric rise to the status of leading female literary voice from Latin America and best-selling female writer in the world.

The appearance in late 1994 of Allende's autobiographical memoir *Paula*, written as a farewell letter to Paula Frías, her recently deceased daughter, marked the publication of Allende's sixth book in a dozen years. Allende's books have topped the best-seller lists in Europe, Latin America, and the United States, selling an estimated eleven million copies in thirty languages (including pirated editions in Turkish, Vietnamese, and Chinese); her first two novels, *The House of the Spirits* and *Of Love and Shadows*, have already been filmed.[2] Indeed, as several interviews in this volume make clear, in one sense Isabel Allende has merely switched roles since the distant day of her fateful meeting with Pablo Neruda: she has gone from celebrity interviewer to celebrity interviewee.

* * *

Isabel Allende is a disarming and often hilarious interview subject—and her humor, which is seldom remarked on by critics of her writing, is on full display in her interviews. For instance, she confesses her "passion" for writing, declaring that she prefers it over all other activities. Then she pauses: "Well, what I like most is making love! But then second: writing. Writing too!" Later, in a more serious vein, she responds to a question about critical assessments of her *oeuvre*: "I don't know how to answer in an intelligent, academic, scholarly way. I can only tell you how I feel. I write [my work] with feelings. . ." (no. 16).

Or, as a character in *Eva Luna* remarks about the art of stories and storytelling: "If you start analyzing them, you ruin them."[3]

Although Allende's experience with and sophistication toward the role of interviewee have increased as the occasions have multiplied through the 1990s, her fundamental openness and straightforwardness as an interview subject are apparent in all the conversations in this volume. Such a collection is a kind of "biography on the pulse," both corresponding closely to the dominant events of the moment in her life and serving as a running history of her rapidly changing circumstances between the mid-1980s and mid-1990s. As such, it is an invaluable complement to *Paula*, amounting *in toto* to an informal autocritique that sheds further light on Allende's life and art: another, quite different and more spontaneous, oral form of storytelling by a master storyteller.

Or as Allende herself puts it in a 1994 interview (no. 25), explaining that her interviewing skills from her journalism days have proven indispensable to her as a fiction writer, and that she still occasionally conducts interviews to enrich her settings and enliven her character portraits: "Through interviews you can come up with things that you will never find in a book."[4]

The same is sometimes true about Allende's life, as the interviews in *Conversations with Isabel Allende* testify. They variously provide biographical details, extended self-interpretations, or glimpses into states of mind and feeling not contained in Allende's own books: e.g., her heady life in the early 1970s as a Chilean celebrity, her struggles with anger and perfectionism, and her spiritual awakening in the aftermath of her daughter's death in 1992. Thus, the interviews collected here supplement and complement *Paula*, sometimes filling in "gaps" not addressed in the memoir or even (as yet) transmuted into art in Allende's fiction.

* * *

But should we take everything that Allende says in her interviews at face value? *Paula* was released as "fiction" in Germany and the Netherlands;[5] and perhaps even Allende herself is unsure of its genre. As she remarked of *Paula* in one pre-publication interview (no. 25): "It's a sort of memoir. I think it's nonfiction; however, it reads like fiction." And Allende issues the interviewer a warning:

If you ask me to tell you my life, I will try, and it will probably be a bag of lies because I am inventing myself all the time, and at the same time I am inventing fiction, and through this fiction I am revealing myself.

Caveat lector!

Let us heed that warning and, rather than approach an Allende interview as prosaic journalistic reportage, conceive it as a literary genre in its own right, featuring "Isabel Allende" as protagonist (see no. 20).[6] For Allende is not only drawing on memory and expressing opinion, but also engaging in imaginative acts of self-transformation: they are part of the performative repertoire of a prose fabulist and unprosaic romancer.

Indeed Allende's mythic sensibility—or mythomania (or "bag of lies," as she calls it)—is part of her Romantic sui generis project of endless self-reinvention—whereby even her confession about "lying" may itself be a "lie": still another of the tale-teller's telltale tricks. Implicitly confirming Pablo Neruda's judgment of her, Allende readily admitted to one interviewer (see no. 6) her irresistible urge to embellish, recalling her experience in a Santiago publishing house as a translator of Barbara Cartland-style romances:

I changed the dialogue a little bit at the beginning so that the heroine wouldn't be so stupid. Then I changed the plot a little bit. By the end, I had the man helping Mother Teresa in Calcutta and the heroine selling weapons in Algeria!

Allende sometimes gives different interviewers different versions of major events in her life—versions that also differ from her account in *Paula*. One example are her "different stories" of how she first met her second husband, William Gordon, which range from her jumping from the Golden Gate Bridge to save him from drowning to her walking up to him at a restaurant table and asking him to dine with her.[7] Or as Allende puts it in *Paula*, speaking of her first night of lovemaking

---

with him: "I am tempted to invent wild erotic rites to adorn my memoirs, as I suppose others do, but in these pages I am trying to be honest." Still, she adds: "We can invent memories that fit our fantasies. . . . [Paula's death] has given me this silence in which to examine my path through the world . . . to recover memories others have forgotten, to remember what never happened and what still may happen."[8]

So Allende's claim that she is indeed the Latin American Scheherazade—"In a weird way, Eva Luna is me or I am Eva Luna" (see no. 25)—should thus be taken not just as biographical testimony (Eva Luna—*C'est moi*! Or *Soy yo*!). It is also yet another warning to the unguarded or ingenuous interviewer. As Eva Luna herself puts it: "One word from me and, abracadabra!, reality was transformed."[9]

Should *Conversations with Isabel Allende* itself, therefore, be classified as "fiction"? Acknowledging the relevance of the question, the careful reader may, I think, suspend an answer and move on to enjoy Allende's performance as interviewee. Whatever their genre, the interviews in this volume offer, at minimum, rich insight into the evolving self-images of Isabel Allende as storyteller, fabulist, exile, writer, memoirist, woman, wife, and mother. I hope that they will also assist the scholar-critic's understanding of the relationship between Allende's life and work—and meet the general reader's desire to know more about the lives of authors: the author as heroine in her own life drama. The interviews in this volume address both of these purposes: they enrich our appreciation of the autobiographical aspects of Allende's art and reveal the woman behind the literary characters. As such, these conversations constitute, however informally, part of what the novelist George Garrett has called "the scholarship of experience."[10]

Organized chronologically by date of publication—to highlight both the development of Allende's literary career and the evolution of her political and social thought—the thirty-four interviews in *Conversations with Isabel Allende* divide themselves roughly into three periods.

The first period covers the mid-1980s and constitutes chiefly literary interviews by well-informed scholar-teachers of Latin American literature, most of whom are frank admirers fascinated by Allende's rise to international success. Living in exile in Venezuela during this period, Allende published *La casa de los espíritus* (1982; *The House of the Spirits*, 1985) and *De amor y de sombra* (1984; *Of Love and Shadows*, 1987).

A second group of interviews—which might be termed the "Eva Luna years"—spans the late 1980s to 1991. These years witnessed the publication of *Eva Luna* (1987; *Eva Luna*, 1988) and *Cuentos de Eva Luna* (1990; *The Stories of Eva Luna*, 1991) and coincide with Allende's second marriage in 1988, her relocation to San Rafael in California, and her transition to American life. Interviewers' questions during this period turn increasingly biographical, now that Allende has become not only a literary celebrity, but also an American resident.

Finally, a third phase of interviews opens in 1991, and it spans the sickness of Allende's daughter Paula during 1991 and 1992, the appearance of *El plan infinito* (1991; *The Infinite Plan*, 1993), and the publication of *Paula* (1994; *Paula*, 1995). In this period, interviewers focus above all on Allende's relationship to Paula, who died in December 1992 of a rare metabolic disorder. Quite often, the interviews from these years are not just biographical but frankly personal, even intimate; Allende reveals that she wrote *Paula*, a mother's heart-rending memoir about her existence before and after her only daughter's death, partly to assist other families who have suffered similar overwhelming losses—and that she regards the sharing of herself in her interviews and public engagements as a chance to aid her readers.

1984-1987:
A Latin American Literary Celebrity Is Born

Isabel Allende's first book, *The House of the Spirits*, created an immediate sensation on the international literary scene in the early 1980s, and by the time of its English translation in mid-1985, Allende's novel had occupied the best-seller lists in several European countries for more than a year. The novel was quickly chosen as a Book-of-the-Month Club selection and given a royal welcome by the *New York Times*: "With this spectacular first novel," began Alexander Coleman in his rave review, "Isabel Allende becomes the first woman to join what has heretofore been an exclusive male club of Latin American novelists."[11] During these years—the early and mid-1980s—though she traveled frequently and even accepted a guest appointment for a semester's teaching at Montclair State College in New Jersey, Allende was still living in Venezuela.

As the *New York Times* review suggests, the American as well as European press took immediate note of Allende: feature stories in *People* accompanied author profiles in Spain's *El Pais* and Germany's *Der Spiegel*; *Vogue* serialized chapters of *The House of the Spirits*. Because most of the interviews from the mid-1980s were conducted by academics and published in literary or scholarly journals, however, the literary interview—rather than the personal or celebrity interview—predominates, with questions focusing on the imaginative worlds of *The House of the Spirits* and *Of Love and Shadows*, or the relationship between the novels and Allende's family history.

Broadly speaking, two related themes pervade interviews from this first period of Allende's reception: Allende's status as both a successful female writer and as a relative of former Chilean President Salvador Allende.

For instance, in the opening interview in this volume, Allende herself emphasizes that one of her major goals is to write to and for women—and as a Latin American woman. Speaking to Marjorie Agosín, a Chilean-born poet-critic and professor of Latin American literature at Wellesley College (see no. 1),[12] Allende emphasizes the femininity of her feminist characters: "I chose extraordinary women who could symbolize my vision of what is meant by *feminine*, characters who could illustrate the destinies of women in Latin America." Noting that *The House of the Spirits* had already been reprinted twelve times by 1984 in its original Spanish edition, Agosín asks probing questions about Allende's family background and literary imagination, so that her interview serves as an excellent introduction of the novelist to her growing international public.

Agosín's in-depth interview (conducted in 1984)—which was translated into English even before the publication of the novel in English—is characteristic of the expertise exemplified by scholar-interviewers in the mid-1980s. Here, in the Agosín interview, as well as in subsequent conversations, Allende discloses the autobiographical dimensions of *The House of the Spirits*, as she reminisces about her childhood in her grandparents' home and reflects on how her maternal grandmother served as the model for Clara del Valle in *The House of the Spirits*. Nor is Allende reticent here about making political pronouncements, predicting that "Pinochet and the evil ones who are with him" represent merely "an accident in the long life of my country. They will go into history as a misfortune that darkened the sky, but they will go."

Such political statements constitute the most controversial elements of Allende's interviews during the mid-1980s, which were conducted before the 1988 plebiscite that removed General Augusto Pinochet Ugarte from power in Chile. In these interviews, Allende's ideological/ feminist critique of Latin American power politics revolves around a cluster of attributes, among them "feminine solidarity," the "military mentality," and *machismo* (no. 2). Commenting on themes that soon would be apparent in her second novel, *Of Love and Shadows*, Allende elaborates on these interconnections in an interview published in 1986 (no. 3): "I have two obsessions, two recurrent phantoms: love and violence, light and darkness. . . . They are always present in my life like two antagonistic forces." Allende asserts here that her "natural tendency" is "toward socialism." As a member of "a privileged social class," she insists, she feels "a double responsibility" to campaign for social justice.

As Allende became a more visible figure in the United States, above all in American university departments of Spanish and Latin American literature, and also a more available one—especially after ending her twenty-five-year marriage to Chilean engineer Miguel Frías and publishing *Of Love and Shadows* in 1987—U.S. interviewers addressed themselves to Allende's political responsibilities deriving from her dual status as an Allende family member and a now-famous woman writer. Increasingly, interviewers cast her not just as a feminist voice but as a spokeswoman for Latin America. Challenged in 1987 by two conservative student journalists to advise U.S. youth on how to approach Latin American culture and politics, she replies: "Try and be open-minded . . . because I'm a very intolerant person. I have only become tolerant after suffering. And probably you will never suffer that much" (no. 4).

As this pronouncement suggests, Allende occasionally rose to the invitation extended by her interviewers to speak as a political authority or Latin American voice. The line of interviewers' questions discloses how utterly Americans were fascinated, from the very outset of her literary career, both by the Allende surname—which functioned as a brand-name tag to endow her with the aura of Revolutionary by Blood Connection—and by her conception of the political legacy she had thereby inherited. The glow from Allende's family heritage radiated outside left-wing academic and political circles into the literary sphere, where, simply because she was an "Allende," critics and reviewers occasionally treated her with awe, lavishly praising her work as comparable to that of Cervantes, James Joyce, and Edith Wharton, not to mention Gabriel García Márquez.[13] Or they approached her as if she were the incarnation of Salvador Allende himself, a phoenix arisen from the ashes to hurl down verbal thunderbolts on the murderous Pinochet tyranny.[14]

Most academic interviewers did not treat her with such awe. Quite accurately, they presented her as the newest addition and only woman in the "exclusive male club" of first-rank Latin American writers of the postwar "Boom," a literary movement whose members combined realism and fantasy to produce what became known as "magical realism" (e.g., Jorge Luis Borges, Alejo Carpentier, Julio Cortázar, Carlos Fuentes, Gabriel García Márquez, and Mario Vargas Llosa). Unfortunately, especially in later years when journalists have subjected her to variants of the "celebrity" interview, many interviewers' questions tend to cast Allende less as a serious writer than as a "personality"—a famous exile, the "niece" of a fallen Marxist hero,[15] the first and only woman writer in Latin America who has ascended to international prominence, or the only Latin American feminist writer who has employed magical realist techniques to depict her continent's history.

To indicate Allende's popularity, I have included a few samples of such "celebrity" interviews in *Conversations with Isabel Allende* (nos. 6, 7, 12, 21, and 30), even though such approaches, of course, beg the issue of the quality of her work, leaving such serious matters to the scholarly journals that Allende's vast public are unlikely to read. Whether deliberately or not, such "celebrity" interviews—given that they have been delivered against the backdrop of the great historical sweep of Allende's real-life drama and the saga of *The House of the Spirits*—have helped confer upon her an outsized, even mythical image that the scholars too have had to confront.

It also bears noting that, in the literary interviews in this volume, Allende frequently addresses the topic of her public image (nos. 12, 16, 17, 19). Already by the mid-1980s, Isabel Allende was known not just as Latin America's leading female voice but in some circles—quite exaggeratedly—as a socialist (or even quasi-Marxist) spokeswoman and feminist revolutionary.

The questions comparing Allende with the Latin American Boom writers also reflect, however, the interesting topic of her literary debts and writing habits. Allende's most extensive, substantive conversations on these topics during the mid-1980s occurred in three interviews with Michael Moody, who met with Allende in Caracas. Speaking with Moody in an interview published in autumn 1986 and included in this volume (no. 3), Allende addresses the influences on her of García

Márquez, of the family sagas of writers such as Russian-born Henri Troyat, and of Neruda. Asked whether she is "bothered" by the frequent comparisons between her first novel and García Márquez's *Cien años de soledad* (1967; *One Hundred Years of Solitude*, 1970)—an analogy soon to be so relentlessly voiced that it would indeed annoy her in later years—Allende says, "Not in the least. I admire him. I love him dearly."[16]

Allende discusses, with mixed emotions, the effects of fame on her work life. Feeling both excited and ambivalent, she acknowledges that she is starting to get frequent invitations to travel, and that this involves the challenge of balancing writing against other activities. "Literature is like love, a full-time occupation. It does not accept distractions" (no. 3). Allende also discusses her workmanlike, journalistic sensibility, noting that she has no fear of "the blank page" (no. 2). And she mentions work habits that she applied during the composition of *Of Love and Shadows*—habits that continue to intrigue her interviewers into the mid-1990s. Among them are her "research method"—i.e., clipping bizarre stories from newspapers and popular magazines (no. 3)—and her self-admitted "superstition" that January 8—the date on which she began composition of *The House of the Spirits* and thereafter started to write all her books—is her "lucky day" (no. 8).[17]

And here too, as yet another Allende interview crosses self-reflexively into the subject of interviewing itself (e.g., nos. 15, 19, and 20), Allende stresses the importance of interviewing to gather "research" for constructing her fictional universes. To write *The House of the Spirits* and *Of Love and Shadows*, she made use variously of letters to her mother, old diaries and notebooks of her grandmother, journalistic articles and recordings from her days as a reporter, and conversations with fellow Chilean exiles in Venezuela.

While following Neruda's advice and becoming a novelist, therefore, Allende nevertheless has also remained a journalist—and even an interviewer.

1987-1991: The Eva Luna Years

"I try to live my life as I would like . . . like a novel," says the title character of *Eva Luna*, a TV soap opera heroine, near the novel's close.

Eva's creator has often said that her own life resembles a novel—or, indeed, a magical realist *telenovela* [soap opera]—and never was this truer than in the *annus mirabilis* of 1988, when the plot twists and character changes in Isabel Allende's life story took a radical new turn—and world events impinged, oddly and yet again, on her personal history. "Out of Venezuela" might serve as a suitable title for a memoir of Allende's life during these years.

How much Allende maintained a "narrative control" over these narrative leaps is hard to say, but fueling the headlong changes was her love life: Ironically, just a few months before the Chilean plebiscite of December 1988 that ended Pinochet's rule—and which would have facilitated Allende's return from her self-imposed exile to Santiago—she fell in love with William Gordon, a San Francisco attorney. Now that she could easily go back home and live in a more hospitable political climate, surrounded by her extended family and old friends, her life seemed elsewhere—in California, *El Norte*. Choosing love over politics, she married Gordon in July 1988 (after sending the lawyer "a contract, listing all my demands, and the few concessions I was willing to make"—and giving him twenty-four hours to think it all over.[18] And then, Allende—despite her publisher's worries that her imaginative juices would desiccate in California suburbia (no. 8)—resolved to build a new life in the United States as a writer, wife, and stepmother of two young boys.

Allende's relocation to the United States and the Spanish publication in 1987 of her third novel, *Eva Luna*—the similarity of Allende's own whirlwind romance to her title character's epic love adventures and storytelling gift prompted critics to dub the author "The Chilean Scheherazade"[19]—ushered in a second, more biographically oriented phase of interviewers' concerns. Allende's life changed radically and the focus of interviewers' questions altered accordingly. This period—

which I am terming "the Eva Luna years"—featured numerous explorations of Allende's relationships to her characters, especially Eva Luna herself,[20] and reflected the international acclaim in 1989 through 1991 that greeted the appearance of Allende's first story collection, *The Stories of Eva Luna*. Approaching her work as "woman's writing," interviewers highlighted her treatment of the complex relations between feminism and femininity. American press interviewers—no longer were most of her interviewers Latin American literature specialists—hailed her work as much for what it said directly to Americans, especially to women (who comprise Allende's chief audience, as she herself notes in these interviews) as for its relationship to Latin American politics and history.

Because her transition to American life was so hectic and her professional and family responsibilities so many, Allende said, she did not immediately attempt to write another novel, but rather limited herself to stories, which could be written in short bursts of concentration (no. 12). She began writing the exotic tales that eventually would form *The Stories of Eva Luna*. Permanently settled in the United States, she now also felt that invitations to teach and lecture in the United States did not greatly interfere with her work; during 1988-1989 alone, for instance, she taught at the University of Virginia, Barnard College, and the University of California at Berkeley. One also notes her increasing comfort with English during this period; after 1990, even with native Spanish speakers, she conducts most interviews for English-language publications in English, preferring to speak English rather than have her words translated from Spanish.

A central theme in Allende's interviews is the consequence of her new American life for her international status as a Latin American voice. In a *Mother Jones* interview in late 1988 (no. 8)—conducted when she was halfway to completion of *The Stories of Eva Luna*— Allende identified three major practical changes in her daily life entailed by her move to the United States, all of which posed immediate and significant challenges for reorganizing her work life: her new role as a suburban housewife and mother, without the benefit of the inexpensive live-in household help that she enjoyed in Santiago and Caracas; her sudden accessibility to the American media and academy; and her "split life" linguistically, i.e., as a day-to-day English speaker and Spanish author.

Allende chose to stress the last two issues, seeking to transform them into opportunities: More consciously and deliberately than before, she would embrace the role that Fate had granted her and address Americans on political and social issues. She would step up to the world stage and, standing on the raised platform of literary fame, speak out on the topic of "politics and the writer" in a Latin American vs. North American context (see no. 12).[21]

One representative example is her statement in *The Kenyon Review* (no. 16), in the immediate aftermath of the 1988 Chilean plebiscite. Asked if she has "something special" to say to U.S. readers, Allende replies:

> Yes. You do not live in a bubble. You are not privileged. You are very spoiled. You think you will be saved when this globe explodes. You will not. We all share the same planet; this is a rock lost in space. We are all parts of it. There are no superior races. . . . [Latin Americans are] not [living on] another planet. They are not on Mars. It's our planet. It's our land, and these borders are just illusions. We trace them on a map, but they don't exist. We all share the same planet.

Or as she told *New Perspectives Quarterly* in 1991, responding to the interviewers' comment that Americans possess a Disneyesque outlook whereby "everything will have a happy ending," "The attraction of Disney is undeniable. . . . I have been living in the U.S. for three years and what I really miss about my Latin American culture is the sense I had there of belonging in a common project, of being part of a coherent group, with a common set of values. . . . Due to our history we have a sense of fate, or destiny, that the U.S. lacks" (no. 17).

Such political outspokenness has elicited sharp and sometimes condescending rebukes, especially from a few conservative critics, who deride Allende's politics as black-and-white and simplistic. It is easy to see how her summary of the history of the Pinochet regime in *New Perspectives Quarterly*, a left-liberal magazine, could contribute to such dismissals: "All the violence, repression, and brutality came from the military. And the people responded with nonviolence, pacific protests, solidarity, and organization." But Allende is unfazed by critics' hostility toward her work, whether political or literary. Responding to charges that her work is kitschy, she says: "What do I do with my truth? I write it" (no. 16). Indeed she even goes so far as to run through a dismissive catalogue of her critics' complaints:

Contradictory things are said all the time. I couldn't please everybody, and I shouldn't even try. . . . One "bad" thing people say is that I discovered a very attractive mixture of melodrama, politics, feminism, and magic realism and I throw it all together. . . . Another "bad" thing is that I'm very sentimental and that I'm not detached, I'm not cold; therefore I can be very kitschy, very campy sometimes. What other bad things can I remember? Oh yes, that it resembles García Márquez. (no. 8)[22]

Despite her cooperativeness with individual critics, Allende makes it clear that she takes a dim view of them as a species:

Critics are terrible people. They will label you no matter what, and you have to be classified. I don't want to be called a feminist writer, a political writer, a social writer, a magical realism writer, or a Latin American writer. I am just a writer. I am a storyteller. (no. 25)

Allende acknowledges in interviews after 1988 that her transition to American life has put her at a mental as well as geographical distance from political events in Latin America. But she holds that "exile" yields literary advantages. In general, exile is "good" for a writer, Allende believes, precisely *because* it generates imaginative space and multiplies perspectives—and because one learns to "understand that your roots are within yourself."[23] Allende herself possesses a "double perspective" by living in the United States and writing from her Latin American past; she says she now has a valuable distance from both places. Another advantage of "exile" is, however paradoxical it may sound, the upheaval it creates in one's life. Allende says that her own crises have shaken her complacency and made her a more questioning, self-aware person and artist (no. 32).

Not only U.S. but also Latin American interviewers have addressed the topic of Allende's adaptation to life in California. Indeed it is interesting to see the changing response of selected Latin American interviewers to Allende after her relocation to the United States. In some cases, they begin to look upon her less as one of their own than as a cultural mediator and spokeswoman for U.S.-Latin American relations, i.e., they start to treat her much as did the American press in the early 1980s. One example of Allende's elevation to the status of cultural spokeswoman in a Latin American interview appears in her 1991 conversation in the journal *Mester*. Asked to assess the "future" of Latin America, Allende says that the continent has an important role to play in the evolving "collective consciousness" of the world (no. 15).

Related to the Latin American motif during this second period of Allende interviews is the topic of her feminism and what might be termed her "personal mythology." The publication of Allende's two *Eva Luna* books gave both U.S. and Latin American interviewers the opportunity to explore Allende's fantasy life as a real-life Scheherazade, a spinner of magical Latin American stories. Not only do interviewers express curiosity about Allende's family background, therefore, but also about her powerful and compelling identification with her autobiographical heroine, Eva Luna.

As we have already seen, Allende freely acknowledges that she identifies with Eva Luna. She has often described how she used to read stealthily what her family ordained to be "forbidden literature"—

above all, the Arabian romance *A Thousand and One Nights*—all of it stashed in her stepfather's closet in Beirut, which was off-limits to her. (In *Eva Luna*, the heroine herself carries a copy of the romance with her, deeming it "essential baggage for my travels through life," and *The Stories of Eva Luna* begins and ends with quotations from *A Thousand and One Nights*.) To several interviewers, it does indeed seem as if Allende's tumultuous life were a seamless story, reality transformed; i.e., from *reading* about Scheherazade as a girl to *becoming* "the Chilean Scheherazade" as an adult woman.

Allende is well aware that her image as a humorous, ironic Scheherazade accounts in part for her tremendous international following, particularly her high standing with educated American women. Diffidently yet forthrightly, she explains to *Mester* in 1991 that her U.S. popularity is "partly due to the great interest that there is here for women's literature," partly attributable to the Anglo-Saxon fascination with magic realism, and partly because her work is not "baroque" and therefore "easy to read in comparison to other Latin American novels"—all of which has led to her books being "read and studied in universities" (no. 15). By 1991, Allende had published five best-sellers in twenty-seven languages. Asked to explain her phenomenal international reception, Allende generously, and with a touch of humor, attributes it to her excellent translators, who invariably "improve my books" (no. 12).

While interviewers of the early 1990s are chiefly concerned with the topics of Allende's feelings in the present and her adjustment to U.S. life, they also plumb her past more deeply than in the previous decade. Much of the curiosity stems from the simple desire to know who Allende was *before* she metamorphosed—Abracadabra!—into the Eva Luna of San Rafael and began weaving her Scheherazade-like fantasies.

Where did this extraordinary woman come from? readers now wanted to know. Some interviewers, therefore, concentrate on Allende's background, inquiring about Allende's Chilean days, i.e., the years before her international celebrity; for example, the writer Alberto Manguel asks about her writing before the 1973 coup, including her activities as a playwright. Manguel also addresses her participation as a contributor and staff member on publications such as *Magazine Ellas* and *Paula*, the latter of which was the first Chilean publication to address taboo social topics such as abortion, divorce, and drugs; and also her involvements with the children's magazine *Mampato* and her TV programs and short films. Already at the age of twenty-nine, in 1971, Allende had a much-discussed play, *El embajador* [The ambassador], performed in Santiago, along with a play titled *La balada del medio pelo* [The parvenu's ballad] (no. 13). One literary/biographical interview (no. 19) shows Isabel Allende to possess a wide variety of expressive gifts, and here she delves into her literary and theatrical activities in Santiago in greater detail than in *Paula* or her fiction (see also no. 13).

The main outcome of the "Eva Luna years" for Allende herself was that she came to feel more comfortable with herself as a woman and as a writer. As she confides in a 1988 interview, the writing of *Eva Luna* vouchsafed her "a new attitude about being a woman": "I had to finally accept that I was always going to live in this body with this face and be the person I am." And she had taken significant steps to confront and cope with her "anger" toward her grandfather and the oppressive patriarchy of her Chilean years (no. 8). In a 1991 interview, she speaks of an "enraged intimacy" between herself and her maternal grandfather (the model for Esteban Trueba, the family patriarch of *The House of the Spirits*). "We never agreed on anything but we adored each other. I saw him every day while I was in Chile, until 1975" (no. 13). She had also refused to take her husband's family name because of her anger. "My anger towards male authority . . . continued even after my marriage. And it endures even today" (no. 13). This is another topic that Allende takes up at greater length after Paula's death (no. 32).

Allende also affirms that *Eva Luna* led to her self-acceptance as a "narrator of stories," i.e., as a professional creative writer (no. 11). With *Eva Luna* and *The Stories of Eva Luna*—and just as she is starting to write *The Infinite Plan*—Allende finally judges her apprenticeship as an imaginative writer to be over. With increasing confidence, she discusses her admiration for the work of Borges and Cortázar, disavows critics' speculations that she deliberately parodied García Márquez's *One Hundred Years of Solitude*, concedes the admittedly limited capacity of writers to affect world events, and replies to feminist critics who find her female characters stereotyped or weak (no. 11). She also admits in a 1991 interview that life in an English-language environment is affecting her writing: "My sentences are shorter, there's less ornamentation, fewer adjectives. The language is more straightforward, and . . . the text is more restrained" (no. 12). Working on *The Infinite Plan* in 1991, Allende notes that, as she has switched from Latin American and Caribbean settings in her first four works of fiction to a California setting in *The Infinite Plan*, she has moved away from magic realism to a more straightforward literary realism (no. 12).

One final comment of Allende's about her writing merits emphasis here, a comment that leaps out at the reader and makes it seem as if, once again, Allende's life of upheaval is a seamless story that reflects a storyteller's careful design. As though Allende were anticipating her daughter Paula's tragic fate and her own decision to write *Paula* partly just to cope with the loss, she speaks in May 1991—fully five months before Paula falls ill and is hospitalized, and with no awareness of her daughter's impending sickness—about writing (in the characterization of her interviewers) as an "act of remembering to forestall death." Thus does the topic that will dominate interviews of the mid-1990s arise explicitly here for the first time: spirituality. "I believe that there is a spirit, a spirit of life in everything that surrounds me," Allende says. "I try to be in touch with that" (no. 20).

1991-1995: Paula and the Beyond

But the Spirit of Death was to envelop Isabel Allende and her family first. Attending a Barcelona book party on December 8, 1991, for the publication in Spain of *El plan infinito* [*The Infinite Plan*], she received word of a cataclysmic event that would alter her life abruptly: her twenty-seven-year-old daughter, Paula, who had fallen sick on December 6 and entered a Madrid hospital, had slipped into a coma. Paula would die precisely one year later to the day. Like Alba in *The House of the Spirits*, who followed the advice of the spirit of her grandmother Clara, and wrote to "survive" the ordeal of her rape and her family's anguish, Allende coped with Paula's death by heeding the counsel of her mother, who told her: "If you don't write, you'll die."[24] Allende explains of the note-taking that led to *Paula*: "I was not thinking of publishing . . . my only goal was to survive; that is the only time that I have written something without thinking of a reader" (no. 25).

The interviews from this third period focus on Allende's personal life and on her loss of Paula; even the interviews conducted before the appearance in 1994/1995 of *Paula* devote attention to Allende's loss. Indeed, given that Allende's two books during this period are based on her husband's life (Willie Gordon is the model for Gregory Reeves, the protagonist of *The Infinite Plan*) and on Allende's relationship to her daughter, it is unsurprising that interviewers highlight Allende's roles as wife and mother.[25] What emerges is less the outsized heroic, even "magical realist" portrait of the feminist and socialist in the mid-1980s, or the exotic Chilean Scheherazade of the late 1980s and early 1990s, but rather a more subdued, humanized figure.

Put another way, it is as if we see Allende close up in this most recent round of interviews, rather than against the giant mural of Latin American history or through the gossamer fantasia of Eva Luna. The mid-1990s mark what might be called "the family period" of Allende's interviews. Some of these interviews have a familiar, even confidential tone, making them truly "conversations"; more so than in earlier years, we encounter the private woman behind the public persona. Allende says several times in these interviews that the death of her daughter had "changed" her; one interviewer remarks that Allende's recent experience had "erased all the unnecessary barriers that separate human beings" (no. 26). During my own interviews with her in April and May 1995 (nos. 31, 32, and 33) I found Allende to be a noticeably different woman—more reflective, less goal-directed, more self-revealing, less guarded—than I had in my earlier interview, conducted in 1988. At fifty-two, Isabel Allende seemed suddenly to have taken a mystical turn—and discovered a new House of the Spirits.

And with that discovery have come "lessons" that Allende has drawn from the harrowing year of Paula's sickness: the words "destiny," "trust," "acceptance," and "openness" come up again and again in interviews after Paula's death. Indeed one notes that the whole cast of her conversation has shifted to the spiritual realm:

> Life is like a very short passage in the long journey of the soul. It is just an experience that we have to go through, because the body has to experience certain things that are important for the soul. But we shouldn't cling to life and the world so much: we shouldn't cling to the material aspects of the world, because you can't take them with you. You will lose them no matter what. (no. 24)[26]

Throughout her book tours of 1994/1995 to promote *Paula*, Allende spoke about learning to "let go." As she put it in one interview: "When I said, *dead*, [Paula's death] became real and I could deal with it" (no. 23).

Elsewhere Allende has spoken of another, more mundane "death," or form of "clinging," with which she also still copes: literary ambition. "Ambition is like a bottomless pit," Allende says. After the publication of *The House of the Spirits*, she "had the sensation that I had done something in my life and I could now die in peace," but soon the hydra-headed monster returned to haunt her: "One becomes ambitious and wants more and more" (no. 13).

Asked in another interview to sum up what she has learned as a result of Paula's passing, Allende makes her spiritual discovery even more explicit:

Your approach to the world is different. . . . You become more detached. . . . You gain a sort of spiritual dimension that opens up completely your world. (no. 28)

Or as Allende put it in another interview: "I finally understood what life is about; it is about losing everything. Losing the baby who becomes a child, the child who becomes an adult, like the trees lose their leaves. So every morning we must celebrate what we have."[27]

Allende is speaking about learning a different kind of exile—a leavetaking of the temporal world—and it seems that she is approaching the sense of peace and acceptance implied in the words told to Eva Luna just moments after the death of her mother: "Everyone dies, it's not so important."[28] For Allende, the death of Paula eventually became—the paradox is only apparent—both all-important and "not so important." "Godspeed, Paula, woman. Welcome, Paula, spirit," Allende closed *Paula*. Paula Frías had merely gone to her spiritual home, joining those intrepid women who govern the Trueba mansion—or, even better, those beneficent ghosts that watch over them.

But perhaps Allende's spiritual turn has not occurred quite so suddenly as it might appear, nor been precipitated by Paula's death alone. For Allende was already working through her fiction on the "lessons" that the harrowing year of 1991/1992 would bring home conclusively. Indeed the lessons from Paula's death that Allende draws in her interviews—Destiny, Trust, Acceptance, Openness—are all thematized (though treated somewhat skeptically) in the quasi-New Age evangelical Christianity propounded by preacher Charles Reeves in *The Infinite Plan*, whose title Allende borrowed from a book of that title written by her husband's itinerant mystic-father, upon whom the character of Charles Reeves is based. Reeves proselytizes and peddles "The Infinite Plan, or The Course That Will Change Your Life," a package of lectures designed to put the recipient in tune with Cosmic Forces. Listeners flock to Reeves, and are "comforted by the certainty that their misfortunes [are] part of a divine plan, just as their souls [are] particles of universal energy."[29] And indeed, when Allende speaks in the interviews about "karma" and "Fate," it is as if she is sometimes quoting Charles Reeves—but this time sincerely, not ironically or parodically. It is as if she were preparing herself for the news about Paula—and the writing of *Paula*.

"I believe that there is a destiny. I also believe that you can do much to modify it," Allende remarks in one interview (no. 26). And so she ultimately comes to an opposite conclusion from that of her protagonist, Reeves's son Gregory, who says at the novel's close to the Allende-like author-narrator:

> I realized that the important thing was not, as I had imagined, to survive or be successful; the most important thing was the search for my soul. . . .
>
> [I never imagined] that one day I would meet you and make this long confession. Look how far I've come to reach this point and find there is no infinite plan, just the strife of living. . . .[30]

I have the impression that Isabel Allende might today say instead: "Look how far I've come, only to realize that there's more to life than the strife of living—there may even be some Infinite Plan!" I find her openness to a change of heart in matters of the spirit both courageous and refreshing.

Allende's "courage" resides, I think, precisely in her heightened awareness and commitment to relinquish tight self-control and open herself to the possibilities of a providential Design beyond her own will. And such a change does seem to be one of "heart" rather than "head"—or rather, a form of growth reflecting a greater capacity to connect her heart and head. For Allende already, by the time of composing *The Infinite Plan*, seems to have possessed the cognitive ability to recognize the existence of an Infinite Plan; Gregory Reeves reports that the Allende-like author-narrator had countered his chastened conclusion that "there is no infinite plan, just the strife of living," with words of hope: "Maybe . . . maybe everyone carries a plan inside, but it's a faded map that's hard to read and that's why we wander around so and sometimes get lost."

Allende's courage and openness have also extended to a greater capacity for self-disclosure about her private demons. Fearlessly yet modestly, she now abandons reticence in her interviews and discusses her struggles to renounce perfectionism, to nourish intimacy, and to silence her stern, unrelenting conscience and "inner voices" of Authority (no. 32). In these later interviews, readers gain a deeper understanding of the paradoxical woman behind the work: a woman who, though private, likes to be seen and noticed; who luxuriates in solitude yet possesses a flamboyant, extroverted sensibility and lives life intensely; who is a careful planner yet glories in the moment; who has a steadiness and an iron will dedicated to work, and yet also a spontaneous emotional life and a tendency to act on impulse; who has a shrewd pragmatism and keen sense of responsibility, and yet is ruled by passion and does not wait for Life to happen but rather provokes her Destiny.

And yet: What also about the other Allende—the writer behind the woman? How has she been affected "after Paula"—and after *Paula*?

"All sorrows can be borne," Isak Dinesen once wrote, "if you put them into a story or tell a story about them." In advising Allende to write about the agony of Paula's dying, Allende's mother seemed intuitively to have grasped Dinesen's insight—and indeed, writing the story of her confrontation with Paula's death has not only effected her spiritual transformation, but also affected Allende's writing. As yet, she is not quite sure how, except that she is less concerned with the literary "product" (no. 32).

In several interviews of the mid-1990s, Allende is, understandably, in a backward-looking, pensive mood—not only because she is discussing *Paula*, but also because she has built a substantial body of work—six books in a dozen years—that she wants to assess, especially now that she has learned to grant herself the honorific title "writer." Summing up her literary development in the 1980s, Allende told one interviewer that "each one of my books corresponds to a very strong emotion." She associated *The House of the Spirits* with "longing," a desire to recapture a lost world; *Of Love and Shadows* with "anger" in the face of the abuses of dictatorships; and *Eva Luna* with "accepting myself, finally, as a person and a writer" (no. 13).

The early and mid-1990s were also a time for Allende to reflect in her literary interviews on both her vocation as a writer and her literary successes and shortcomings. Implicitly conceding the force of some critics who found the politics of her second novel intrusive, Allende says: "If I were to write *Of Love and Shadows* again, I would do it differently. It is not subtle enough and I feel it is too direct" (no. 13). Although she says that it is easier to be a woman in the United States than in Latin America—since the feminist movement has advanced farther in the United States, Allende tells her feminist critics: "I don't invent characters so that they serve as models for radical feminists or young women who want to be feminists, but I simply tell how life is. Life is full of contradictions" (no. 26). More extensively than before, she also discusses the autobiographical background of *The Infinite Plan*, particularly the similarities between her husband William Gordon and the novel's protagonist, Gregory Reeves. Gordon served as the "model" for Reeves, who "is a survivor. In real life Willie is too. . . . The people who bend but never break are always fascinating to me" (no. 23).[31]

In the aftermath of the American publication of *The Stories of Eva Luna* in 1991, Allende was often asked about her plans to write more short fiction. She tells one interviewer that she's not going to write any more short stories. "I would much rather write a thousand pages of a long novel than a short story" (no. 25). And also: "I'm scared of short stories, very scared" (no. 23). Allende confesses that she has difficulty writing "erotic" scenes. "Every writer of fiction," Allende asserts, "should confront these three challenges: write short stories, an erotic novel, and children's literature" (no. 13). Allende has already written a story collection and a children's book; although she has certainly written several erotic scenes in her fiction, and devoted a whole new book

(*Aphrodite*) to sex and food, the challenge of the erotic novel remains. "I really would like to write erotic novels. Unfortunately, I was raised as a Catholic, and my mother is still alive, so it's difficult. However, I feel that there is a part of me as a person that is extremely sensuous and sexual" (no. 25; see also no 23).[32] As so often, Allende's tone is overtly quite sober—and yet also slightly playful. The reader is not certain how seriously to take her—which is doubtless the way she wants it.

A related topic that engaged interviewers was Allende's response to the film versions of *The House of the Spirits* and *Of Love and Shadows*, both productions of which she admired and enjoyed. Allende's statement to one interviewer on seeing the film version of *The House of the Spirits* attests again to her necromancer sensibility:

> Now the fiction has replaced the real story of the family, and we live this sort of fantasy that these things happened. When I saw the movie, I realized immediately that the fiction of the film is ten times bigger than the fiction of the book. Very soon, we will have the photographs of Jeremy Irons and Meryl Streep on the piano. They will be my grandparents. I will have all these famous people as my relatives.

Like Eva Luna, Allende also said that she would one day like to try her hand at writing screenplays herself. But, for now, prose fiction—novel length—is enough. And through all the vicissitudes of her romantic and family life, novel writing remains the great solace and tonic for Allende. "Writing is never a burden," she says. "It is pure joy. Life tends to be a burden, because it has very grave moments, with a very heavy karma." But she still jokes that she'll never discuss work in progress—as if such a lack of reticence might also boomerang with karmic vengeance: "It's like boasting about a boyfriend—someone may take him away from you."[33]

Life is loss, Allende admits—but she insists that she will not accept losses without putting up a good fight.

Although the leitmotif of this third period of interviews is less literary than spiritual, less humorous than contemplative, the "lessons" that Allende draws from the loss of Paula also have to do with love. Whereas in earlier interviews Allende had invariably used the word "love" in connection with sexual passion, she speaks after Paula's death also of maternal and filial love. For example, Allende says that, before Paula's death, she had practiced only conditional love, but that through Paula's departure she learned true "love" as "giving":

> I even rarely trust a lover. . . . It is very difficult for me to open up, to fully abandon all in an intimate relationship. I begin from the premise that I will be betrayed. . . .
>
> Up [until the last days of Paula's illness], all my relationships, even the relationships with my children, had been a two-way road. . . . But I was left with the everlasting treasure of the love that I gave her and that I know I am capable of giving. (no. 22)

This knowledge has been acquired by Allende at a very painful price, and for this reason she values even the pain itself: "I do not want to lose this pain," she says. "It makes me a better person" (no. 22).

In speaking of herself as a "better person," Allende is not referring to virtue in the ordinary sense, but rather to a perception that she is humbler, more clear-sighted, more forgiving, more empathic. The loss of Paula also taught Allende to let go of the urge to plan life; her new attitude of fearlessness and openness to the future is a marked change:

> I have no plans for the future. . . . If you have no plans for the future, you cannot fear it. You are not afraid of being unable to carry out those plans. I try to live today as best I can. That way I have the feeling that I have finished everything. (no. 22)

And Allende observes in an interview published in December 1994:

My daughter died, and she's with me in a way that she never was when she was alive because she had a life of her own and she had a destiny of her own. She still has them, in the spiritual world she's doing things, but the memory of her lives in me. I carry it with me and it's part of my life in a very vivid way. So vivid, in fact, that when I come here every morning I light a candle for her. I have her photograph and her ashes there and I feel her presence very strongly. There's a lot of sadness still going on, but I know that I will get over that and there will be a point when I will understand the spiritual life better and will not be stuck in the loss. I will probably be connected better to who she is now. (no. 28)

Or as Olga says in *The Infinite Plan*:

The dead go hand in hand with the living.

By the time of the appearance of *Aphrodite: A Memoir of the Senses* in April 1998, Allende no longer seemed "stuck in the loss" of Paula's horribly tragic death. Although she had told at least one interviewer in 1995 that she might never write again (no. 33), the act of composing *Aphrodite*, as Allende explained during her U.S. book tour in the spring of 1998, helped her rediscover a capacity to live in the present. She had written her memoir of her daughter's death; now she would write a celebration of life: a "memoir of the senses." *Aphrodite* is, she said in one interview, her "healthy reaction to mourning and writer's block" that followed Paula's death.[34]

In another interview, she discussed her struggle to emerge from her "long tunnel" of grieving,[35] a battle that forms a prominent theme in *Aphrodite*: "After the death of my daughter, I spent three years trying to exorcise my sadness with futile rituals. Those years were three centuries filled with the sensation that the world had lost its color and that a universal greyness had spread inexorably over every surface. I cannot pinpoint the moment when I saw the first brush strokes of color, but when my dreams about food began, I knew that I was reaching the end of a long tunnel of mourning and finally coming out the other end, into the light, with a tremendous desire to eat and cuddle once again."[36]

On Allende's own account, she recovered her artistic powers and her feeling for the sensuality of language by immersing herself joyously in the world of amour and appetite. Revive the senses and the imagination, counsels Allende, and you will revive the spirit too! So Isabel Allende affirmed life by relishing two of its earthiest appetites—sex and food—and in a light, delicate, feminine, playfully poetic way. "When I wrote *Paula*, about her death, I cried every day," Allende told an interviewer for *Ms*. "Now, when I was putting together *Aphrodite*, I finally laughed. A lot. . . ."[37] Mixing the carnal and the culinary, *Aphrodite* connects Allende's love of writing to the prime drives that create and perpetuate life and make it pleasurable—and thereby reconnects the author to her deepest creative wellspring as a storyteller.

In literary terms, *Aphrodite* is virtually unclassifiable.[38] Viewed biographically, however, it is clear that this lavishly illustrated cookbook served as a literary aphrodisiac for Allende's dormant literary powers. And here we can witness the Latin American Scheherazade assuming the persona of the Greek goddess of love and beauty. Indeed the new work is the author-grandmother's personal recipe for summoning the love goddess within, a self-help book on how to recover a keen taste for life's sweetness—and, yes, its bittersweetness.

As in the case with her earlier books, Allende credits her family—and her familial House of Spirits—with assisting her completion of her new book (most of the recipes were developed by her mother, Panchita Llona). And, she insists, they have also guided her through the "tunnel of mourning" into "the light": "I don't believe in ghosts. But I do believe in memory. When I say somebody's spirit helps me, I mean that when I need poetic inspiration, I think of my grandmother and the crazy character she was. When I need something to be from the heart, I think of Paula, who had such generosity. When I need courage, my grandfather, this stubborn Basque, carries me through. I have photographs of them, all over.[39]

Memory, of course, is the memoirist's prize resource. And it is significant that Allende's two books in the mid-1990s have been memoirs, i.e., that Allende wrote another work of "non-fiction"—rather than fiction—after *Paula*. While memory had returned, aided by her family spirits, the imaginative powers through which her novels emerged still had not. Indeed, as Allende admitted to one interviewer, throughout the mid-1990s she simply could not write fiction, because "it just wouldn't come": "Fiction, for me, just happens, I let the story unfold itself. I don't think of a plot, an outline, characters. I allow them to appear before me. After Paula died, it just wouldn't come like that. So I did nonfiction: first I wrote about her illness and her death. And now, this" (*Aphrodite*).[40]

Allende has always maintained that while her nonfiction—like her journalism—is an act of will, her fiction "just comes," arriving unbidden and on its own schedule, a gift from beyond. The gift of fiction had been absent from Allende's life for a long time. Eventually, however, it did "just come." In 1998, having emerged into "the light," Allende started her sixth novel—once again, on January 8.

Notes

1. *Paula* (New York: HarperCollins, 1995), 181, 182.

2. For information about these productions, see the following: Sarah Provan, "The Shooting of 'Spirits,'" *Europe: Magazine of the European Community*, no. 327 (June 1993): 41-42; Brian D. Johnson, Review of *The House of the Spirits*, *Macleans* 107, no. 15 (April 11, 1994): 69; John Powers, Review of *The House of the Spirits*, *New York* 27, no. 15 (April 11, 1994): 56; and Bodo Fruendt, "The Chilean Tragedy," *Süddeutsche Zeitung*, October 5, 1994.

3. *Eva Luna* (New York: Knopf, 1988), 223. That admonition, of course, could have come from Allende herself, and it warrants mention here how much Allende's feelings resemble those of her fictional characters. In numerous author profiles with

the mass media she speaks through the voices of her characters, straightforwardly quoting one of her fictional characters' statements, without "attribution," as an explanation of her own ideas or states of mind—and which interviewers then cite accordingly, unaware that the line actually comes from one of Allende's literary characters.

Consider, for instance, the following statement that Allende made in a 1988 interview with Susan Benesch ("Mixing Fantasy, Reality," *St. Petersburg Times*, December 11, 1988, 7D): "Writing novels is my private orgy. I'm never afraid of the white paper. It is something like a clean sheet recently ironed to make love."

The interviewer concludes her profile with that stunning metaphor, apparently unaware (despite the title of her article) that the line comes from the mouth of Eva Luna herself: "I took a clean white piece of paper—like a sheet freshly ironed for making love—and rolled it into the carriage. Then I felt something odd. . . . I wrote my name, and immediately the words began to flow, one thing linked to another and another" (224).

4. So not only are we readers indebted to Allende's willingness to "put up with" interviews; Allende herself is also indebted to the numerous men and women she has interviewed to sharpen her understanding of events or round out characters' personalities. Allende has noted that Rolf Carlé (in *Eva Luna*) is based on the son of an SS officer whom she interviewed in Hamburg; and especially in her research on portions of *The Infinite Plan* (New York: HarperCollins, 1993), Allende has acknowledged her debt to interview subjects—the most important of whom was her own husband, who served as the model for the novel's protagonist Gregory Reeves. She elaborated in her 1994 interview with Farhat Iftekharuddin: "It is much better to research with interviews of real people who have experienced the event, whatever that event may be, than going to a library and looking at books. . . . Journalists are in the streets hand in hand with people talking, participating, and hearing."

Understandably, given Allende's professional past, the topic of interviewing itself surfaces occasionally in her interviews. Her interviewers like to ask how it feels to have the tables turned on her, now that she must answer, rather than ask questions. And one sometimes also has a sense that Allende may be playing with the interview, sometimes embroidering or inventing episodes, or just testing out new *personae*—much as Jorge Luis Borges was wont to do.

Indeed, Allende's "reinvention" of herself in her interviews places her within an already well-established Latin American literary tradition. As Ted Lyon remarks: "Borges turned the interview into a literary genre, a game, a personal art form that he often controlled more directly than the interviewer." And, of course, the tradition is not just Latin American; William Faulkner was famous for telling tall tales and conflicting stories (including even various statements about his birthdate) to interviewers.

On Borges, see Ted Lyon, "Jorge Luis Borges and the Interview as Literary Genre," *Latin American Literary Review* 22, no. 4 (July-December 1994): 74-89. On Faulkner, see James B. Meriwether and Michael Millgate, eds., *Lion in the Garden: Interviews with William Faulkner 1926-62* (New York: Random House, 1968).

5. For one German reviewer's puzzlement over *Paula*'s classification, see "'Paula' ein Hymnus an das Leben," *Focus Magazin*, 28 March 1995.

6. When the interviewers for *Contemporary Literature* suggested to Allende,

however, that her interviews constituted "a kind of storytelling for readers interested in literary interviews," Allende responded: "Let them read fiction."

Perhaps oddly, Allende maintains that interviews themselves—especially literary interviews—hold little interest for her. Told by *Contemporary Literature* (no. 20) that she was becoming "a best-selling interview subject," Allende claimed that she herself "would never read a literary interview." She is only interested in the interview for journalistic purposes—to provide information or to aid her construction of fictional worlds: "I'm not interested in what other writers have to say, only what they write."

Allende does acknowledge, however, that many people are as interested in what she says as in what she writes, and that her frankness with her interviewers sometimes yields unsettling results. For example, Allende relates this funny story: "A man who said he was a doctor came over after a lecture and said he'd listened to several of my interviews, read several interviews, listened to me on the radio, and now he'd heard me in this lecture, and he was convinced that there was something wrong with me. That I didn't have a line between reality and fantasy; that that had a name in psychology; and that I should see a therapist!" For her part, Allende reflects, she would rather remain "sick" than become "cured"—because then she would have no neurosis out of which to write (no. 20).

But Allende is indeed indebted to the interview genre for her new career: She willingly and often recounts for interviewers the aforementioned story of her encounter with Pablo Neruda—which she confirms was a "turning point" in her life—and sometimes does so in an even more spontaneous, ingenuous way than in the already-quoted passage from *Paula*. In a breathless style that is echoed by the star-struck commentary of some of her own interviewers of the 1990s, Allende tells *Confluencia* in 1990: "We had lunch, and when I was driving there, I thought, 'This guy won the Nobel Prize. The most important poet, the most important writer of Latin America, and maybe in the world wants me to interview him!' Of all people, me! I always thought that I was great, I had a big ego at that time. After lunch, I said, 'I'm ready for the interview.' He said, 'What interview?' I said, 'Well, the interview.' He said, 'What interview? Look, my child, I would never be interviewed by you, you are the worst journalist in this country. You never tell the truth. You are always in the middle of everything, you are never objective, why don't you switch to literature.' Neruda was right" (no. 11).

Allende's homage to Neruda has been open and frequent. For instance, she quotes Neruda as the opening epigraph of *The House of the Spirits* and mythologizes him simply as "the Poet" in that book's poignant funeral scene. And the epigraph to the Spanish edition of *Of Love and Shadows* is a famous line about Chile from Neruda: "I carry our nation wherever I go, and the oh-so-far-away essences of my elongated homeland live within me."

7. Allende in a 1991 interview (no. 20): "I'm always inventing my own life, so I find that in different interviews I tell different stories about the same subject. My husband says that I have twenty versions of how we met, and I'm sure the twenty versions are true! His version is not true! So I can't tell you if they are accurate or not. My life is fiction too." By 1994 (no. 23), the story had grown: "I have fifty versions of how I met Willie, my husband. He says they are all true."

8. *Paula*, 231.

---

9. *Eva Luna*, 15.

10. Quoted in William Butts, ed., *Interviews with Richard Wilbur* (Jackson: University of Mississippi Press, 1990), xiv. Commenting on the emergence of the literary interview as an independent genre, Butts notes: "The form of the literary interview has come into its own, with no less potential for strengths and weaknesses than any other form" (xiii).

11. Alexander Coleman, "Reconciliation among the Ruins," *New York Times Book Review*, May 12, 1985, 1.

12. Agosín is also a human rights activist and fiction writer. Perhaps her best-known works are two short-story collections, *Happiness* (1993) and *Woman in Disguise* (1996). Agosín, a Chilean-born German Jewish writer who was educated in the United States, is sometimes classified with Allende as a Latin American "magical feminist"—along with such writers as the Puerto Rican Rosario Ferré and the Argentine Luisa Valenzuela.

13. Patricia Hart, "*The Stories of Eva Luna*," *The Nation*, March 11, 1991, 316.

14. And such heroine-worship sometimes provoked a reaction among left-oriented critics, one of whom called *The Stories of Eva Luna* "the populist pipe dreams of a bourgeois Latin American leftist who struggles to recover through literature a lost link with the exotic native culture she somewhat disingenuously claims as her own." Daniel Harris, "*The Stories of Eva Luna*," *Boston Review* 16, no. 2 (April 1991): 28.

15. Allende's father, Tomás Allende, who abandoned the family when Isabel was a small child, was actually the first cousin of Salvador Allende. Isabel Allende is thus actually a second cousin of Salvador Allende, who was also her godfather and, as the *paterfamilias* of the Allende clan, gave her away at her 1962 wedding. But Allende made it clear to me in a personal communication (May 6, 1998) that she and her relatives have always thought of (and referred to) Salvador Allende as her "uncle."

16. A few years later, however, she would become visibly frustrated by critics' imputations that *The House of the Spirits* was derivative, a mere knockoff of *One Hundred Years of Solitude*, with García Márquez's Macondo transposed into Allende's unnamed, semi-mythical "half-forgotten country at the end of the earth."

On this view, Allende has written a family chronicle that is merely imitation García Márquez, right down to the magical realist techniques and even its parallel characterization, with Rosa the Beautiful based on Remedios the Beautiful, Clara on Úrsula, Nicolás and Esteban on José Arcadio Buendías, Blanca on Amaranta, and Tío Marcos on Melquíades.

As Allende's defenders have noted, however, such dismissals ignore the feminist perspective—what Patricia Hart has called Allende's "magical feminism"—and the journalistic sensibility informing *The House of the Spirits*. For instance, Allende stresses that she takes historical documents or reportage and uses them as background for her fiction. Máximo Pacheco Gómez's book *Lonquén* (1980), which summarizes an independent investigation of the disappearance of fifteen Chileans in the village of Lonquén, served as the source material for *Of Love and Shadows* (see nos. 3, 5, 11, and 13).

17. Allende discusses the significance of January 8 in *Paula* (p. 280), and in nos. 2, 19, 21, 23, 24, and 31 in this volume.

18. Elizabeth Mehren, "Allende Weaves Novels of Private Pain, Public Passion," *Los Angeles Times*, February 10, 1988.

19. See, for instance, Alan Ryan, "Scheherazade in Chile," *Washington Post Book World*, October 9, 1988, 1-2.

20. In some ways, these explorations constituted a new round of legend-building: an opportunity for Isabel the Storyteller to engage in a different form of self-mythologization. As she confessed in 1988: "What I dream at night is sometimes more important than what happens during the day. When I met my husband, I recognized that I had dreamt of and written about someone like him in *Eva Luna*. I invented him before I met him" (no. 7).

Or as she closed another 1988 interview: "Writing *Eva Luna* was imagining how the world could be if I accepted myself—and if I had love. I imagined that happening for Eva Luna, and then it happened to me—a year later."

To which the interviewer deadpans: "Please be very careful about what you write next" (no. 8).

21. As she declared in an address, titled "Why I Write" and delivered at the University of Virginia in April 1988: "I write about the things I care about: poverty, inequality, and social problems are part of politics, and that's what I write about. . . . I just can't write in an ivory tower, distant from what's happening in the real world and from the reality of my continent. So the politics just steps in, in spite of myself."

The language, the social commitment, the will to bear witness, and even the artist's reluctance to make a political statement echo George Orwell's famous essay of the same title. (Allende later published the address as "Writing As an Act of Hope," in *Paths of Resistance: The Art and Craft of the Political Novel*, ed. William Zinsser [New York, 1989], 39-63.) She elaborated on this theme in an interview published in 1994: "I feel I have a mission. I belong to the lowest of the low in the social classes in this country. I am Latina and I am a woman. But I have a platform to speak in English about my culture" (no. 22).

22. By contrast, she is contrite about some difficulties in her personal life, e.g., the breakup of her first marriage and her decision to divorce her husband: "There was no reason for not loving him, he deserved love, but you know, love has no rules" (no. 8).

That 1988 comment, which marks Allende's first reference to Miguel Frías in any published interview, also points to the paradoxical fact that, while Allende does openly cultivate a myth of herself, she also insists on her privacy. She keeps a low public profile and does not associate much with other writers, let alone California celebrities; she draws a tight circle around parts of her private life and does not expose them to public inspection.

23. Elizabeth Mehren, "Private Pain, Public Passion," 5.

24. *Paula*, 45. Allende adds: "It was destiny—and it was bad luck. After they told me, I went on writing because I could not stop. I could not let anger destroy me."

25. Noting that Gordon's reading *Of Love and Shadows* had piqued his interest in Allende and led to his wanting to make her acquaintance, Allende deadpans: "I am convinced he married the book, not me" (no. 13).

26. Such remarks may smack of watered-down New Age mysticism to skeptical or sophisticated, academically oriented readers. But Allende's confessional tone pos-

sesses both credibility and charismatic power precisely because she has lived through an agony—the loss of a child—that moves people deeply. I witnessed just how deeply people are moved during Allende's dramatic presentation at the University of Texas in April 1995. Many listeners in her audience of twelve hundred were left alternately weeping and laughing by her emotional honesty, as she addressed topics ranging from dying to karma to the non-causal "synchronicity" of events—topics that are rarely touched upon in public by literary figures, particularly in academic settings.

27. Margot Hornblower, "Paula," *Time*, July 10, 1995, 65.

28. *Eva Luna*, 41.

29. *The Infinite Plan* (New York: HarperCollins, 1991), 15.

30. *The Infinite Plan*, 381, 379.

31. Allende interviewed her husband formally and informally, along with others (especially one Vietnam veteran) whose stories might enrich her narrative. She became a journalist again—but now with a substantial difference: not only were her reportorial skills again put in the service of her emerging fictional worlds, but she now relied on interviews to create characters, gain cultural literacy about American history, and fill in large knowledge gaps (e.g., she interviewed several people about topics such as the California counterculture and the antiwar protest movement of the 1960s).

32. On this theme in Allende's work, see Maureen E. Shea, "Love, Eroticism, and Pornography in the works of Isabel Allende," *Women's Studies* 18, no. 2-3 (September 1990): 223-231.

33. William A. Davis, "The Magic Realism of Isabel Allende," *The Boston Globe*, April 14, 1991, A40.

34. Zillah Bahar, review of *Aphrodite*, *The San Francisco Examiner*, May 20, 1998, 13.

35. Diane Carman. "Recipe of Sensuality Focuses on the Physical," *Denver Post*, April 5, 1998, F5.

36. *Aphrodite*, 24-25.

37. Claudia Dreifus, "On Erotic Recipes, Love and Grief, Writing, and Life," *Ms.*, March/April 1998, 39-40.

38. The genre is, however, not unknown in Latin America (though it is usually associated with fiction). The best-known example is Laura Esquivel's *Como agua para chocolate* (*Like Water for Chocolate*), published in 1992.

39. Fred Kaplan, "Angel of Gluttony and Lust," *The Boston Globe*, April 1, 1998, D1.

40. Dreifus, "On Erotic Recipes," 39.

RESOURCES

Chronology of Isabel Allende's Life _____

1942	Isabel Allende is born in Lima, Peru, on August 2 to Tomás Allende and Francisca Llona Barros.
1945	Tomás and Francisca separate, and Francisca moves with her children to Santiago, Chile, to live with her parents.
1953-1958	Francisca marries Ramón Huidobro, a Chilean diplomat, and the family lives in Bolivia, Beirut, and Europe.
1958	Allende is sent to Chile to complete her education when the Suez Canal crisis causes political unrest in Beirut. She meets Miguel Frías, an engineering student at the University of Chile in Santiago.
1959	Allende begins working for the United Nations Food and Agriculture Organization (FAO).
1962	Allende marries Frías, who is now working as an engineer.
1963	Allende's daughter, Paula, is born.
1964-1965	Allende travels through Europe with Miguel and Paula on behalf of the FAO. The family lives in Brussels and Switzerland.
1966	Allende's son, Nicolás, is born in Chile.
1967-1974	Allende works as a journalist, editor, and advice columnist for various magazines.
1970	Allende begins working as a television host and interviewer. Salvador Allende, Isabel's first cousin once removed, is elected president of Chile in September. A Marxist, Allende begins to transition the country into a socialist economy.
1972	Allende interviews the poet Pablo Neruda, who tells her she ought to quit journalism and write fiction.
1973	A military coup overthrows Salvador Allende's presidency.

1974	Augusto Pinochet is appointed president of Chile, and he transitions the country into a military dictatorship.
1975	After her family receives death threats from Pinochet supporters, Allende emigrates to Venezuela, settling in Caracas. She again works as a journalist.
1979-1982	Allende works as an administrator at a Caracas secondary school.
1981	Allende begins writing *La casa de los espíritus* (*The House of the Spirits*) on January 8.
1982	*The House of the Spirits* is published.
1984	*De amor y de sombra* (*Of Love and Shadows*) is published.
1987	*Eva Luna* is published. Allende is divorced from Frías and moves to California.
1988	Allende marries William Gordon, an attorney.
1990	Democratic elections force Pinochet out of the Chilean presidency, and Allende visits Chile to receive the Gabriela Mistral Prize. *Cuentos de Eva Luna* (*The Stories of Eva Luna*) is published.
1991	*El plan infinito* (*The Infinite Plan*) is published. An attack of porphyria causes Paula to fall into a coma. After a medical error, she suffers brain damage and falls into a vegetative state.
1992	Paula dies on December 6.
1994	*Paula* is published.
1997	*Afrodita* (*Aphrodite*), a memoir-cum-cookbook, is published.
1998	Allende is awarded the Dorothy and Lillian Gish Prize.
1999	*Hija de la fortuna* (*Daughter of Fortune*) is published.
2000	*Retrato en sepia* (*Portrait in Sepia*) is published.

2002	*Ciudad de las bestias* (*City of the Beasts*), a novel for young adults, is published.
2003	*El reino del dragón de oro* (*Kingdom of the Golden Dragon*), a novel for young adults, and *Mi país inventado* (*My Invented Country*), a memoir, are published. Allende becomes a U.S. citizen.
2004	*El bosque de los Pigmeos* (*Forest of the Pygmies*), a novel for young adults, is published.
2005	*Zorro* is published.
2006	*Inés del alma mía* (*Inés of My Soul*) is published.
2007	*La suma de los días* (*The Sum of Our Days*), a memoir, is published.
2009	*La isla bajo el mar* (*Island Beneath the Sea*) is published.

Works by Isabel Allende

Long Fiction
La casa de los espíritus, 1982 (*The House of the Spirits*, 1985)
De amor y de sombra, 1984 (*Of Love and Shadows*, 1987)
Eva Luna, 1987 (English translation, 1988)
El plan infinito, 1991 (*The Infinite Plan*, 1993)
Hija de la fortuna, 1999 (*Daughter of Fortune*, 1999)
Retrato en sepia, 2000 (*Portrait in Sepia*, 2001)
Zorro, 2005 (English translation, 2005)
Inés del alma mía, 2006 (*Inés of My Soul*, 2006)
La isla bajo el mar, 2009 (*Island Beneath the Sea*, 2010)

Short Fiction
Cuentos de Eva Luna, 1990 (*The Stories of Eva Luna*, 1991)

Nonfiction
Civilice a su troglodita: Los impertientes de Isabel Allende, 1974
Paula, 1994 (English translation, 1995)
Conversations with Isabel Allende, 1999, 2004 (John Rodden, editor)
Mi país inventado, 2003 (*My Invented Country: A Nostalgic Journey Through Chile*, 2003)
La suma de los días, 2007 (*The Sum of Our Days*, 2008)

Children's/Young Adult Literature
La gorda de porcelana, 1984 (*The Porcelain Fat Lady*, 1984)
Ciudad de las bestias, 2002 (*City of the Beasts*, 2002)
El reino del dragón de oro, 2003 (*Kingdom of the Golden Dragon*, 2004)
El bosque de los Pigmeos, 2004 (*Forest of the Pygmies*, 2005)

Miscellaneous
Afrodita: Cuentos, recetas, y otros afrodisíacos, 1997 (*Aphrodite: A Memoir of the Senses*, 1998)

Bibliography

Allende, Isabel. 1999. *Conversations with Isabel Allende*. Ed. John Rodden. Austin: University of Texas Press, 2004.

Amago, Samuel. "Isabel Allende and the Postmodern Literary Tradition: A Reconsideration of *Cuentos de Eva Luna*." *Latin American Literary Review* 28.56 (2000): 43-60.

André, Maria Claudia. "Breaking Through the Maze: Feminist Configurations of the Heroic Quest in Isabel Allende's *Daughter of Fortune* and *Portrait in Sepia*." *Latin American Literary Review* 30.60 (2002): 74-90.

Bloom, Harold, ed. *Isabel Allende*. Philadelphia: Chelsea House, 2003.

Carvalho, Susan. *Contemporary Spanish American Novels by Women: Mapping the Narrative*. Woodbridge, England: Tamesis, 2007.

_____. "The Craft of Emotion in Isabel Allende's *Paula*." *Studies in Twentieth Century Literature* 21.2 (2003): 223-38.

_____. "The Male Narrative Perspective in the Fiction of Isabel Allende." *Journal of Hispanic Research* 2 (1994): 269-78.

_____. "Transgressions of Space and Gender in Allende's *Hija de la fortuna*." *Letras Femeninas* 27.2 (2001): 24-41.

Coddou, Marcelo, ed. *Los libros tienen sus propios espíritus: Estudios sobre Isabel Allende*. Xalapa: Universidad Veracruzana, 1986.

Correas Zapata, Celia. *Isabel Allende: Life and Spirits*. Trans. Margaret Sayers Peden. Houston, TX: Arte Público Press, 2002.

Cox, Karen Castellucci. *Isabel Allende: A Critical Companion*. Westport, CT: Greenwood Press, 2003.

Davies, Lloyd. *Allende: "La casa de los espíritus."* London: Grant & Cutler, 2000.

Dulfano, Isabel. "The Mother/Daughter Romance—Our Life: Isabel Allende in/and *Paula*." *Women's Studies* 35 (2006): 493-506.

Feal, Rosemary G., and Yvette E. Miller. *Isabel Allende Today: An Anthology of Essays*. Pittsburgh, PA: Latin American Literary Review Press, 2002.

Frenk, Susan. "The Wandering Text: Situating the Narratives of Isabel Allende." *Latin American Women Writing: Feminist Readings in Theory and Crisis*. Ed. Anny Brooksbank Jones and Catherine Davies. Oxford: Clarendon Press, 1996. 66-84.

Frick, Susan R. "Memory and Retelling: The Role of Women in *La casa de los espíritus*." *Journal of Iberian and Latin American Studies* 7.1 (2001): 27-41.

Fuchs, Miriam. "Autobiographical Discourse as Biographical Tribute: Isabel Allende's *Paula*." *The Text Is Myself: Women's Life Writing and Catastrophe*. Madison: University of Wisconsin Press, 2004.

Gough, Elizabeth. "Vision and Division: Voyeurism in the Works of Isabel Allende." *Journal of Modern Literature* 27.4 (2004): 93-120.

Gregory, Stephen. "Stories as Aphrodisiacs: The Price of Seduction in Isabel Allende's Storytelling." *Journal of Iberian and Latin American Studies* 8.2 (2002): 225-40.

Hart, Patricia. "Magic Feminism in Isabel Allende's *The Stories of Eva Luna*." *Multicultural Literatures Through Feminist/Poststructuralist Lenses*. Ed. Barbara Frey Waxman. Knoxville: University of Tennessee Press, 1993. 103-36.

_____. *Narrative Magic in the Fiction of Isabel Allende*. London: Associated University Presses, 1989.

Hart, Stephen M. *Allende: "Eva Luna" and "Cuentos de Eva Luna."* London: Grant & Cutler, 2003.

Lagos, María Inés. "Female Voices from the Borderlands: Isabel Allende's *Paula* and *Retrato en sepia*." *Latin American Literary Review* 30.60 (2002): 112-27.

Levine, Linda Gould. "Defying the Pillar of Salt: Isabel Allende's *Paula*." *Latin American Literary Review* 30.60 (2002): 29-50.

_____. *Isabel Allende*. New York: Twayne, 2002.

_____. "Weaving Life into Fiction." *Latin American Literary Review* 30.60 (2002): 1-25.

Lindsay, Claire. "Re-reading the Romance: Genre and Gender in Isabel Allende's 'Niña perversa.'" *Romance Studies* 19 (2001): 135-47.

McNeese, Tim. *Isabel Allende*. New York: Chelsea House, 2006.

Main, Mary. *Isabel Allende: Award-Winning Latin American Author*. Berkeley Heights, NJ: Enslow, 2005.

Piña, Juan Andrés. *Conversaciones con la narrativa chilena*. Santiago, Chile: Editorial Los Andes, 1991.

Ramblada-Minero, María de la Cinta. *Isabel Allende's Writing of the Self: Trespassing the Boundaries of Fiction and Autobiography*. Lewiston, NY: Edwin Mellen Press, 2003.

Riquelme Rojas, Sonia, and Edna Aguirre Rehbein, eds. *Critical Approaches to Isabel Allende's Novels*. New York: Peter Lang, 1991.

Rivero, Eliana S. "Of Trilogies and Genealogies: *Daughter of Fortune* and *Portrait in Sepia*." *Latin American Literary Review* 30.60 (2002): 91-111.

Swanson, Philip. "California Dreaming: Mixture, Muddle, and Meaning in Isabel Allende's North American Narratives." *Journal of Iberian and Latin American Studies* 9 (2003): 57-68.

_____. "Latin Lessons for Young Americans: Isabel Allende's Fiction for Children." *Revista de estudios hispánicos* 41.2 (2007): 173-89.

_____. "Magical Realism and Children's Literature: Isabel Allende's *La ciudad de las bestias*." *A Companion to Magical Realism*. Ed. Stephen M. Hart and Wen-chin Ouyang. Woodbridge, England: Tamesis, 2005. 168-80.

_____. *The New Novel in Latin America: Politics and Popular Culture after the Boom*. Manchester: Manchester University Press, 1995.

_____. "Tyrants and Trash: Sex, Class, and Culture in *La casa de los espíritus*." *Bulletin of Hispanic Studies* 71 (1994): 217-37.

Weldt-Basson, Helene C. "Irony as Silent Subversive Strategy in Isabel Allende's *Cuentos de Eva Luna*." *Revista de estudios hispánicos* 31.1 (2004): 183-98.

CRITICAL
INSIGHTS

About the Editor

John Rodden has taught at the University of Virginia and the University of Texas at Austin. He has published *Conversations with Isabel Allende* (1999, 2004), along with numerous articles devoted to Isabel Allende and Latin American literature. He has also written widely on British and American intellectual history, German politics and culture, human rights abuses, and European cultural history. Among his recent books are *The Worlds of Irving Howe: The Critical Legacy* (2005), *Every Intellectual's Big Brother: George Orwell's Literary Siblings* (2006), *The Cambridge Companion to George Orwell* (2007), *The Walls That Remain: Eastern and Western Germans Since Reunification* (2008), and *Dialectics, Dogmas, and Dissent: Stories from East German Victims of Human Rights Abuse* (2009).

About *The Paris Review*

The Paris Review is America's preeminent literary quarterly, dedicated to discovering and publishing the best new voices in fiction, nonfiction, and poetry. The magazine was founded in Paris in 1953 by the young American writers Peter Matthiessen and Doc Humes, and edited there and in New York for its first fifty years by George Plimpton. Over the decades, the *Review* has introduced readers to the earliest writings of Jack Kerouac, Philip Roth, T. C. Boyle, V. S. Naipaul, Ha Jin, Ann Patchett, Jay McInerney, Mona Simpson, and Edward P. Jones, and published numerous now classic works, including Roth's *Goodbye, Columbus*, Donald Barthelme's *Alice*, Jim Carroll's *Basketball Diaries*, and selections from Samuel Beckett's *Molloy* (his first publication in English). The first chapter of Jeffrey Eugenides's *The Virgin Suicides* appeared in the *Review*'s pages, as well as stories by Rick Moody, David Foster Wallace, Denis Johnson, Jim Crace, Lorrie Moore, and Jeanette Winterson.

The Paris Review's renowned Writers at Work series of interviews, whose early installments include legendary conversations with E. M. Forster, William Faulkner, and Ernest Hemingway, is one of the landmarks of world literature. The interviews received a George Polk Award and were nominated for a Pulitzer Prize. Among the more than three hundred interviewees are Robert Frost, Marianne Moore, W. H. Auden, Elizabeth Bishop, Susan Sontag, and Toni Morrison. Recent issues feature conversations with Salman Rushdie, Joan Didion, Norman Mailer, Kazuo Ishiguro, Marilynne Robinson, Umberto Eco, Annie Proulx, and Gay Talese. In November 2009, Picador published the final volume of a four-volume series of anthologies of *Paris Review* interviews. *The New York Times* called the Writers at Work series "the most remarkable and extensive interviewing project we possess."

The Paris Review is edited by Philip Gourevitch, who was named to the post in 2005, following the death of George Plimpton two years earlier. A new editorial team has published fiction by André Aciman, Colum McCann, Damon Galgut, Mohsin Hamid, Uzodinma Iweala, Gish Jen, Stephen King, James Lasdun, Padgett Powell, Richard Price, and Sam Shepard. Poetry editors Charles Simic, Meghan O'Rourke, and Dan Chiasson have selected works by John Ashbery, Kay Ryan, Billy Collins, Tomaž Šalamun, Mary Jo Bang, Sharon Olds, Charles Wright, and Mary Karr. Writing published in the magazine has been anthologized in *Best American Short Stories* (2006, 2007, and 2008), *Best American Poetry, Best Creative Non-Fiction*, the Push-cart Prize anthology, and *O. Henry Prize Stories*.

The magazine presents two annual awards. The Hadada Award for lifelong contri-bution to literature has recently been given to Joan Didion, Norman Mailer, Peter Matthiessen, and, in 2009, John Ashbery. The Plimpton Prize for Fiction, awarded to a debut or emerging writer brought to national attention in the pages of *The Paris Re-view*, was presented in 2007 to Benjamin Percy, to Jesse Ball in 2008, and to Alistair Morgan in 2009.

The Paris Review was a finalist for the 2008 and 2009 National Magazine Awards in fiction, and it won the 2007 National Magazine Award in photojournalism. The *Los Angeles Times* recently called *The Paris Review* "an American treasure with true inter-national reach."

Since 1999 *The Paris Review* has been published by The Paris Review Foundation, Inc., a not-for-profit 501(c)(3) organization.

The Paris Review is available in digital form to libraries worldwide in selected aca-demic databases exclusively from EBSCO Publishing. Libraries can contact EBSCO at 1-800-653-2726 for details. For more information on *The Paris Review* or to sub-scribe, please visit: www.theparisreview.org.

John Rodden has taught at the University of Virginia and the University of Texas at Austin. He has published *Conversations with Isabel Allende* (1999, 2004), along with numerous articles devoted to Isabel Allende and Latin American literature.

Amanda Hopkinson is Professor of Literary Translation and Director of the British Centre for Literary Translation. She translates from Spanish, Portuguese, and French and has won the International Dagger Award for her cotranslation (with Ros Schwartz) of *Lorraine Connection* by Dominique Manotti. She also writes extensively on Latin America and has written numerous books on photography.

Michael Wood is Charles Barnwell Straut Class of 1923 Professor of English and Professor of Comparative Literature at Princeton University and the author of celebrated books on Stendhal, Gabriel García Márquez, Vladimir Nabokov, and Franz Kafka, among others. He is a frequent contributor to the *London Review of Books* and the *New York Review of Books*.

Beth E. Jörgensen is Associate Professor of Spanish at the University of Rochester. Her monograph *The Writing of Elena Poniatowska* was published in 1994, and she is the coeditor of *The Contemporary Mexican Chronicle* (2002).

Charles Rossman is Professor of English and Distinguished University Teaching Professor at the University of Texas, Austin, where, since 1968, he has taught courses on modern British, Irish, and European literature and modern Latin American narrative. He has published widely on James Joyce, D. H. Lawrence, and Latin American novelists of the so-called Boom. He has been a member of the editorial boards of the *James Joyce Quarterly*, the *Journal of Modern Literature*, and the *D. H. Lawrence Review*. His publications include three coedited volumes, one each on Mario Vargas Llosa, Carlos Fuentes, and Samuel Beckett, and he has also edited two special journal issues dealing with Latin American literature, one on Gabriel García Márquez and one titled "The Boom and Beyond," as well as a special issue on the Gabler edition of Joyce's *Ulysses*.

María Roof is Assistant Professor of Spanish at Howard University. Her publications on Latin American contemporary literature often deal with fiction from the Southern Cone and Central America and the connections between Latin America and Africa.

Carrie Sheffield is a lecturer in English at the University of Tennessee, Knoxville. She earned her doctorate from Purdue University, and her research interests encompass contemporary American literature and Native American literatures.

Sara E. Cooper is Associate Professor of Spanish and Multicultural and Gender Studies at California State University, Chico. She is the author of numerous articles, many of which have appeared in such literary journals as *Cuban Studies*, *Journal of Lesbian Studies*, and *Confluencia*. She has also contributed many reviews to *Choice:*

Current Reviews for Academic Libraries. She is the founder of the MLA Discussion Group on Cuban and Cuban Diaspora Cultural Production.

Barbara Foley Buedel is Professor of Spanish and Director of International Education at Lycoming College in Pennsylvania. Her lectures cover Spanish language, literature, and culture, as well as Latin American literature and Hispanic theater. Her published articles cover such authors as Carmen Resino, Pedro Villora, and Delgado Salas.

Linda S. Maier is Associate Professor of Spanish at the University of Alabama in Huntsville. She is the author of *Woman as Witness: Essays on Testimonial Narrative by Latin American Women* (2004). Her articles have appeared in *Romance Quarterly*, *Anthropos*, *Hispanófila*, and *Hispanic Journal*. Her current work in progress is *Buñuel's Literary Lens: The Origins of a Cinema Poet.*

Cherie Meacham is Professor of Spanish and Director of the Faculty of Cultural Studies at North Park University, where she teaches courses on the Spanish language and the literature of Spain. She has published widely on women's literature, especially the works of Isabel Allende, Rigoberta Menchú, and Julia Alvarez.

Nadia Avendaño is Assistant Professor of Hispanic Studies at the College of Charleston. She is the author of "Chicana Sexuality and Gender: Cultural Refiguring in Literature, Oral History, and Art" (2009) and *The Contemporary Feminist Bildungsroman in Angeles Mastretta, Isabel Allende, and Lucha Corpi* (2003).

Linda Gould Levine is Professor of Spanish and Chair of the Spanish/Italian Department at Montclair State University (New Jersey) and former Director of the Women's Studies Program at MSU. She received her Ph.D. in Romance languages and literatures from Harvard University, and her areas of interest are contemporary Spanish fiction and film, Spanish and Latin American women writers, and feminist literary criticism. She is the author of *Isabel Allende* (2002), as well as *Juan Goytisolo: La destrucción creadora* (1976), and editor of two critical editions of Goytisolo's acclaimed novel *Don Julián* (1985, 2004). She is also coauthor of *Feminismo ante el franquismo: Entrevistas con feministas de España* (1980) and *Spanish Women Writers: A Bio-bibliographical Source Book* (1993). She has published extensively on contemporary Spanish literature and Spanish and Latin American women writers and is a member of the board of directors of the International Institute in Spain.

Vincent Kling is Professor of German and Comparative Literature at La Salle University in Philadelphia. He has written scholarly essays on Hugo von Hofmannsthal, Ödön von Horváth, Heimito von Doderer, Gert Jonke, W. G. Sebald, the art of literary translation, and the Austrian "Robin Hood," Johann Breitwieser. He has translated fiction and poetry by Jonke, Doderer, Hofmannsthal, and Heimrad Bäcker for Ariadne, Counterpath, and Dalkey Archive Presses and by Gerhard Fritsch for the journals *Calque* and *Literary Imagination.*

Philip Swanson is Hughes Professor of Spanish at the University of Sheffield. He has published numerous articles and books on the topics of Latin American literature and Hispanic cinema, including *Latin American Fiction: A Short Introduction* (2004),

The Companion to Latin American Studies (2003), and *The New Novel in Latin America: Politics and Popular Culture After the Boom* (1995). He is President of the Association of Hispanists of Great Britain and Ireland and an editorial board member of the journals *New Novel Review, Aracnofiles,* and *Arifex.*

Luz María Umpierre is a Puerto Rican poet, scholar, speaker, and consultant who has taught at Bates College and Ithaca College. She has focused much of her research on bilingualism, lesbianism, and the immigrant experience, and she is the author of seven books and hundreds of articles. She is the recipient of several awards for human rights advocacy and her work in the inclusion of issues of sexual orientation, gender, class, race, and ethnicity into the curriculum.

Don Latham is Associate Professor in the School of Library and Information Studies at Florida State University. He has published on Lois Lowry, Isabel Allende, and Laurie Halse Anderson, and he is the author of *David Almond: Memory and Magic* (2006). He is currently working on a three-year project that will investigate information literacy skills and develop interventions for addressing the needs of low-skilled students.

Acknowledgments _____

"The *Paris Review* Perspective" by Michael Wood. Copyright © 2010 by Michael Wood. Special appreciation goes to Christopher Cox, Nathaniel Rich, and David Wallace-Wells, editors at *The Paris Review*.

"'Un puñado de críticos': Navigating the Critical Readings of Isabel Allende's Work" by Beth E. Jörgensen. From *Latin American Literary Review* 30, no. 60 (July-December 2002): 128-146. Copyright © 2002 by the Latin American Literary Review Press. Reprinted with permission of the Latin American Literary Review Press.

"Maryse Condé and Isabel Allende: Family Saga Novels" by María Roof. From *World Literature Today* 70, no. 2 (1996): 283-288. Copyright © 1996 by *World Literature Today*. Reprinted with permission of *World Literature Today*.

"Voices from the Political Abyss: Isabel Allende's *The House of the Spirits* and the Reconstruction and Preservation of History and Memory in 1970s Chile and Beyond" by Carrie Sheffield. From *Proteus: A Journal of Ideas* 19, no. 2 (2002): 33-38. Copyright © 2002 by Shippensburg University. Reprinted with permission of Shippensburg University.

"Family Systems and National Subversion in Isabel Allende's *The House of the Spirits*" by Sara E. Cooper. From *Interdisciplinary Literary Studies: A Journal of Criticism and Theory* 10, no. 1 (2008): 16-37. Copyright © 2008 by *Interdisciplinary Literary Studies*. Reprinted with permission of *Interdisciplinary Literary Studies*.

"Magical Places in Isabel Allende's *Eva Luna* and *Cuentos de Eva Luna*" by Barbara Foley Buedel. From *West Virginia University Philological Papers* 53 (2006): 108-117. Copyright © 2006 by West Virginia University. Reprinted with permission of West Virginia University.

"Mourning Becomes *Paula*: The Writing Process as Therapy for Isabel Allende" by Linda S. Maier. From *Hispania: A Journal Devoted to the Teaching of Spanish and Portuguese* 86, no. 2 (2003): 237-243. Copyright © 2003 by the American Association of Teachers of Spanish and Portuguese. Reprinted with permission of the American Association of Teachers of Spanish and Portuguese.

"The Metaphysics of Mother/Daughter Renewal in *La casa de los espíritus* and *Paula*" by Cherie Meacham. From *Hispanófila*, no. 131 (January 2001): 93-108. Copyright © 2001 by the University of North Carolina. Reprinted with permission of the University of North Carolina.

"Isabel Allende, Fortune's Daughter" by John Rodden. From *Hopscotch: A Cultural Review* 2, no. 4 (2001): 32-39. Copyright © 2001 by Duke University Press. All rights reserved. Used by permission of the publisher.

"*La hija de la fortuna*: Cross-Dressing, Travel, and Gendering the Self" by Nadia Avendaño. From *Cuaderno Internacional de Estudios Humanísticos y Literatura: CIEHL* 7, no. 1 (2007): 113-127. Copyright © 2007 by La Federación Española de

Ingeniería Sin Fronteras. Reprinted with permission of Universidad de Puerto Rico en Humacao.

"Self-Portrait in Sepia? Isabel Allende's Technicolored Life" by John Rodden. From *Society* 42, no. 3 (March/April 2005): 62-65. Copyright © 2005 by Springer New York. Reprinted with permission of Springer Science and Business Media.

"Z/Z: Isabel Allende and the Mark of Zorro" by Philip Swanson. From *Romance Studies* 24, no. 3 (2006): 265-277. Copyright © 2006 by Maney Publishing. Reprinted with permission of Maney Publishing.

"Unscrambling Allende's 'Dos palabras': The Self, the Immigrant/Writer, and Social Justice" by Luz María Umpierre. From *MELUS: Journal of the Society for the Study of the Multi-Ethnic Literature of the United States* 27, no. 4 (Winter 2002): 129-136. Copyright © 2002 by MELUS/University of Connecticut. Reprinted with permission of the journal.

"The Cultural Work of Magical Realism in Three Young Adult Novels" by Don Latham. From *Children's Literature in Education* 38, no. 1 (2007): 59-70. Copyright © 2007 by Springer Science and Business Media. Reprinted with permission of Springer Science and Business Media.

"'I Am Inventing Myself All the Time': Isabel Allende in Her Interviews" by John Rodden. From *Conversations with Isabel Allende*, rev. ed., edited by John Rodden (2004), pp. 1-42. Copyright © 2004 by the University of Texas Press. Reprinted with permission of the University of Texas Press.

Soto, Tránsito (*The House of the Spirits*), 56

"Spirits Were Willing, The" (Allende), 90

Stories of Eva Luna, The (Allende), 4, 19, 133, 279, 312, 319

Straayer, Chris, 201

Suárez, Inés (*Inés of My Soul*), 221, 249

Suleiman, Susan, 175

Sulsona, Violeta, 43

Sum of Our Days, The (Allende), 23

Suma de los días, La. See *Sum of Our Days, The*

Swanson, Philip, 48, 116, 119, 145

Talmor, Sascha, 127

Tao Chi'en (*Daughter of Fortune*), 202, 214, 226

Themes; coming-of-age, 289; death and dying, 60, 71, 184, 234, 241, 243, 297; duality, 264; feminism, 31, 39, 55, 89, 105, 132, 164, 217, 230, 331; immigration, 5, 21, 191, 195, 220, 281; imprisonment and torture, 16, 65, 69, 90, 95, 125; justice, 46, 271; Latina Scheherazade, 4, 146, 188, 311, 318, 322-323; male-female relationships, 54, 61, 63, 176, 189, 203, 231, 233, 272; motherhood, 47, 89, 150, 163; political violence, 60, 70, 79, 86, 110, 170, 228; resurrection, 241; sensuality, 5, 62, 138, 168-169, 188, 250, 332, 335; social-class tensions, 61, 70, 79, 117; writing and documentation, 26, 58, 71, 91, 93, 96, 133, 137, 206, 280

Thousand and One Tales of the Arabian Nights, A, 146, 236, 323

Tompkins, Jane, 290

Toulouse Valmorain. *See* Valmorain, Toulouse

Tránsito Soto. *See* Soto, Tránsito

Travel literature, 195, 216, 220

Tree of Life (Condé), 76, 78, 81

Tres Marías, 53, 114, 118

Trites, Roberta Seelinger, 289

Trueba, Alba (*The House of the Spirits*), 55, 81, 88, 170, 212, 230, 243, 245

Trueba, Blanca (*The House of the Spirits*), 55, 81, 88, 168, 230, 249

Trueba, Clara del Valle (*The House of the Spirits*), 54, 109, 165, 216, 242, 253

Trueba, Esteban (*The House of the Spirits*), 52, 56, 79, 112, 230, 245, 324

Urbina, Nicasio, 34

Valdivieso, L. Teresa, 47

Valmorain, Toulouse (*Island Beneath the Sea*), 232

Vargas Llosa, Mario, 50

Violette Boisier. *See* Boisier, Violette

Watzlawick, Paul, 107

Wesley, Marilyn C., 195, 197

Whitehead, Colson, 252

Wilder, Thornton, 240

Williams, Raymond L., 145

Winfrey, Oprah, 193, 211

Women; marginalization of, 197, 234; portrayals of, 31, 46, 51, 82, 89, 105, 132, 163, 189, 216, 221, 249, 313; violence against, 60-61, 65, 67, 80, 91, 122, 170, 232, 243

Woolf, Virginia, 253

Yarbro-Bejarano, Yvonne, 168

Yardley, Jonathan, 218

Zamora, Lois Parkinson, 288

Zarité (*Island Beneath the Sea*), 232

Zorro (Allende), 22, 221, 235